Discourse Markers in Romance Languages. Crosslinguistic Approaches in Romance and Beyond

Cecilia-Mihaela Popescu / Oana-Adriana Duţă (eds.)

Discourse Markers in Romance Languages. Crosslinguistic Approaches in Romance and Beyond

PETER LANG
Berlin - Bruxelles - Chennai - Lausanne - New York - Oxford

Library of Congress Cataloging-in-Publication Data
A CIP catalog record for this book has been applied for at the Library of Congress.

Bibliographic information published by the Deutsche Nationalbibliothek
The Deutsche Nationalbibliothek collects this publication in the Deutsche Nationalbibliografie; detailed bibliographic data are available on the Internet at .Nationalbibliografie; detailed bibliographic data are available on the Internet at http://dnb.d-nb.de.

ISBN 978-3-631-89851-2 (Print)
E-ISBN 978-3-631-89852-9 (E-PDF)
E-ISBN 978-3-631-89853-6 (E-PUB)
DOI 10.3726/b20640

Published by Peter Lang GmbH, Berlin, Deutschland

info@peterlang.com - www.peterlang.com

Table of Contents

Foreword 7

List of Contributors 11

I Discourse Markers: Theories and Methods

Adriana Costăchescu
1 How the Study of Discourse Markers Changes Pragmatic Theories of Discourse 15

Chiara Ghezzi
2 *Adunque* and *Dunque* in Old Italian between Free and Patterned Variation: The Role of English Translation in Pragmatic Analysis 37

II Discourse Markers and Their Relation to Other Semantic and Pragmatic Categories

Pierre Lejeune, Amália Mendes
3 A Study on the French Functional Equivalents of some Modal and Metadiscursive Uses of the European Portuguese Marker *lá* 61

Federica Cominetti, Doriana Cimmino
4 The Semantic and Pragmatic Meanings of Italian *davvero* through Text Types 83

Viviana Masia
5 The Evidentiality Dimension of the Italian Discourse Marker *sai* between Subjectification and Intersubjectification Processes 103

Claudia Timoci
6 The Use of *ştii, ştiţi, vezi, vedeţi* and *înţelegi, înţelegeţi* as Discourse Markers in Spoken Romanian. A Quantitative Analysis 123

Anna de Marco, Emanuela Paone
7 Discourse Markers in Complaints and Apologies: A Comparison between Native and Non-Native Speakers of Italian 141

III Corpus-Based Approaches to Discourse Markers

Rogelio Nazar, Irene Renau, Hernán Robledo
8 Dismark and Text·a·Gram: Automatic Identification and Categorization of Discourse Markers in Texts 165

Bianca Maria Alecu
9 Digital Discourse Markers in Romanian Forum Communication: The Case of *welp, TBH (to be honest)* and *TBF (to be fair)* 185

Heejung Kim
10 Reformulation Markers, Linguistic Typology and Rhetorical Conventions: The Case of Spanish and Korean 207

Fátima Silva, Fátima Oliveira, Ana Sofia Pinto
11 On Discourse Reformulation Markers with the Structure *More + Adverb* in European Portuguese: A Corpus-Based Study 227

Anna de Marco, Mariagrazia Palumbo
12 Interactional Discourse Markers in a Corpus of Italian Migrants in Munich 247

Alice Ionescu
13 Discourse Markers *si vous voulez* in French and *dacă vreți* in Romanian: A Comparative Analysis 267

Louise Behe
14 *Même* Discourse Marker? A Study of Its Argumentative Uses 285

Foreword

This volume reunites a selection of the papers presented in the international conference *Discourse Markers in Romance Languages: Crosslinguistic approaches in Romance and beyond* (DISROM7), organized at the University of Craiova, Romania, during 16–18 June 2023. This conference continued the series of prestigious scientific events devoted to discourse markers in Romance languages (Madrid, 2010; Buenos Aires, 2011; Campinas, 2012; Heidelberg, 2015; Louvain-la- Neuve, 2017; Bergamo, 2019), and served as a platform for internationally renowned linguists and young researchers alike to exchange views and ideas and to broaden their research perspectives.

Roughly defined as words and phrases that are used to manage and organise the structure of discourse, discourse markers form a heterogeneous functional class that can be analysed and reviewed from a wide array of points of view (syntactically, semantically, pragmatically, etc.), on both a monolingual and cross-linguistic level, in synchrony and diachrony, and so on. Starting from these considerations, the authors of the 15 papers – organised in three thematic sections – propose a substantial and enriching range of reflections and interpretations of discourse markers.

The first section of the volume is devoted to the discussion of theories and methods in the analysis of discourse markers. Adriana Costăchescu's contribution, *How the Study of Discourse Markers Changes Pragmatic Theories of Discourse*, focuses on three categories of discourse markers (of disagreement, of topic shift and of reformulation), in order to see whether any adjustments should be done to two of the main pragmatic theories of dialogue, Grice's conversation theory (1975) and the relevance theory (Sperber & Wilson, 1986). The second contribution in this section, Chiara Ghezzi's *Adunque* and *dunque* in Old Italian between free and patterned variation: the role of English translation in pragmatic analysis, considers patterns of use of the Italian discourse markers *adunque* and *dunque* in texts dating from the 14th century and confronts them with their English translation in order to map the functional spectra of forms and establish their semantic-pragmatic fields.

The second section deals with the relationship between discourse markers and other semantic and pragmatic categories. In their *Study on the French Functional Equivalents of some Modal and Metadiscursive Uses of the European Portuguese Marker* lá, Pierre Lejeune and Amália Mendes explore some typical uses of the marker *lá*, such as locative, temporal, modal, etc., by using a monolingual corpus of Portuguese and two bilingual corpora. Federica Cominetti and Doriana Cimmino's contribution, *The Semantic and Pragmatic Meanings of Italian davvero through Text Types*, discusses the various values of the adverb *davvero*, such as the dialogic feature of reacting to an interlocutor's statement, reinforcing or questioning it, as well as the expression of agreement, surprise and courtesy, mostly in spontaneous spoken Italian. In *The Evidentiality Dimension of the Italian Discourse Marker* sai *between Subjectification and Intersubjectification Processes*, Viviana Masia argues that the Italian discourse marker *sai* has acquired a new evidential meaning – expressing mutually shared knowledge – through a pragmaticalization process. Other discourse markers with an intrinsic evidential nature are analysed and classified in Claudia Timoci's contribution, *The Use of* ştii, ştiţi, vezi, vedeţi *and* înţelegi, înţelegeţi *as Discourse Markers in Spoken Romanian. A Quantitative Analysis.* In *Discourse Markers in Complaints and Apologies: a Comparison between Native and Non-native Speakers of Italian*, Anna de Marco and Emanuela Paone analyse the uses and functions of discursive markers (DMs) in complaints and apologies performed by learners of Italian as L2 and native speakers of Italian engaged in dyadic interactions, providing useful information on the language teaching level.

The third section includes papers discussing corpus-based approaches to discourse markers. Rogelio Nazar, Irene Renau and Hernán Robledo present a methodology for the compilation of a taxonomy of discourse markers using a parallel corpus in *Dismark and Text·a·Gram: Automatic identification and categorization of discourse markers in texts.* Bianca Maria Alecu deals with *Digital Discourse Markers in Romanian Forum Communication: the Case of* welp, TBH (to be honest) *and* TBF (to be fair) and proposes an investigation of the forms and functions of discourse markers occurring in forum interactions, as well as of the interaction between English borrowings and code-switching sequences in the case of discourse markers. In *Reformulation Markers, Linguistic Typology and Rhetorical Conventions: the Case of Spanish and Korean*, Heejung Kim conducts a contrastive study of reformulation markers between Spanish and Korean taking into account linguistic typology and the contrastive rhetorical features of these two languages. The contribution by Fátima Silva, Fátima Oliveira and Ana Sofia Pinto, *On Discourse Reformulation Markers with the Structure* More + *Adverb in European Portuguese: a Corpus-Based Study*, discusses the role of *more* + adverb markers in a typology of European Portuguese reformulation markers, based on three written and two oral corpora. Anna de Marco and Mariagrazia Palumbo propose an analysis of *Interactional Discourse Markers in a Corpus of Italian Migrants in Munich*, exploring the variation in the use of interactional discourse markers in terms of functional space across two generations of Italian migrants.

Discourse Markers si vous voulez *in French and* dacă vreți *in Romanian: a Comparative Analysis*, by Alice Ionescu, undertakes a comparative review of two equivalent discourse markers which introduce sequences of speech presented as virtual, by means of a corpus of literary and journalistic texts. Finally, in Même *Discourse Marker? A Study of Its Argumentative Uses*, Louise Behe aims at showing that the French adverb *même* can be classified as a discourse marker, based on its argumentative uses that introduce a feature of unexpectedness.

Due to their dynamic pragmatic properties, discourse markers are a perpetually-evolving subfield of linguistics, inciting new research approaches and points of view. This volume aims at furthering scientific research on discourse markers, proposing up-to-date frames of quantitative and qualitative analysis, detailed reviews of their semantic and pragmatic features and thorough corpus surveys.

Cecilia-Mihaela Popescu and Oana-Adriana Duţă

List of Contributors

Louise Behe
École des hautes études en sciences sociales, e-mail: louisebehe@yahoo.fr

Doriana Cimmino
Independent researcher, e-mail: dorcimm@hotmail.com.

Federica Cominetti
Università dell'Aquila, Italy, e-mail: federica.cominetti@univaq.it

Adriana Costăchescu
University of Craiova, Romania, e-mail: acostachescu@gmail.com

Oana Adriana Duță
University of Craiova, Romania, e-mail: oana.duta@edu.ucv.ro

Chiara Ghezzi
University of Bergamo, Italy, e-mail: chiara.ghezzi@unibg.it.

Alice Ionescu
University of Craiova, Romania, e-mail: alice.ionescu@yahoo.com

Heejung Kim
Universidad Autónoma de Madrid, Spain, e-mail: heejung.kim2506@hotmail.com

Pierre Lejeune
Universidade de Lisboa, e-mail: lejeunepierre@hotmail.com

Anna de Marco
Università della Calabria, Italy, e-mail: demarco.anna@gmail.com

Bianca Maria Alecu
University of Bucharest, Romania, e-mail: bianca-maria.alecu@litere.unibuc.ro

Viviana Masia
Università Roma Tre, Italy, e-mail: viviana.masia@uniroma3.it

Amália Mendes
Universidade de Lisboa, e-mail:amaliamendes@letras.ulisboa.pt

Cecilia Mihaela Popescu
University of Craiova, Romania, e-mail: cecilia.popescu@edu.ucv.ro

Rogelio Nazar
Pontificia Universidad Católica de Valparaíso, e-mail: rogelio.nazar@pucv.cl

Fátima Oliveira
University of Porto, e-mail: moliv@letras.up.pt

Mariagrazia Palumbo
Università della Calabria, Italy, e-mail: mariagraziapalumbo@yahoo.it

Emanuela Paone
Università del Salento, Italy, e-mail: emanuela.paone@unisalento.it

Irene Renau
Pontificia Universidad Católica de Valparaíso, e-mail: irene.renau@pucv.cl

Hernán Robledo
Pontificia Universidad Católica de Valparaíso, e-mail: hernan.robledo@pucv.cl

Fátima Silva
University of Porto, e-mail: mhenri@letras.up.pt

Ana Sofia Pinto
University of Porto, e-mail: sofiapinto.as@hotmail.com.

Claudia Timoci
'Al. Ioan Cuza' University of Iaşi, Romania, e-mail: timociclaudia@gmail.com

I Discourse Markers: Theories and Methods

Adriana Costăchescu

1 How the Study of Discourse Markers Changes Pragmatic Theories of Discourse

Abstract: Discourse markers have been studied lately from a wide range of theoretical perspectives (politeness theory, argumentation, conversation, etc.) and within distinct fields of linguistics (semantics, sociolinguistics, pragmatics). This study focuses on three categories of discourse markers that we have studied before (of disagreement, of topic shift and of reformulation), in order to see whether any adjustments should be done to two of the main pragmatic theories of dialogue, Grice's conversation theory (1975) and the relevance theory (Sperber & Wilson 1986). Markers of disagreement (*assez* 'enough', *tais-toi/ taisez-vous* 'shut up', *ça suffit* 'that's enough', *arrête!* 'stop!') cast doubts on the first part of the wording of the cooperative principle. Topic shift markers (*à propos* 'by the way', *d'ailleurs* 'besides', *quant à* 'as for', *concernant* 'regarding', *au sujet de* 'with respect to') show that dialogue frequently exceeds the framework traced by the second part of the cooperative principle and by the Maxim of Relation. As for markers of reformulation (*c'est-à-dire* 'that is', *à savoir* 'namely', *disons* 'let's say', *je veux dire* 'I mean'), they show that some postulates regarding communication, concepts expressed by Martinet (1960), by Grice (1975) or by Sperber and Wilson (1986), are not always applicable.

Keywords: discourse markers, disagreement, topic shift, reformulation, pragmatic theories

1. Introduction

A considerable amount of research has been devoted to discourse markers, which have been described, in the last quarter of century, as one of the 'great encounters of linguistics' (Dostie & Pusch, 2007). Such research is based on a wide range of approaches, such as politeness theory, argumentation, dialogue frameworks, etc. It is not only the theories that differ, but also the field of reference: pragmatics, semantics, sociolinguistics, psychology. These studies have analysed discourse markers (DMs) from a wide range of languages, but they show some common traits: they are generally based on corpus extraction and, due to the nature of the topic, they focus on the interpersonal and textual meaning of the DMs.

When examining certain categories of DMs in terms of the postulates proposed by the pragmatic theories of communication, in general, and of conversation, in particular, we see the need to supplement, amend and adjust several of these principles. We focus on three categories of DMs (of disagreement, of topic shift and of reformulation), in order to see whether any adjustments should be done to two of the main pragmatic theories of dialogue, Grice's conversation theory (1975) and the relevance theory (Sperber & Wilson, 1986).

DMs are generally characterised by at least one of the following particular traits: they do not contribute to the semantic propositional content of the sentences (to their truth value), they tend to be independent from the syntactic structure of the phrase, their use is optional, their function is manifested beyond the phrase, at the level of discourse relations between sentences (Dostie & Pusch, 2007: 4). DMs are the outcome of a de-categorization and re-categorization of target elements which, before, had no discourse meaning (Dostie, 2004; Pusch, 2007: 33), but which seem to bear pragmatic potential, especially in their metaphorical or connotative meanings. This process is quite vaguely termed as 'pragmaticalization', following the term for 'grammaticalization', as both developments are based on category change.

For some linguistic units (adverbs, prepositions, interjections, nouns, verbs, phrases and even sentences), the conversion to DMs may be under way, as re-categorization takes place gradually, which sometimes makes it difficult to establish whether a certain linguistic form is a full or partial DM.

The three classes of DMs that have inspired our reflections have the following discourse characteristics: (i) markers of disagreement (*assez* 'enough', *arrêtez* 'stop', *silence* 'silence', etc.) show that one of the speakers does not accept the topic or the direction of the conversation; (ii) topic shift markers (*au sujet de* 'with respect to', *quant à* 'as for', *d'ailleurs* 'besides', etc.)[1] show that one of the participants in the conversation changes the topic or the direction of the discussion; (iii) markers of reformulation (*c'est-à-dire* 'that is', *autrement dit* 'in other words', *soit* 'namely', etc.) show that the speaker is not happy with the message s/he has just uttered and 'corrects' it.

Besides the use of discourse markers, speakers can signal this kind of reorientation of a conversation by using 'ordinary' words, i.e. by using words, phrases or sentences in their meaning, as ascribed by the linguistic code. In certain contexts, such sequences also acquire pragmatic meaning, similarly to DMs. These elements also seem to have undergone pragmaticalization.

Let us look at some examples. A specific DM may show that the same information is expressed again, but amended or modified, representing an explanation,

1 Grice noticed that the formulation of the Maxim of Relevance ('Be relevant') 'conceals a number of problems' (Grice, 1975: 48), such as the issue of topic shifting during the conversation.

as a spontaneous choice of the speaker or as the outcome of a demand from the receiver:

(1) a. MISTRESS GREY : « – … si tu tombes malade à ton tour, qui te soignera ? » LE DOCTEUR : « – Bonsoir, Anna. » MISTRESS GREY : « – **C'est-à-dire que** je t'ennuie, n'est-ce pas ? » (Dumas, in *TLFi*, s. v. *c'est-à-dire*)
'MISTRESS GREY: '(…) if you become sick too, who will look after you?' THE PHYSICIAN: 'Good evening, Anna.' MISTRESS GREY: '**You mean** I annoy you, right?"[2]

b. Si je savais qu'une telle publication toucherait la cible, **c'est-à-dire** soulèverait des discussions, je le ferais. Mais c'est l'improbable. (Valéry, in *TLFi*, s. v. *cible*)
'If I knew that such a publication would touch a nerve, **that is**, it would generate discussions, I would do it. But it's unlikely.'

c. Je rejoins ici ma notion cardinale à cet égard que je dois avant tout à mes deux années de vie parmi mes réfugiés, à ce qu'il y a de meilleur chez Gide, et à ce qui fut la doctrine constante de Tchekhov – **à savoir** toujours me mettre à la place de l'autre et essayer non seulement de voir, mais, dans la mesure du possible, de penser et de sentir comme lui. (Du Bos, in *TLFi*, s. v. *cardinal*)
'Here I emphasize my seminal idea in this regard, which I owe above all to my two years of life among my refugees, to what is best in Gide and to what was Chekhov's constant doctrine – **namely** I always put myself in the other person's shoes and try not only to see, but, as far as possible, to think and feel like him.'

The consulted corpus has shown that the change of direction in the development of the dialogue may be signalled by a phrase such as *vouloir dire* 'mean', which acts as a pragmatic equivalent of DMs of reformulation (*c'est-à-dire* 'that is', *à savoir* 'namely', *autrement dit* 'in other words', *pour mieux dire* 'to be more specific', etc.):

(2) a. – Bien ! – Comment, bien, que **voulez-vous dire** ? – Je **veux dire** qu'en me demandant ma signature, n'est-ce pas, vous me laissez absolument libre de ma personne ? (Dumas in *TLFi*, s. v. *absolument*)
"Well!' '**What do you mean** by well?' '**I mean** that, by requesting my signature, you do set me absolutely free, right?"

b. Et qu'on ne me parle pas, après cela, du travail, je **veux dire** de la valeur morale du travail. (A. Breton, in *TLFi*, s. v. *après*)
'And do not even talk to me, after this, about work, **I mean**, about the moral value of work.'

2 Unless otherwise mentioned, all the translations of texts in other language than English belong to the authors of the relevant chapters.

The disagreement or the refusal to pursue the conversation may be announced by an imperious DM (*assez !* 'enough', *la ferme !* 'hold your tongue', etc.), but also by a form of the verb *se taire* 'shut up' or by one of its synonyms, usually in the imperative:

(3) a. Il disait volontiers dans les dernières années que Paris était une porcherie : « – **Taisez-vous**, je ne veux pas vous entendre, regardez les autres capitales. » (Barrès, in *TLFi*, s. v. *porcherie*)
'In the last years, he was happily saying that Paris was crap: '**Shut up**, I don't want to hear you, look at the other capitals."

b. « – Qui est là ? » s'écria celle-ci en entendant Rodolphe frapper à ses carreaux. « – **Silence** », répondit-il, « ouvrez… » (Murger, TLFi, s. v. *celui-ci*)
"Who is there?' she yelled, hearing Rodolphe knock on the door. '**Silence**', he answered, 'open up…"

c. « -Pourquoi qu'tu prépares tes valises ? … » « -Ta **gueule** !… Occupe-toi d'tes fesses ! » (Le Breton, in *TLFi*, s. v. *fesse*)
"Why are you preparing your luggage?' '**Shut up**! Mind your own business!"

In order to emphasize disagreement, the speaker may combine the two possibilities (the imperative of a verb commanding silence and DMs repeating the order), to underline his/her attitude:

(4) « – **Ferme la** ! **la ferme** ! **Tais-toi.** » « – Je m'fous pas mal de c'que tu dis ou d'c'que tu n'dis pas. » (Barbusse, in *TLFi*, s. v. *fermer*)
"**Stop! Stop! Shut up!**' 'I could not care less about what you are or are not saying."

In (4) the speaker uses both DMs (*ferme la! la ferme!* « stop ») and a PolyM, the imperative form of the verb *se taire* «to stop speaking» (*tais-toi!* «shut up! »). All these utterances have the same function: make the addressee stop speaking. Here l'imperative of the verb is a PolyM. In other contexts, this verb behaves differently (*Marie s'est tue toute la soirée* « Mary said nothing all evening», *les gens ont refusé de se taire* «people refused to be silent!», *le droit de se taire* «the right to silence», etc.). Our study deals with changes of discourse focus, i.e. changes of direction that seem to contradict some hypotheses of the above mentioned pragmatic theories. These changes are easily accepted by the speakers when signalled. We have seen that pragmatic developments provide speakers with two major categories of means: (i) specific DMs, resulting from a more or less advanced process of pragmaticalization; (ii) phrases with an identical or close meaning to their usual linguistic one, which acquire a contextual discursive value. Since the terminology of the field is quite diverse[3], we shall use for this second category the

3 For instance, Dostie and Pusch (2007: 3), working in French, mention the following synonyms for *marqueurs du discours/ discursifs* 'discourse markers': *mots du discours*

term of 'polyfunctional marker' (PolyM), as they have conserved their meaning and have enriched their usage with a discourse-based dimension.

2. The Cooperative Principle and the Laws of Discourse

The study of the three categories of DMs and of PolyMs with an equivalent discourse function shows that it is necessary to revise and adjust the fundamental principle of the conversation theory, the cooperative principle, as well as certain details of discourse principles theorized by Grice under the form of maxims (Grice, 1975). The analysis of the functions of the examined DMs/PolyMs also shows the need to rectify some premises of cognitive pragmatics, i.e. the relevance theory (Sperber & Wilson, 1986).

Grice's theory is based on two correlated principles: (i) the speaker's wish to contribute to an efficient exchange of information; (ii) the recipients' capacity of deducing what the speaker intends to communicate, what s/he 'means' beyond the literal meaning of the words. Thus, the participants in the verbal exchange should cooperate and should be willing to have a constructive contribution, because there will be no conversation after all if they refuse to participate. Afterwards, this fundamental principle is nuanced and specified by the four conversational maxims.

The cooperative principle details a more general human trait that is seen not only in communication, since the collaboration between individuals is the expression of rational social behaviour. This way of acting facilitates a range of complex activities, suitably implemented so that a large or small number of persons (workers, technicians, engineers, physicians, architects, sportsmen, actors, musicians, etc.) could take part in the performance of a certain activity (erecting a building, making an object, a match against another team, a theatre performance, a surgery, a concert, etc.) (Bracops, 2006; Costăchescu, 2013).

Here is Grice's definition for the essential postulate of his communication theory – the cooperative principle:

> Make your conversational contribution such as is required, at the stage at which it occurs, by the accepted purpose or direction of the talk exchange in which you are engaged. One might label this the COOPERATIVE PRINCIPLE. (Grice, 1975: 45)

'discourse words', *particules discursives/ énonciatives* 'discourse/enunciative particles', *connecteurs* 'connectors'. The French *Wikipedia* adds *jalon de discours* 'discourse milestone', *marqueur pragmatique* 'pragmatic marker', *particule discursive* 'discourse particle' or *connecteur discursif* 'discourse connector'.

The study of how the three examined groups of discourse markers operate in symptomatic contexts shows us the limits of defining both the cooperative principle and the four maxims of conversation (quantity, quality, relation and manner), which should be extended and nuanced. This is also applicable to the fundamental concept of cognitive, pragmatics, i.e. relevance.

2.1. DMs/PolyMs of Disagreement

The Cooperative Principle corresponds to an ideal exchange, in a world of harmony and agreement, but it leaves out a wide array of conversations between persons with different, even contrary, opinions and/or purposes, who unwillingly accept the topic or the direction of the conversation. This is the case of verbal exchanges such as a contradictory investigation driven by the police or the prosecution, where the investigator and the suspect have contrary interests. Another less harmonious type of conversation is that of various polemic dialogues, of an argumentative nature, for instance those of politicians belonging to different political parties during television debates or electoral campaigns (Costăchescu, 2014).

By means of items expressing disagreement, the participants to the discourse can express their opposition to the words or actions of their interlocutor(s). If the opposition refers to the verbal behaviour, the speaker may refuse to pursue the conversion or s/he proposes a different topic.

By refusing to pursue the exchange, the speaker somehow suspends the cooperative principle and this attitude is frequently shown by a DM (*assez* 'enough', *zut* 'damn'), by a PolyM (*tais-toi* 'shut up') or by a pragmatic phrase with a similar discourse function, which occupies an intermediary position between the two categories, in terms of linguistic status (*ça suffit comme ça* 'that's enough', (*fais*) *silence* ! 'silence/be quiet!').

The consulted corpus reveals two types of situations. In the first one, the speaker abruptly interrupts the discussion:

(5) a. « – **Ça suffit**! Je ne veux plus rien entendre! » (*WordReference*)
'**Enough!** I don't want to hear any more!'

b. « -**Tais**-toi, ami, **tais**-toi, **arrête**. » (A. de Vigny in *TLFi*, s. v. *arrêter*)
'**Shut up**, my friend, **shut up**, **stop**.'

c. « – Sang du Christ! **assez de paroles** », s'écria l'évêque. (E. Sue, *Les mystères du peuple*, VII, 305)
"For God's sake! **No more speaking**', the bishop cried.'

d « – **Taisez-vous**, Armand, **taisez-vous** ! » (Ponson du Terrail, *Rocambole*, *Le club*… II, 833)
'**Shut up**, Armand, **shut up**!'

In the second case, the speaker justifies the interruption. There are several types of explanations. The refusal to pursue the conversation is frequently motivated by the (moral or intellectual) disgust triggered by the interlocutor(s), which is often shown by an injurious appellative:

(6) a. « – **Tais-toi, infâme** ! s'écria le marquis. **Tais-toi, Satan** ! » (Ponson du Terrail, *Rocambole, Le club…* II, 464)
"**Shut up, you idiot**! the marquis cried. **Shut up, Satan**!"
b. « -**Taisez-vous!** Vous êtes un **vilain** ! » (Pailleron, in *TLFi*, s. v. *follet*)
'**Shut up!** You are **disgusting**!'
c. « – Allons, **silence, crapules**! » (Macé, in *TLFi*, s. v. *poivrière*)
'Come on, **silence, you scoundrels**!'
d. « – **Brigands, tenez-vous donc tranquilles**! »… Nous ne sommes pas ici pour banqueter. (Balzac, in *TLFi* s. v. *colleter*)
'**Brigands, keep quiet!**… We are not here to party.'

Sometimes, the speaker explains his/her negative attitude towards the pursuit of the discourse through a critical evaluation of the dialogue. For instance, s/he questions the seriousness of the conversation. In many situations, such an estimation results in the interruption of the conversation, so the interlocutors no longer talk to each other:

(7) « – C'est pousser trop loin la **plaisanterie**, monsieur. Veuillez me laisser seule! » (Maupassant, in *TLFi*, s. v. *plaisanterie*)
'This **joke** has gone too far, sir. Please leave me alone.'
b. « – Assez de **bavardages** ! » *(Grand Robert*, s. v. *bavardage)*
'No more **chitchatting!**'
c. « – Allons, **tais-toi**, vieux, tu **radotes**! » (Erckmann-Chatrian, in *TLFi*, s. v. *radoter*)
'Come on, **shut up**, old man, you are **rambling**!'
d. « – Dis donc pas **de conneries.** » (Fallet, in *TLFi*, s. v. *vérité*)
'Don't talk **rubbish**.'

The interruption of the verbal exchange may be justified by other reasons: the invocation of norms of civil or military behaviour (soldiers must keep silent when the call is made), the intention to do something else, a reaction from another speaker:

(8) a. « -**Assez, assez** », dit-elle, « allez-vous-en, il est minuit, **respectons les convenances.** » (Balzac, in *TLFi*, s. v. *assez*)
"**Enough, enough**', she said, 'go away, it's midnight, **let's observe the conveniences.**"
b. ALCMÈNE : « -**Tais-toi,** s'il te plaît, Sosie, **je vais dormir**… » (Jean Giraudoux, *Amphitryon 38*, 58–59)
'**Shut up**, please, Sosie **I want to sleep**…'

c. « -**Arrêtez**, monsieur, **c'est assez d'effroi pour une femme**. » (A. de Vigny, *Chatterton*, 71)
'**Stop**, sir, **that's scary enough for a woman**.'

d. Le brigadier lançait avec autorité la phrase coutumière « – **Silence** à l'appel! » (Courteline, in *TLFi*, s. v. *garer*)
'The brigadier yelled with authority the customary phrase: '**Silence** at the roll call!"

In other contexts, the speaker explicitly rejects the proposed topic and/or direction of the dialogue, which makes him/her interrupt the conversation:

(9) a. « – La religion… » commença-t-il. Le prêtre lui coupa brutalement la parole. « – Vous n'allez pas recommencer !? **Taisez-vous**. Toutes vos arguties, je les balaye d'un geste. » (H. Barbusse, *l'Enfer*, 329)
"Religion…' he began. The priest cut him off abruptly. 'Surely you won't begin again?! **Shut up**. I sweep away all your quibbles with one gesture."

b. PONTAGNAC : « -Alors, quand le ciel met sur ma route une créature exquise, divine ! … » LUCIENNE (*passant à gauche*) : « – **Assez, monsieur** ! **assez, sur ce chapitre** ! » (Feydeau, *Le dindon*, 28–29)
'PONTAGNA: 'Then, when the sky makes me meet an exquisite, a divine creature!' LUCIENNE: '**Enough, sir! Enough on this!**"

c. Ah, là là ! quand est-ce qu'il aura fini ! **en v'là assez** ! nous **en avons assez** de toutes ces histoires ! la barbe ! qu'il nous laisse tranquille ! (P. Claudel, in *TLFi*, s. v. *ah!*)
'Oh, oh! When will it end! **It's been enough**! We've **had enough** of all these stories! Such a liar! Why won't he leave us alone?'

The proof that expressions of disagreement are deeply rooted in language is not provided only by their frequency, but also by their presence at all stylistic levels, including the familiar and vulgar one, since disagreement frequently generates a feeling of exasperation or fury:

(10) a. J'**en ai plein les bottes** de vos histoires qui ne mènent jamais à rien. (*Wiktionnaire*)
'**I'm sick and tired** of your stories, that never lead to anything.'

b. **Ta gueule**! T'as compris ?! **Ta gueule**! J'veux plus l'entendre, ta valise ! (Éric Durnez, à <https://www. lalanguefrancaise.com/>)
'**Shut your big mouth!** Do you understand? **Shut your big mouth!** I don't want to hear it any more, you deal with it!'

c. J'**en ai ras le bol** de tes **conneries**. (*Reverso*)
'**I'm sick and tired** of your **crap**.'

We also notice that all DMs/PolyMs of disagreement appearing in the above examples work as guidelines used by the speaker to trigger speech acts with significant perlocutionary force.

2.2. DMs/PolyMs of Topic Shift

As we have shown in note 1 above, Grice signalled that he failed to integrate topic shift in his theoretical framework. The preservation of topic and of the direction of the conversation during the verbal exchange is related not only to cooperation, but also to discourse coherence and to the speakers' subjective capacity of becoming aware of this thematic unity, which explains why Grice's considerations are related to the maxim of relation. The transition to a new topic is a complex phenomenon, which can only manifest itself in certain conditions, in whose absence the interlocutor can protest against the lack of coherence in the speaker's speech.

In everyday language, speakers frequently change the topic of their dialogue, as our brain works based on associations of ideas or on sequences of mental representations, which have been studied in psychology, psychiatry or philosophy. When the topic shift is signalled by a DM or a PolyM, the change in direction does not raise an issue, as the presence of the discourse marker removes the suspicion of incoherence in the speaker's discourse. Phrases such as *à propos de* 'speaking of', *au sujet de* 'with respect to', *quant à* 'as for', *d'ailleurs* 'besides' frequently show that the speaker intends to deviate somehow from the main direction of the discourse. In other cases, the speaker considers that the correlation between his/her sentences is clear for the interlocutor(s), even in the absence of a specific DM/PolyM, as s/he considers that the association of ideas is obvious.

In order to see how the topic of the conversation changes, let us look at an excerpt from a novel written by a master of dialogue, Alexandre Dumas-père. It is a conversation between two friends, the prior of the Jacobin monastery, Don Modeste Gorenflot, and a witty and highly cultured Gascon gentleman, Chicot. The discussion takes place over lunch. The prior recounts how he stifled the protests of his monks who, exhausted by military exercises, demanded a more substantial meal:

(11) « – Enfin, pour couronner l'œuvre, j'ai commandé un nouvel exercice, voulant terrasser l'hydre de la révolte : les psaumes disent cela, vous savez ; attendez donc : *Cabis poriabis diagonem*, eh ! vous ne connaissez que cela, mordieu ! » « – *Proculcabis draconem* », fit Chicot en versant à boire au prieur. « – *Draconem*, c'est cela, bravo ! **À propos de dragon**, mangez donc de cette anguille, elle emporte la bouche, c'est merveilleux ! » (A. Dumas père, *Les Quarante-cinq*, 285)
"Finally, to complete the work, I ordered a new exercise, wanting to bring down the hydra of revolt: the psalms say that, you know; wait then: *Cabis poriabis diagonem*, eh! you only know that, for God's sake!' '*Proculcabis draconem*', Chicot said, pouring the prior a drink. '*Draconem*, that's it, well done! **Speaking of the dragon**, eat this eel, it sweeps you off your feet, it's wonderful!"

The first topic shift occurs when don Gorenflot wants to provide the exact quotation of the metaphor in the psalms, describing the defeat of enemies. He makes an association of ideas that is normal for a churchman, who wants to show that his actions are in agreement with the stipulations of the Sacred Scripture. His approximate knowledge of Latin does not allow him to accurately quote the verse of Psalm 90, which emphasizes the power that God has awarded to the faithful. Chicot provides a correct, but approximate form,[4] but the word that is meaningful for the pursuit of the conversation and for the subsequent associations of ideas is *draconem*, making Gorenflot think of the eel dish on the table. He makes the association *dragon – serpent – eel*, which is motivated by the wider narrative context. In the previous chapter, the author made us witness a discussion between Gorenflot, Chicot and the monk-cook about the breeding of eels in the monastery: when very well fed, the eels they reach a considerable size, comparable to that of a large serpent[5]. Thus, in (11), the MD *à propos* 'by the way' fulfils a double function: it shows the topic shift and refers, as a textual anaphor, to a previous fragment of the text.

A quick look at our corpus shows that the adverbial phrase *à propos* is closely connected to the topic of the conversation, generally focusing on the relevant subject, with some additional mentions spontaneously provided by the speaker or requested or sometimes assumed by the interlocutor:

(12) a. « – Tu vois, dit-il (= Blazius) au tyran, combien mes prévisions **à propos** de la petite lumière rouge étaient logiquement déduites. » (Théophile Gautier, *Capitaine Fracasse*, 364)
'You see, he [Blazius] told the tyrant, that my forecasts **regarding** the small red light were logically deducted.'

b. « – Continuez, je vous prie ! Que disiez-vous ? » « – Ces messieurs me querellaient », répondit l'abbé. « – **À propos** de quoi ? » « – Sur la sainte Écriture, monsieur le Comte ! » (Gustave Flaubert, *Buvard et Pécuchet*, 112)
"Go on, please! What were you saying?' 'Those gentlemen were quarrelling with me', the abbot replied. '**About** what?' 'About the Sacred Scripture, Count!"

---

4 The actual form of the verse is *conculcabis leonem et draconem* 'and thou shalt trample under foot the lion and the dragon'. The wording of Chicot is approximate, as he replaces the verb *conculcare* by *proculcare*, but the new phrase is correct, the two verbs are partial synonyms.

5 'The one [the eel] that I will offer to the lord prior today, for example, weighs nine pounds.' 'It's a snake then', Chicot said. 'It swallowed a six-day-old chicken in one bite.' (A. Dumas-père, *Les quarante-cinq*, 280)

c. « – Et tous ces gens-là vous persécutent pour la même raison ? Sans doute **à propos** de ce secret que vous possédez en dehors d'eux ? » (Maurice Leblanc, *La demoiselle aux yeux verts*, 107)
'And all these people are going after you for the same reason? Undoubtedly **because of** that secret you have?'

As a discourse marker, the adverbial phrase *à propos* signals the topic shift as a consequence of an association of ideas. The consulted corpus has provided two types of associations: either justified by the extralinguistic situation (examples 12a, 12b, 12c), or by a linguistic element (example 11).

Sometimes, the associations triggered by extralinguistic circumstances lead the speaker to ask for additional information, to draw up a request, etc.:

(13) a. « – Va te camper sous son balcon à huit heures. » « – J'y serai comme j'y suis chaque jour, mais sans plus d'espoir que les autres jours. » « – **À propos** ! l'adresse au juste ? » (A. Dumas-père, *Les quarante-cinq*, 46)
"Go camp under his balcony at eight o'clock.' 'I will be there as I am there every day, but without more hope than the other days.' '**By the way**! What is the exact address?"

b. « – Ah ! Joyeuse m'accompagne toujours. Il était avec moi à la Grève aujourd'hui, lui, Joyeuse. » « – Eh bien ! moi j'étais ici, sire, et Votre Majesté voit que je ne perdais pas mon temps. » « – Merci, Lavalette. » « – **À propos**, sire », fit d'Épernon, après un silence d'un instant, « j'avais une chose à demander à Votre Majesté. » (A. Dumas-père, *Les Quarante-cinq*, 99)
'Ah! Joyeuse always accompanies me. He was with me at La Grève today.' 'Well! I was here, sire, and Your Majesty sees that I was not wasting my time.' 'Thank you, Lavalette.' '**By the way**, sire' d'Épernon said, after a moment's silence, 'I had something to ask your Majesty."

c. Antoine sortit une enveloppe de sa poche et s'approcha de son frère : « – Voilà la lettre pour le notaire. Tu la cachetteras… **À propos**… Toi, en cas de guerre ? … Tu as été ajourné, n'est-ce pas ? Mais… si on mobilisait ? » (R. Martin du Gard, *Les Thibault, L'Été*, 446)
'Antoine took an envelope out of his pocket and approached his brother: 'Here is the letter for the notary. You will have the notary seal it… **By the way**… You, in case of war? … You have been adjourned, have you not? But… what if France were to mobilize?"

d. « – Dans dix minutes j'en aurai fini avec mon bonhomme. Dans vingt minutes je te rejoins… Ah ! **à propos**, tu m'as envoyé l'auto ? Parfait. À tout à l'heure. » (Maurice Leblanc, *Arsène Lupin – 813*, 41)
'In ten minutes, I'll be done with my man. In twenty minutes, I'll join you… Ah! **By the way**, did you send me the car? Perfect. See you soon.'

The topic of the dialogue (13a) is a serenade that the duke Anne de Joyeuse intends to organize in order to help his brother, Henri, to court a lady. He realizes that he doesn't know her address, so he abandons the topic of the serenade for a moment, in order to request this address. Example (13b) I significant for a category of dialogues between persons with distinct social positions, such as the king and one of his favourites, the duke d'Épernon. After having discussed about a service provided to the king (the organization of the forty-five guardsmen), the duke immediately thinks of asking him for a favor, so he makes the association 'a job done for someone's benefit → a reward'. In excerpt (13c), extracted from the *Les Thibault* cycle, the two brothers, Antoine and Jacques, discuss about their father's succession, on the eve of the outbreak of the Great War. In these circumstances, Antoine moves from the discussion about the transfer of the part of the inheritance which goes to his brother to the situation of Jacques in the event of mobilization. Finally, (13d) is a fragment of a telephone conversation: the speaker announces his arrival, but he changes the topic to make sure that the interlocutor has already sent him the car to get there.

In other cases, the speaker performs a mental association that takes him outside the main direction of the conversation, due to a presence of a word in the immediate context of the sentence, as already shown in (11):

(14) a. – Et vous m'avez déjà considérablement servi, monsieur Robert Briquet, j'ose le dire ; oh ! ma femme vous bénira. Mais, **à propos**, ma pauvre femme ! ô mon Dieu, mon Dieu ! elle va être étouffée dans cette foule. (A. Dumas-père, *Les Quarante-cinq*, p. 5)
'And you have already served me considerably, Mr Robert Briquet, I dare say it; Oh! My wife will bless you. But, **by the way**, my poor wife! Oh my God, my God! she's going to be suffocated in this crowd'

b. LUCILE : « – Comment, tu connais le piano ? » BAPTISTE : « – Oui, Mademoiselle. Ma mère en avait un vieux au village. » LUCILE : « – Allons donc ! Et tu t'en servais ? » BAPTISTE : « De garde-manger, oui, Mademoiselle. Au pays, nous n'avons pas les moyens de gâcher des pianos pour en faire des instruments de musique. » LUCILE : « – Ah ! **À propos** de musique, il viendra tout à l'heure un monsieur. » (Georges Feydeau, *Amour et piano*)
'LUCILE: 'What, do you know what a piano is?' BAPTISTE: 'Yes, miss. My mother had an old one in the village.' LUCILE: 'Come on! And did you use it?' BAPTISTE: 'As a pantry, yes, miss. In the country, we cannot afford to waste pianos to make musical instruments.' LUCILE: 'Oh! **Speaking of** music, a gentleman will come later."

c. « – (Les forçats) n'osent pas grogner, commandant… Du reste, premier qui rouspète, je lui brûle la boîte au sel ! » « – C'est le règlement, sergent », approuva Chéri-Bibi. « **À propos**, capitaine, qu'est-ce qu'on a fait de mon règlement ? » (Gaston Leroux, *Les cages flottantes*, 243)
"(The convicts) don't dare to growl, Commandant… Anyway, the first one to complain, I'll deck his noggin!' 'It's the rules, sergeant', Cheri-Bibi agreed. '**By the way**, captain, what have they done with my rules?"

In (14a), the speaker, a Parisian bourgeois named Jean Friard, expresses his gratitude for having been saved from a stampede, evoking the blessings Robert Briquet will receive from his wife. He changes the topic, as he was at the Saint Antoine gate to wait for his wife, who was also in danger of being crushed by the crowd. For the conversations in (14b–c), the words *musique* 'music' and, respectively, *règlement* 'rules' trigger a change in direction, always signalled by this DM.

The discourse marker *d'ailleurs* 'besides, what's more' signals a broadening of the topic, an additional piece of information that is not strictly related to the main theme, but which has arisen in the speaker's mind by association of ideas:

(15) a. « – Le fait est que si mon inconnue est aussi aimable qu'elle est belle, je vous déclare que je me fixe à Rome pour six semaines au moins. J'adore Rome, et **d'ailleurs** j'ai toujours eu un goût marqué pour l'archéologie. » (A. Dumas-père, in *TLFi*, s. v. *adorer*)
'The fact is that if my stranger is as lovable as she is beautiful, I declare to you that I am settling in Rome for at least six weeks. I love Rome, and, **besides**, I've always had a strong taste for archaeology.'

b. « – Mulot a été condamné pour faux témoignage. Injustement **d'ailleurs**. » (André Gide, dans *TLFi*, s. v. *ouais*)
'Mulot was convicted of perjury. Wrongly **by the way**.'

c. « – Cette chère enfant ! » soupira la maîtresse de pension de sa voix la plus tendre. « Je crains qu'elle ne vous fatigue. **D'ailleurs,** vos moments sont précieux. » (Anatole France, *Le crime de Sylvestre Bonnard*, 121)
"That dear child!' the boarding school mistress sighed in her most tender voice. 'I'm afraid she will tire you. **Besides**, your moments are precious."

Another interesting marker is *quant à* 'as for', which focuses on a new topic, often subsidiary to the previous one or on a specific detail of the main subject of discussion.

(16) a. « – Des papiers ! des actes de naissance ! » s'écrièrent les ennemis de Rozaine, « mais Arsène Lupin vous en fournira tant que vous voudrez ! **Quant à** la blessure, c'est qu'il n'en a pas reçu… ou qu'il en a effacé la trace ! » (Maurice Leblanc, *Arsène Lupin*, 18)
"Papers! Birth certificates!' Rozaine's enemies cried, 'but Arsène Lupine will supply you with as much as you want! **As for** the injury, he did not get one… or he erased the trace of it!"

b. « – **Quant à** ma bénédiction, je m'en vais vous la donner tout de suite ! » et le vieux ouvrit ses bras pour l'accueillir. (André Gide, dans *TLFi*, s. v. *bras*)
'**As for** my blessing, I am going to give it to you immediately! and the old man opened his arms to welcome him.'

c. « – Combien connaissez-vous de sortes de vin, **quant à** la couleur ? » « – Il y a deux sortes de vin : le vin blanc et le vin noir. » (Georges Duhamel, dans *TLFi*, s. v. *combien*)

"How many kinds of wine do you know, **as for** colour?' 'There are two kinds of wine: white wine and black wine."

This discourse marker also has the more special capacity of focusing on a change in the interlocutor or of individualizing the person of the relevant group. It can also mark a contrast between the addressee and the speaker, as in (17d):

(17) a. « – Restez donc tranquilles! » continuait le professeur indigné. « **Quant à** vous, le nouveau, vous me copierez vingt fois le verbe *ridiculus sum.* » (Gustave Flaubert, in *TLFi*, s. v. *copier*)
"So stay calm!' the indignant teacher pursued. '**As for** you, the new one, you will copy the verb *ridiculus sum* twenty times."

b. « – Antoinette, adieu ! » reprit madame de Beauséant, « soyez heureuse. **Quant à** vous, vous l'êtes, vous êtes jeune, vous pouvez croire à quelque chose », dit-elle à l'étudiant. (H. de Balzac. *Père Goriot*, 474)
"Antoinette, farewell!' Madame de Beauseant resumed, 'be happy. **As for** you, you are already happy, you are young, you can believe in something', she told the student.'

c. Qu'on me tienne au courant chaque minute. J'attends ici les messages. **Quant à toi**, président, cours au-devant des émeutiers, et, de ta voix la plus enthousiaste, fais-leur part de la nouvelle. (Jean Giraudoux, *Électre*, 225)
'Let me know every minute. I am waiting for the messages here. **As for** you, President, run to the rioters, and, in your most enthusiastic voice, tell them the news.'

d. **Elle** prenait un enfantin plaisir au spectacle. **Quant à moi** je le suivais à peine. (Gide in *TLFi*, s. v. *acrobate*)
'**She** took a childish pleasure in the show. **As for me**, I barely followed it.'

2.3. DMs/PolyMs of Reformulation

We have shown that phenomenon of reformulation, studied for a long time under the name of 'paraphrase', seems to contradict both the principle of economy and the idea that, after the message is uttered, the inferences are only made by the receivers.

When developing his theoretical framework, Grice (1975, 1978) tried to explain the gap between the conventional meaning of a phrase according to the linguistic code and the contextual meaning of the message ('non-natural meaning'), a gap that is reduced and sometimes even cancelled by the receivers' inferences. This gap may be more or less wide and the Relevance Theory attributes to receivers the (relative) capacity of 'thought reading', i.e. the ability to confer to the speaker certain thoughts and/or (communicative) intentions, which helps them understand the message correctly.

The existence of paraphrases and, more specifically, of DMs of reformulation shows that there are, however, situations when the receiver is not sure of having understood well or s/he realizes that s/he has not grasped the full meaning of the message. This is frequently due to phenomena studied by lexical pragmatics.[6] Deirdre Wilson presents semantic phenomena such as narrowing or specification (for instance, in *all doctors* ***drink***, the verb *drink* convey not the encoded sense 'drink liquid' but, more specifically, 'drink alcohol', or 'drink significant amounts of alcohol'), extension (for a fashion text, in the phrase *brown is the new* ***black*** the adjective *black* evokes the category of staple colours in a fashion wardrobe) approximation (*this coat cost* ***1,000*** *dollars.* means ' it costs about 1,000 dollars', etc.) (Wilson, 2003).

Lexical pragmatics recovers and capitalizes concepts proposed by psychologists, for instance by Lawrence Barsalou (1987, 1992), who has shown that, sometimes, the meaning of an item is built on the spot, ***ad hoc*** and depending on a certain context. *Ad hoc* concepts have been integrated in a second phase in the development of cognitive pragmatics, a theory trying to explain their elaboration (Sperber & Wilson, 1998; Wilson & Kolaiti, 2017). However, the theory has not changed the concept of 'relevance', which is still defined as the stimulation of cognitive processes appraised in terms of costs and benefits. The theory continues to applaud low costs for information processing efforts (perception, memory and inference efforts) in relevance-theoretic comprehension procedure: the greater the processing effort expended, the lower the relevance of the input to the individual at that time (Wilson & Sperber, 2004: 609). The existence of the paraphrase and of DMs of reformulation shows that the speaker sometimes decides to make additional efforts in order to obtain the intended cognitive efforts, an issue which still remains outside the theory.

If the speaker uses linguistic expressions in a particular, contextual, meaning, i.e. *ad hoc*, the interlocutor may ask him/her to 'reformulate' the message, to clarify it:

(18) a. « – Admets, si tu veux, que je sois un sous-traitant. » « – **C'est-à-dire?** » « – [C'est-à-dire] que je fais une besogne que d'autres signent. » (Éduard Estaunié, in *TLFi*, s. v. *c'est-à-dire*)
"Admit, if you will, that I'm a subcontractor.' '**What do you mean?**' '[I mean] that I am doing the job that is signed off by others."

---

6 'Lexical pragmatics is a rapidly developing branch of linguistics that investigates the processes by which linguistically-specified ("literal") word meanings are modified in use' (D. Wilson 2003: 2003).

b. « – Votre âge? » « – Vingt ans. » « – Votre profession? » « – Agiteur de bottes. » « – **Comment?** » « – Agiteur d'bottes. » « – **Qu'est-ce que c'est que ça?** » (E. et J. de Goncourt, in *TLFi*, s. v. *agiteur*)
"Your age?' 'Twenty' 'Your job?' 'Boot shaker.' '**What?**' 'Boot shaker.' '**What is that?**"[7]

c. « – [Son écriture, sur la carte-vue] je ne l'ai pas imitée. » « – **Vous voulez dire** ? » « – Qu'il l'a écrit lui-même. » (G. Simenon, in *TLFi*, s. v. *admiratif*)
"[His handwriting, on the postcard] I did not imitate it.' '**What do you mean?**' 'That he wrote it himself'."

On the other hand, DMs/PolyMs of reformulation show that, sometimes, the speaker acts like a second hearer, i.e. s/he hears his/her own message and evaluates it according to two parameters: (i) his/her own thoughts, thus verifying the congruity of the message with what s/he had intended to communicate; (ii) the transparency of his/her message in relation to the interlocutor's/interlocutors' (actual or supposed) capacity of understanding it. If s/he considers that one of these two aspects is not satisfactory, s/he reformulates his/her message, thus performing an additional effort (Costăchescu, 2022). This waste of energy, however, is not useless, but rather motivated, as shown by the following examples, which illustrate spontaneous reformulations of the speaker, who provides synonyms or explanations:

(19) a. L'abus des narcotiques **c'est-à-dire** leur usage habituel, contribue beaucoup à hâter cette vieillesse précoce. (Pierre Jean Georges Cabanis, dans *TLFi*, s. v. *abus*)
'The abuse of narcotics, **that is**, their habitual use, contributes a lot to hasten this early aging.'

b. Je viens du bureau des échevins, **autrement dit** bureau de la ville. La municipalité vous refuse votre alignement. (Louis Reybaud, in *TLFi*, s. v. *ville*)
'I come from the office of the aldermen, **in other words** the town office. The municipality refuses your alignment.'

c. Toute peinture hollandaise est concave; **je veux dire** qu'elle se compose de courbes décrites autour d'un point déterminé par l'intérêt, d'ombres circulaires autour d'une lumière dominante. (Eugène Fromentin, dans *TLFi*, s. v. *concave*)
'All Dutch painting is concave; **I mean**, it is composed of curves drawn around a point determined by interest, of circular shadows around a dominant light.'

7 In slang French, the phrase *agiteur de bottes* '*lit.* boot shaker' is the name of the person whose job was to intimidate the clients of brothels who wanted to leave without paying by waving boots tied to a string, a gesture which signalled the arrival of the bouncers.

In other situations, the speaker considers that his/her previous statement does not convey an accurate piece of information, so the reformulation brings a correction:

(20) a. « – Monsieur Bonacieux, vous avez une femme ? » « – Oui, monsieur; **c'est-à-dire**, j'en avais une. » (Alex. Dumas père, *Les trois mousquetaires*, 328)
"Monsieur Bonacieux, do you have a wife?' 'Yes, sir; **that is to say**, I had one."

b. « – Une moustache grise – **je veux dire**, grisonnante. » (Marcel Pagnol, in *TLFi*, s. v. *grisonnant*)
'A grey moustache – **I mean**, grizzled.'

c. « – Ces fleurs sont d'un rose vraiment céleste », dit Legrandin, « **je veux dire** couleur de ciel rose. Car il y a un rose ciel comme il y a un bleu ciel. » (Marcel Proust, in *TLFi*, s. v. *ciel*)
"These flowers are a truly heavenly pink', Legrandin said. '**I mean**, the colour of a pink sky. Because there is a pink sky, as there is a blue sky."

d. « -Tu patientes ou pour **mieux dire**, tu ajournes, tu diffères, tu retardes, quoi? » (Henri-Frédéric Amiel, in *TLFi*, s. v. *ajourner*)
'You wait or, **to put it better**, you postpone, you differ, you delay, what?'

Frequently, when a phrase has a very general meaning, the reformulation specifies its precise contextual meaning through semantic narrowing:

(21) a. Sans doute, **la dernière molécule sociale, à savoir le village**, est bien encore un clan transformé. (Émile Durkheim, in *TLFi*, s. v. *molécule*)
'Undoubtedly, **the last social molecule, namely the village**, is still a transformed clan.'

b. Quand il l'eut reposée chez elle, il revint dans la chambre de son fils prendre **ce qu'il désirait, c'est-à-dire** les dossiers qui chargeaient le battant d'un secrétaire … (Maurice Druon, in *TLFi*, s. v. *battant*)
'After he had taken her home, he went back to his son's room to take **what he wanted, that is to say** the files that loaded the door of a desk…'

c. Le « miracle grec » c'est beau, mais **le miracle français, je veux dire** notre expansion au treizième siècle, ce n'est pas mal non plus. (Maurice Barrès, in *TLFi*, s. v. *miracle*)
'The 'Greek miracle' is beautiful, but **the French miracle, I mean** our expansion in the thirteenth century, is not bad either.'

Our corpus has also provided sentences including rare expressions, idioms or metaphorical sequences, whose exact meaning should be explained:

(22) a. Madame mère **faisait de la chaise longue** de principe. **Je veux dire** qu'elle y était assise. (Hervé Bazin, in *TLFi*, s. v. *chaise*)
'My mother **was doing** her usual **sun lounger**. **I mean** she was sitting on it.'

b. Des **déserteurs à la deuxième puissance, je veux dire** des hommes qui ont déserté d'abord le drapeau de l'Allemagne et ensuite le drapeau de la France. (Jean Jaurès, in *TLFi*, s. v. *déserter*)
'From **double deserters, I mean** men who first deserted the flag of Germany and then the flag of France.'

c. **Je casse une canne, autrement dit** je m'esbigne, ou, comme on dit à la cour, je file. (Victor Hugo, in *TLFi*, s. v. *esbigner*)
'**I make my getaway, in other words** I'm off, or, as they say at court, I leave quickly. (Victor Hugo, in *TLFi*, s. v. *esbigner*)'

Contextual *ad hoc* meanings are frequently so particular that the speaker explains them spontaneously, as, if s/he does not make this additional effort, there is a risk that s/he may not be understood:

(23) a. « – Avez-vous **joué** Phèdre? **Je veux dire** le rôle de Phèdre. » (Georges Duhamel, in *TLFi* s. v. *rôle*)
'Have you **played** Phaedra? **I mean** the role of Phaedra'

b. … j'appris **la discipline, à savoir** : que le caporal a toujours raison lorsqu'il parle au soldat, le sergent lorsqu'il parle au caporal. (Erckmann-Chatrian, in *TLFi*, s. v. *deux*)
'I learned **discipline, namely**: that the corporal is always right when he speaks to the soldier, the sergeant when he speaks to the corporal.'

c. Ma passion pour **quitter Grenoble, c'est-à-dire lui** [= mon père], et ma passion pour les mathématiques, seul moyen que j'eusse de quitter cette ville que j'abhorrais et que je hais encore me jeta dans une profonde solitude. (Stendhal, in *TLFi*, s. v. *abhorrer*)
'My passion for **leaving Grenoble, that is him** [= my father], and my passion for mathematics, the only way I could leave this town which I abhorred and which I still hate threw me into a deep loneliness.'

3. Conclusion

The examination of the functions of DMs/PolyMs belonging to various category is likely to suggest changes, sometimes small linguistic adjustments to pragmatic theories that have a philosophical and/or logical origin. Here, we have dealt with Grice's conversational theory and with the Relevance Theory.

DM/sPolyMs of disagreement show that (i) during the conversation, one of the speakers may refuse to continue the verbal exchange, thus temporarily suspending the Cooperative Principle; (ii) the negative reaction of a participant to the conversation may be less abrupt, as s/he may just request to change the topic or the direction of the talk. We consider that the Cooperative Principle should be formulated so as to suggest these two possibilities. This remark is reinforced by the existence of specific DMs/PolyMs, such as *au sujet de* 'with respect to', *quant à* 'as for', *d'ailleurs* 'besides', *je veux dire* 'I mean', etc., which show the shift in the topic or in the course of the conversation.

The presence of DMs/PolyMs of reformulation in discourse make us doubt the role assigned to the principle of economy in verbal communication, a role presented by Martinet (the principle of least effort), Grice (the Maxim of Quantity) and Sperber/Wilson (in a part of the definition of the notion of 'relevance', which stipulates that the less effort is needed to process the information, the higher the relevance of the message). Reformulation shows, to begin with, that the speakers do not always assign the same importance to the maxims drawn up by Grice, as the Maxim of Relation and of Manner prevail over the Maxim of Quantity, i.e. the speaker is willing to make additional efforts in order to express a relevant and clear message. The same remark is applicable to the theoretical framework of cognitive pragmatics, since, in order to obtain optimal cognitive effects, the speakers frequently make additional efforts, which does not reduce the relevance of the message, quite the contrary.

Secondly, the phenomenon of reformulation requires reconsidering a common principle of the two pragmatic theories – the receivers' inferences. For Grice, the receivers make inferences in order to infer the non-natural meaning of the message, a meaning that corresponds to what the speaker means, beyond the proper meaning of the phrases in his/her message. For Sperber and Wilson, the receiver's inferences are a part of the (cognitive) efforts required to understand and interpret the message. Pragmatics should study the speaker's inferences too, since, after having said the sentence, the speaker judges it, as if s/he were a second receiver, checking whether what s/he has said matches what s/he means and whether the sentence is understandable to the interlocutors. If s/he is not satisfied with one of these aspects, s/he may provide a paraphrase, repeating in other words what s/he has just said.

The study of DMs/PolyMs enriches and clarifies not only the prerequisites for a proper functioning of the dialogue, but also the logical mechanism of formation of presuppositions. This is a situation that emphasizes once more the need for corpus linguistics and dialogue linguistics to take into account the philosophical and logical approaches adopted in the last decades.

References

Barsalou, L. (1987). The instability of graded structure. Implications for the nature of concepts. In Neisser, U. (ed.), *Concepts and conceptual development: Ecological and intellectual bases of categories* (pp. 101–140). Cambridge University Press.

Barsalou, L. (1992). Frames, concepts, and conceptual fields. In A. Leehrer & E. Feder Kittay (eds.), *Frames, fields and contrasts. New essays in semantic and lexical organization* (pp. 21–74). L. Erlbaum Associates.

Bracops, M. (2006). *Introduction à la pragmatique*. De Boeck.

Costăchescu, A. (2013). *La pragmatique linguistique : Théories, débats, exemples. Lincom Studies in Pragmatics*, 24.

Costăchescu, A. (2014). On disagreement markers in French and Romanian dialogue. In C. Ghezzi & P. Molinelli (eds.), *Discourse and pragmatic markers: From Latin to Romance languages* (pp. 41–60). Oxford University Press.

Costăchescu, A. (2022). A self-critical speaker: The Romanian reformulation marker *adică* 'I mean/namely'. In L. Ionescu-Ruxăndoiu, M.-V. Constantinescu, G. Stoica & Ş. Harturar (eds.), *Attitude and stances in discourse* (pp. 292–315). Cambridge Scholar Publishing.

Dostie, G. (2004). *Pragmaticalisation et marqueurs discursifs. Analyse sémantique et traitement lexicographique*. De Boeck-Duculot.

Dostie, G. & Pusch, G. (2007). Présentation. Les marqueurs discursifs. Sens et variation. *Langue française* 2/154, 3–12. https://www.cairn.info/article.php?ID_ARTICLE=LF_154_0003

Grice, H. P. (1975/1979). Logic and conversation. In P. Cole & J. L. Morgan (éds.), *Syntax and semantics, vol. 3: Speech Acts* (pp. 41–58). Academic Press. https://www.persee.fr/doc/comm_0588-8018_1979 _num_30_1_1446

Grice, H. P. (1978/1989). Further notes on logic and conversation. In P. Cole (éd.), *Syntax and semantics, vol. 9: Pragmatics* (pp. 113–128, pp. 41–57). Academic Press. Reprinted in Grice, H. P. (ed.) (1989). *Studies in the way of words*. Harvard University Press.

Martinet, A. (1960). *Éléments de linguistique Générale*. Armand Colin.

Pusch, C. (2007). Faut dire : variation et sens d'un marqueur parenthétique entre connectivité et (inter)subjectivité. *Langue Française* 2/154, 29–44.

Sperber, D. & Wilson, D. (1986). *Relevance, communication and cognition*. Harvard University Press.

Sperber, D. & Wilson, D. (1998). The mapping between the mental and the public lexicon. In P. Carruthers & J. Boucher (eds.), *Language and thought: Interdisciplinary themes* (pp. 184–200). Cambridge University Press.

Wilson, D. (2003). Relevance and lexical pragmatics. *Rivista di Linguistica* 15/2L, 273–291. https://linguistica.sns.it/RdL/15.2/03.Wilson.pdf

Wilson, D. & Kolaiti, P. (2017). Lexical pragmatics and implicit communication. In P. Cap & M. Dynel (eds.), *Implicitness: From lexis to discourse* (pp. 147–175). John Benjamins.

Wilson, D. & Sperber, D. (2004). Relevance theory. In L. Horn & G. Ward (eds.) *The Handbook of Pragmatics* (pp. 607–632). Blackwell Publishing.

Corpus

Balzac, H. de. (1855). *Le père Goriot*. Bibliothèque électronique du Québec.

Barbusse, H. (1925). *L'enfer*. Bibliothèque électronique du Québec.

Dumas, A. (1844). *Les trois mousquetaires*. Bibliothèque électronique du Québec.

Dumas, A. (1847). *Les Quarante-cinq*. Bibliothèque électronique du Québec.

Feydeau, G. (1883). *Amour et piano*. https://fr.wikisource.org/wiki/ Amour_et_piano

Feydeau, G. (1896). *Le dindon*. Bibliothèque électronique du Québec.

Flaubert, G. (1881). *Buvard et Pécuchet*. Bibliothèque électronique du Québec.

France, A. (1880). *Le crime de Sylvestre Bonnard*. Bibliothèque électronique du Québec.

Gautier, T. (1889). *Le capitaine Fracasse*. Bibliothèque électronique du Québec.

Giraudoux, J. (1929). *Amphitryon 38*. Bibliothèque électronique du Québec.

Giraudoux, J. (1937). *Électre*. Bibliothèque électronique du Québec.

Grand Robert de la langue française. (2005). (2nd ed.) Le Robert.

https://fr.wiktionary.org/wiki/Wiktionnaire

https://www.reverso.net/traduction-texte

https://www.wordreference.com/

Leblanc, M. (1910). *Arsène Lupin – 813*. Bibliothèque électronique du Québec.

Leblanc, M. (1927). *La demoiselle aux yeux verts*. Bibliothèque électronique du Québec.

Leroux, G. (1913). *Les cages flottantes*. Bibliothèque électronique du Québec.

Martin du Gard, R. (1936). *Les Thibault*, tome VII, *L'Été 1914*. Bibliothèque électronique du Québec.

Ponson du Terrail, P. A. (1858). *Rocambole, Le club des Valets-de-Cœur* II. Bibliothèque électronique du Québec.

Sue, E. (1849). *Les mystères du peuple*, tome VII. Bibliothèque électronique du Québec.

Vigny, A. de. (1835). *Chatterton*. https://www.academia.edu/42192660/Chatterton_Alfred_de_Vigny

Chiara Ghezzi

2 *Adunque* and *Dunque* in Old Italian between Free and Patterned Variation: The Role of English Translation in Pragmatic Analysis

Abstract: From earliest records, the Italian *adunque* and *dunque* 'then, therefore' are used apparently in free variation as they both translate Lat. *igitur*, *ergo*, *itaque*. If the first is more frequent until the end of the 16th century, the second increases steadily until the 20th century when it totally substitutes *adunque*. Despite their very long use, the history of the two forms is very difficult to reconstruct. The core uses of both forms are those of correlative and resultative connectives. However, in earlier texts, some differences emerge as only *adunque* can have the temporal meaning of 'at that time' and it is more frequently used in bridging contexts whose reading is also compatible with that of discourse and pragmatic marker. This study considers patterns of use of the two forms in texts dating to the 14th century, when the variant *adunque* was still very frequent. By considering the use of both forms in Boccaccio's *Decameron* and Catherine of Siena's letters, it confronts these texts with their English translations. The analysis of English translations equivalents of both forms proves a rewarding way of mapping the functional spectra of forms and serves as a heuristic tool to establish their semantic-pragmatic fields.

Keywords: *adunque*, *dunque*, Italian discourse markers

1. Introduction[1]

From earliest written records, two Italian variants *adunque* and *dunque*, which can both be translated with Eng. 'then, therefore, so' and Lat. *igitur, ergo, itaque*, are used apparently in free variation. However, if the form *adunque* is more frequent until the end of the 16th century, the turning point being 1592 according to Google Books Ngram Viewer (see Figure 2.1), *dunque* increases steadily until the 20th century, and today it has totally substituted *adunque*, which is considered an archaic literary variant of *dunque* (IT Zingarelli, 2020, s.v.).

---

1 This work has been carried out thanks to the funding of PRIN 2017 project 'Writing expertise as a dynamic sociolinguistic force' coordinated by Piera Molinelli, University of Bergamo. The author hereby thanks Piera Molinelli, Pierluigi Cuzzolin and the anonymous reviewer for their help in the discussion of this paper.

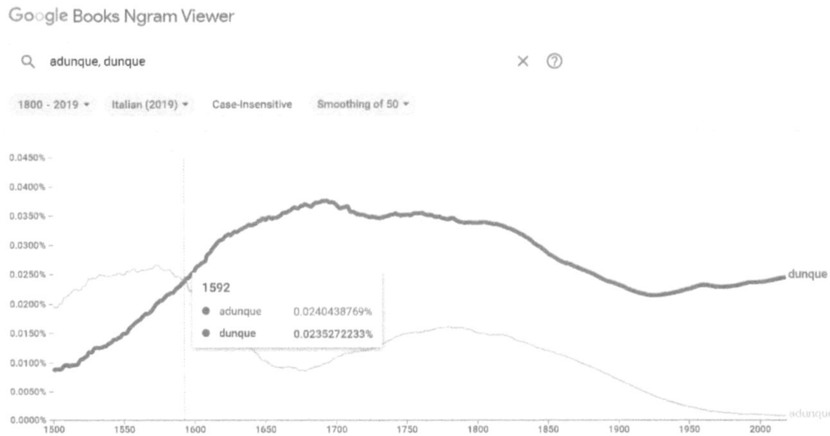

Figure 2.1. Trajectory and frequency of adunque and dunque in Google Books Ngram Viewer

However, despite their very long use, the history of the two forms is very difficult to reconstruct (see for instance Fedriani & Molinelli, 2021 for a discussion on the etymology of It. *dunque* or Hansen 1997: 163 and Badiou-Monferran, 2008 for similar consideration on Fr. *donc*).

In Contemporary Italian etymological dictionaries, *adunque* is generally treated as a variant of *dunque*, which is considered the main lemma (e.g., DELI and TLIO, s.v.). Yet, if one considers earlier dictionaries, the situation is reversed. For instance, the *Dizionario degli Accademici della Crusca*, one of the oldest dictionaries of the Italian language, in its first 1612 edition, describes the lemma *dunque* simply as referring to *adunque*, which is, contrary to todays' etymological dictionaries, the main lemma (*Dizionario Accademici della Crusca*, s.v.). Along similar lines, Patota (1987: 97) while commenting on the use of *dunque* by the writer Ugo Foscolo at the closure of the 18th, underlines how in actual use *dunque* is more common, even though for the lexicographers of the time as the *Crusca,* D'Alberti and Tramater *adunque* is the main lemma.

As regards the functions of *adunque* and *dunque* in the language, moving from Old Italian, both forms perform similar discourse-pragmatic functions, their core use being that of correlative and resultative connectives 'then, therefore, thus, so' (Salvi & Renzi, 2010). However, especially in dialogic texts, as novellas, narrative texts with dialogic sequences, and letters, both forms can also be used as discourse or pragmatic markers[2], as exemplified by *adunque* in (1a) and *dunque* in (1b) below. The example in (1a), from Virgil's *Aeneid* and its vulgar Italian version, both Lat. *ergo* and O.It. *adunque* operate as pragmatic markers as they appear in injunctive contexts, co-occurring with an imperative, and have the function of urging Anchise, Aeneas' father, to be carried by his son in order to escape from a burning Troy. Note, in this regard, the presence of the injunctive marker *age* 'come on' in the original Latin version. Instead the example in (1b), from Seneca's the Younger letter to his friend Lucilius, both Lat. *ergo* and O.It. *dunque* are used in questions and invite the interlocutor to make an inference.

(1)

(a)

Lat.	**Ergo** age, care pater, cervici imponere nostrae; ipse subibo umeris, nec me labor iste gravabit; (Virgilio, *Eneide*, II, 707)
O.It.	**Adunque**, o caro padre, ponete al nostro collo. Io succederò con li omeri, né mi gravarà questa fatica (OVI, K513 l.2, 245.4, *Eneide volgarizzata*)
	'Come **then**, dear father, clasp my neck: I will carry you on my shoulders: that task won't weigh on me'

(b)

Lat.	Quid **ergo** est? non puto pauperem cui quantulumcumque superest sat est (Sen. Ep. 1–15, ep. 1)
O.It.	**Dunque**, che ssarà? Io non credo che quelli sia povero a cui basta quello che gli è rimaso, (OVI, *Pistole di Seneca* (red. I), 1308/25 (fior.))
Eng.	'What is the state of things, **then**? It is this: I do not regard a man as poor, if the little which remains is enough for him.'

In later centuries the situation is similar. For instance, at the beginning of the 19th century, as exemplified in (2) and (3) both *adunque* and *dunque* are used to close a letter. The example in (2), with *dunque*, is written by the writer Ugo Foscolo to his dear friend Silvio Pellico, while the second, in example (3), is from Giuseppe Grassi, a great admirer of Foscolo. It is possible to hypothesise, as regards the register of the two letters, that if Foscolo had a higher degree of intimacy with his dear friend Silvio, which can also be seen in the use of the diminutive to refer to Stefano, his relation with Grassi was not as intimate.

2 Discourse markers are intended here as functional units which index the structure of discourse/text, while pragmatic markers are units which index the relation of interlocutors and the speakers' stance (cf. Ghezzi, 2014).

(2) Addio **dunque** mio Silvio: Stefanino ti abbraccia (Ugo Foscolo, *Epistolario*, October 1812, Ugo Foscolo to Silvio Pellico)
'Goodbye **then** my Silvio. Little Stefano hugs you'

(3) [...] altre novità letterarie non abbiamo. Addio **adunque** mio caro Foscolo; [...]. (Ugo Foscolo, *Epistolario*, 8 January 1817, Giuseppe Grassi to Ugo Foscolo).
'We do not have any other news. Goodbye **then** my dear Foscolo.'

Apparently, therefore, the two forms, at least in the 19th century, could be used as register variants based on the formality of the context, i.e. *adunque* would be more formal, while *dunque* less formal.

Yet, a century later, it is possible to identify examples as (4), where both forms co-exist in the same context.

(4) Concretezza politica **adunque**, e **dunque** concezione integrale, totalitaria, etica dello Stato (1937, *Rivista di filosofia neoscolastica*, 19, 634)
'Politic concreteness **then**, and **therefore** an integral, totalitarian and ethic conception of State'

In (4), an extract from a journal of philosophy dating to the middle of the 20th century, the two forms do not seem two operate as mere variants, rather they perform different, although partly overlapping, connective functions. *Adunque* has a resultative value and is positioned in the right periphery of the sentence, while *dunque* has a consecutive value and is positioned in the left periphery of the sentence.

Studies on the discourse-pragmatic domain of use of the two forms show that as early as Old Italian, another functionally concurrent form is developing, i.e., *allora* (from Lat. *illa ora* 'at that time'), which is gradually taking over parts of the discourse-pragmatic functions of *(a)dunque*, especially in its uses as discourse and pragmatic markers. (cf. Ghezzi & Molinelli, 2021).

Therefore, moving from these preliminary data and hypothesis, this contribution will attempt to answer a series of questions. Firstly, it describes the uses of *adunque* and *dunque* in Old Italian; secondly, it discusses whether the two forms have (partially) different functions, or they are used in free variation; thirdly, it considers if it is possible to identify a sort of personal patterned variability which can be associated with a writers' history of usage. In that case *(a)dunque* would be part of a repertoire of resources for writers to express their stance in discreet speech events (Jaffe, 2009).

Discourse and pragmatic markers, as is the case of some uses of *adunque* and *dunque*, are mostly polyfunctional items whose different discourse-pragmatic functions are often difficult to pinpoint and separate clearly. As Bazzanella (2001) notes, they tend to be polyfunctional both sintagmatically (*in praesentia*) and paradigmatically (*in absentia*). In this regard, a number of studies stress how translation data can be used to gain insight into the precise meaning of the linguistic forms under study (Noël, 2003; Degand, 2009). As Aijmer et al. (2006: 111) note, translations of pragmatic markers can serve as a heuristic for discovering contextual dimensions or for making more fine-grained divisions in these dimensions, because the translations force one to account for the contextual factors that lead to particular choices.

This cross-linguistic method can lead to establishing semantic-pragmatic fields. By taking the translator's profile as a starting point, one is likely to acquire some information on the original propositional content of the message and on the potentially accompanying pragmatic implicatures, together with very relevant information of the functional domains of use of the forms (Mortier, 2007: 144).

These heuristic data become precious especially in the analysis of functional domains of forms, as is the case of those under analysis here, which share (partially) overlapping meanings and functions. In this sense, one last objective of this study is to find out whether translation can be of help in uncovering different patterns of use of *adunque* and *dunque*.

Moving from these premises and these questions, the aim of this study is to uncover patterns of use of *adunque* and *dunque* in two dialogic genres of texts written during the 14th century, when the variant *adunque* was still very frequent (i.e., a selection of letters written by Saint Catherine of Siena and novellas in Boccaccio's *Decameron*) and to confront them with their English translations. The English translations will be used on one hand to map the functional spectra of both forms and, on the other hand, to establish their semantic-pragmatic fields (Degand, 2009: 174).

The corpus built for the analysis comprises the novellas in Boccaccio's *Decameron* (1–5th day) and a selection of Catherine of Siena's letters, together with their English translations. Both the Italian editions of the two texts and their English translations are synthesised in Table 2.1.

Table 2.1. Italian and English versions of texts

Italian	**English**
Branca, Vittorio (a c. di). 1992. *Decameron.* Torino, Einaudi.	Rigg, James M. (ed.) 1903. *Decameron.* Digireads.
Meattini, Alberto (a c. di). 1993. *Lettere di Caterina da Siena.* Milano, Paoline Editoriale Libri.	Dutton Scudder, Vida (ed.). 1905. *Saint Catherine of Siena as seen in her letters.* London, New York: J.M. Dent and E.P. Dutton.

This paper is therefore structured as follows. In Section 2 a discussion of the etymology of the two forms is given, in Section 3 the functions of the two forms in the corpus is described, while Section 4 offers an overview of the distribution of the forms together with their English translations. Section 5 discusses some conclusions.

2. The Etymology of *adunque* and *dunque*

For the expression of consecution, between the 13th and 14th century, two sets of forms in *ad-* or *d-* compete with each other. One includes a paradigm in *dunque*, another a paradigm in *adunque*. In the corpus OVI, which comprises texts written in those two centuries, the two paradigms include the following variants:

(1) *dunque: ddunque, deoncha, doca, domcha, domqua, domque, donca, doncha, donche, donka, donqu', donqua, donque, dumqu', dumqua, dumque, dunca, duncha, dunche, duncqua, dunka, dunqu', dunqua, dunquano, dunque, dûnque, duunche.*

(2) *adunque: addonqua, addonque, addunca, addunqu', addunqua, addunque, adomqua, adonca, adonch, adoncha, adonche, adonka, adonqu', adonqua, adonque, adumgua, adumqua, adumque, adunca, aduncha, adunche, adunco, adunka, adunqu', adunqua, adunque, andonca, andoncha, andonqua, andunqua, andunque, aunque;*

Depending on the position of scholars on the etymology of the forms, it is possible to identify a third set of forms in *id-*, much less frequent in the OVI corpus, represented by *idunque*.

Rather interestingly, if one considers the distribution of the functional competing form, which at the time was just beginning to gain momentum, i.e. It. *allora,* derived from Lat. *(ad) illa(m) hora(m)* 'at that time/hour', one notices how a similar set of paradigms was present. The more common variant with *al-* (i.e. It. *allora*), which was derived from the Latin prepositional phrase *ad illa(m) hora(m)*, coexisted with the one in *l-* (i.e. It. *lora*), derived from the Lat. noun phrase *illa(m) hora(m)*. Yet, it is true that this second form was peripheral in Old Italian (only 45 hits in the OVI corpus vs 21907 of *allora*) and was used mostly in Northern varieties or in texts with a strong influence of French, where instead the sets *lors* and *alors* where much more widespread (cf. Badiou-Monferran, 2008). However, for the pair *adunque* and *dunque* this does not seem to be the case, as their frequencies and distribution are much more even (8273 hits for *dunque* and 8906 for *adunque*).

The reconstruction of the etymology of the forms, together with their functional values, is extremely complicated as it has its roots in the changes that were developing in Latin and Vulgar Latin within the complex system of correlative deictic temporal adverbs which gradually disappeared in a long process of erosion (e.g. *cum* 'when' – *tum* 'then', *nunc* 'now' – *tunc* 'then') (Lüdtke, 2015: 544).

Particularly relevant for the development of *(a)dunque* and other Romance forms (e.g. Fr. *(a)donc*, Sp. *entonces*, Port. *então*, Rom. *atunci*) is the opposition between *nunc* 'now', which denotes the moment of speaking or writing, and *tum* – *tunc* 'then', which denote the moment before or after an immediate situation. Both *nunc* and *tunc* could also be used with the meaning 'nowadays' and 'at that time', respectively, and could refer to a wider situational field. These adverbs disappeared in Vulgar Latin. The classical terms and popular innovations coexisted for some time, but are documented only occasionally e.g. in *ad tunc* 'at that time' in (5) and (6), or can be reconstructed based on Romance evidence, as in the case of **(in)tunc(ce)* > Sp. *entonces* 'then' (RAE, s.v., cf. also Bazzanella & Borreguero, 2011) and Port. *então* 'then', or of *(ac/as) tunc (ce)* > Rom. *atunci* 'then' (Puscariu, EWRS, s.v., cf. also Popescu, 2014).

(5) Sidera in judicio videbuntur obscura, etc., **usque ad tunc** fiet quod idem propheta alibi dicit (**Anselmus Laudunensis et schola (1050 – 1117),** ***Evangelium secundum Lucae: Prooemium Lucae***, II)
'The stars will appear dark in judgement, etc., **until then** it will happen what the prophet says elsewhere'

(6) 47. **a tunc** inter Toronicos cives bella civilia surrexerunt (Gregorius Turonensis (573–594) – *Historiarum libri X*, 7, 47, 366, 6)
'**From that time** civil wars arose between the Toronic citizens'

Another relevant change which developed in the Latin system of temporal adverbials is that independent *cum* 'when' is largely replaced by *dum* 'while', a temporal particle marking the simultaneity of two actions taking place. *Dum* progressively overlaps with *cum* and encroaches on it especially in Late Latin (Fedriani & Molinelli, 2021, cf. also Adams, 1976: 77).

A series of hypothesis on the etymology of It. *adunque* and *dunque* consider the paradigm in *-d* (It. *dunque* or Fr. *donc*). The first of these focus on the cross-breeding in Imperial times of *dum* and *tunc*. It. *dunque* and Fr. *donc* would have developed from Lat. *dunc*, originally with the temporal meaning of 'at that time', which in turn would have developed analogically from *dum* 'while', as in the pair *tum/tunc* (DELI, s.v.; cf. also Rohlfs 1969: § 948), or from later *donec* (Rosen, 2009). However, as Fedriani and Molinelli (2021) have highlighted convincingly, this would be an extremely improbable evolution, since Lat. *dunc* is only marginally attested as epigraphic variant of *dum*.

Another, more convincing, hypothesis considers that Lat. *dum* functionally replaced *tunc* in its meaning of 'then, hence'. Latin *dumque*, from which It.

dunque and Fr. *donc*, originates from the merging of *dum* ('while') with the clitic coordinating conjunction *que* ('and'). *Dum* in Latin is polyfunctional as it can function as an adverb or as a conjunction introducing a temporal subordinate, which points to simultaneity or immediate succession (Fedriani & Molinelli, 2021: 196).

This hypothesis would also have a functional corroboration as *dum* in Latin can be found in injunctive contexts, especially co-occurring with imperatives. This use of *dum* with imperatives is archaic, colloquial and comic (TLL s.v. *dum*, 5.1.2201-8-25). For instance the idiomatic *agedum* 'come on now!', from the interjection *age* 'come on' + *dum*, where the use of *dum* reinforces the interjection, is attested for a wide range of authors, including Seneca (TLL s.v. *ago*, 1.1405.67-6.11).[3] As it will be discussed in detail in Section 3, the use of It. *dunque* is also rather common in injunctive contexts, although this is a functional trait also shared by *adunque*.

Other scholars consider the evolution from *dum* with *tum, tunc* (*tunc* = *dum* TLL loc. cit., 2214, 14) (Hofmann-Szantir, 1963: 617, § γ), while TLIO (s.v.) considers both forms as derived from Lat. *dunc umquam* 'one day, sometimes'.

Instead, another group of studies discusses the development of the paradigm in *ad-* (It. *adunque,* Fr. *adonc,* Rom. *Atunci*) or of that in *id-* (Sp. *entonces*, Port. *entaõ*) from Lat. *tum* > *tunc*, with the meaning of 'at that time'. This development would have evolved as follows: Lat. *tum* > *tunc* > Lat. *ad tunc* > O.It. *adonqua,* O. Fr. *adonc*, Ro. *atunci*; Lat. *tum* > *tunc* > Lat. *in tunc* > Sp. *entonces* (cf. Lüdke, 2015: 544). Therefore, other forms would have derived from different prepositional variants, as Lat. *in tunc* > O.It. *idunque* (cf. OVI). In this regard, Diez (1864, s.v.) notes that *a tunc* and *ad tunc* can still be found in older Italian documents. Within this line of research, Tommaseo and Bellini (1861, s.v.) consider both *adunque* and *dunque* as derived from Lat. *ad hunc* 'for this', with ellipsis of *modum* 'way' or *finem* 'aim', etc.

Let us now move to consider the discourse-pragmatic functions of the two forms in the corpora.

3. Functions of *Adunque* and *Dunque* in Old Italian

The discourse-pragmatic functions of the forms in the corpora cluster around three main uses of *adunque* and *dunque* which can operate as (a) connectives,

---

3 A similar expression, with the same meaning, can still be found today in the vernacular spoken in the Bergamo area, i.e. the injunctive *'dòm doca*, from *'dòm* 'go.IMP.1PL' + *doca* 'then' (cf. Tiraboschi, 1873, s.v.).

(b) discourse markers, or (c) pragmatic markers. In the sections below each of these uses in the corpora is described in detail.

3.1. *Adunque* and *Dunque* as Connectives

As mentioned in the discussion on the etymology of the forms (see Section 2), the temporal values of both Lat. *dum* 'while' and *tunc* 'then' are exploited in the connecting uses of *(a)dunque* which can function as markers of concomitance. When they operate as connectives, they exploit this capacity to mark concomitance by representing the causal link as a necessary link, which is thus posited as existing outside the discourse that represents it. In other words, their connective uses are fundamentally consensual, and their assumption becomes co-enunciative.

The core uses of both forms revolve around a resultative meaning (cf. examples 7 and 8).

(7) [...]occultamente si fece venir Ruggieri e nella sua camera il mise e dentro il vi serrò in fino a tanto che certe altre persone della casa s'andassero a dormire. Standosi **adunque** Ruggier nella camera e aspettando la donna [...] gli venne nella finestra veduta questa guastadetta d'acqua (Boccaccio, *Decameron*, IV, 10)
'[she] brought Ruggieri in privily, and locked him in her chamber until certain other folk that were in the house were gone to sleep. Ruggieri, **therefore**, being in the chamber, awaiting the lady [...], caught sight of the bottle containing the water'

(8) Il peccato non procede da altro, che amare quello che Dio odia, e odiare quello che Dio ama: **dunque** amando le cose transitorie del mondo, [...], offende, perocchè è quella cosa che Dio odia, [...]. (Santa Caterina da Siena, *Lettere*, XXIX, A Madama moglie di Bernabò Visconti)
'Sin proceeds from nothing other than loving what God hates, and hating what God loves: **therefore** loving the transitory things of the world, [...] he offends, for it is that thing which God hates'

In dialogic sequences in Boccaccio, *adunque* is often used in bridging contexts, as in (9), whose interpretation is also compatible with that of a discourse-structuring marker, with a specialized resultative meaning. This is far less common in the case of *dunque*.

(9) Il re[...] disse: "Damigella, voi avete ben guadagnato il marito". A cui ella rispose: "**Adunque**, monsignore, ho io guadagnato Beltramo di Rossiglione". (Boccaccio, *Decameron*, III, 9).
'the King [...] said: "Damsel," said the king, "well have you won your husband." She answered: "**In that case**, Sire, I have won Bertrand de Roussillon" '

The two forms can also be used with a causal value to indicate a transition in the text, typically a succession of events in a narrative sequence (example 10).

(10) Al romor della donna corsero molti, li quali, vedutala e udita la cagione del suo gridare, non solamente per quello dieder fede alle sue parole, ma aggiunsero la leggiadria e la ornata maniera del conte, per potere a quel venire, essere stata da lui lungamente usata. Corsesi **adunque** a furore alle case del conte per arestarlo; (Boccaccio, *Decameron* II, 8, 24).
'The lady's cries brought not a few to her aid, who, observing her plight, not only gave entire credence to her story, but improved upon it, alleging that the debonair and accomplished Count had long employed all the arts of seduction to compass his end. **So,** they rushed in hot haste to the Count's house, with intent to arrest him'

In Old Italian, only *adunque* can have a temporal value with the meaning of 'at that time', as in (11) from Dante's *Comedy* (cf. also Rohlfs, 1969: 285, § 983). None of these uses were however found in the two corpora under analysis here.

(11) Facemmo **adunque** più lungo viaggio (Dante, *Inferno* 31, 82)
'**At that time** we made a longer journey'

Other uses of *adunque* and *dunque* can be compatible with an interpretation of consecutive values, as in hypothetical structures, although these uses are more common in argumentative contexts, rather than in the dialogic contexts in focus here, where the forms have rather a conclusive connotation.

3.2. *Adunque* and *Dunque* as Discourse Markers

The discourse functions of *(a)dunque* reflect the status of the forms as the 'original' distal members of the pair *now – then*. In such uses they mark the speakers' progression through discourse of an idea, unit, orientation, and/or participation framework. They mark a reference time, i.e., a linguistic event prior to speaking time. When used anaphorically, they establish a temporal relation between two linguistic events internal to discourse.

Moving from this general function, it is possible to identify two main functions of the two forms.

The first relates to the management of textual cohesion and coherence: in these contexts, *adunque* or *dunque* highlight the process of text construction. The forms typically refer to the discourse context and focus on an event or a change in the narrative perspective, as in the passage in (12) from Catherine's letters.

(12) [...] scrivo a voi con desiderio di vedervi pastore buono, considerando me, babbo mio dolce, che el lupo infernale ne porta le pecorelle vuostre e non si trova chi le remedisca. Ricorro **dunque** a voi, padre e pastore nostro, pregandovi [...] che voi impariate da lui. (Santa Caterina da Siena, *Lettere*, CXCVI, A papa Gregorio XI)

'[I] write to you with desire to see you a good shepherd. For I reflect, sweet my "Babbo," that the wolf is carrying away your sheep, and there is no one found to help them. **So** I hasten to you, our father and our shepherd, begging you to rescue that lost sheep'.

Along similar lines, in these contexts, information can be presented as a discourse consequence, which refers to what mentioned in a previous turn. The presence of the discourse marker invites the interlocutor to infer something from the information provided before. This is the function of *adunque* exemplified in (13), from Boccaccio's *Decameron*, where the servant refers to Cisti's previous turn in which he mentions the fact that he was not sent by Messer Geri.

(13) Al quale Cisti rispose: – Per certo, figliuol, non fa. – **Adunque** – , disse il famigliare – a cui mi manda? Rispose Cisti: – Ad Arno. (Boccaccio, *Decameron*, IV, 2)
'"Son," answered Cisti, "Messer Geri does, for sure, not send thee to me." "To whom **then**," said the servant, "does he send me?"'

A second type of use relates to topic management, in these contexts the discourse markers introduce new topics, as in (14) where *adunque* marks the beginning of the actual narration. In these passages the forms have a cohesive function. In the *Decameron* the structure *dico adunque che* 'I therefore say that'marks the passage from the prologue to the actual narration. The form is of scholastic origin and translates Lat. *dico igitur quod* (or *dico enim quod*), in that context it was used by the author to take responsibility for what he said (Dardano, 2011: 47). In the texts under analysis here, *adunque* is commonly used with this function.

Similarly, both *adunque* and *dunque* can also be used to signal a transition to a subtopic or a change of frame, as in (15), or the closure of a topic/subtopic, as in (16) where *dunque* closes a sequence in which the narrators of the *Decameron* are discussing which rules to follow in telling their stories.

(14) Fu **adunque** in Pisa un giudice, piú che di corporal forza dotato d'ingegno, il cui nome fu messer Riccardo da Chinzica (Boccaccio, *Decameron*, II, 10, 5)
'**Know then that** there was in Pisa a judge, better endowed with mental than with physical vigour, by name Messer Ricciardo of Chinzica'

(15) La giovane di buona fede rispose: "O padre mio, poscia che io ho il ninferno, sia pure quando vi piacerà". Disse allora Rustico: "Figliuola mia, benedetta sia tu; andiamo **dunque**, e rimettiamlovi sì che egli poscia mi lasci stare". (Boccaccio, *Decameron*, III, 10)
'In good faith the girl made answer: "As I have hell to match your Devil, be it, my father, as and when you will." Whereupon: "Bless thee, my daughter," said Rustico, 'go we **then**, and put him there, that he leave me henceforth in peace'

(16) Le donne parimente e gli uomini tutti lodarono il novellare. "**Adunque**", disse la reina, "se questo vi piace, per questa prima giornata voglio che libero sia a

ciascuno di quella materia ragionare che più gli sarà a grado." E rivolta a Panfilo [...] piacevolmente gli disse che con una delle sue novelle all'altre desse principio. (Boccaccio, *Decameron*, I)
'The queen's proposal being approved by all, ladies and men alike, she added: " [if this] So please you, **then**, I ordain, that, for the first day, we be free to discourse of such matters as most commend themselves, to each in turn." She then addressed Pamfilo, [...] bidding him with a gracious air to lead off with one of his stories'

3.3. *Adunque* and *Dunque* as Pragmatic Markers

(A)dunque can also be used as pragmatic marker(s) in two different contexts.

The first is in injunctive contexts (PIC), where the forms co-occur with imperatives and are used to urge the interlocutor to perform an action, as exemplified in (17) and (18).

(17) Venite **dunque**, venite e non più indugiate (Caterina da Siena, *Lettere*, A maestro Raimondo ad Avignone)
'**Come, then**; you ought to come'

(18) -Va **dunque**, – disse la donna -e chiamalo, e digli che qua se ne venga al fuoco [...]. (Boccaccio, *Decameron*, II, 2).
'Go **then**, call him,' said the lady, 'tell him to come hither to the fire [...].'

They can also be used to manage turns in interrogative contexts as in (19), where they also operate as holophrases.

(19) Or non conosci tu [...]questa giovane convenirsi avere in quella reverenza che sorella? Che **dunque** ami? Dove ti lasci trasportare allo 'ngannevole amore? Dove alla lusinghevole speranza? (Boccaccio, *Decameron*, X, 8)
'Don't you know [...] it behoves thee to have his betrothed in even such pious regard as if she were thy sister? Whither art thou suffering beguiling love, delusive hope, to hurry thee?'
lit. 'Don't you know you had better consider her as your sister? **Then,** why do you love her? Where do you let yourself being carried by beguiling Love? Where by flattering Hope?'

Table 2.2 summarizes the different values of *(a)dunque* in the texts considered.

Table 2.2. *Values of* adunque *and* dunque *in the corpora*

	(a)dunque
Temporal adverb ('at that time') [T]	-
Connective	
Temporal ('at that time', 'and then')	-
Causal connective ('As a consequence, therefore, so (that)')	7, 8

Table 2.2. Continued

	(a)dunque
Consecutive (*se…(a)dunque* 'then, in this/that case')	-
Resultative ('then, therefore')	10
Discourse marker	
Reference to discourse context	12
Invitation to inferential process	13
Introduction of a new topic/subtopic	14, 15
Closure of interactional sequence	16
Pragmatic marker	
Injunctive contexts	17,18
Turn exchange/questions	19

Moving from these functions let us now consider their distribution in the texts considered.

4. Distribution of *Adunque* and *Dunque* in Letters and Novellas

If one takes into consideration the overall frequency of the two forms in the two text genres, an interesting picture emerges. If *adunque* is more common in Boccaccio, *dunque* is more frequent in Saint Catherine's letters (cf. Table 2.3).

Table 2.3. *Absolute and relative frequencies of* adunque *and* dunque

	letters		**novellas**	
	AF	RF (per million words)	AF	RF (per million words)
adunque	362	683	269	841
dunque	596	1124	45	140

As regards the discourse-pragmatic uses of the forms, it is possible to identify some differences in the two genres (see Figure 2.2).

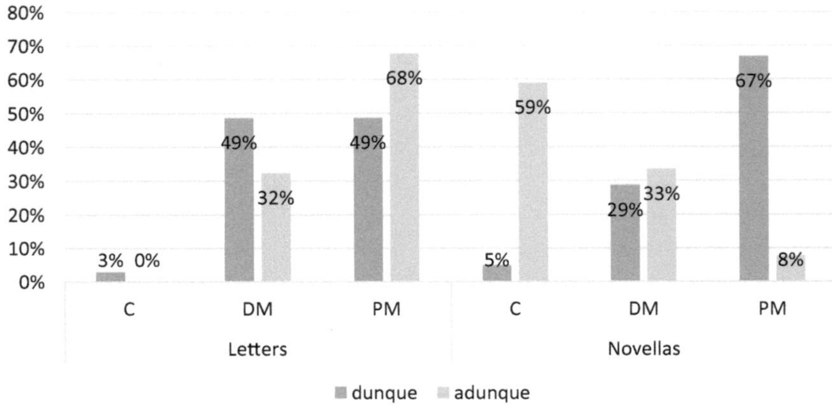

Figure 2.2. *Discourse-pragmatic functions of* dunque *and* adunque *in letters and novellas*

As regards letters, the connective uses (C) of the forms are marginal: while *adunque* is never used as connective, a few uses of *dunque* can be found. Most frequent functions of both forms cluster around discourse (DM) or pragmatic marking (PM). It is however possible to identify some differences in these uses. *Dunque* functions with similar frequencies as discourse or pragmatic marker, while *adunque* is more commonly a pragmatic marker, especially in injunctive contexts, which are a characterising trait of Saint Catherine's letters.

As for novellas, instead, *adunque* more frequently functions as causal connective, especially in transitions in the text, which are a characterising trait of narrative sequences. In dialogic sequences *dunque* and *adunque* alike can function as discourse markers, while *dunque* is far more common than *adunque* as pragmatic marker, especially in questions.

What emerges form Italian data, therefore, hints at a more marked use of *adunque* as connective, especially in novellas where it often occurs in narrative sequences. It is not possible to compare this use in letters, due to lack of narrations in that specific genre. Instead, if the discourse structuring functions of the two forms is evident in both genres, more marked differences emerge in relation to their pragmatic uses, as *dunque* characterises novellas, while *adunque* and *dunque* alike are used in letters.

A more fine grained picture can be found considering the English translation of the two forms.

On a general level both *adunque* and *dunque* are translated with inferential or implicative connectives and/or discourse/pragmatic markers which include forms as *so, therefore, thus, then, hence*, etc. Although in English grammars and/or dictionaries, the forms are generally considered synonyms, as Fraser (2015) notes, *so* functions with a primary implicative value, as it stresses the S1 should be used by the hearer to justify the content of S2, leaving aside any specific reason. By contrast, *thus, hence, therefore, then*, function as secondary discourse/pragmatic markers and connectives as they are used to refine the relationship between S1 and S2. *Thus, hence, therefore* would signal that there is some logical correlational grounds to conclude that S2 should be taken as true or relevant, while *then* would signal two interpretations on which speaker of S2 is drawing a conclusion, implying that 'If S1, *then* S2 follows.' The semantic meaning of *then* is exploited to indicate discourse time, as it refers to prior discourse time and establishes a succession between events or units of talk (ideas, topics, actions). In this sense, it is used to refer to discourse time as a source of information for upcoming talk.

Both *adunque* and *dunque* can also be found translated with Eng. *now* or *well*. As for *well*, Schiffrin (1987: 230) notices how it usually situates and restores both discourse participants and utterances at those points where conversational coherence is considered in danger, while *now* usually functions as a deictic presentative. Its discourse function in English reflects its status as the proximal member of the pair *now-then*. This property is exploited to mark the progression through discourse time by displaying attention to an upcoming idea, unit or orientation.

Moving from these functions of English translations, the data in the two corpora offer some interesting glimpses.

As regards Saint Catherine's letters, the bulk of translations for both *dunque* and *adunque* include Eng. *then* (see Figures 2.3 and 2.4 below).

As for *dunque*, for the majority of its uses as connective, discourse or pragmatic marker it is translated with *then*. This include the totality of uses as connective, the majority of uses as discourse or pragmatic marker (see Figure 2.2).

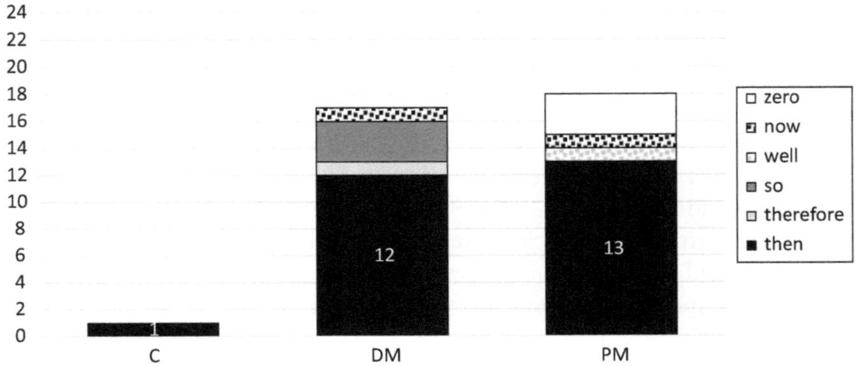

Figure 2.3. *English translations of* dunque *in letters*

When *dunque* is used as discourse marker, the second most frequent translation is *so.* Instead, when used as pragmatic marker, which includes uses in injunctive contexts and questions, *so* is not used and the translator often opts for not translating *dunque,* a sign of the difficulty of transposition of this value in English.

As regards the use of *adunque* in letters (see Figure 2.3), the situation is very similar to that of *dunque* when it operates as a discourse marker; instead, when it functions as pragmatic marker it is also translated with *so,* in addition to *then*, which represent the only two options of translations used.

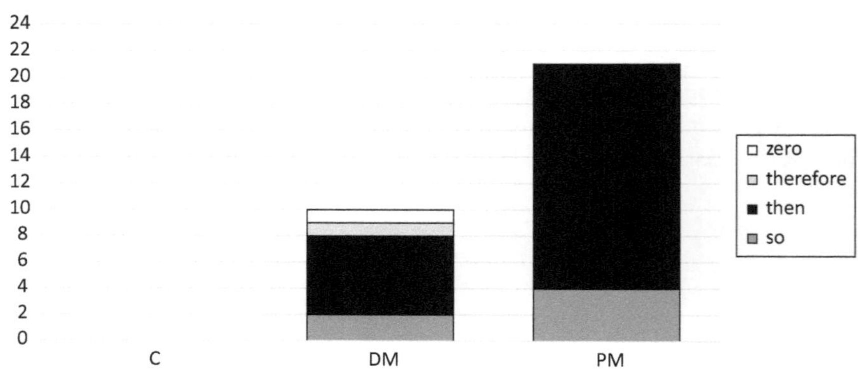

Figure 2.4. *English translations of* adunque *in letters*

As regards, instead, the translations of the two forms in novellas, different patterns of uses emerge (see Figures 2.5 and 2.6 below).

As for *dunque* (see Figure 2.5), its role as text-structuring marker emerges clearly in translations which include general *then*, but also *know then*, which typically introduces the actual narration, and less frequently *so*. When used as pragmatic marker, it is mostly translated with *then*, *so*, or it is not translated at all, another indication of the difficulty of the translator in finding an English equivalent for these uses.

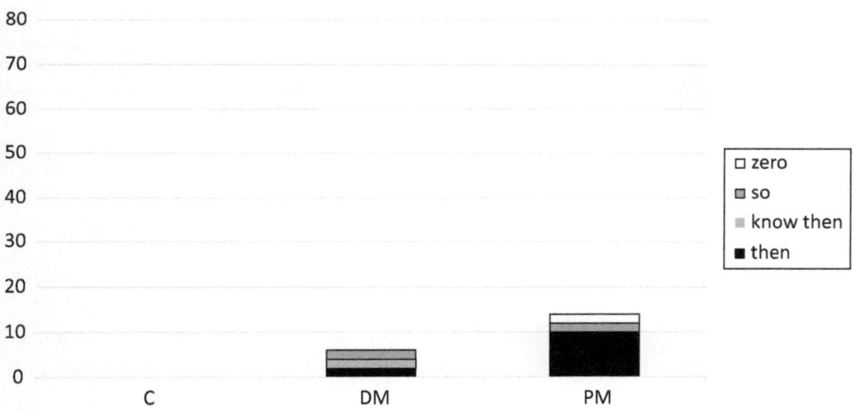

Figure 2.5. *English translations of* dunque *in novellas*

As for the translations of *adunque* in novellas (see Figure 2.6), when used as a connective, apart from the translation with *then*, it is more frequently translated with forms implying some kind of causal relation as *so*, mostly, or *thus, therefore, wherefore*. When it is used as a discourse marker, translations tend to be more varied depending on the function. For instance, *know then* is the typical translation when the actual narration of the story begins, while *now* is quite common in the closing of topics.

Instead, when *adunque* is used as a pragmatic marker, it is more frequently translated with *then* or zero, again an indication of difficulty for the translator.

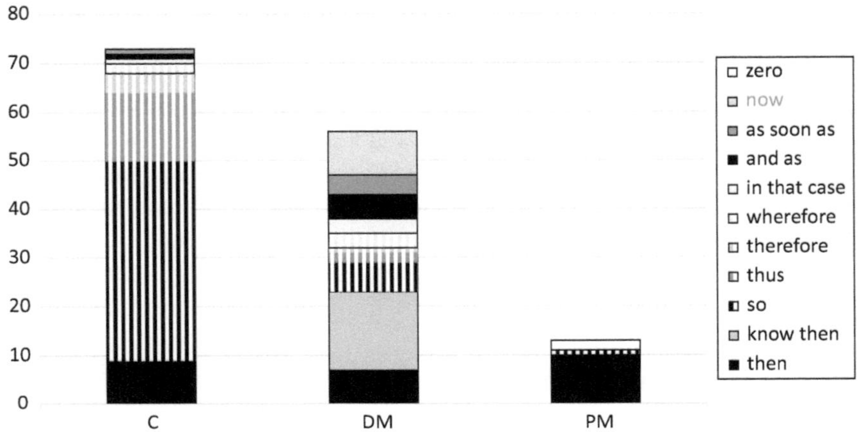

Figure 2.6. *English translations of* adunque *in novellas*

5. Some Conclusions

The analysis of uses of *adunque* and *dunque* in letters and novellas, together with their English translations, offers a preliminary insight into their uses and functions.

Although the etymology of the forms is very much debated, the data show that in Old Italian *adunque* and *dunque* already shared a discourse-pragmatic domain, they were used as connectives, discourse and pragmatic markers with substantially similar functions. Yet, their discourse-pragmatic uses are not completely overlapping. For instance, *adunque* is the connective in Boccaccio, while *dunque* is more frequent as pragmatic marker in Saint Catherine's letters.

Their uses vary depending on the genre considered. This relates both to forms, as *adunque* is more common in Boccaccio and *dunque* is more frequent in Saint Catherine, and to functions performed, as *adunque* is more frequently used as connective in novellas, while *dunque* is more frequent as pragmatic marker. In this regard, the analysis of other textual genres, and consequent discourse traditions, might show different patterns. For instance, interesting genres to consider might be argumentative texts, where the causal and resultative values of the forms might emerge more clearly, or poetry, where rhythm might play a relevant role in the choice of one or the other form.

What emerges clearly from the analysis of the two texts considered is that both Boccaccio and Saint Catherine show a personal patterned variability in the use of the forms, as they move from one form to another to express their stances in discreet speech events. However, it remains to identify which parameters play relevant roles in the choice of one or the other form. For instance, the correlation between the use of one form, its position within the sentence, and the function performed may be one of these parameters. Another interesting parameter to investigate relates to social stratification, as in some letters only *adunque* is used, while in others both forms are present. This would imply considering the role of patterned variability and, with it, the role of *individuals* in language variation and change (cf. e.g. Petré, 2016; Petré & Van de Velde, 2018). Individuals may adopt new uses in different ways and with different degrees. Their role in language variation and change has been underscored in historical sociolinguistic research. For instance Raumolin-Brunberg (2009: 166) stresses how " the understanding of the diffusion of linguistic changes requires research on the behaviour of individuals".

As regards English translations, on a heuristic level they prove extremely helpful in the interpretation of functions of forms, for instance specific translations emerge in relation to functions. This is the case of the text-structuring value, as *adunque* and *dunque* are often translated with *know then*, when they introduce actual narration, or with *now*, when they index the progression of discourse. Moreover, a rich variety of translations, as is for instance the case of the discourse marking functions of the forms in novellas, is helpful in understanding the degree of polyfunctionality of the form when used with a specific function (e.g. discourse marker *vs* connective). Lastly, similar patterns of translations across textual genres proved helpful in highlighting the substantial overlap of the bulk of the functions of the two forms as early as Old Italian.

In conclusion, the study of these two forms raised more questions than it answered. Both their origin and their uses need to be further analysed. As for the origin, considering the changes that developed from Latin into the different Romance languages within the system of time adverbials, it extremely difficult to identify without doubt the Latin antecedent of the forms, what seems more plausible is that these forms developed at the beginning of the Middle Ages, when Latin was no longer the mother tongue of speakers. As for the functions, although the two variants *adunque* and *dunque* are both attested from earliest written records, already in Old Italian the original temporal meaning 'at that time' is only characteristic of *adunque* and is peripheral. From this may follow that the Italian time adverbial *allora* 'at that time' took over as a temporal deictic adverb as a consequence of (a)*dunque* having assumed additional meanings, different from the original temporal value.

All these hypotheses remain speculations, that need to be corroborated by further studies.

References

Primary Sources

DELI: Cortelazzo, M. & Zolli, P. (1979). *Dizionario etimologico della lingua italiana*. Zanichelli.

Diez, F. C. (1864). *An etymological dictionary of the Romance languages: Chiefly from the German of F. Diez*. Williams and Norgate.

Dizionario degli Accademici della Crusca. http://www.lessicografia.it

EWRS: Puşcariu, S. (1905). *Etymologisches Wörterbuch der rumänischen Sprache*. Carl Winter's Universitätbuchhandlung.

IT Zingarelli 2020: Zingarelli, N. (2019). *Lo Zingarelli 2020. Vocabolario della lingua italiana*. Zanichelli.

Leumann, M., Hofmann, J. B. & Szantyr, A. (1963). *Lateinische Grammatik auf der Grundlage des Werkes*. Beck.

OVI: *Corpus OVI dell'italiano antico*, http://gattoweb.ovi.cnr.it

RAE: *Real Academia Española*. https://dle.rae.es

Tiraboschi, A. (1873). *Vocabolario dei dialetti bergamaschi antichi e moderni*. Bolis.

TLIO: *Tesoro della lingua italiana delle origini*. http://tlio.ovi.cnr.it/TLIO/

TLL: Estienne, R. & Estienne, H. II. (1743). *Thesaurus linguae latinae*. E. & JR Thurnisiorum fratr. https://thesaurus.badw.de/tll-digital/tll-open-access.html

Tommaseo, N. & Bellini, B. (1861). *Dizionario della lingua italiana*. https://www.tommaseobellini.it/

Secondary Sources

Adams, J. N. (1976). *The text and language of a vulgar Latin chronicle (Anonymus Valesianus II)*. Bulletin Supplement of the Institute of Classical Studies of the University of London, 36.

Aijmer, K. et al. (2006). Pragmatic markers in translation: A methodological proposal. In K. Fischer (ed.), *Approaches to discourse particles* (pp. 101–114). Brill.

Badiou-Monferran, C. (2008). Les disparitions de formes sont-elles des épiphénomènes?. In J. Durand et al. (éds.), *Congrès Mondial de Linguistique Française – CMLF'08* (pp. 147–158). Institut de Linguistique Française.

Bazzanella, C. (2001). Segnali discorsivi e contesto. In C. Heiss & W. Heinrich (a c. di) *Modalità e substandard* (pp. 1–24). Clueb

Bazzanella, C. & Borreguero Zuloaga, M. (2011). *Allora* e *entonces*: problemi teorici e dati empirici. *Oslo Studies in Language* 3/1, 7–45.

Dardano, M. (2011). *Dico adunque che….* In A. Overbeck, W. Schweickard & H. Völker (hrsg.) *Lexikon, Varietät, Philologie. Romanistische Studien. Günter Holtus zum 65. Geburtstag* (pp. 47–57). De Gruyter.

Degand, L. (2009). On describing polysemous discourse markers. What does translation add to the picture? In M. Stef Slembrouck et al. (eds.), *From will to well. Studies in linguistics offered to Anne-Marie Simon-Vandenbergen* (pp. 173–183). Academia Press.

Fedriani, C. & Molinelli, P. (2021). Functional expansions of temporal adverbs and discursive connectives: From Latin *tum, tunc, dumque* to Old Italian *dunque. Journal of Historical Pragmatics* 21/2, 182–208.

Fraser, B. (2015). The combining of Discourse Markers – A beginning. *Journal of Pragmatics* 86, 48-53.

Ghezzi, C. (2014). The development of discourse and pragmatic markers. In C. Ghezzi & P. Molinelli (eds.), *Discourse and pragmatic markers from Latin to Romance languages* (pp. 10–26). OUP.

Ghezzi, C. & Molinelli, P. (2021). Connectives and cyclicity. From the Latin temporal phrase *illa hora* to the Italian discourse marker *allora. Journal of Historical Pragmatics* 21/2, 208–235.

Hansen, M.B. (1997). *Alors and donc* in spoken French: A reanalysis. *Journal of Pragmatics* 28, 153-187.

Jaffe, A. (2009). The Sociolinguistics of Stance. In A. Jaffe (ed.), *Stance: Sociolinguistic Perspectives (pp.* 1-28*)*. Oxford Academic.

Lüdtke, J. (2015). From Latin and Vulgar Latin to Romance Languages. In K. Jungbluth & F. Da Milano (eds.), *Manual of Deixis in Romance Languages* (pp. 537-557). De Gruyter.

Mortier, L. (2007). *Perspectives on grammaticalization and speakers' involvement. The case of progressive and continuative periphrases in French and Dutch.* Unpublished PhD dissertation, University of Leuven.

Noël, D. (2003). Translations as evidence for semantics: An illustration. *Linguistics* 41/4, 757–785.

Patota, G. (1987). L'*Ortis* e la prosa del Secondo Settecento. *Studi di grammatica italiana* XIII, 97–247.

Petré, P. (2016). Unidirectionality as a cycle of convention and innovation: Micro-changes in the grammaticalization of [*be going to* INF]. *Belgian Journal of Linguistics* 30, 115–146.

Petré, P. & Van de Velde, F. (2018). The real-time dynamics of the individual and the community in grammaticalization. *Language* 94, 867–901.

Popescu, M. (2014). Romanian *atunci* and French *alors*: Functional and discourse properties. In C. Ghezzi & P. Molinelli (eds.), *Discourse and pragmatic markers from Latin to Romance languages* (pp. 222–236). OUP.

Rohlfs, G. (1969). *Grammatica storica della lingua italiana e dei suoi dialetti*. Il Mulino.

Rósen, H. (2009). Coherence, sentence modification, and sentence-part modification–the contribution of particles. In P. Baldi & P. Cuzzolin (eds.), *New perspectives on historical Latin syntax* 1 (pp. 317–442). De Gruyter.

Raumolin-Brunberg, H. (2009). Lifespan changes in the language of three early modern gentlemen. In A. Nurmi, M. Nevala & M. Palander-Collin (eds.), *The language of daily life in England (1400–1800)* (pp. 165–196). Benjamins.

Salvi, G. & Renzi, L. (a c. di) (2010). *Grammatica dell'italiano antico*. Vol. 2. Il Mulino.

Schiffrin, D. (1987). *Discourse markers*. CUP.

II Discourse Markers and Their Relation to Other Semantic and Pragmatic Categories

Pierre Lejeune, Amália Mendes

3 A Study on the French Functional Equivalents of some Modal and Metadiscursive Uses of the European Portuguese Marker *lá*

Abstract: The translation of polysemous discourse markers is a challenge, since the additional meaning they contribute to sentences is abstract and subtle, quite difficult to preserve in translation. A dilemma appears whether to ignore this additional meaning (which is economical, but inaccurate) or to paraphrase it (which is accurate, but burdensome). There is a possible way in-between, to resort to a range of local functional equivalents. As a locative adverb, *lá* is included in a double system of markers: a ternary one (*aqui, aí, alí*), which is fundamentally deictic, and a binary one (*cá, lá*), which is based on alterity: *cá em Lisboa* 'here in Lisbon' vs *lá em Paris* 'there in Paris'. A wide range of modal and metalinguistic uses have been described from a pragmatic perspective (Duarte, Marques) or a syntactic one (Martins). Thus, by using a monolingual corpus of Portuguese (CRPC) and two bilingual corpora (Europarl and the original Portuguese version and the French translation of Cardoso Pires' novel *Balada da praia dos cães*), we shall look at some typical uses of the marker *lá*, such as locative, temporal, modal, etc.

Keywords: discourse markers, translation, equivalence

1. Introduction

Languages have discrete multifunctional discourse units whose specific contribution to meaning in context is difficult to isolate, e.g. Discourse particles (DP)[1].

Instead of listing the pragmatic values of a DP seen as the object of "semantic bleaching", it might be of interest to try to individualize a sort of core meaning / semantic identity of a DP, which is necessarily quite abstract and should account for its contextual values that are the result of the bidirectional interaction between the DP and its context.

Arriving at the semantic identity of a unit requires a progressive abstraction that makes use of what is called 'epilinguistic activity' by A. Culioli, according to whom the term refers to:

1 By Discourse Particle, we mean a discourse marker with a single argument (as opposed to connectives, which have two) and a modal value added to the propositional or semantic content of the argument.

> the unconscious metalinguistic activity of any subject and is thus distinct from deliberate metalinguistic activity. Epilinguistic glosses form a large part of our daily discourse and play an important role in the explicative discourse of an informer who tries to explain the meaning of a phrase in a foreign language or the sense of a misinterpreted utterance. (1999: 74)[2].

Some epilinguistic activity is intralingual, some is interlingual, translation being part of the latter[3]. As such, translation interests the linguist describing a unit of a given language.

Morphologically very similar, two adverbs with locative, temporal and modal uses, European Portuguese (EP) *lá* and French (FR) *là* are a good example of problematic linguistic units for translators and interpreters that are rarely functional equivalents. Starting with a short description of the general locative and temporal value of those two units, we will then focus on their modal uses, relying for that purpose on the following corpus:

(a) Europarl, 'a large multilingual corpus containing the minutes of the debates at the European Parliament' (Cartoni et al., 2013): Portuguese, French and English versions – EUR;
(b) the Portuguese 20th century novel *A balada da praia dos cães*: European Portuguese original and French translation by Michel Laban (occurences of *lá* analysed in Duarte, 2005) – CP;
(c) the monolingual European Portuguese corpus CRPC (Corpus de Referência do Português Contemporâneo).

We will also use monolingual examples (mainly oral) drawn from linguistics literature on EP *lá* and FR *là* (with our own translations), as well as a few made up examples (in the introductory part)[4].

2 Translation by G. Granger.

3 [...] it remains that the synonymy between units of the same language, or the translation of one unit for one (or several) other(s) between different languages often forms an empirically well-established relation. These are frequent, instable cases that rely on the joining of two conditions: (1) two sequences formed completely or partly of different words produce a meaning felt to be close; (2) the formal difference can be focused on an easily noticeable lexical nucleus. (Franckel, 2005 : 83) (our translation)

4 Where a translated/parallel version is not available the translation is ours and in square brackets.

2. *Là* and *lá* in Their Locative Uses[5]

2.1. FR *Là*

Various authors (Kleiber, 1995; Barbéris, 1987 and 1998; Corblin & Asic, 2016) have pointed out that as a locative adverb FR *là* ('there') cannot be described in the same terms as *ici* ('here') and *là-bas* ('over there').

Ici can be deictic – referring in some way to the place where the enunciator[6] is (examples 1 and 2) – or demonstrative, referring by pointing to the place where the object is (3) – values.

(1) Je suis ici depuis une heure.
'I have been here – where I am now – for an hour'
(2) Tu es ici en vacances ?
'Are you here on holiday?'
(3) Appuyez ici.
'Press here' (next to the arrow)

Là-bas refers to a place distinct from the situation of uttering (enunciator «I» / co-enunciator «you»), whether visually accessible to the co-enunciators (4) or not (5).

(4) Regarde là-bas: un lapin !
'Look over there: a rabbit!'
(5) Il est resté là-bas dix ans.
'He stayed there for ten years.'

Là has a variety of uses that make it difficult to identify stable values. Dialogues such as (6) are often seen as puzzling for non-native speakers, giving the idea that *là* designates the enunciator´s, the co-enunciator´s and even the potential object's location (7):

On the phone, when the interlocutor is silent.

(6) – Tu es *là* ? – Oui je suis *là*.
'Are you there? Yes, I am here.'

---

5 Because they show more spectacular contrasts than endophoric uses, we will concentrate on exophoric uses of both markers.

6 In what follows, the term *enunciator* will refer to the subjective origin of the enunciative system, whose presence in the text can be signalled by first person pronouns and determiners (*I*, *me*, *my*, *mine*). *Co-enunciator* means the enunciator's counterpart in the situation of uttering, whose presence in the text can be signalled by second person pronouns and determiners (*you*, *your*, *yours*). *Co-enunciators* (in the plural form) means the enunciator plus the co-enunciator.

(7) - Où est-ce que je mets le livre ? – Dépose-le là.
'- Where do I put the book? – Put it there.' (pointing at the book's intended location)

A unitary description of *là* by the authors listed above involves taking into account shared mental representations. For instance, Grobet (2021) refers to *là* as targeting the prior discourse, and simultaneously realizing a spatio-temporal or interpretative framework associated with a change of topic or participation framework. Kleiber (1995) describes *là* as generally anaphorical. He uses a very loose concept of anaphora, according to which the antecedent does not have to be a specific location: you just need a reference to a situation where the notion of space has been previously activated.

> *Là* is an anaphorical adverb, which is only used in connection with a situation already activating the notion of place, either to refer to an already prominent place (explicit or implicit), or to introduce a new place. *Là* denotes the category of spatial referents.[7] (Kleiber, 1995: 25)

One might find that there is an ad hoc, somewhat forced side to this kind of explanation, which is necessary to account for examples such as (8)

(8) Regarde là ! Un lapin !
'Look there! A rabbit' (the rabbit is closer to the co-enunciators than in 4)

Barbéris (1998) proposes a somewhat more convincing enunciative description of *là*. She refuses the traditional dichotomy *ici* enunciator included vs *là* enunciator excluded. She sees a deictic value, including the enunciator in both *íci* and *là*. But according to her, they correspond to two distinct kinds of subjects: for *ici*, an 'ipse subject', where the subject signals their presence as a specific individual, distinguished from the other (*alter*); on the contrary, *là* is associated with a collective subject, not individualized as ego, an 'inseparable intersubjective complex, implying at the same time an enunciator and a co-enunciator that are indissociable, not individualized as specific positions'. This description echoes the impression of vagueness and distancing one has sometimes with *là*. For instance, (9) and (10) can be said by the same person talking about the neighbourhood where they live, showing a stronger sense of belonging in (9) than in (10).

(9) J'habite ici depuis dix ans.
'I have lived here for ten years.'
(10) J'habite là depuis dix ans.
'I have lived here for ten years.'

---

7 Our translation.

As for Corblin and Asic (2016), they establish a parallelism between the conditions of use of *là* and of definite articles in definite NP (Noun phrases):

> The general idea is that interpreting an expression as definite consists of using its definite content to single out a referent, looking for a frame accessible to discourse participants, in which that content selects a single individual. (2016: 35)

For those authors, the description above is applicable mutatis mutandis – *là* refers to a specific referent, a location – to *là*. Here again we find a reference to a location 'accessible to discourse participants', in other words the space of co-enunciation, to which the enunciator necessarily belongs. This description of locative *là* seems to us quite compatible with the mainly temporal deictic value of FR *là* that we find in (11), where *là* means something like 'At the moment and in the situation in which I am speaking' (a value that we do not find with EP *lá*).

(11) - Qu'est-ce que tu fais? – *Là* je prends mon petit déj sur la terrasse.
'- What are you up to? – I am having breakfast on the terrace.'

We share the common view advocated by those various authors that *là* in its locative uses:

- never excludes the enunciator;
- implies a context of pre-existing location available in the co-enunciation space;
- establishes a subjective distance from the enunciator, something that does not happen with *ici*.

We believe that FR *là*'s modal values will share those features shown by locative *là*

2.2. EP lá

Contrarily to French, which has a single, even if heterogeneous, locative system (*ici*, *là*, and *là-bas*), European Portuguese has two competing systems of locative adverbs, one ternary (*aqui*, *aí* and *ali*), the other binary (*cá* and *lá*). A comparative study of those markers is complex, requiring comparisons between markers within the same system (e.g. *cá* vs *lá*) or across systems (e.g. *aqui* vs *cá*; *ali* vs *lá*) that are far beyond the reach of this study. Here we will just give a schematic presentation of the two systems, illustrating with a few made up examples.

We can describe the systems in terms of abstract location operations (Culioli, 1999) that can be used for instance to describe subjective locations: identification with the enunciator (I), differentiation (you) and disconnection – or detachment (*he, she, they*).

Regarding the EP ternary locative system, *aqui* corresponds to identification with the enunciator operation, *aí* to differentiation and *ali* to disconnection.

Typically, they refer to the enunciator's location (12), to the co-enunciator's (13) and to third parties' (14).

(12) Fico aqui no escritório à tua espera.
'I will stay here in the office waiting for you'.
(13) Fica aí até eu chegar.
'Stay where you are until I get there'.
(14) Põe a tua mala alí na mesa ao lado do João.
'Put your case there on the table next to João'.

But things are more complicated than that, as locative operations always combine with subjective perception and positioning (Marques, 2018). This can account for examples like the following.

(15) O João mora aqui perto
'João lives not far from here'.
(16) O João vem aí
'João is coming / about to get here' (Pereira, 2009)
(17) Aí está o João
'João is here / has just arrived' (ibid.)

In terms of locative operations, the binary system is simpler: identification for *cá*, disconnection for *lá*, as in (18).

(18) Cá em Portugal, gostamos de peixe. E lá na Roménia?
'Here in Portugal we like fish. What about you in Romania?'

A possible FR translation of (19) would be 'Ce week-end je reste là' (location including the enunciator) whereas replacing 'cá' by 'lá' in the EP version would modify the meaning («in that other place where I am not at the moment»)

(19) Este fim-de-semana fico cá.
'This week-end I will stay here /where I am'

Generally speaking, the ternary system is better suited for reference to physical locations than the binary. In the latter, the abstract location operation is never only a question of signalling a physical location relative to the enunciator's (quantitative determination). It combines with a qualitative/modal location.

This contrast between the two systems is visible in (20) and (21): (20) refers to the school as an institution as much as a location whereas (21) is about physical location.

(20) A ministra da Educação vem *cá* (?*aqui*) à escola.
'The Education Secretary is coming soon to the school.' (Pereira, 2009)
(21) Vai ser recebida *aqui* (**cá*) nesta sala onde nos encontramos.
'She will be welcomed in this very room where we are at the moment.' (ibid.)

We agree with the comment made by Pereira (2009) when contrasting (22) and (23) (said by someone who is not in Aveiro, in Porto, for instance).

(22) *Ali* para os lados de Aveiro ainda se recolhe o moliço.
'There, near Aveiro, they still collect seaweed.'
(23) *Lá* para os lados de Aveiro ainda se recolhe o moliço.
'There, near Aveiro, they still collect seaweed.'

He states that in (22), 'deictic *ali*, not only signals a relative proximity to the enunciator's location, but also seems to express a relative familiarity with the referred location, presented as more definite concrete and circumscribed', whereas in (23), '*lá* means a location that is more remote, undetermined or vague, more generic and more abstract'[8].

Those examples help us understand why *cá* and *lá* are good candidates to express modal values. In particular *lá* will be associated with modal values marking some sort of distancing between the enunciator and the situation described («nothing to do with me») and will not be able to acquire the temporal value of identification we find for FR *là* (example 11 partly reproduced hereafter as 24). The only possible value for temporal *lá* is anaphoric, as in (25).

(24) Là je prends mon petit déj sur la terrasse.
'I am having breakfast on the terrace'.
(25) Vou de férias em Agosto. Até lá fico em casa.
'I will go on holiday in August. Until then, I will stay at home.'

We disagree with Marques (2018: 258) when she states that *cá* refers to the common space of co-enunciation where *lá* would signal a disconnection between the referred space and the space of co-enunciation. In our opinion, the contrast should be between *cá* – identification with the enunciator – and *lá* -disconnection from the enunciator – (according to the context, the co-enunciator's location will be identified with the enunciator's or disconnected from it).[9] We believe this issue to be crucial when it comes to relating *lá*'s locative and modal values.

3. *Là* and *lá* in Their Modal Uses

In this paper, we assume that modal values of FR *là* and EP *lá* are manifestations of having a core meaning related in some way to the use of the same linguistic units in non-modal (in this case mainly locative) contexts. From that core

8 Our translation.
9 Our position on this issue is quite similar to that assumed by Teixeira (2005) for locative uses.

meaning, contextual values should be explained, taking into account criteria such as scope, position of the marker and prosody. At this stage we cannot propose a systematic review of the influence of each of these factors of variation. Nevertheless, we think that a general unitary description can be arrived at. Schematically, the following can be said:

(a) Modal uses of FR *là* reflect the behaviour of the locative marker as a definite expression related to a preconstructed representation involving both poles of co-enunciation;
(b) Modal uses of EP *lá* reflect the opposition between *cá* (identification with the enunciator) and *lá* (disconnection from the enunciator), with varied semantic-pragmatic effects:
  - 'This does not /concern me' (non-endorsement, responsibility left to the co-enunciator or to other subjective entities, indetermination, indifference)
  - 'This has no value' (what is not mine has no value, is bad)

3.1. Modal Uses of FR *là*

Here, we will just mention two sorts of modal values assumed by FR *là*, the second of which seems to be but is not the same as a value taken by EP *lá*.

3.1.1. Signalling the Crossing of a Limit

This is the qualitative counterpart of the temporal value ('at this moment') identified at the end of Section 1.1. EP *lá* is impossible here, for the same reason as the one mentioned for the temporal value (the disconnection from the utterer's situation signalled by *lá*). FR *là* signals the coincidence /conformity between a subjective ('it is expected, wanted') and a temporal ('it has happened') construction of the predicative relation. If the subjective construction comes first, we get a positive value (what was wanted has happened), as in (26).

(26) (After a few unsuccessful attempts to fix a bicycle, eventually it works)
LÀ, <u>c'est bon</u>
'It is OK now' (EP *lá está / já está)

If the temporal location comes first, a subjective negative value is constructed retrospectively ('It was bound to happen')[10], as in (27).

---

10 Those two ways by which a coincidence between a subjective and a temporal value occurs are called by Franckel (1989: 277) teleonomy (good value) and antiteleonomy (bad value)

(27) LÀ, j'en ai assez, je m'en vais.
'I've had enough. I am off' (EP *Lá estou farto / Estou mesmo farto/farta)

In both cases,

- There is a pause between *là* and the remaining sentence
- *Là* could occupy the final position in the sentence, with a flat, low pitch and a slightly different value - introduction of the situation as new in the first case, preconstruction (mutual salience) in the latter.

3.1.2. Construction of a Common Representation in Oral Interactions

In this type of situation, FR *là* means something like «If you know what I mean» or «Try to remember» as in (28) and (29).

(28) (description of urban space) ces grandes tours du Nouveau Monde LÀ[11] / beige brunes et Bordeaux
'Those big Nouveau Monde blocks, beige, brown and bordeaux' (Barbéris, 1987)

(29) Tu sais le prof de l'année dernière LÀ. 'You know, that teacher we had last year' (Wissner, 2017)

We find very similar uses of EP *lá*, as in (30) and (31).

(30) Elias dispõe dum fornecedor de lagartas de confiança na pessoa prestimosa do dono do lugar de fruta LÁ do bairro.
'Elias has a reliable caterpillar supplier in the helpful person of the owner of the fruit place in the neighborhood' (CP)

(31) Aqui até diziam que era da… Devia ter cavalariça. Não é? Do tempo LÁ dos padres. Não sei.
'Here they even said it was from… There must have been a stable, don't you think? From the time of the priests. I don't know' (Marques & Duarte, 2017)

However, there are two differences, one semantic, the other formal, between the two kinds of examples. Semantically, whereas with FR *là* we have the construction of a common ground, EP *lá* signals the enunciator's indifference/distancing ('I am telling you just in case, it doesn't really matter'). Formally, the postponed position of FR *là* (relative to its scope) contrasts with the frontal position of EP *lá*.

11 From now on, in the examples, the marker will appear in small capitals and the underlined segments will signal its semantic scope, in order to make reading easier. In FR or EN translations or linguistic versions we will identify *lá*'s functional equivalent but this will not always be possible.

3.2. Modal Uses of EP *lá*

Most of the modal values of EP *lá* described in this section have already been identified from a syntactic (Martins, 2010) or pragmatic (Pereira, 2009; Duarte, 1989, 2005, 2010; Duarte & Marques, 2018; Marques & Duarte, 2015, 2017) perspective. Only in Duarte, 2005 do we find a contrastive EP / FR analysis, based on Cardoso Pires's novel *Balada da praia dos cães* and its translation. As stated earlier, contrarily to those authors we have tried to identify for EP *lá* a semantic core value that is common to its locative and modal uses. By presenting bilingual examples, we hope that the French translation equivalents will contribute to better comprehension of the local modal values assumed by *lá*, connecting them with the general characterization of the marker. As much as possible we will try to group the uses that have similar values.

3.2.1. Approximation

In this type of use, *lá* corresponds to a metalinguistic comment: the description of a place (32) / time (33) is not accurate or the words used, which represent a position on a scale (role of *muito* (much)) are not the most suitable (34). *Lá* is part of fixed expressions (*lá para* in the case of spatial and temporal descriptions, *não […] lá muito* para inaccurate wordings). In (33) 'pas si' in the French version suggests that the criticized formulation is not the enunciator's but someone else's.

(32) […] LÁ PARA os sótãos numa gaiola de telhado.
[…] LÀ-HAUT, QUELQUE PART au grenier, dans une cage du toit.
'SOMEWHERE AROUND the attic, in a roof cag' (CP)

(33) Em segundo lugar, a senhora Comissária afirmou que teremos resultados LÁ PARA o final de 2001.
Deuxièmement, vous avez dit que nous aurions des résultats vers la fin 2001.
Secondly, you said we would have the results BY the end of 2001. (EUR)

(34) Senhor Presidente, Senhor Comissário, indústria farmacêutica não vai LÁ muito bem.
Monsieur le Président, Messieurs les Commissaires, l'industrie pharmaceutique ne se porte pas SI bien.
Mr President, Commissioners, the pharmaceutical industry is not doing ALL THAT well. (EUR)

3.2.2. The So-Called Negative Value

Sentences like *Sei lá* (I know 'lá'), with *lá* in post-verbal position, seems to be semantically equivalent to the same sentences without *lá* in the negative form. Martins (2010) has shown convincingly that in this sort of situation *lá* is to be understood in terms of metalinguistic negation, which does not focus 'on the truth or falsity of a proposition, but on the assertability of an utterance' (Horn, 1989 ap. Martins, 2010). Nevertheless, there is something more to it than sheer negation. The general value of disconnection from the enunciator, a general feature of *lá*, has at least two side effects: the absence of endorsement of the predicative relation by the enunciator and an expression of indifference ('This is hardly my problem'). In the framework of Culioli's theory, this corresponds to an operation of scanning between the predicative relation's complementary values (in this case positive and negative), without stabilization on one of them. In the French and English versions, we do not find negative statements but some unanswered questioning ('who knows', 'on se demande pourquoi') (35) or a reference to God (You cannot find a human being who knows) (36), both typical of the scanning operation.

(35) Senhor Presidente, penso que o facto de se dizer que se não se realiza o debate no âmbito do processo de urgência se pode encontrar uma outra forma constitui um problema fundamental, porque, sempre que se diz isso, depois – sabe-se LÁ porquê – as comissões competentes nada fazem.
Monsieur le Président, je pense que le fait de dire que, si on ne décide pas l'urgence, on peut trouver une autre manière, constitue un problème fondamental parce que toutes les fois que l'on dit cela, ensuite – on se demande pourquoi – les commissions compétentes ne font rien.
Mr President, in my opinion, saying that there are other ways to deal with a matter besides holding a topical and urgent debate is a fundamental problem, for every time we say this – and who knows why – the committees responsible do nothing at all. (EUR)

(36) Aí abordou-me um reformado tunisino que, sabe-se LÁ como, tinha sabido que, no Parlamento Europeu, represento os reformados italianos, e perguntou-me: "[---]"
C' est là qu' un retraité Tunisien s' est approché de moi qui, DIEU sait comment, avait appris que je représente les pensionnés italiens au Parlement européen et m' a demandé : "[---]"
While I was there, a Tunisian pensioner came up to me – GOODNESS knows how he had found out that I represent the Italian pensioners in the European Parliament – and he said to me: "[---]" (EUR)

3.2.3. *General Extenders*

General extenders (Overstreet, 1999) are vague expressions that appear as the last element of lists. They can be adjunctive (introduced by *and*, as in *and stuff*) (37), or disjunctive (introduced by *or*, as in *or anything*) (38). In EP, we find *lá* in fixed expressions that have a function of general extenders. In these expressions, *lá* (in frontal position) signals here again a scanning operation. In (37) the general extender has the form of a question in the FR version and in (38) in both the FR and the EN versions, adding a nuance of the enunciator's indifference.

(37) De facto, considero que o que a Suíça fez com a reestruturação da Swissair em Crossair, em Swiss Airlines, ou seja LÁ o que for, é claramente um caso de ajuda directa.
Car j'estime en effet que ce que la Suisse a fait lors de la restructuration de Swissair en Crossair, en Swiss Airlines ou que sais-je, c'est clairement de l'aide directe.
I believe that what Switzerland has done with regard to the restructuring of Swissair into Crossair, Swiss Airlines or whatever is clearly a subsidy case. (EUR)

(38) Assim, à rede judiciária europeia, à academia de polícia europeia, à rede de prevenção de crimes europeia, já existentes, a Europa quer sobrepor uma rede europeia de protecção de personalidades, um procurador europeu, um código penal europeu, eu sei LÁ!...
Alors au réseau judiciaire européen, au collège de police européen, au réseau de prévention des crimes européens existant déjà, l'Europe veut superposer un réseau européen de protection des personnalités, un procureur européen, un code pénal européen, que sais-je encore... ?
Thus, in addition to the European legal network, the European police college, and the European crime prevention network, all of which already exist, Europe now seeks to impose a European network for the protection of public figures, a European public prosecutor, a European penal code, and what else, I wonder? (EUR)

3.2.4. *Absence of Endorsement*

The fixed expression 'É *lá* contigo / com ele' (It is your/their affair), by rejecting the responsibility for a situation on the co-enunciator or on third parties, expresses implicitly the enunciator's non-commitment / indifference. This has to be related to the general disconnection value of *lá*. In (39), FR 'Libre à eux' explicitly leaves the choice of decision to third parties, concerning quite characteristically an action that is valued negatively (water polluting). In (40), we put the words *leur* and *their* in capital letters to simulate a contrastive stress, which entails as implicit a lack of enunciator commitment ('their affair, not mine').

(39) [...] por ocasião da Cimeira de Edimburgo, Helmut Kohl e John Major disseram um ao outro: "Não precisamos de uma política comunitária no domínio da água; se os espanhóis quiserem contaminar a sua água, é LÁ com eles".
[...] au Sommet d'Édimbourg, Kohl et Major se déclaraient mutuellement: nous n'avons pas besoin d'une politique européenne dans le domaine de l'eau. Si les Espagnols veulent polluer leur eau, LIBRE à eux.
[...] at the Edinburgh Summit nearly ten years ago, Mr Kohl and Mr Major assured one another that there was no need for a European water policy. If the Spanish wish to pollute their water, they should do JUST that. (EUR)

(40) Que as grandes empresas reestruturem, é LÁ com elas. Mas o que é inadmissível e revoltante é que o façam condenando os trabalhadores ao desemprego e à pobreza.
Que les grandes entreprises restructurent, c'est LEUR affaire. Mais ce qui est inadmissible et révoltant, c'est qu'elles le fassent en condamnant leurs travailleurs au chômage et à la pauvreté
If big companies wish to restructure, that is THEIR affair, but what is inadmissible and revolting is that they should do it by condemning their workers to unemployment and poverty. (EUR)

3.2.5. Suspended Endorsement

Two constructions with *lá* in frontal position, *lá que P* and *lá porque P* correspond to what Culioli calls an operation of fictive location, that we find for example in hypothetical utterances. The meaning is something like 'let us assume temporarily that P', where there is no enunciator endorsement and P is preconstructed (role of *que* in both EP expressions), generally as dialogical. With *lá que P* (41), P is later endorsed by the utterer in the main clause (identification between the utterer's and the preconstructed position). With *lá porque P*, found in argumentative contexts (42), the pattern is different. P's truth is neither assumed nor negated, but the consequence Q of P is discarded (P is not a sufficient reason to accept Q). In the FR version, the expression 'du simple fait' (42), 'fait' ('fact') is illustrative of a lack of personal endorsement and of the construction of a fictive location[12].

(41) É, talvez, uma informação que não corresponde à realidade , porventura e seguramente bem-intencionada mas que não corresponde à verdade .Mas LÁ que a li nos jornais , isso é verdade.
'Il peut s'agir d'une information qui ne correspond pas à la réalité et si ça trouve sûrement bien intentionnée mais qui ne correspond pas à la vérité Mais le fait est que je l'ai lue dans le journal /en tout cas, je l'ai lue dans le journal.'
'It may be information that does not correspond to the truth, in all probability with the best intentions, but not corresponding to the truth. But that I read it in the newspapers, that's true.' (CRPC)

(42) Não podemos pressupor que LÁ porque um problema está controlado na União Europeia, está também universalmente controlado.

12 By saying 'le fait que P' the enunciator does not necessarily endorse the truth of P. A symptom of this is that the sentence 'Je ne reconnais pas les faits' (I do not acknowledge the facts [I am accused of]), uttered by someone accused of a crime, is not nonsensical.

Nous ne pouvons pas nous imaginer que, DU SIMPLE FAIT que l'Union européenne contrôle un aspect, celui-ci soit universellement sous contrôle.
We cannot assume that JUST because we have something under control in the European Union it is universally under control. (EUR)

3.2.6. Lá *Verb Subject Configuration*

In this section, we show uses of *lá* where:

- *lá*'s scope is a predicative relation;
- *lá* occupies a frontal position;
- the predicate comes before the subject (inversion of the canonical order);
- there is no pause between *lá* and the remaining utterance.

This configuration shares some characteristics of the 'signalling a limit' value of FR *là* (Section 2.1.1), with a coincidence between a subjective and a temporal location. But there are important differences. In the French 'signalling a limit' configuration, *là*, contrarily to EP *lá*, can occupy both the frontal and the final position, and in the frontal position is followed by a pause, without V-S inversion: this suggests a higher degree of syntactic integration of the EP *lá*. In the French 'signalling a limit' configuration, *là* refers to a representation constructed as shared by the enunciator and the co-enunciator, something that does not occur with EP *lá* due to its general disconnection value. On the other hand, with EP *lá*, there is no subjective good value. What is observed (temporal location) necessarily comes before the subjective location, with a semantic effect of inevitability (it was bound to happen), necessity, lack of control by a subjective instance, undesirability.

In (43) in the FR and EN versions there is no direct equivalent of *lá* because the context provides the idea of inevitability ('sabe Deus com que vontade', and its equivalents 'Dieu sait avec quelle envie', 'however unwillingly').

(43) Foi primeiro mudar de roupa e depois LÁ desceu à sala, sabe Deus com que vontade.
Elle alla d'abord changer de vêtements et ensuite descendit au salon, Dieu sait avec quelle envie?
'First she went to change her clothes and then came down to the living room, however unwillingly.' (CP)

In (44) with *lá* we get a 'it took time, but it was bound to happen sooner or later' connotation (quite well rendered by FR 'finalement').

(44) O único problema é que nem sequer tem um balde para ir buscar água. Com o fundo especial para situações de crise, LÁ conseguimos os baldes e congratulo-me verdadeiramente com o facto.
Le seul problème, c'est qu'elle ne dispose même pas d'un seau pour puiser l'eau. Grâce au fonds spécial consacré aux situations de crise, les seaux ont FINALEMENT pu être acquis et je m'en réjouis vraiment.
The only problem is that it does not even possess buckets with which to draw water. With the rapid reaction facility, the Union has now acquired some buckets AT LEAST, and I do welcome that. (EUR)

In (45), *lá*, as part of the fixed expression *lá se vai*, signals that what makes the argument fall apart is the observed PPE-DE's group behaviour (temporal location), not the utterer's counter-argumentation, becoming unnecessary. In the FR version, the temporal location is signalled by 'voilà'.

(45) Senhor Presidente, queria apenas assinalar – uma vez que o faminto senhor deputado Beazley se referiu às votações nominais – que, em cada relatório, todas as votações nominais foram solicitadas pelo Grupo PPE-DE. LÁ se vai esse argumento!
Monsieur le Président, je veux juste signaler – puisque notre affamé M. Beazley a fait une remarque au sujet des votes par appel nominal – que, sur le rapport suivant, chacun des votes par appel nominal a été demandé par le groupe PPE-DE. VOILÁ ce qu'il en est pour celui-là! [*Voilà un de vos arguments qui s'écroule* !]
Mr President, I just want to point out – since hungry Mr Beazley made a point about the roll-call votes – that, on the following report, every roll-call vote was requested by the PPE-DE Group. SO MUCH for that one! (*original version*) (EUR)

In (46), *lá*, part of the fixed expression *já lá vai*, signals the determinism of the world's evolution, the predominance of temporal over subjective location. The French 'Il est fini' renders the idea that a point of no return has been reached.

(46) Senhora Presidente, conforme referiu o orador que me precedeu, JÁ LÁ VAI o tempo em que a gestão de um negócio era uma questão de lucro.
Madame la Présidente, comme vient de le déclarer l'orateur précédent, IL EST FINI le temps où gérer une entreprise consistait simplement à gagner plus d'argent.
Madam President, as the previous speaker mentioned, THE TIME IS PAST when running a company was just about earning more money. (EUR)

In (47), *lá* is part of the semi-fixed expression *lá vem ele*, and we get a typical example of antiteleonomy: the head of the section's reference to censorship is heard by the inspector (temporal location) and retrospectively constructed as predictable (he has mentioned the censorship so many times that you would expect him to mention it again). The FR translation 'le revoilà' contains two elements: *voilà* (same value as in 45) and the prefix -re with an iterative value (the fact that it is not the first time is made manifest).

(47) Por escrito, Covas, essas coisas fazem-se por escrito, disse o inspector. Por escrito ou por falado é preciso que a Censura deixe passar, disse o chefe de brigada. E pronto, disse o inspector, LÁ vem ele com a censura.
Par écrit, Fosses, ces choses-là se font par écrit, dit l'inspecteur. Par écrit ou verbalement, il faut que la Censure laisse passer, dit le chef de brigade. Ça y est, dit l'inspecteur, LE REVOILÁ avec la censure.
"In writing, Covas, these things are done in writing, the inspector said. In writing or verbally, it has to pass through censorship, the head of the section said. HERE WE ARE, the inspector said, HERE HE COMES AGAIN with censorship." (CP)

These examples show similar semantic patterns (something happens and is retrospectively constructed as predictable). At this stage, we are unable to give a satisfactory and comprehensive explanation but our intuition is that this is an effect of the combination of the general value of *lá* (disconnection) and the syntactic construction (frontal position of *lá*, V S inversion, absence of pause between *lá* and the verbal predicate).

3.2.7. Intersubjective Modality

This section deals with examples where the following pattern is to be found:

- sentence with a verb in the imperative form (corresponding to a request, an order, a suggestion, etc.);
- *lá* in immediate post-verbal position without pause between the verb and *lá*;
- without *lá*, the sentence would remain grammatical and meaningful; this feature allows manipulation in order to isolate the specific contribution of *lá* to the sentence's meaning.

This construction has been analysed by various authors from a pragmatic perspective, in terms of speech acts and illocutionary values (Pereira, 2009; Marques & Duarte, 2015; Duarte & Marques, 2018). Our approach consists of trying to understand how *lá*'s general abstract identity (marker of disconnection from the enunciator) combines with this particular configuration.

Formally, an utterance in the imperative form entails the existence of intersubjective modality. A good value of the predicative relation is selected by the enunciator (subjective location), the realization of which (temporal location) depends on the co-enunciator's behaviour.

On the other hand, *lá* signals that responsibility for the execution is left to the co-enunciator (it is up to him). According to the context, which includes prosody (an important element to which our written corpus does not give access and which up to now, as far as we know, has not been analysed systematically), we will get a variety of pragmatic values (e.g.: exhortation, challenge, threat, face saving, advice «if I were you», etc.).

There is another effect of the presence of *lá* in the utterance. In most cases, it seems to imply that the complementary value of the predicative relation (non P) has already been selected by the co-enunciator (attitude of refusal, deliberate absence of initiative). This feature probably accounts for some pragmatic effects (enunciator's impatience, exhortation, etc.). It would be interesting to establish a relation between this observation and the general characterization of *lá*.

(48) is a good example of a situation where the responsibility for seeing the situation as it is, is left to co-enunciators (in this case members of the European Parliament), something that is rendered in the French version by 'Rendez-vous compte'. The situation is already there but the members of the EP have not realised it yet (non P position).

(48) A política de asilo e de imigração é, hoje em dia, vaiada – vejam LÁ os senhores! – em todo o mundo.
La politique d'asile et d'immigration est conspuée aujourd'hui, rendez-vous compte, partout dans le monde.
You realise that people all over the world are booing asylum and immigration policy. (EUR)

In (49), non P consists of some MPs' refusal to recognize what the Council's real aim is. The expression «Allons» found in the FR version is an expression of exhortation, typical of situations where non P has been selected by the co-enunciator.

(49) O que pretende o Conselho quando se opõe a essa base jurídica? Pretende afastar (V.Ex.ª dir-nos-á que o poderia fazer) o Parlamento Europeu do processo de co-decisão. É esse o objectivo. Vamos LÁ, não vale a pena abanar a cabeça! Estão a recusar-nos a co-decisão.
Que veut le Conseil en s'opposant à cette base juridique ? Il veut écarter (vous nous direz qu'il le pourrait) le Parlement européen de la procédure de codécision. C'est cela, l'enjeu. ALLONS, pas de hochements de tête ! Vous nous refusez la codécision.
[…] what is the Council after in opposing this legal base? It is seeking to take the European Parliament out of the codecision procedure (you will tell us that it could do this). That is what is at issue. So, do not shake your head! You are rejecting our right to take part in codecision. (EUR)

4. Back to Locative Values of lá and là: A Very Limited Convergence

The analysis of two parallel corpora (*Balada da Praia dos Cães* and Europarl) has allowed us to elicit that, despite their morphological resemblance, situations in which locative FR *là* and EP *lá* are functional equivalents are extremely rare, something that does certainly not correspond to the intuition of most bilingual speakers of FR/EP. One of those situations is to be found in (50).

(50) Elias tem uma visão barroca do Avenida Palace: colunas e criados velhos, um sítio inconcebível para dois predestinados se conhecerem. Mas era LÁ que o pai da moça fazia o ponto com os amigos, entre os quais o major enviado de belzebu, e daqui para a frente está tudo dito, Elias deixa correr a conversa.
Elias a une vision baroque de l'Avenida Palace : colonnades et valets vieillots, incroyable que deux destinées se soient croisées en un tel lieu. Mais c'était LÀ que le père de Mena faisait le point avec ses amis, parmi lesquels le major envoyé du diable, et à partir de là, tout a été dit, Elias laisse couler la conversation.
'Elias has a baroque impression of the Avenida Palace: columns and old servants, unbelievable that two people should be destined to meet each other there. But that was WHERE Mena's father caught up with his friends, among them the major sent by the devil, and from then on everything has been said, Elias lets the conversation run its course.' (CP)

Here, both markers have the value of locative anaphora (antecedent: the Avenida Palace [hotel]).

For EP *lá,* it is hardly surprising: a locative adverb signalling disconnection from the utterer should be available for anaphora. The fact that also FR *là* can be used in such contexts, even though it signals a – loose – identification with the enunciator, has to do with the idiosyncrasies of narrative genres: in those genres an autonomous system of location, independent of the enunciator/narrator, is set up, so that the constraint of non-disconnection from the enunciator becomes irrelevant[13]. Local synonymy is achieved between the two markers, but it is contingent.

(51) is a case of a translation that is acceptable even if it tells a slightly different story from the original. *Balada da praia dos cães* is a crime story. A witness, a bricklayer has reported an episode mentioning an attic room window in the house. The journalist has gone to the house in order to check the window's existence. EP 'Está lá' and 'Elle est là' are not complete synonyms: the Portuguese utterance is a case of locative anaphora (The window is effectively part of the house), the French is more a question of presence/absence, as in utterances like 'Est-ce que tu es là?' (example 6 above): the journalist checks that there is indeed an attic room window, suggesting that the bricklayer had been telling the truth. Each one of the meanings is compatible with the markers' core meaning.

13 D. Lebaud (personal communication).

(51) O jornalista e o pedreiro-testemunha enfrentam-se no terreiro à entrada da vivenda, dali quase não se vê a janela da mansarda porque fica um tanto recolhida em relação à fachada. Mas que a janela existe, existe. Está LÁ, [...]
Journaliste et maçon-témoin sont face à face sur le terre-plein, à l'entrée de la maison ; de là on ne voit presque pas la fenêtre de la mansarde qui est un peu en retrait par rapport á la façade. Mais qu'elle existe, ça ne fait aucun doute. Elle est LÀ, [...].
[The journalist and the bricklayer face each other on the ground in front of the house; from there you can hardly see the attic window which sits back from the front wall of the house. But there is a window, without a doubt. It is THERE.] (CP)

5. Conclusion

In the first part of this paper, using mainly made-up examples, we have tried to identify the basic location operations underlying the diversity of uses of FR *lá* and EP *là*.

We have mentioned the existence in EP of a double spatial location system (vs a single one in FR: *ici*, *là*, *là-bas*), one more concrete (*aqui*, *aí*, *ali*), the other more abstract (*cá. lá*). For all those adverbs, the locative operation never rules out subjectivity completely (for instance the notion of distance – what is near or far – depends on subjective factors). But we can say that because it belongs to the more abstract system, *lá* has a stronger subjective component than for instance *ali*. This makes it more available for modal uses. FR does not have that more abstract system. Therefore, it is hardly surprising that EP *lá* assumes a much wider range of modal values than FR *là*. The basic locative operations that we have found for FR *là* (signalling of a pre-existing location available in the co-enunciation space) and EP *lá* (disconnection from the enunciator) are very different. This might account for the fact that we have not found a single modal value common to FR *là* and EP *lá*.

We have tried to make some progress towards identifying an abstract – covering locative, temporal and modal values – core meaning of FR *là* and EP *lá*. Our assumption is that beyond local values that can be very different, discourse particles have a stable semantic identity. It relies on the fact that a native speaker of a language develops very early the ability to use DPs in a wide variety of idiomatic contexts, without having to think much about them, which suggests an interiorized and intuitive knowledge of the DPs' semantic identity. This happens for instance with EP *lá*, whose uses are very difficult to acquire for a learner of EP as a foreign language. We believe that, being the trace of some epilinguistic activity, translations can provide some insights into that semantic identity. Trying to explain the fact that two expressions (one in the source text, one in the target text) are functional equivalents relying on semantic units' core meaning in both languages is not an easy task but is worth the effort. We are aware of the fact that our contribution is most of the time very limited. Still, it will be of some use if it stimulates further debate and analysis. Research is always a work in progress.

References

Barbéris, J.-M. (1987). Deixis spatiale et interaction verbale: un emploi de *là*. *Cahiers de Praxématique* 9, 23–48.

Barbéris, J.-M. (1998). Identité, ipséité dans la deixis spatiale: *ici* et *là*, deux appréhensions concurrentes de l'espace?. *L'Information grammaticale* 77, 28–32.

Cartoni, B., Zufferey, S. & Meyer, T. (2013). Using the Europarl corpus for linguistic research. *Belgian Journal of Linguistics* 27, 23–42.

Corblin, F. & Asic, T. (2016). Une nouvelle approche de l'opposition ici / là et ovde / tu. *Travaux de Linguistique* 72, 29–48.

Culioli, A. (1999). *Pour une linguistique de l'énonciation. Formalisation et opérations de repérage*. Tome 2. Ophrys.

Duarte, I. M. (1989). *Alguns operadores de agulhagem comunicativa* (na prosa narrativa de Eça de Queirós e José Cardoso Pires). MA Thesis. University of Porto.

Duarte, I. M. (2005). Palavras do falar desataviado de todos os dias em *Balada da Praia dos Cães. Semear*, 11, 97–125.

Duarte, I. M. (2010). La dimension modale de *cá* et *lá* en portugais. *Studii și Cercetări Lingvistice* LX, 179–195.

Duarte, I. M. & Marques, M. A. (2018). Funções discursivas das construções com a partícula *lá*. In J. Veloso, J. Guimarães, P. Silvano & R. Sousa-Silva (eds.), *A Linguística em Diálogo* (pp. 195–211). Centro de Linguística Universidade do Porto.

Franckel, J.-J. (1989). *Études de quelques marqueurs aspectuels du français*. Droz.

Franckel, J.-J. (2005). De l'interprétation à la glose : vers une méthodologie de la reformulation. In D. Lebaud (ed.), *Actes du colloque D'une langue à l'autre*, Besançon, 5-6-7 septembre 2002. Presses Universitaires de Franche-Comté.

Grobet, A. (2021). *Ça* et *là* : formes privilégiées de reprise méta-discursive dans l'interaction orale. *Langue française* 210, 59–76.

Horn, L. R. (1989). A Natural History of Negation. CSLI Publications. 2001.

Kleiber, G. (1995). D'*ici* à *là* et vice-versa: pour les aborder autrement. *Le Gré des Langues* 8, 8–27.

Marques, M. A. (2018). Les expressions déictiques *aí* et *praí*. Registre colloquial, approximation et responsabilisation énonciative. *Studia UBB Philologia* LXIII/2, 2018,

Marques, M. A. & Duarte, I. M. (2015). *Cá* e *lá*: atenuação, reforço e outros valores modais em PE. *Acta Semiotica et Lingvistica* 20/2, 115–128.

Marques, M. A. & Duarte, I. M. (2017). *Lá*, atenuador em interações informais do Português Europeu. *Studia Universitatis Babeş-Bolyai, Philologia* LXII/4, 17–34.

Martins, A. M. (2010). Negação metalinguística (*lá*, *cá* e *agora*). In A. M. Brito et al. (eds.), *XXV Encontro Nacional da Associação Portuguesa de Linguística. Textos Seleccionados* (pp. 567–587). APL.

Overstreet, M. (1999). *Whales, candlelight and stuff like that. General extenders in English discourse*. Oxford University Press.

Pereira, M. (2009). *Aspectos Semânticos e Pragmáticos de aqui, aí, ali, cá e lá em Português Europeu*. MA Thesis, University of Porto.

Teixeira, J. (2005). De *cá* para *lá* e de *aqui* para *aí*: rede de valores semânticos dos marcadores espaciais *cá*/*lá*/(*acolá*) e *aqui*/*aí*/*ali*. In G. M. Rio-Torto, O. M. Figueiredo & F. Silva (coord.), *Estudos em Homenagem ao Professor Doutor Mário Vilela* (Vol.1, pp. 449–460). Faculdade de Letras da Universidade do Porto.

Wissner, I. (2017). Le marqueur *là* en français actuel dans l'espace francophone: quelle description lexicographique pour quel(s) usage(s)?. *Revue de Sémantique et Pragmatique, Cadrage sur la variation, le changement lexical et le changement grammatical en français actuel*, 79–97.

Federica Cominetti, Doriana Cimmino

4 The Semantic and Pragmatic Meanings of Italian *davvero* through Text Types

Abstract: It is generally maintained that, as a modal adverb, Italian *davvero* 'really' signals the degree of certainty attributed by the speaker to the modified linguistic material or expresses its positive evaluation (De Cesare, 2002a, b; Ricca & Visconti, 2014). Differently from other modal adverbs (e.g., *probabilmente* 'probably'), in its absolute use, *davvero* can react to an interlocutor's statement, reinforcing it or questioning it, thus expressing an epistemic judgment on an already existing assertion (De Cesare, 2003). We suggest that *davvero* retains this inherently dialogic feature in certain monologic texts, both spoken and written: in particular, we have considered a large corpus of Italian political monologues (the IMPAQTS corpus) and an ad hoc corpus of Italian tweets written by politicians and a large corpus of news reports (Repubblica). Our analysis shows that in these types of texts and in some specific linguistic configurations, *davvero* expresses a negative epistemic judgment and the overall polemic attitude of the speaker. Furthermore, *davvero* is able to trigger a presupposition of existence of a first voice responsible for an already shared content. On the contrary, in spontaneous spoken Italian (Kiparla corpus), the pragmatic functions performed by *davvero* seem quite different, being related not to persuasive functions, but to the expression of agreement, surprise and courtesy.

Keywords: discourse marker, epistemic values, pragmatics, *davvero*, Italian

1. Introduction[1]

This paper focuses on the semantic and pragmatic meanings of the Italian adverb *davvero* 'really', showing that under peculiar textual circumstances it triggers specific pragmatic enrichments. In particular, we describe the pragmatic meanings conveyed by *davvero* in a range of text types, including spontaneous spoken language, spoken political discourse, political tweets and written news report. The data collected from different corpora are analysed both quantitatively and qualitatively, to provide a description of the role of the adverb in the organization of discourse, focusing on its pragmatic use(s) in different text types.

The paper is organized as follows: in Section 2 the state of art is presented; in Section 3 the reference corpora and the methodology adopted are introduced; in

---

1 For academic purposes, FC should be considered responsible for Sections 4.2.2, 4.2.3, 4.2.4, 6; DC for Sections 1–3, 4.1, 4.2.1, 5, 7.

Section 4 data are analysed; in Section 5 we focus on the manipulative potential of the structures introduced in Section 4; in Section 6 a discussion of the findings is provided; in Section 7 conclusions are drawn.

2. State of the Art

At least since Traugott (1995), adverbs are acknowledged to be a class of words which easily get additional pragmatic meanings[2]. The pragmatic enrichment triggered by Italian *davvero* in some specific linguistic configurations has been firstly described by Cimmino and Cominetti (2023a), while previous studies on the adverb have focused on its syntactic, semantic and textual features, with no specific reference to the pragmatic meanings (De Cesare, 2000, 2002a, 2002b, 2003; Ricca & Visconti, 2014). Cross-linguistically, the pragmatic enrichment triggered by adverbs whose meaning is comparable to that of *davvero* has been studied. In particular, the work of Paradis (2003) and Romero and Han (2004) on the English adverb *really*, and the work of Yuan (2015) on Chinese *zhende* 'really' show pragmatic behaviours for some aspects similar to those of *davvero*.

In this work, we wish to describe some of the pragmatic meanings of *davvero* as implicitly conveyed contents: in particular, we will show that *davvero* – under some specific textual circumstances – is able to trigger either a conversational implicature, or both a conversational implicature and a presupposition. In fact, the pragmatic enrichment triggered by discourse or pragmatic markers can be analysed not only as a speech act marker or context marker, but also as implicit content (Lagerwerf, 1998; Karagjosova, 2001; Zeevat 2004; Yuan, 2015).

Since we will refer to the notions of presupposition and implicature to describe the pragmatic meanings triggered by *davvero*, let us clarify to which definitions of these categories we are relying on. For presupposition, we are adopting the definition by Stalnaker (2002: 701): 'to presuppose something is to take it for granted, or at least to act as if one takes it for granted, as background information – as common ground among the participants in the conversation'. Presupposition is considered a heterogeneous category (Levinson, 1983: 217; Sbisà, 2007). A long tradition has described many different linguistic triggers, including definite descriptions (Frege, 1892), change of state predicates (Sellars, 1954; Karttunen, 1973), factives (Kiparsky & Kiparsky, 1971; Karttunen, 1971), iteratives (Levinson, 1983: 182), and more. Recently, particles, conjunctions

2 In the domain of Romance languages, some relevant studies are collected in Ghezzi and Molinelli (2014).

and discourse markers have also been described as presupposition triggers (Lagerwerf, 1998; Karagjosova, 2001; Zeevat, 2004; Yuan, 2015). Typically, presupposed content refers to the existence and/or unicity of some entity, the being in place of some state of affairs, or the happening of an action. However, presupposed content may also include expectations and pre-requirements.

As for implicatures, we are adopting the milestone definition by Grice (1975): implicatures are propositions that in specific contexts can be communicated through an utterance without being explicitly said. According to Grice, conversational implicatures arise as a consequence of the speakers' compliance to the *cooperative principle*: 'Make your contribution such as is required, at the stage at which it occurs, by the accepted purpose or direction of the talk exchange in which you are engaged'. The apparent violation in discourse of one of the four *maxims of conversation*, which jointly express the cooperative principle, can also lead to the activation of an implicature.

3. Corpora and Methodology

In order to investigate the role of *davvero* in the organization of discourse, we considered different text types, using four corpora of Italian as a source of data: the IMPAQTS corpus of political monologic discourse (Cominetti et al., 2022), the Kiparla corpus of spontaneous spoken conversation (Mauri et al., 2019), the Repubblica corpus of written journalistic prose (Baroni et al., 2004); finally, we considered an *ad hoc* corpus of political tweets. The textual variation of this collection of corpora was conceived to allow disentangling the pragmatic use(s) of *davvero* from specific discourse traits. In particular, we want to gauge the impact of diamesic and diaphasic variation, as well as of the different communicative aims of the text. For this reason, not only are the selected corpora varied diamesically (spoken vs written) and diaphasically (spontaneous vs planned), but they are generally expected to represent a more (IMPAQTS and tweets corpora) or less (Repubblica and Kiparla) persuasive text type[3].

The IMPAQTS corpus of Italian political discourse, currently under construction, includes monologues uttered by 150 Italian politicians in different public contexts (chambers of the Parliament, meetings, rallies, press conferences, etc.) from 1946 to present. For the purposes of the present work, we interrogated the available section of the corpus, amounting to 763 speeches and 1,470,144

---

3 Cimmino and Cominetti (2023a) already hypothesize a relation between the mentioned variation traits and the use(s) of *davvero*. However, their data are not based on a variety of text types, and accordingly do not allow to (dis)confirm such hypothesis.

tokens. To obtain a comparable amount of data representative of other text types, we considered the entire Kiparla corpus (1,125,977 tokens) and a section of Repubblica corpus, choosing the portion of data produced in the year 2000 in the 'news' section[4], amounting to 1,421,721 tokens. Finally, we considered a corpus of around 382,000 words, composed of 11,450 tweets twitted by the official accounts of four Italian politicians[5]. The corpus was collected in the month of February 2022 by automatically downloading the 3000 most recent tweets published by each of the four considered people: accordingly, the tweets cover a time span from the beginning of 2013 to February 2022.

The four corpora were automatically searched for occurrences of the adverb *davvero*. The retrieved occurrences were then manually analysed. More precisely, we annotated: the type of sentence in which the adverb occurs; the semantic reading of the adverb (cf. Section 4.2.1); whether the adverb triggers a pragmatic enrichment; in case the adverb has a pragmatic meaning, what this meaning is.

4. Data Analysis

4.1. Quantitative Comparison of the Four Corpora

Interestingly, the four corpora represent quite different uses of the adverb *davvero*, both from a quantitative and qualitative point of view. The data emerged from a first quantitative analysis are reported in Table 4.1:

4 By choosing the 'news' genre, we have excluded from our corpus other journalistic text types, such as editorials, interviews and reportages, so as to collect a sample of texts whose main aim is not argumentative, but informative, and accordingly provide a sample of texts qualitatively different from political discourse, as for their communicative aim.

5 Namely: Maria Elena Boschi, Giorgia Meloni, Matteo Renzi, Matteo Salvini. The politicians were chosen so as to grant a balance for gender and political orientation: they indeed are one left-wing woman, one right-wind woman, one left-wing man and one right-wing man. They were also chosen because they are particularly active on social media. More details on the Tweet corpus composition may be found in Cimmino and Cominetti (2023b).

Table 4.1. The frequency of *davvero* in the four corpora

	Tokens	Occurrences of *davvero*	Frequency per million tokens
Tweet	382,000	123	321.98
IMPAQTS	1,470,144	466	316.97
Kiparla	1,125,977	255	226.47
Repubblica	1,421,721	103	72.45

Let us first notice that the adverb has its highest frequency in the Tweet corpus (321.98 occurrences per million tokens), followed by IMPAQTS (316.97) and Kiparla (226.47), while Repubblica represents the lowest frequency (72.45). This last datum is the one that most dramatically diverges from the other ones. It should however be considered that in the whole Repubblica corpus (380,823,725 tokens), the frequency of the adverb is 165.44 per million: still lower than that of the other corpora, but not so dramatically. The difference between the selected sub-corpus and the whole corpus may be partly related to the specific text type represented by the sub-corpus 'news', which excludes the editorials, the parts of the newspapers where journalists are driven by an argumentative aim and may accordingly express personal opinions. The fact that one of the functions of *davvero* is to express a subjective point of view (Ricca & Visconti, 2014) may be related to this deviation of the frequency of the adverb in the sub-corpus compared to the whole corpus.

A first qualitative analysis of the data reveals that Kiparla shows a very different use of the adverb if compared to all the other corpora. In fact, more than half of the occurrences of *davvero* in the Kiparla corpus – precisely 147 out of 255 – are holophrastic. On the contrary, no holophrastic occurrences are attested in the IMPAQTS and in the Tweet corpus and only one in Repubblica, in a reported speech.

4.2. Types of Meaning

4.2.1. Semantic Meanings

De Cesare (2000) brings forth a semantic analysis of *davvero*, according to which the adverb can have an intensifying, an emphasizing or a modal reading. The intensifying reading is in place when the adverb has scope on a gradable adjective or adverb and has the function of signalling that the modified property is in place at its greatest degree, as in the following example:

(1) Per questo vorrei che abbandonassimo le due [ideologie] che più danneggiano il nostro paese oggi. La prima è quella di un liberismo che ha poco a che fare, *davvero* poco, con la cultura liberale. IMPAQTS
'Thus, I would like us to abandon the two [ideologies] that mostly damage our country today. The first one is that of a liberalism that has little to do, *really* little, with liberal culture.'
[Intensifying reading: 'This liberalism has very little to do with liberal culture.']

The emphasizing reading is in place when *davvero* is used to signal that the characteristics of a certain concept are actually in place. For example, in (2) *davvero* underlines that Rome has to be a capital not only in name but also in fact:

(2) E allora se Roma Capitale deve essere *davvero* capitale e deve trainare l'Italia, beh, deve poterlo fare e deve poterlo fare alla pari con le altre. [IMPAQTS]
'So, if Roma Capitale has to be *really* capital and has to drag Italy, well, it has to be allowed to do that, and has to be allowed to do that at the same conditions of the others.'
[Emphasizing reading: 'Roma has to be truly, authentically capital.']

De Cesare (2002a) notices that emphasizing *davvero* is typically pronounced with a prosodic emphasis: for example, with reference to (2) 'Se Roma Capitale deve essere *DAVVERO* capitale' 'If Roma Capitale REALLY has to be the capital'.

Finally, the modal reading is recognized when the speaker wants to stress the truth-conditional traits of the sentence:

(3) Le elezioni di domenica sembreranno a molti di voi lontane, e invece sono elezioni importanti, perché l'Europa *davvero* sembra distante e invece qui, pesa sulla condizione di lavoro, di vita di ognuno di noi. [IMPAQTS]
'Sunday's elections seem very distant to many of you, but on the contrary, they are important, because Europe *really* seems distant, but instead it matters on work and life conditions of each of us'.
[Modal reading: 'It is indeed true that Europe seems distant'.]

De Cesare's classification is very clear, and prototypical examples are not hard to find. Nonetheless, many occurrences found in the corpora are difficult to classify accordingly. This is often the case with written data, but it can also happen in spoken examples and the prosody may not be of help. In some cases, it is difficult to decide between an emphasizing and a modal reading[6]:

6 Such difficulty may be enhanced by the presence of verbs of opinion, especially when inflected in the first person, like in (4). We are grateful to an anonymous reviewer for this observation.

(4) Spero *davvero* che coloro a cui Parisi rivolge il suo appello rispondano con lo stesso coraggio. [Repubblica]
'I *really* hope that those to whom Parisi addresses his plea answer with the same courage'.
[Emphasizing reading: 'I do really hope so', 'I truly, authentically hope so'.
Modal reading: 'Really, I hope so', 'It is indeed true that I hope so'.]

Other examples are ambiguous between an emphasizing and an intensifying reading:

(5) Ci spiace dirlo, ma sono *davvero* irresponsabili. [IMPAQTS]
'We are sorry to say, but they are *really* irresponsible'
[Emphasizing reading: 'They are truly, authentically irresponsible'.
Intensifying reading: 'They are very irresponsible'.]

Considering the presence of numerous ambiguous examples, we are not providing any statistics of the distribution of the three semantic readings of *davvero* in the examined corpora.

4.2.2. Contrast Implicatures

In many of the occurrences where *davvero* has a clear emphasizing reading, the adverb activates an implicit content, by establishing a contrast between the mentioned state of affairs and another one relevant in context. Let us consider the following example:

(6) Contiamo nella riconversione ecologica della nostra industria, senza più ricatti tra salute e occupazione, che scelga *davvero* le energie rinnovabili al posto del carbone. [IMPAQTS]
'We count on the ecologic reconversion of our industry, with no more blackmails between health and employment, that *really* chooses renewable energies over coal'.

In (6), the presence of *davvero* activates the content that in other relevant situations renewable energies were said to be chosen over coal, but they actually were not. Depending on the context, such implicated content could be referred to previous governments, opposing parties or other specific situations that the addressees are likely to be able to infer, thus resulting in an implicit attack. If we manipulate the example to delete the adverb, we notice that this implicit attack is no longer present:

(6a) Contiamo nella riconversione ecologica della nostra industria, senza più ricatti tra salute e occupazione, che scelga le energie rinnovabili al posto del carbone.
'We count on the ecologic reconversion of our industry, with no more blackmails between health and employment, that chooses renewable energies over coal'.

While 'no more blackmails' still activates the implicit content that blackmails were used in the past, the fact that the promise to switch to renewable energies was failed in the past is no longer recognizable in (6a).

This kind of 'contrast implicature' appears to be relatively frequent in the Tweet, IMPAQTS, and Repubblica corpora, but extremely rare in the Kiparla. Example (6) above is taken from IMPAQTS, while examples from the other corpora are provided after the table:

Table 4.2. Percentage of occurrences of *davvero* activating a contrast implicature in the four corpora

	Contrast implicature	**Total**	**Percentage**
Tweet	59	123	48 %
Repubblica	31	103	30 %
IMPAQTS	30	100[7]	30 %
Kiparla	1	255	0,4 %

(7) Il segno che qualcosa è cambiato *davvero*, nel ménage tra Berlusconi e Fini, è stato, ieri, una frase del leader di Alleanza nazionale: "Con i sondaggi si incartano le patate". Repubblica
'The sign that something has *really* changed, in the ménage between Berlusconi and Fini, was, yesterday, an utterance by the leader of Alleanza nazionale: "You can use polls to wrap potatoes"'.

(8) 23 anni fa ci lasciava Pinuccio Tatarella, ispiratore di una destra moderna, forte e capace di governare. Il suo pensiero continua a guidare la nostra azione politica. Per questo lavoriamo per dare alla Nazione un governo di patrioti in grado di rappresentare *davvero* gli italiani. [Tweet]
'23 years ago, Pinuccio Tatarella left us, who was inspirer of a modern, strong and capable of governing right-wing. The thought of him continues to lead our political action. This is why we work to give the Nation a government of patriots capable of *really* representing the Italians'.

(9) Tutti ci vestiamo. E soprattutto oggi con la diffusione della moda *davvero* di massa, fast fashion e la possibilità di acquistare capi vintage a basso costo. Kiparla
'We all get dressed. And especially today, with the diffusion of a *really* mass fashion, fast fashion and the possibility of buying vintage pieces at a low price'.

---

7 A qualitative analysis of *davvero* in the IMPAQTS corpus is conducted only on the 100 occurrences sample considered in Cimmino and Cominetti (2023a) and not in all the 466 occurrences.

Example (7) activates the implicature that in other circumstances where a change in the relationship between Berlusconi and Fini was announced or expected, such change had not actually happened. Example (8) implicates that the actual government does not represent the Italians. Example (9) implicates that before today fashion was not actually mass fashion.

In all the corpora, contrast implicatures are activated by emphasizing *davvero*. On the contrary, it is not true that all the occurrences of emphasizing *davvero* trigger a contrast implicature, as it may be observed in (10). Accordingly, the emphasizing reading is a necessary but not sufficient condition for the triggering of a contrast implicature.

(10) E il referendum viene ultimo. E ha la sua importanza anche per questo aspetto, proprio perché la Casa delle Libertà vuole trovare in questo un rimedio per le ripetute sconfitte che ha avuto durante tutti questi mesi. E lo vuol fare su un documento che *davvero* distrugge la nostra carta costituzionale. [IMPAQTS]
'The referendum comes last. It is important also for this aspect, precisely because the Casa delle Libertà wants to find in this a remedy to the several defeats it has undergone during all these months. And it wants to do that on a document that really destroys our Constitution'.

In example (10), *davvero* has an emphasizing reading: the document truly, authentically destroys the Constitution. However, it does not activate the implicature that some other relevant documents did not really destroy the Constitution.

4.2.3. Polemic Polyphony

When occurring in some specific linguistic configurations, *davvero* appears to trigger a quite complex pragmatic meaning that we shall label 'polemic polyphony[8]'. In order to describe it, let us consider the following examples:

(11) Spero tuttavia che questo dibattito, che si svolge oggi, possa essere utile per parlare finalmente del ruolo della cultura in un Paese come il nostro, del ruolo che essa può avere per lo sviluppo economico, e non soltanto, civile e democratico di un Paese come il nostro. Ma voi, onorevoli deputati della sinistra e dell'opposizione che avete presentato la mozione di sfiducia, siete *davvero* interessati a discutere della cultura? [IMPAQTS]
'Anyway, I hope that this debate, which is taking place today, can be useful to finally discuss the role of culture in a Country like ours, of the role that it can have for the economic, civic and democratic development of a Country like ours. But

8 The notion of polyphony, to refer to the presence of a plurality of voices in a text, is first introduced in Ducrot (1972) and further discussed in Carel and Ducrot (2009).

do you, honorable colleagues of the left and of the opposition, who have presented the motion of no confidence, are you *really* interested in talking of culture?'

(12) Basterà *davvero* questo stop al traffico per migliorare la qualità dell'aria che respiriamo? [Repubblica]
'Will this traffic stop *really* be enough to improve the quality of the air we breathe?'

(13) *Davvero* qualcuno crede che per i 16enni oggi la priorità sia il diritto di voto e non all'istruzione, alla socialità, alla libertà? Le forze di maggioranza si occupino di fronteggiare epidemia e crisi economica per tornare il prima possibile alla normalità, anziché fare demagogia. Tweet
'Is there *really* someone who believes that today's 16-years-olds have as a priority the right to vote and not the right to education, sociality and freedom? The majority forces should take care of fronting the epidemic and the economic crisis to go back to normal as soon as possible, instead doing demagogy'.

First, let us consider (11), taken from an official assembly of the Parliament. The speaker, a Minister against whom a motion of no confidence was tabled by the opposition, directly addresses his opposing colleagues in the Chamber. By asking whether they are really interested in talking of culture, he implicitly conveys two further contents: (i) he suggests that they have mentioned that they are interested in talking of culture; (ii) he suggests that he does not believe that they are interested in talking of culture. The presence of the two contents can easily be verified by manipulating the example to delete the adverb:

(11a) Spero tuttavia che questo dibattito, che si svolge oggi, possa essere utile per parlare finalmente del ruolo della cultura in un Paese come il nostro, del ruolo che essa può avere per lo sviluppo economico, e non soltanto, civile e democratico di un Paese come il nostro. Ma voi, onorevoli deputati della sinistra e dell'opposizione che avete presentato la mozione di sfiducia, siete interessati a discutere della cultura?
'Anyway, I hope that this debate, which is taking place today, can be useful to finally discuss the role of culture in a Country like ours, of the role that it can have for the economic, civic and democratic development of a Country like ours. But do you, honorable colleagues of the left and of the opposition, who have presented the motion of no confidence, are you interested in talking of culture?'

In (11a), the two implicit contents present in (11) are no longer recognizable: it is no longer suggested that the members of the opposition have mentioned that they are interested in discussing culture and neither is it suggested that the speaker does not believe that they are.

Examples (12–13) convey comparable implicit meanings. In (12), it is implicitly encoded that someone mentioned that the traffic stop will be enough to improve the quality of the air, and that the writer does not think that the traffic stop will be enough. In (13), it is implicitly encoded that someone mentioned that they believe that for 16-years-olds the right to vote is a priority, and that the speaker does not believe that to be true.

The polemic polyphony can be described as the sum of two implicit contents: the *presupposition* of the mentioning of the content of the utterance by someone, and the *conversational implicature* that the source does not believe that the content of the utterance is true. For the pragmatic analysis which leads to this conclusion we refer to Cimmino and Cominetti (2023a).

The polemic polyphonic dynamic is activated in dialogue mimicking contexts, such as questions (11–13), while it is interestingly not attested in the actual dialogues of the Kiparla corpus, for reasons that will be discussed in Sections 5–6.

Another linguistic configuration where the polemic polyphonic dynamic is found to be activated is the hypothetical clause. This may be linked to the fact that both questions and hypothetical clauses are typically used to build counter-argumentative moves (Calaresu, 2022: 67, cf. Section 5):

(14) Le risorse messe a disposizione dall'Europa non sono poche. Certo, bisognerebbe avere però le idee chiare su come utilizzare queste risorse. Ad oggi, tutte le categorie produttive sono insoddisfatte dei provvedimenti varati dal governo. Lo hanno detto chiaramente, Ministro, nelle audizioni che abbiamo ascoltato ieri, eppure il presidente del Consiglio e lei avreste la strada segnata se *davvero* voleste rimettere in moto l'economia. [IMPAQTS]
'The resources made available by Europe are not little. Of course, one should have clear ideas on how to use them. At the moment, all the productive categories are unsatisfied with the motions voted by the government. They have clearly said so, Minister, in the auditions we have listened to yesterday, and still the Prime Minister and you would have an open way if you *really* wanted to restart the economy'.
[Polemic polyphony: it is presupposed that the Ministers mentioned that they want to restart the economy and it is implied that the speaker does not believe that to be true.]

The polemic polyphony seems to be triggered exclusively by the modal *davvero*, and it is found in all the corpora, with the exception of Kiparla. It appears to be less frequent than contrast implicatures, as may be noticed comparing Tables 4.2–4.3: the deviation of occurrences in the corpora will be discussed in Section 6.

Table 4.3. Percentage of occurrences of *davvero* activating the polemic polyphony in the four corpora

	Polemic polyphony	Total	Percentage
Tweet	21	123	17 %
Repubblica	16	103	16 %
IMPAQTS	7	100	7 %
Kiparla	0	255	0 %

4.2.4. Agreement, Surprise and Courtesy

As mentioned in Section 4.1, in spontaneous spoken Italian, represented in our study by the Kiparla corpus, the most common use of *davvero* seems to be the holophrastic one. In such cases, the function of the adverb is explicitly guiding the interaction with the interlocutor, as the speaker expresses agreement.

(15) A: Guarda, c'è delle ingiustizie, una cosa spaventosa.
B: *Davvero.*
'A: Look, there are such injustices, it is terrible.
B: *Really*'.

In such cases, the pragmatic meaning is compatible with the semantic modal one, with which it overlaps: *davvero* in (15) could be paraphrased as 'I agree with you', but also as 'It is indeed true that there are terrible injustices'. Prosody and non-verbal communication may help disambiguating between these two interpretations, but not always. Indeed, in holophrastic occurrences the semantic use of the adverb seems to be typically intertwined with a pragmatic function.

The interpretation is different in questions, even more common than holophrastic affirmative sentences. Let us consider (16):

(16) A :Il riso alla cantonese non esiste in Cina.
B: No e non è così soprattutto. È piccantissimo.
A: *Davvero*?
'A: Cantonese fried rice does not exist in China.
B: No, and moreover it is not like that. It is super spicy.
A: Really?'

Asking '*Davvero*?', the speaker is typically not inquiring whether the interlocutor has a high degree of certainty on the truth value of the sentence, but is expressing her surprise. Interrogative holophrastic occurrences may also have the pragmatic function of casting doubts on the truthfulness of the interlocutor's utterance. However, no occurrences with this pragmatic meaning were found in the corpora.

When it is not holophrastic, in the Kiparla corpus *davvero* often acquires another interactional function as a collaborative strategy, aimed at showing one's willingness to cooperate in conversation:

(17) A: Volevo dirle tutto in piemontese.
B: Ma non si preoccupi parli come come preferisce non…
A: Ah eh a attualmente preferisco in italiano.
B: Va benissimo ita come come preferisce *davvero*. [Kiparla]
'A: 'I wanted to tell you all in Piedmontese.
B: Don't worry speak as you like, don't…

A: Well at the moment I prefer Italian.
B: It is perfect Ita… as, as you like, *really*'.

In (17), the speaker uses modal *davvero* not (only) to stress the truth-conditional traits of the sentence, but to ease the interaction, by signaling to the interlocutor her full openness and friendliness.

5. Persuasive Power

The pragmatic enrichments described in Sections 4.2.2 and 4.2.3 can be exploited as linguistic strategies to ease the manipulation of the addressees. This is due to the presence of implicit strategies, which are acknowledged to be useful resources to the purpose of persuasion (Givón, 1982; Sbisà, 1999, 2007; Macagno, 2015; Lombardi Vallauri, 2016a, 2016b, 2019). More specifically, implicit strategies have the power of reducing the epistemic vigilance of the addressees and take advantage of cognitive mechanisms such as the egocentric bias (Reboul, 2011: 17). Accordingly, if a speaker/writer uses an implicit strategy to encode contents which are not *bona fide* true, an attempt of manipulation can be spotted.

In the specific case considered in this paper, both the contrast implicature and the polemic polyphony can be considered a manipulative attempt – provided that the contents they encode are not *bona fide* true. Let us consider as a first example (8), discussed in Section 4.2.2. In the case of this Tweet, published by a member of the opposition, it is implied that the current government does not represent the Italian citizens. This content is clearly non *bona fide* true: being packaged implicitly, as a conversational 'contrast' implicature, it is more likely to be accepted as true by the addressees than if it had been explicitly affirmed.

The polemic polyphony provides a more subtle and complex strategy of persuasion due to the overlapping of two implicit strategies. In particular, an attempt of manipulation can be spotted when the polemic polyphonic dynamic is activated, but the presupposed content is not *bona fide* true: on the contrary, it is exaggerated, or false altogether, as in (18):

(18) Beppe Grillo rilancia il referendum sull'euro: avrebbe conseguenze devastanti sulla nostra economia. Spero che il Governo smentisca. O vogliono *davvero* un'estate con l'Italia sotto il tiro dei mercati? [Tweet]
'Beppe Grillo relaunches the referendum on euro: it would have devastating consequences on our economy. I hope that the government denies that. Or do they *really* want a summer with Italy under the fire of markets?'

In (18) it is presupposed that the government deliberately acted as if they wanted to let Italy under the fire of markers for the summer. This content is not a shared truth, but the writer's personal opinion, and accordingly its framing as a presupposition is illegitimate and can be considered a manipulative attempt on the part of the writer. Being encoded as a presupposition, not as an explicit assertion, this content has more chances of eluding the epistemic vigilance of the addressees, which will be less likely to notice the exaggeration of the content and more likely to end up believing that the government has acted very stupidly.

Interestingly, in polemic polyphonic occurrences, when the presupposition is not *bona fide* true, the other implicit content, the conversational implicature, is on the contrary quite obvious. In (18), for example, it is implied that the writer does not believe that the government wants to leave Italy under the fire of markets for all the summer. Since the presupposed content is exaggerated, the implied content that the source does not believe that true becomes on the contrary easily shareable. Accordingly, the addressees will be more likely to find themselves in agreement with the source.

Notwithstanding the truth value of the contents encoded implicitly, the polemic polyphony and – less markedly – the contrast implicatures appear to be triggered in texts (or stretches of texts) characterized by a persuasive aim. Not by chance, the polyphonic dynamic is labelled 'polemic': even if the implicit contents are true, the intent of the speaker is always to express a disagreement. Also contrast implicatures can be used to denigrate a scenario by comparing it with a preferable alternative, as noticed in (6) and (8). This aspect is likely to play a role in the distribution of the pragmatically enriched *davvero* in the different corpora, as it will be discussed in the next section.

6. Types of *Davvero* and Text Types

After analysing the types of pragmatic enrichments triggered by *davvero*, their relation with the semantic reading of the adverb and the manipulative potential of this dynamic, we wish to discuss the differences observed in the different corpora.

As observed in Tables 4.2 and 4.3, both contrast implicatures and polemic polyphonic occurrences are comparatively more frequent in the Tweet corpus, followed by Repubblica and IMPAQTS, while Kiparla is practically void of this kind of pragmatic enrichments, showing a dramatic difference in the use of the adverb with respect to all the other corpora. As suggested in Cimmino and Cominetti (2023a), we believe that the presence of the pragmatic meanings is related to the persuasive aim of the text, which – as described in Section 5 – can be enhanced by the presence of implicit strategies. Accordingly, it comes as no surprise that the pragmatic enrichment is particularly frequent in the Tweet corpus: political tweets are often used to propagandistic purposes, and not by chance they provide a rich source of implicit strategies (Garassino et al., 2019, 2022; Pietrandrea, 2021).

What may actually be surprising is that implicit strategies are slightly less frequent in the IMPAQTS corpus than in Repubblica. Political discourse is indeed expected to represent a more persuasive text type than news report. However, we believe that the deviation can be explained considering another important difference between the two corpora. In fact, IMPAQTS is a spoken corpus, while Repubblica is written. While it is true that a large part of the IMPAQTS corpus represents a very controlled variety of spoken language, especially as far as official speeches are concerned, some texts on the contrary bear evidence of more spontaneous language:

(19) Oggi voglio ringraziare di cuore Matteo Renzi: grazie *davvero*. [IMPAQTS]
'Today I want to thank Matteo Renzi from the heart: *really* thanks'.

(20) Quindi faccio un grande in bocca al lupo a Marta, lo faccio a tutti voi, perché so che se la eleggerete, le cose che ha detto – non conosco la vostra città come la conoscete voi e come la conosce lei, come la conosce Francesco, Renato Soru – ma dalle cose che ascoltavo, mi sembravano vere, mi sembravano sensate, giuste, e se la eleggerete incomincerete a farle con lei e penso che cambierà il volto di questa città e di questa parte della Sardegna, quindi in bocca al lupo *davvero*. IMPAQTS
'So good luck to Marta, on behalf of all of you, because I know that you will elect her, the things that she has said – I don't know your city as you do and as she does, as Francesco and Renato Soru do – but from the things I was listening to, they seemed true, they seemed sensible, right, and if you elect her you will start to do those things with her and I think that the face of this city and of this part of Sardinia will change, so *really* good luck'.

Examples (19–20) are taken from election rallies in which the two politicians spontaneously address their audiences. These examples are indeed very similar to many retrieved in the Kiparla corpus, like (17) and (21):

(21) Va bene, io ti ringrazio tantissimo per il tempo. Grazie mille *davvero*. [Kiparla]
'Ok, I thank you very much for your time. Thank you a lot, *really*'.

These modal or modal/emphatic occurrences of *davvero* perform the collaborative function described in Section 4.2.4. They are typical of spontaneous spoken language: in fact, they are numerous in the Kiparla corpus, but their frequency is not negligible in IMPAQTS either. Crucially, they concur to interactional functions, but not to persuasion. Coherently with our model, they in fact do not trigger contrast implicatures nor polemic polyphony. Thus, they reduce the overall figure of the occurrences of *davvero* responsible for an implicit pragmatic enrichment in the IMPAQTS corpus.

The comparatively high frequency of the instances of *davvero* triggering implicit contents in Repubblica is still quite surprising, since it is expected that news reports do not include potentially manipulative linguistic strategies. However, a qualitative analysis of the occurrences shows that the polemic polyphony in Repubblica is typically activated in two situations: reported speeches (22) and provocative questions addressed to the readers (23), which typically get an answer in the remainder of the article:

(22) Ogni cosa mi dà motivo di piangere: la guerra che abbiamo subito e la pace che subiremo allo stesso modo. Era *davvero* necessario tutto questo? (Dal Diario di Belgrado del 3 giugno 1999). [Repubblica]
'Everything gives me a reason to cry: the war we have endured and the peace we will endure in the same way. Was all this *really* necessary?' (From the Diary of Belgrade of June 3, 1999).
[Polemic polyphony: it is presupposed that someone mentioned that the war was necessary and it is implied that the writer does not believe that to be true.]

(23) Bresci è arrestato e condannato all'ergastolo. Petacco ripropone un testo pubblicato già anni fa, aggiornato però secondo numerose rivelazioni. Bresci, per esempio, dichiara di non essere al servizio di nessuno. Ma era davvero un isolato? Petacco sembra non pensarla così grazie a nuovi rilevanti documenti. [Repubblica]
'Bresci was arrested and condemned to life sentence. Petacco proposes again a text published years ago already, updated with many revelations. Bresci, for example, declares not to be at anyone's service. But was he *really* isolated? Petacco seems to disagree thanks to new relevant documents.'
[Polemic polyphony: it is presupposed that someone mentioned that Bresci was isolated and it is implied that the writer does not believe that to be true.]

7. Concluding Remarks

In this paper we have compared the pragmatic meanings acquired by the Italian adverb *davvero* in a variety of text types. In particular, we have identified two kinds of pragmatic meanings which can be described as implicit contents, in line with the works of Lagerwerf, 1998; Karagjosova, 2001; Zeevat, 2004; Yuan, 2015. In one case, *davvero* triggers what we label a 'contrast' implicature, implying the existence of a relevant scenario opposed to the one depicted by the sentence including the adverb. In another case, *davvero* triggers what we propose to call a 'polemic polyphony' (Cimmino & Cominetti, 2023a), produced by the sum of two implicit contents: a presupposition of previous mentioning of the content of the utterance and an implicature conveying the disbelief of the source on said content. Both these types of pragmatic contents can be exploited by the source to the purpose of persuading the addressees.

Probably as a consequence of their manipulative potential and of their general polemic aim, the acquisition of implicit pragmatic meanings is most frequent in the political Tweet corpus. Political tweets are indeed a text type often used for expressing opinions (also polemic ones) and persuading the addressees. On the other hand, these strategies are less frequent in the IMPAQTS corpus of political discourse. Although political discourse is a text type generally aimed at persuasion, the deviation in the exploitation of *davvero* to potentially manipulative purposes is related to the fact that the corpus is spoken. Accordingly, the overall use of *davvero* is partly contaminated by typically spoken traits, with the adverb acquiring a pragmatic meaning related to the expression of courtesy. Data extracted from the spontaneous spoken corpus Kiparla do indeed confirm this tendency, since no instances of contrast implicatures or polemic polyphony could be retrieved.

The most surprising datum is the one regarding the Repubblica journalistic corpus, where the instances of potentially manipulative pragmatic uses were more frequent than in the IMPAQTS corpus. This datum – despite partially mitigated by the occurrence in reported speeches – can be added to other suggesting that Italian news report is a text type not void of persuasive attempts (cf. Labinaz & Sbisà, 2018; Meluzzi et al., 2021; De Cesare, 2021; Coppola et al., forthcoming), opening to further research.

References

Baroni, M., Bernardini, S., Comastri, F., Piccioni, L., Volpi, A., Aston, G., & Mazzoleni, M. (2004). Introducing the 'la Repubblica' corpus: A large, annotated, TEI(XML)-compliant corpus of newspaper Italian. *Proceedings of LREC 2004.*

Calaresu, E. M. (2022). *La dialogicità nei testi scritti. Tracce e segnali dell'interazione tra autore e lettore*. Pacini Editore.

Carel, M. & Ducrot, O. (2009). Mise au point sur la polyphonie. *Langue française* 2009/4, 33–43.

Cimmino, D. & Cominetti, F. (2023a). Italian davvero ('really') as a trigger of implicit contents in persuasive discourse. In E. Lombardi Vallauri, L. Baranzini & D. Cimmino (eds.), *Journal of pragmatics, 211 (2023): 84-95.* Special Issue 'The dynamic contribution of implicit meaning to the context: Variability in real usage'.

Cimmino, D. & Cominetti, F. (2023b). La dialogicità di *davvero* nell'e-taliano di Twitter. Un confronto con l'inglese. In A.-M. De Cesare, A. Ferrari, L. Lala, F. Pecorari (eds.), Forme della scrittura italiana contemporanea in prospettiva contrastiva. La componente testuale. Firenze, Franco Cesati Editore, 31-44.

Cominetti, F., Lombardi Vallauri E., Panunzi A., & Gregori L. (2022). IMPAQTSS: un corpus di discorsi politici italiani annotato per gli impliciti linguistici. In E. Cresti & M. Moneglia (a cura di), *Corpora e Studi linguistici. Atti del LIV Congresso della Società di Linguistica Italiana* (Online, 8–10 settembre 2021) (pp. 151–164). Officinaventuno.

Coppola, C., Cimmino, D., Cominetti, F., Giunta, G., Lombardi Vallauri, E., Mannaioli, G., & Masia, V. (forthcoming). The role of implicitness in persuasive argumentation. Looking at different text genres. *Conference proceedings of the European Conference on Argumentation, 30 September 2022.*

De Cesare, A.-M. (2000). Sulla semantica di alcuni tipi di intensificazione in italiano: '*Davvero*, è proprio molto interessante!'. *Romanistisches Jahrbuch* 51, 87–107.

De Cesare, A.-M. (2002a). *Intensification, modalisation et focalisation. Les différents effets des adverbes* proprio, davvero *et* veramente. Peter Lang.

De Cesare, A.-M. (2002b). Gli usi e le funzioni dell'avverbio proprio. *Italica* 79/4, 453–465.

De Cesare, A.-M. (2003). Les adverbes italiens *davvero* et veramente: propositions de description. *Revue Romane* 38/1, 29–52.

De Cesare, A.-M. (2021). Opinion shaping in the context of the 'Me too movement'. An investigation of the presupposition triggered by additive focus adverbs in traditional and social media. In E. Lombardi Vallauri, F. Cominetti & V. Masia (eds.), *Journal of pragmatics*. Special Issue 'Persuasive and manipulative power of implicit communication'.

Ducrot, O. (1972). *Dire et ne pas dire: Principes de sémantique linguistique*. Hermann.

Frege, G. (1892). Über Sinn und Bedeutung. *Zeitschrift für Philosophie und philosophische Kritik* 100, 25–50.

Garassino, D., Brocca, N., & Masia, V. (2022). Is implicit communication quantifiable? A corpus-based analysis of British and Italian political tweets. *Journal of Pragmatics* 194/5, 9–22.

Garassino, D., Masia, V., & Brocca, N. (2019). Tweet as you speak. The role of implicit strategies and pragmatic functions in political communication: Data from a diamesic comparison. *RILA*, 187–208/2019, 2–3.

Ghezzi, C., Molinelli, P. (2014, eds.). Discourse and Pragmatic Markers from Latin to the Romance Languages. Oxford University Press.

Givón, T. (1982). Evidentiality and epistemic space. *Studies in Language* 6/1, 23–49.

Grice, P. (1975). Logic and conversation. In P. Cole & J. Morgan (eds.), *Syntax and semantics*, vol. 3: Speech acts (pp. 41–58). Academic Press.

Karagjosova, Elena. (2001). Towards a comprehensive meaning of German *doch*. *Proceedings of the ESSLLI 2001 Student Session.*

Karttunen, L. (1971). Some observations on factivity. *Paper in Linguistics* 4, 55–69.

Karttunen, L. (1973). Presupposition of compound sentences. *Linguistic Inquiry* 4, 169–193.

Kiparsky, C. & Kiparsky, P. (1971). Fact. In D. D. Steinberg & L. A. Jakobovits (eds.), *Semantics: An interdisciplinary reader* (pp. 345–369). Cambridge University Press.

Labinaz, P. & Sbisà, M. (2018). Argumentation as a dimension of discourse. The case of news articles. *Pragmatics & Cognition* 25, 602–630.

Lagerwerf, L. (1998). Causal connectives have presuppositions. Effects on discourse structure and coherence. *LOT International Series* 10.

Levinson, S. C. (1983). *Pragmatics*. Cambridge University Press.

Lombardi Vallauri, E. (2016a). Implicits as evolved persuaders. In K. Allan, A. Capone & I. Kecskes (eds.), *Pragmemes and theories* (pp. 725–748). Cham: Springer.

Lombardi Vallauri, E. (2016b). The 'exaptation' of linguistic implicit strategies. *SpringerPlus* 5, 1106.

Lombardi Vallauri, E. (2019). *La Lingua Disonesta*. Il Mulino.

Macagno, F. (2015). Presupposition as argumentative reasoning. In A. Capone & J. L. Mey (eds.), *Interdisciplinary studies in pragmatic, culture and society* (pp. 465–487). Springer.

Mauri, C., Ballarè, S., Goria, E., Cerruti, M., & Suriano, F. (2019). KIParla corpus: A new resource for spoken Italian. In R. Bernardi, R. Navigli & G. Semeraro (eds.), *Proceedings of the 6th Italian Conference on Computational Linguistics CLiC-it.*

Meluzzi, C., Valvason, E., Pinelli, E., & Zanchi, C. (2021). Responsibility attribution in gender-based domestic violence: A study bridging corpus-assisted discourse analysis and readers' perception. In E. Lombardi Vallauri, F. Cominetti & V. Masia (eds.), *Journal of pragmatics*. Special Issue 'Persuasive and manipulative power of implicit communication'.

Paradis, C. (2003). Between epistemic modality and degree: The case of really. In R. Facchinetti, M. Krug & F. Palmer (eds.), *Modality in contemporary English* (pp. 191–222). Mouton de Gruyter.

Pietrandrea, P. (2021). *Comunicazione, dibattito pubblico, social media*. Carocci.

Reboul, A. (2011). A relevance-theoretic account of the evolution of implicit communication. *Studies in Pragmatics* 13, 1–19.

Ricca, D. & Visconti, J. (2014). On the development of the Italian truth adverbs *davvero* and *veramente*. In I. Taavitsainen, A. Jucker & J. Tuominen (eds.), *Diachronic corpus pragmatics* (pp. 133–153). John Benjamins.

Romero, M. & Han, C.-H. (2004). On negative yes/no questions. *Linguistics and Philosophy*, 27, 609–658.

Sbisà, M. (1999). Ideology and the persuasive use of presupposition. In J. Verschueren (ed.), *Language and ideology: Selected papers from the 6th International Pragmatics Conference* (pp. 492–509). International Pragmatics Association.

Sbisà, M. (2007). *Detto non detto. Le forme della comunicazione implicita*. Laterza.

Sellars, W. (1954). Presupposing. *The Philosophical Review* 63, 197–215.

Stalnaker, R. (2002). Common ground. *Linguistics and Philosophy* 25, 701–721.

Traugott, E. (1995). *The role of the development of discourse markers in a theory of grammaticalization*. Paper presented at ICHL XII, Manchester 1995.

Yuan, M. (2015). *Chinese discourse adverbs as presupposition triggers*. PhD Thesis. City University of Hong Kong.

Zeevat, H. (2004). Particles: Presupposition triggers, context markers or speech act markers. In R. Blutner & H. Zeevat (eds.), *Optimality theory and pragmatics* (pp. 91–111). Palgrave Macmillan.

Viviana Masia

5 The Evidentiality Dimension of the Italian Discourse Marker *sai* between Subjectification and Intersubjectification Processes

Abstract: The Italian DM *sai* differs from other verb-based DMs for an additional epistemic value it adds to a proposition. This value is grounded in its intrinsic evidential nature, which rests on its function of intersubjectifying information. Notably, it is argued that sentence-initial *sai* behaves like an evidential marker, and particularly signals that some knowledge is mutually shared. This also explains why initial *sai* is mostly compatible with subjective utterances (such as assertions or orders) and weakly compatible with interrogative ones. It is argued that this newly acquired evidential meaning has emerged through a pragmaticalization process which led *sai*, in its function as a DM, to comply with the purpose of placing a proposition within the epistemic domain of all participants in an interaction.

Keywords: *sai*, subjectivity, intersubjectivity, evidentiality, mutual knowledge.

1. Introduction

Current research on Discourse Markers (DM) has profoundly benefited from both diachronic and synchronic analyses, either across linguistic types or linguistic genealogies (Hansen, 1998; Waltereit, 2006; Ghezzi, 2012; Heine et al., 2021, inter alia). On the one hand, these analyses have contributed to shedding some light on the theoretical and functional status of DMs – still on its way to be exhaustively defined –; on the other hand, they raised new empirical issues related to their identifying traits, categorial differences and terminological boundaries. These three aspects are in fact interrelated and, so far, the criteria to refer to DMs with the most appropriate term (pragmatic markers, discourse particles, connecting adverbials, among many others) are still hazy and not applicable throughout both within a single language system and on cross-linguistic grounds (Schiffrin, 1987, 2001; Brinton, 1990; Foolen, 1996; Hansen, 1998; Schourup, 1985; Fischer, 2006; Fraser, 2009). Instead, what can be taken to be an incontrovertible feature of their status in communication is the fact that they typically encode procedural meanings (Wilson, 2011), in the sense that they impose operational constraints on the construction of intended contexts and cognitive effects (see also Hansen's instructional semantics approach in this respect, cf. Hansen, 1998).

Within the Romance language group, the study of DMs has received a remarkable impulse, both synchronically and diachronically. Earlier and more recent lines of investigation have succeeded in unveiling common patterns of specific categories of Romance markers, but also some unshared peculiarities of their syntactic distribution and use in conversation (Cuenca & Marín, 2012; Khachaturyan, 2011).

The present chapter wishes to contribute to this flourishing thread of research with a focus on the Italian verb-based DM *sai* ('you know'), with a view to recasting it as an evidentiality marker (Chafe & Nichols, 1986; Willett, 1988; Aikhenvald, 2004). It will be argued that at the basis of its procedural meaning is its property of signalling different commitment and sourceness degrees of the speakers in an interaction. It will also be put forth that this function of *sai* essentially hinges on its capability of modulating the speaker's epistemic positioning towards a proposition by turning a subjective statement into an intersubjective one (Traugott, 1989; Traugott, 2010; Nuyts, 2012; Visconti, 2013). The evidentiality of *sai*, as it will be profiled in this chapter, allows enlisting the form among those which, according to Traugott (2010: 35), encode meanings centered on the addressee, thus indicating the speaker's interactive stance towards the hearer.

In the light of the foregoing, the chapter will be structured as follows. Section 2 will outline the state-of-the-art literature on *sai* and its interpretation as DM. Some working hypotheses on how *sai* makes an assertive statement (which is pragmatically subjective) acquire an intersubjective status in an interaction are reported in Section 3, where also the results on a pilot rating questionnaire on the relation that *sai* bears to commitment attribution are discussed. Section 4 highlights how the use of *sai* intersects with the coding of subjectivity and intersubjectivity in language, while Section 5 correlates the use of the DM to the coding of mutual evidentiality. Finally, in Section 6 some concluding remarks are fleshed out.

2. Some State of the Art

The category of verb-based DMs in Italian and in other Romance languages has been the bulk of discourse analyses for quite a long time. As for Italian, verb forms such as *guarda* 'look', *senti* 'hear', *ascolta* 'listen', among others, have been found to comply – fairly consistently – with those requirements which Heine (2013: 19) associates to the use of a linguistic expression as DM, namely the condition of prosodic and syntactic independence from the environment and the non-restrictive and mostly procedural meaning ('procedural' is here intended in Wilson's sense brought up before). In all, these features allow deriving some expectations on their semantic and formal behaviour. On the semantic level, verbs used as DMs do not have a valency structure, namely they do not select neither obligatory nor facultative argument roles associated with participants in the event, because they actually do not refer to any tangible event at all, nor are they heads of a sentence phrase. Prosodically, they are usually separated from the rest of the sentence by a virtual pause – which may surface in the use of commas in the written language. Finally, they display fewer (if any) positional constraints. To clarify the above properties, below some examples of *guarda*, *senti*, *vedi* and *ascolta* both as full verbs and as DMs are reported from the LIP corpus.[1]

(1a) e di fatti **guarda** quelle statuine. Io c'ho, io ce l'ho entrambe nel corrido io sul mobile [FB14347A, LIP]
'…and, indeed, **look at** those statuettes. I have, I have both on my hallway furniture'

(1b) Io spero che domani si faccia chiarezza, **guarda**, spero proprio [FB1158B, LIP]
'**Look**, I hope someone will shed some light, I really hope so'

(2a) mhmh, **senti** il tuo fidanzato… [FB12161A, LIP]
'mhmh, you should **hear from** your boyfriend…'

(2b) Bè, **senti**, lui c'ha il sei stiracchiato [FB12242B, LIP]
'Well, **listen**, he barely scores 6'

(3a) Se **vedi** come scrive: che precisione di linguaggio, che descrizioni… [FB12227A, LIP]
'If you **see** how he writes: what precision in his language, what descriptions…'

(3b) Senz'altro, infatti, **vedi**, son stata zitta, non ti ho detto niente [FE15354G, LIP]
'Of course, in fact, **you see**, I held my tongue, I have not said anything'

(4a) **Ascolta** me, **ascolta** me. No, Cesare, fammi parlare…[FB14248A, LIP]
'**Listen to** me, **listen to** me. No, Cesare, let me speak'

(4b) **Ascolta**, sei libera oggi? [FB911A, LIP]
'**Listen**, are you free today?'

Depending on their core meaning, these verbs behave either as turn-taking or as attention-getting devices. In (b)-sentences, for example, the speaker is more likely to have the addressee focus attention on a subsequent or a previous proposition. With respect to certain discourse-regulatory functions, *sai* ('you know') parallels the other verb forms, yet its use as DM adds further epistemic implications to the propositional meaning of an utterance, which do not seem to remarkably characterize the meaning of the DMs in (1) through (4). We shall seek to address this issue in detail later.

---

1 The LIP (Lessico di frequenza dell'italiano parlato) was gathered in the early 1990s with the aim to create a frequency lexis of spoken Italian.

Within the Italian tradition of studies, *sai* was first described by Bazzanella (1995) as performing a phatic function, notably signalling an existing common ground between participants in an interaction. In other contributions on the subject, the functions of *sai* have been differentiated based on the positions it can occupy in a sentence. Based on a study on the use of *sai* in the North-East regional variety of Italian, Biasio and Del Fante (forthcoming) suggested to view clause-initial and clause-final *sai* as correlated with different expectations of the speaker, what they call positive and negative presuppositions: initial *sai* would entail a negative presupposition (the speaker does not expect a proposition to already hold in the common ground of the conversation), while final *sai* entails a positive presupposition, in that the speaker expects a proposition to be in the background knowledge of the receiver.[2] Within generative frameworks, Cardinaletti (2015) has recast the initial and final positions of *sai* as hinging on their being merged in different layers of the clausal spine. In this view, clause-initial *sai* (ex. ***Sai***, *non credo che verrà alla tua festa*) is outlined as merging with a constituent of the Complementizer Phrase layer, while clause-final *sai* (ex. *Non credo che verrà alla tua festa,* ***sai****?*) would be merged in the Inflectional Phrase layer, similarly to other sentence-internal particles. A few more considerations on the relation between the syntactic position and the different functional properties of *sai* would be in order, and these specifically concern *sai* combinability and compatibility with different utterance types. Some examples will clarify this point. Always from the LIP corpus, below some occurrences of sentence-initial (5), sentence-medial (6) and sentence-final *sai* (7) are provided.

(5) Sì, **sai**, è figlio di notaio, non è che non faccia [FA1038B, LIP]
'**You know**, he is son of a notary, it's not that he doesn't do anything'
(6) Della morale boh io non so niente, **sai**? [MB1244, LIP]
'About morality, mh.., I don't know anything, **you know**?'
(7) non ho mica capito **sai** comunque cos'è 'sto ricevimento professori [MB348D, LIP]
'I have not understood, **you know**, anyway, what these professors' office hours are'

That the three syntactic positions correlate with different functions of *sai* more clearly emerges from the effects of combining the DM with assertive, interrogative and imperative speech acts. As a matter of fact, while initial and medial *sai* appear to combine more felicitously with assertive utterances, the same does not seem to hold with interrogative and imperative utterances, as shown in (8)–(13).

2 The authors suggest to chiefly consider this account for the regional variety their investigated, since in Standard Italian these same interpretations may appear less natural.

(8) **Sai**, il sapone si consuma [in modo] differente, la saponetta si consuma tutte le mattine (ASSERTIVE)
'**You know**, liquid soap is used in a different way, while the soap bar is used every morning'
(9) ***Sai**, vuoi venire a cena da me? (INTERROGATIVE)
'***You know**, do you want to come to dinner?'
(10) ***Sai**, non provare a rispondermi in quel modo! (IMPERATIVE)
'***You know**, don't you dare answer me like that!'
(11) *La casa, **sai**, l'hanno comprata? (INTERROGATIVE)
*The house, **you know**, have they bought it?'
(12) ??? Non provare, **sai**, a rispondermi così! (IMPERATIVE)
'??? Don't you dare, **you know**, answer me like that!'
(13) La casa, **sai**, l'hanno comprata due anni fa (ASSERTIVE)
'The house, **you know**, they have bought it two years ago'

Conversely, final *sai* appears to be perfectly compatible with assertive and imperative sentences, but again in no way compatible with interrogative ones.

(14) ...piace anche a noi, **sai**? (ASSERTIVE)
'...we like it too, **you know**?'
(15) Non rispondermi in quel modo, **sai**! (IMPERATIVE)
'Don't answer me like that, **you know**!'
(16) *Vuoi venire a cena da me, **sai**? (INTERROGATIVE)
*Do you want to come to dinner, **you know**?'

So, all in all, *sai* as a DM shows some resistance to utterances with weak assertiveness, like questions. In fact, it should be noted that while initial and medial *sai* do not change the illocutionary type of the utterance, final *sai* is generally perceived as shifting the assertive or imperative illocution of an utterance into an interrogative one, as also evidenced by the rising contour normally associated to the DM in final position. Indeed, the interrogative flip brought about by final *sai* eventuates in a functional doubling of the illocution type featured by the sentence. In other words, a question cannot be followed by a linguistic expression which already has the function of adding an interrogation value to an utterance.

The novelty/givenness degree of the proposition following or preceding *sai* is also another issue worth reflecting on a while. To a certain extent, it can be assumed that *sai* triggers a packaging-driven effect on the interpretation of the proposition uttered within its syntactic scope. Following Chafe (1994), by 'packaging', I mean the particular linguistic features a proposition (or its syntactic components) display, independently of the particular content being conveyed, which, in turn, provides the addressee with specific instructions on how to parse the utterance, viz. how to allocate her processing resources to fit the desired mental representation of the described event. In this view, the type of packaging *sai* ascribes to a sentence is that of presenting it as if it were already part of a shared common ground; in other words, as *information already known by the interlocutor* whatever its actual activation state in its mind. This means that there would not be any prior expectation on the degree of newness of the *sai*-dependent proposition, but only a 'request' to treat any proposition as shared knowledge. Let us consider (17), with sentence-initial *sai*, always taken from the LIP corpus. Now, this sentence could be taken to either fit a situation such as that described in (a) or that described in (b).

(17) **Sai**, la speranza di copiare all'ultimo…
'You know, the hope to copy at the very last moment'
(a) The addressee knows that the speaker has the habit of copying at the very last moment
(b) The addressee completely ignores that the speaker has the habit of copying at the very last moment

In case (a), the complex NP (*la speranza di copiare all'ultimo* 'The hope to copy at the very last moment') would evoke information belonging to an existing common ground; in (b), the same phrase would provide the addressee with entirely new information. Analogous considerations would hold with *sai* in final position, as in (18), with the sole difference that the whole proposition would acquire an overall interrogative nuance, which would not be activated by sentence-initial *sai*.

(18) La speranza di copiare all'ultimo, **sai**?
['The hope to copy at the very last moment, you know?']

On balance, the givenness/newness criterion cannot be taken to be discriminating between the functions of sentence-initial and sentence-final *sai*. On the contrary, it may well mark the difference between the use of *sai* as a DM and other verb-based DMs. In fact, while *sai* can precede sentences conveying both given and new information, as argued for (18), DMs such as *senti*, *guarda* or *ascolta* are more expected to be used with entirely new propositions. Indeed, (19) would appear somewhat odd, if the sentence uttered within the scope of the verbal DMs (be it *senti*, *guarda* or *ascolta*) recalled discourse-available information.

(19) **Senti/guarda/ascolta**, a Lucia non piace questo condimento
['**Look/look/listen**, Lucia does not like this dressing']

To a certain extent, the expected (novel) information status of the statement *a Lucia non piace questo condimento* is justified by the attention-getting function these markers perform in discourse. Thus, it is fairly unlikely that the speaker might want to draw the addressee's attention to information she is already aware of. In this view, their pragmatic profile is more akin to that of a focusing particle, in that they cast focal status to the proposition on which they have scope. Conversely, the function of epistemic positioning of a proposition associated with *sai* makes its use compatible with both novel and old information.[3]

3. Working Hypotheses

The different behaviour of *sai* with respect to the clause type highlights quite astrong interaction between the DM and the illocution level of an utterance. Put otherwise, it seems that, more than discourse-regulatory, turn-taking or attention-getting moves, the use of *sai* entails an epistemically oriented perspective on a proposition, namely a particular attitude of the speaker not only to the proposition being negotiated but also to its addressee. In the remainder of this work, we shall seek to make the point that this particular meaning of *sai*, which is apparently not shared with other verb-based DMs, clings to its intrinsic evidential value, which also underpins its function of shifting the status of the proposition from a subjective to an intersubjective one. To ground this assumption, we have collected judgments from a sample of native speakers of Italian on how strongly they would relate the use of sentence-initial and sentence-final *sai* to an increase or a reduction of the speaker's commitment to an asserted proposition. More details on this pilot study will be zoomed in on in the following section.

3.1. *Sai* and Speaker Commitment

To gauge the level of commitment native speakers of Italian associate to the use of *sai* in a sentence, a battery of 20 context-sentences followed by three continuation answers/options has been created: one represented by a plain assertion (without *sai*), the other two with *sai* both in initial and in final position, as shown in the example item below:

CONTEXT SENTENCE:
Perché non vieni al mare con me?
'Why don't you come to the seaside with me?'
ANSWER/CONTINUATION OPTIONS:

3 Of course, the terms *old* and *given* should not be taken as entirely interchangeable. In cognitive-functional frameworks, such as those of Chafe (1976) and Lombardi Vallauri (2009), *old* refers to knowledge stored in long-term memory, although it has not been introduced in the preceding discourse. *Given*, instead, usually refers to information recently activated in the current discourse and in the addressee's short-term memory. For the purpose of our discussion, we shall use both terms as indicating either one or the other information state.

a. Ho una montagna di compiti da correggere
'I've got loads of tests to correct'
b. **Sai**, ho una montagna di compiti da correggere
'**You know**, I've got loads of tests to correct'
c. Ho una montagna di compiti da correggere, **sai**?
'I've got loads of tests to correct, **you know**?'

3.2. Methods and Participants

40 Italian volunteers (of any age, sex and level of education, in any case not inferior to a high school diploma) completed the test. They received the instruction to choose (upon first reading) the continuation/answer option which – they believed – involved a stronger commitment on the part of the speaker. The options within each item did not always appear in the same order and all items were randomly administered.

Although the three options instantiated an assertive speech act, the expectation was to register some remarkable differences between the sentences with *sai* (in any position) and those without it. Put otherwise, plain assertions (without *sai*) were predicted to be perceived as more committal than those with *sai*.

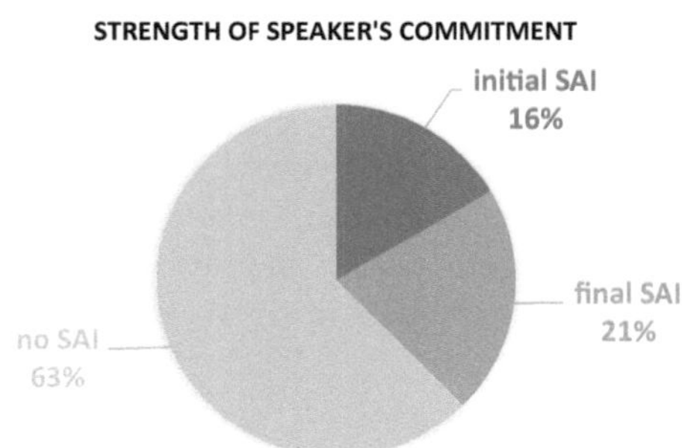

Figure 5.1 Correlation between sai and speaker commitment in participants' judgments

The percentages displayed in the graph in Figure 5.1 point to a more frequent association of plain assertions (without *sai*) to a stronger speaker commitment, as opposed to the options with *sai*. This trend is statistically significant (F(1,58)= 56.4, *p*-value= *0.0001), in line with the above predictions. By contrast, the difference between sentences with initial and those with final *sai* is significantly smaller (F(1,58)=1.27, *p*-value= 0.2) with a slight preference for sentence-final *sai* as indication of stronger commitment on the part of the speaker.

3.3. Discussion

Needless to say, the data gathered from this simple exploratory test do not allow drawing conclusive generalizations on the registered differences. However, a *prima facie* consideration that can be made is that statements with *sai* (in any syntactic position) considerably reduce or weaken the speaker's commitment state towards a proposition. A declarative sentence with *sai* is perceived as being less forcibly imposed on the addressee; in other words, the speaker commits to the proposition to the extent that its truth is also accepted by the receiver which is usually the case when a sentence is uttered within the scope of *sai*. Thus, adding this DM to a declarative proposition may turn into a strategic move to shrink one's authority on a fact and accordingly the likelihood of being held accountable, if attempts to challenge it should obtain.

Although smaller, the difference observed between sentences with initial and final *sai* is also worth some reflections. The fact that assertions with final *sai* are seen as involving a mildly stronger commitment on the part of the speaker may allow thinking of clause-initial *sai* as an interaction-setting/preparatory device through which the speaker is induced to construe whatever follows the DM as entailing weaker commitment of the speaker. Some examples will clarify this point. Let us take (20) and (21), as an illustration.

(20) **Sai**, non credo che Mario abbia gradito la cena di ieri
'**You know**, I don't think Mario liked dinner last night'

(21) Non credo che Mario abbia gradito la cena di ieri, **sai**?
'I don't think Mario liked dinner last night, **you know**?'

In (20), the addressee is first required to mentally construe that the speaker's degree of responsibility for whatever is going to be uttered next (*non credo che Mario abbia gradito la cena di ieri*) is reduced, and that she is only partly committed to its truth. Conversely, in (21), this cognitive representation is accessed only at the end of the sentence, which is first taken to involve a stronger speaker commitment, and only then is such commitment reinterpreted as weaker, because the proposition is – so to say – rethought *as being packaged as already shared*. So, with *sai* in final position, the addressee first construes an assertive statement, bringing with it a stronger commitment (Pagin, 2004), but it is then required to reconsider the speaker's epistemic position as only partly committing to the conveyed proposition.

4. *Sai* between Subjectivity and Intersubjectivity

One way of accounting for the trends emerged from the above questionnaire is also considering the role of subjectification and intersubjectification processes in discourse. As is known, the term subjectivity (*subjectivité*) in language was first used by Benveniste (1971) with regard to those linguistic means with which the speaker refers to herself in an interaction.[4] In a later account, Traugott (1989: 49) delineated subjectification as a process through which the speaker more directly encodes her attitude towards a proposition.

The array of linguistic means languages have to express a more subjective perspective on some information includes a number of different lexical categories, from personal pronouns to verbs, as exemplified in (22), from Nuyts (2012: 55).

(22) In such an unstable situation, **I think** the army will intervene.

The absence of **I think**, or its substitution with a more impersonal expression such as **it is likely** (as in *In such an unstable situation, **it is likely** that the army will intervene*) would mark the sentence as less subjective, because no direct reference to the speaker can be recovered. It should be noticed that, while the subjective meaning in (22) is lexically codified, languages can also express subjectivity through pragmatic strategies. The use of assertive speech acts is a clear example of this. Notably, the use of an assertion, if compliant with the Cooperative Principle (Grice, 1975), licenses the assumption that the speaker has adequate evidence to endorse its truth. In other words, whoever produces the assertion *The cat is on the mat* is expected to have witnessed that particular event and is therefore committing to its truth. So, assertive packaging endows a proposition with a subjective meaning in the sense that it presents the event it describes as first-hand experience of the speaker. In this view, an assertion could be seen as a 'reduced' version of a statement uttered within the scope of a representative predicate like *maintain, say, state, assure*, etc. (belonging to the category of Searle's representative acts – Searle, 1969). So, for instance, if (23) exemplifies a case of lexical subjectivity – as the speaker's epistemic vicinity to the proposition is made explicit by the expression *I can assure* – in (24) the same condition is only indirectly inferred by the use of a simple assertion, which activates the implicature that the speaker is grounding the statement on a witnessed fact (at

4 'The subjectivity we are discussing here is the capacity of the speaker to posit himself as "subject". It is defined not by the feeling which everyone experiences of being himself [...], but as the psychic unity that transcends the totality of the actual experiences it assembles and that makes the permanence of the consciousness. Now we hold that this "subjectivity", whether it is placed in phenomenology or in psychology [...] is only the emergence in the being of a fundamental property of language. "Ego" is he who says "ego". That is where we see the foundation of "subjectivity", which is determined by the linguistic status of "person".' (71: 224)

least this is the impression that assertive packaging gives, no matter the actual belief state of the speaker).

(23) I can assure the cat is eating all your food.
(24) The cat is eating all your food.

The way of subjectifying knowledge exemplified in (24) relies on the pragmatic dimension of the utterance and, notably, on its speech act level. Drawing on De Smet and Verstraete (2006: 384), we shall refer to this case as *pragmatic subjectivity*.[5]

Now, taking assertions to be instances of subjectification also entails that their association with epistemic modulators such as *sai* leads to a downgrading of their assertive strength and consequently of the speaker's commitment to their truth. As a matter of fact, *sai* differs from other verb-based DMs in that it does not draw the receiver's attention to the main proposition; rather, as argued before, it reduces it as it endows that proposition with a 'shared' and 'mutual' status, i.e. the proposition *is required* being understood as already belonging to the interlocutors' common ground.

Many scholars have suggested viewing subjectification as a driving force and trigger of grammaticalization phenomena in natural languages, many of these leading to the formation of discourse markers. Yet, grammaticalized forms are often also the offshoot of a further shift of subjectified meanings to intersubjective ones. Traugott (2010: 35) correlates intersubjectification to linguistic forms which are recruited to encode meanings centered on the addressee. In the development from subjectified to intersubjectified meanings, a linguistic unit marking the relation of the speaker to a proposition becomes marker of the speaker's interactive stance towards the hearer. In a similar vein, Nuyts (2012: 58) outlines subjective modal evaluation as taking place whenever a proposition is presented as being strictly the assessor's sole responsibility.[6] On the contrary, an intersubjective evaluation comes about when a proposition is presented as being shared between the assessor and a wider group of people, possibly but not necessarily including the hearer. The distinction between subjective and intersubjective representation of knowledge could be grasped more sharply drawing on Langacker's model of subjective and objective construal (Langacker, 2008) which, for the sake of clarity, we shall recall with the following illustration.

---

5 De Smet and Verstraete (2006: 384): "[pragmatic subjectivity] is inherent in language use and independent of the semantics of a particular expression".

6 The term 'responsibility' here refers to the speaker's accountability if a given statement should turn out to be false.

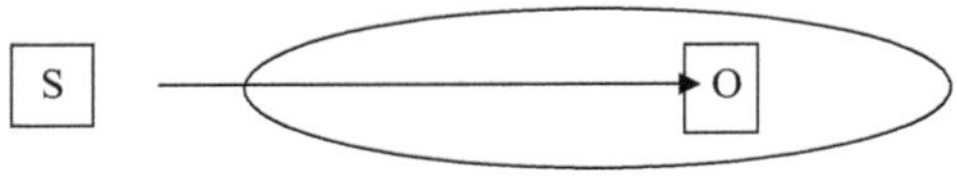

Figure 5.2 Langacker's representation of objective construal (Langacker, 2008)

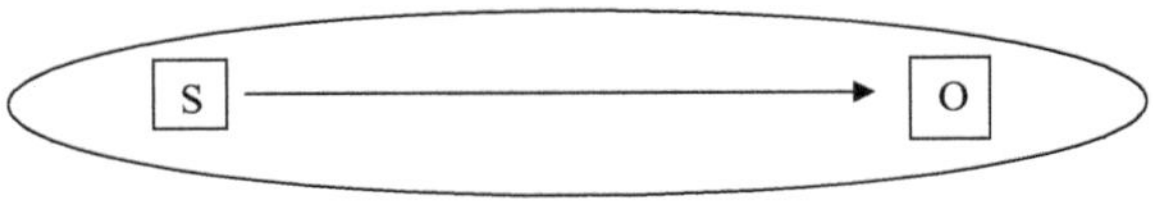

Figure 5.3 Langacker's representation of subjective construal (Langacker, 2008)

The oval space epitomizes the domain of knowledge (or experience) of a subject [S] who beholds a particular state of affairs ([O] Object of knowledge). Thus, [O] is either knowledge [S] has direct experience of (Figure 5.2), or he may get that knowledge objectively, for example as second-hand information (Figure 5.3). This model provides a theoretically-sound scaffolding to also account for the encoding of evidentiality in language, and we shall turn to this in the following sections.

As it can be easily deduced, Langacker's model does not explicitly account for the intersubjective state of knowledge, namely for that condition in which some information is shared between all participants in an interaction (Masia, 2021). This third condition, however, would call for rethinking the components of the representation as follows in Figure 5.4 (Masia, 2021).

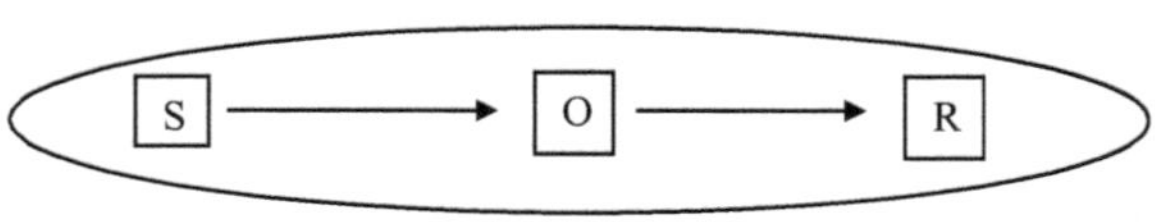

Figure 5.4 Representation of intersubjective construal as sketched in Masia (2021)

5. Evidentiality and Intersubjectivity in Language

Before recasting the DM status of *sai* as intersected with its intrinsic function as evidential marker, a few preliminary aspects on the phenomenon of evidentiality will come in useful. In the mainstream literature, evidentiality is generally described as an experiential category expressing the speaker's source of information (Willet, 1988; de Haan, 1998; Aikhenvald, 2004; among others). Within the current scholarly panorama, two views of evidentiality have caught on, one seeing it as exclusively expressing sourceness degrees (Aikhenvald, 2004), the other connected with the speaker's commitment to the truth of a proposition (Friedman, 1986). Evidentiality of the first type has been called *narrow*, whereas that of the second type *broad* (Chafe & Nichols, 1986). It should be noticed that there has been some skepticism on assuming these two views of evidentiality phenomena, in that the broad type refers to meanings that are usually covered by epistemic modality, which is why some scholars prefer to characterize evidentiality as the sole manifestation of information source. From my viewpoint, a sensible way of looking at evidentiality phenomena is to consider speaker source and speaker commitment as two sides of the same coin (Masia, 2017) since, in a way, manifesting oneself as the source of a proposition is also tantamount to committing to its truth. By the same token, if I present an event as second-hand information, I'm also necessarily deferring any responsibility for its truth to another source. This means that expressing source or epistemic commitment are two simultaneous conversational moves which cling to the same linguistic expression. For this reason, I do not think distinguishing between narrow and broad evidentiality might be of any use; instead, it is probably more reasonable, on both theoretical and empirical grounds, to take evidentiality as encompassing both meanings (Masia, 2017). This is the working definition of evidentiality we shall take on in the remainder of this chapter, namely an experiential category encoding both the speaker's source of some information and degree of commitment to its truth.

Early approaches to evidentiality identified systems with three-fold up to six-fold evidential markers, often, though not necessarily, attached to the verb stem. The tripartite distinction between direct (first-hand), indirect (second-hand) and conjectural/inferential evidentiality is the most common and is largely attested in Native American languages. Some examples are provided below (Aikhenvald, 2004).

CHEROKEE (Iroquian)

(25) wesa u-tlis-**ʎʔi**
cat it-run-**first-hand.past** 'A cat ran' [I saw it running]

(26) u-wonis-**eʔi**
he-speak-**non.first-hand.past** 'He spoke' [someone told me]

WANKA QUECHUA

(27) Daanu pawa-shra-si ka-ya-n-**chr**-ari
field finish-partitive-eventive be-imperfective-3-**inferential**-emphatic
'It (the field) might be completely destroyed' [I infer]

Direct evidentials usually mark some knowledge as first-hand experience of the speaker, indirect evidentials indicate that some information originates from a source other than the speaker and, finally, conjectural evidentials are used when the speaker grounds a proposition on an inference derived from clues available in the communicative situation.

Inquiring about the functioning of evidentiality systems in the Quechua family, Hintz and Hintz (2017) have recently found a further knowledge state signalled through evidential markers. They called this state 'mutual knowledge' as it refers to information that is assumed to be already part of the interlocutors' common ground. Mutual knowledge evidentiality is particularly common in Conchucos Quechua, with traces in other varieties of the language group, and it is normally expressed by the morph *-cha* (Hintz & Hintz, 2017: 20).

Conchucos Quechua

(28) Tsay-pa-**mi** qati-ya-ra-n mama-yki-kuna [direct evidentiality]
that-gen-**dir.ev** follow-pl-pst-3 mother-2-pl
'By that route your ancestors pastured animals' [I affirm]

(29) Tsay-pa-**cha:** qati-ya-ra-n mama-yki-kuna [mutual evidentiality]
that-gen-**mut.ev** follow-pl-pst-3 mother-2-pl
'By that route your ancestors pastured animals' [as we both know]

Using *-cha* in (29) the speaker shares epistemic authority with the receiver, in that it verbalizes the main event (*by that route your ancestors pastured animals*) as an established fact, known by everybody. Thus, while in (28) the fact that 'ancestors pastured animals by that route' is conveyed as first-hand experience of the speaker, in (29) the same fact is presented as something the addressee is already aware of, which presents it as an indisputable fact.

As it can be easily evinced, this knowledge state does not stray very far from what we have seen for the intersubjective construal of concepts in an interaction, which we have devised based on Langacker's original model. More precisely, marking an assertion with *-cha* in Conchucos Quechua amounts to encoding some information as intersubjective, in that the addressee is conceived as sharing the speaker's same *territory of information* (Kamio, 1997). As already hinted at before, Langacker's dichotomic modelling opposing subjective and objective knowledge construal may well be taken to mirror the underlying coding processes of direct and indirect evidentiality, respectively. In this perspective, direct evidentiality would involve a subjective construal of a fact on the part of the speaker – who is depicted as holding inside the domain of experience which the relevant fact belongs to; conversely, indirect evidentiality entails an objective construal of knowledge, because the speaker is not inside that domain of experience, which she only reports as a second-hand source. In the intersubjective condition, instead, both speaker and receiver share the same domain of experience, which means that in an interaction, any information marked as intersubjective will have to be 'accepted as an established fact', and thus as shared consensus between speaker and receiver, and any other participant in the conversation.

The suggested interplay between evidentiality and the coding of subjectivity/intersubjectivity in language may help unveiling the nature and use of *sai* as a DM. If assertive utterances can be characterized as pragmatic strategies of direct evidentiality, it could also be safely assumed that they are expressions of higher subjectivity, in that they increase the speaker's commitment to a proposition and, thus, her personal perspective on it. Conversely, as a DM that modulates the speaker's epistemic positioning to some information, *sai* can be deemed to function as a *subjectivity reducer* when combined with assertive speech acts. Put another way, *sai* turns a subjective utterance (mostly an assertion or an order) into an intersubjective one. In so doing, its function in a sentence ends up paralleling that of the Quechuan *-cha*. *Sai* then endows a sentence with an intersubjective meaning because it presents it as knowledge already in possession of the addressee. This explanation may also account for the observed incompatibility of *sai* with questions, as the speaker cannot commit to information she is only requesting. Questions necessarily involve, to some extent, an objective construal of knowledge, in that the speaker does not have certainty of a fact and needs confirmation from the addressee. On the contrary, assertions and orders are intrinsically committal which means that the speaker can modulate her subjective relation to them. Therefore, while directive and representative speech acts can be intersubjectified, because they are already intrinsically subjective, interrogative acts cannot.[7] Put differently, intersubjectifying some knowledge entails making that knowledge subjective also for the receiver (see the proposed model of intersubjective construal above).

Another factor to consider concerns the function of *sai* in different syntactic positions. For example, how can we explain the fact that *sai* more felicitously combines with imperative sentences (i.e. orders) when it occupies the final position and not when it is in sentence-initial position?

(30) ?? **Sai**, non prenderti gioco di me!
'**You know**, don't make fun of me!'

(31) Non prenderti gioco di me, **sai**?
'Don't make fun of me, **you know**?'

7 This seems to legitimize the view that only those utterances characterized by a high subjectivity degree can be further intersubjectified, namely simultaneously brought into the subjective dimension of the receiver.

A tentative, yet plausible, explanation to such a discrepancy is that while in final position the DM can be analysed as triggering an illocution shift – in that it turns the imperative utterance into an interrogative one (as also typically manifested by a rise in the prosodic curve), initial *sai* seems to behave like an evidentiality marker proper, marking the main proposition as mutual knowledge. On a closer look, this aspect is likely to be at odds with the directive nature of imperative utterances, whose perlocutionary outcome involves having the addressee taking on a particular behaviour or bringing about a particular action. The imperative sentence within the scope of initial *sai* cannot, therefore, be taken as knowledge already possessed by the receiver; rather, it needs to be new information for this latter.

What makes the status of *sai* as an evidentiality marker – and, notably, as a marker of shared knowledge – worth investigating further also concerns the reason why in sentence-final position the DM calls for an interrogative prosodic contour. In fact, in Italian, final *sai* does not usually occur with a descending contour, but with a rising one, as illustrated in (32) and (33).

(32) *Non mi piacciono gli spaghetti, **sai?***
(33) ?? *Non mi piacciono gli spaghetti, **sai**…*
'I don't like spaghetti, **you know** ?/…'

This means that sentence-final *sai* most probably performs a function of a different sort than that associated with sentence-initial *sai*. As a matter of fact, since initial *sai* cannot have an interrogative status in sentence-initial position, what it does in this position is establish a discourse 'footing' between interlocutors to interpret a forthcoming proposition as intersubjective and, in so doing, it would act as a marker of mutual evidentiality. In other words, initial *sai* dispenses a procedural meaning by which the receiver is induced to place a proposition within her epistemic domain, namely as if she, also, were subjectively tied to it. In our view, the same interpretation does not so distinctly emerge from sentence-final *sai*, which seems to act more like an illocution-reducer and, notably, as a subjectivity-reducer: it marks a sentence as no longer subjective (therefore involving the unique engagement of the speaker as information source), but, rather, as intersubjectified (both speaker and receiver are the source of the exchanged proposition).

6. Final Remarks

In previous research work, subjectification was outlined as epitomizing the driving force of most grammaticalization processes in language, especially of those involving the diachronic path of DMs. In the case of *sai*, however, also intersubjectification may have played a crucial role; as a matter of fact, not only does *sai* seem to regulate the speaker's relation to a proposition (establishing the degree of her commitment to its truth), but also her relation to the addressee which, differently from other verbal DMs such as *guarda*, *ascolta*, etc., neither brings about (at least as its primary function) a turn-taking request, nor an attention-getting operation. The function of *sai* as a DM is more epistemic in nature and concerns how the speaker positions a certain proposition within her own domain of knowledge and that of the addressee. This addressee-oriented construal of a proposition uttered within the syntactic scope of *sai* is the very essence of its evidentiality and, marking the condition of mutually shared knowledge, namely intersubjectivity.

The account here proposed did not put forward a clear diachronic profile – which will hopefully be traced in future research work – yet, what can be envisaged is that in gradually moving towards a more subjective meaning, *sai* has also simultaneously gained an intersubjective interpretation. It can then be fleshed out that the reanalysis of *sai* into a DM has been driven by discourse-related constraints and, notably, constraints on the speakers' need to manifest communicative motivations and purposes, epistemically position themselves with respect to negotiated meanings and last, but not the least, comply with politeness, face and cooperation requirements.

Moving from the foregoing, it can be assumed that, more than grammaticalization, *sai* has rather been involved in a pragmaticalization process, through which the verb form has developed an additional pragmatic meaning allowing it to also perform as a discourse marker in given utterance contexts. Within the framework of evidentiality encoding put forth in this work, it can be argued that, to some extent, this newly developed function of *sai* can be paralleled with that of conventional evidentiality markers and, particularly, with those markers expressing mutual knowledge as well as the condition of intersubjective information in dialogic communication.

Although the proposed account of *sai* as a DM would profoundly benefit from firmer typological grounding – besides the one offered by languages of the Quechuan family – the sketched evidential facet of the marker opens a number of unresolved issues, especially in comparison with other verb-based DMs. For this reason, the present work does not claim to draw conclusive generalizations on the place of *sai* in linguistic theory; yet, it is hoped that future reflection on the subject might constructively capitalize on the working hypotheses put forward here and further enrich it within a more empirically-grounded typological purview.

7. Conclusion

The status of *sai* as a DM strongly relies on its intrinsic evidential function. The type of evidential meaning *sai* encodes in a sentence is akin to mutual evidentials in some Quechuan languages, signaling that some knowledge is part of the interlocutors' common ground. Contrary to other verb-based DMs, *sai* has a more direct interface with the epistemic dimension of utterances, in that it positions the speaker with respect to the truth of a given proposition and to the addressee. In so doing, *sai* makes an assertive sentence – which is intrinsically subjective in nature – become more intersubjective – as it shares any commitment to it between speaker and receiver. This intersubjectification process may have been responsible for the emergence of the evidential function of *sai* as well as for its reanalysis as a discourse marker.

References

Aikhenvald, A. Y. (2004). *Evidentiality*. Oxford University Press.

Bazzanella, C. (1995). I segnali discorsivi. In L. Renzi, G. Salvi & A. Cardinaletti (a cura di), *Grande grammatica italiana di consultazione* (vol. 3, pp. 225–257). Il Mulino.

Benveniste, É. (1971). Subjectivity in language. *Problems in general linguistics* 1: 223-230.

Biasio, M. & Del Fante, D. (2021). Once Known, Always Known: Clause-Final SAI in North-East Regional Italian. Paper presented at the workshop *The Pragmatics of Evidentiality: Inter- and intra-linguistic perspectives on pragmatic aspects of evidentiality marking in communication* (Venezia, June 19th–21st 2021).

Brinton, L. (1990). The development of discourse markers in English. In J. Fisiak (ed.), *Historical linguistics and philology* (pp. 45–71). Mouton de Gruyter.

Cardinaletti A. (2015). Italian verb-based discourse particles in a comparative perspective. In J. Bayer, R. Hinterhölzl & A. Trotzke (eds.), *Discourse-oriented syntax* (pp. 71–91). John Benjamins Publishing Company. https://doi.org/10.1075/la.226.04car

Chafe, W. (1976). Givenness, contrastiveness, definiteness, subjects, topics, and point of view. In C. Li (ed.), *Subject and topic* (pp. 25–55). Academic Press.

Chafe, W. (1994). *Discourse, consciousness and time. The flow and displacement of conscious experience in speaking and writing*. Chicago University Press.

Chafe, W. & Nichols, J. (1986). *Evidentiality. The linguistic coding of epistemology*. Ablex.

Cuenca, M.-J. & Marín, M.-J. (2012). Discourse markers and modality in Catalan: The case of *(és) clar*. *Journal of Pragmatics* 44, 2211–2225.

De Smet, H. & Verstraete, J.-C. (2006). Coming to terms with subjectivity. *Cognitive Linguistics*, 17–3, 365–392.

Fischer, K. (ed.). 2006. *Approaches to discourse particles*. Elsevier.

Fraser, B. B. 2009. An account of discourse markers. *International Review of Pragmatics* 1/2, 293–320.

Friedman, V. A. (1986). Evidentiality in the Balkans. Macedonian and Albanian. In W. Chafe & J. Nichols (eds.), *Evidentiality: The linguistic coding of epistemology* (pp. 168–187). Ablex.

Foolen, A. (1996). Pragmatic particles. In J. Verschueren, J.-O. Östman, J. Blommaert & C. Bulcaen (eds.), *Handbook of pragmatics*. John Benjamins.

Ghezzi, C. (2012). Guarda, secondo me stai sbagliando! Marcatori interazionali da verbi di percezione in italiano contemporaneo. In Pîrvu, Elena (ed.), La lingua e la letteratura italiana in Europa, *pp. 143-16. Craiova: Editura Universitaria*. http://hdl.handle.net/10446/152246

Grice, H. P. (1975). Logic and conversation. In P. Cole & J. Morgan (eds.), *Syntax and semantics 3: Speech Acts* (pp. 41–58). Academic Press.

de Haan, F. (1998). *The category of evidentiality*. Unpublished manuscript. https://www.academia.edu/755483/The_category_of_evidentiality

Hansen, M. B. M. (1998). The semantic status of discourse markers. *Lingua* 104, 235–260.

Heine, B. (2013). On discourse markers: Grammaticalization, pragmaticalization, or something else? *Linguistics* 51/6. https://doi.org/10.1515/ling-2013-0048.

Heine, B., Kaltenböck, G., Kuteva, T. & Long, H. (2021). On the rise of discourse markers. In S. Hancil & A. Haselow (eds.), *Studies at the grammar-discourse interface* (pp. 23–55). John Benjamins.

Hintz, D. J. & Hintz, D. M. (2017). The evidential category of mutual knowledge in Quechua. *Lingua* (186–187), 88–109. https://doi.org/10.1016/j.lingua.2014.07.014.

Kamio, A. (1997). *Territory of information*. John Benjamins. https://doi.org/10.1075/pbns.48

Khachaturyan, E. (2011). Discourse markers in romance languages. *Oslo Studies in Language* 3/1.

Langacker, R. (2008). *Cognitive grammar: A basic introduction*. Oxford University Press.

Lombardi Vallauri, E. (2009). *La struttura informativa. Forma e funzione negli enunciate linguistici*. Carocci.

Masia, V. (2017). *Sociobiological bases of information structure*. John Benjamins.

Masia, V. (2021). *The manipulative disguise of truth. Tricks and threats of implicit communication*. John Benjamins.

Nuyts, J. (2012). Notions of (inter)subjectivity. In L. Brems, L. Ghesquière & F. Van de Velde (eds.), *Intersections of intersubjectivity* (pp. 53–76). John Benjamins.

Pagin, P. (2004). Is assertion social? *Journal of Pragmatics* 36/5, 833–859.

Schiffrin, D. (1987). *Discourse markers*. Cambridge University Press.

Schiffrin, D. (2001). Discourse markers: Language, meaning, and context. In D. Schiffrin, D. Tannen & H. E. Hamilton (eds.), *The handbook of discourse analysis* (pp. 54–75). Blackwell.

Schourup, L. (1985). *Common discourse particles in English conversation: Like, well, Y'know*. Garland.

Searle, J. R. (1969). *Speech Acts. An essay on the philosophy of language*. Cambridge University Press. https://doi.org/10.1017/CBO9781139173438

Traugott, E. C. (1989). On the rise of epistemic meanings in English: An example of subjectification in semantic change. *Language* 65, 31–55.

Traugott, E. C. (2010). Revisiting subjectification and intersubjectification. In K. Davidse, H. Cuyckens & L. Vandelanotte (eds.) (pp. 29–73).

Visconti, J. (2013). Facets of subjectification. *Language Sciences* 36, 7–17.

Waltereit, R. (2006). The rise of discourse markers in Italian. A specific type of language change. In K. Fischer (ed.). *Approaches to Discourse Particles*, Vol. I, Studies in Pragmatics (pp. 61–76). Brill.

Willett, T. (1988). A cross-linguistic survey of the grammaticalization of evidentiality. *Studies in Language* 12/1, 51–97.

Wilson, D. (2011). The conceptual-procedural distinction. In M. V. Escandell-Vidal, M. Leonetti & A. Ahern (eds.), *Procedural meaning: Problems and perspectives* (pp. 3–31). Emerald.

Claudia Timoci

6 The Use of *ştii, ştiţi, vezi, vedeţi* and *înţelegi, înţelegeţi* as Discourse Markers in Spoken Romanian. A Quantitative Analysis

Abstract: The article presents a model of quantitative analysis applied to the research on the discourse markers *ştii, ştiţi* 'you know', *vezi, vedeţi* 'you see', *înţelegi, înţelegeţi* 'you understand' in our PhD dissertation. By examining 194 occurrences of the above-mentioned verbal DMs in seven corpora of spoken Romanian, we have proposed, for the beginning, a new organization of the pragmatic-discursive functions they fulfil. The quantitative analysis has outlined a range of general trends, which has allowed us to point to a series of conclusions. By means of tables and charts, we shall present the absolute and the relative frequency of the DMs within the eight subcorpora, depending on the formal/informal register. We have also seen that different types of co(n)text favour the appearance of certain DMs. From this perspective, we emphasize the strongly contrastive uses of *înţelegi* 'you understand', exclusively used in the informal corpus and in media discourse, and *vedeţi* 'you see', with a more frequent use in the ±formal corpora. Finally, we shall research the position of DMs within a speaking turn. As a result of this comparative analysis, we have seen, along with other researchers, that the positional freedom of the DM in a speaking turn is determined by the polyfunctionality of the marker, by the semantics of the original verb and by the degree of desemanticization of this marker.

Keywords: discourse markers, verb, pragmatics, corpus, spoken Romanian

1. Introduction

This paper is based on the fourth chapter of my Ph.D. dissertation *Pragmatica verbului în limba română vorbită actuală* ('Pragmatics of the verb in contemporary spoken Romanian'). The study aimed to investigate the use of the discourse markers (hereinafter DMs) *ştii, ştiţi* 'you know', *vezi, vedeţi* 'you see', *înţelegi, înţelegeţi* 'get it?'/'you understand?' in spoken Romanian. We examined the functions and frequencies of these DMs in eight genres, separated based on the formal/informal distinction. Partially adopting the C-ORAL-ROM Corpus[1] approach, we separated the ± Informal Corpus into three categories or subcorpora: interactions in a family setting, interactions in a public context, and

1 See C-ORAL-ROM (elda.org).

telephone interactions between family members and friends. The ± Formal Corpus was split into three categories: interactions in a natural context (which were further divided into monologue interactions and dialogue interactions), interactions mediated by mass media (which were divided into interviews, reports, talk shows, and political speeches or debates), and formal telephone conversations between individuals who are not closely related or who have a professional or business relationship.

Our findings showed that context can influence DM frequency. Their frequency is higher in the informal register than in the formal one; furthermore, specific DMs appear to occur more frequently in specific contexts.

2. Corpus Design

Seven Romanian language corpora (CLRVA I, CLRVA II, CORPUS POP I, CORPUS POP II, CORPUS POP IV, IVLRA, and IV II) were used to compile the dataset. The fact that the corpora contain a wide variety of text types allowed us to perform an empirical investigation into how a particular context might influence the frequency and use of specific discourse markers. The material under analysis was sampled based on the following set of parameters of variation:

(a) The formal/informal distinction;
(b) The communication environment: direct interaction (face-to-face) vs. interaction mediated by technical means (telephone, radio, television);
(c) The type of communication: dialogic vs. monologic interaction.

This sampling is intended to represent different types of communication, broken down into eight sub-corpora, in order to allow multiple comparisons and cross-comparisons (e.g., planned vs. spontaneous, dialogic vs. monologue), thus complementing past approaches carried out on only two or three different genres.

Figure 6.1 provides a qualitative overview of the corpus design, followed by a quantitative data summary in Table 6.1.

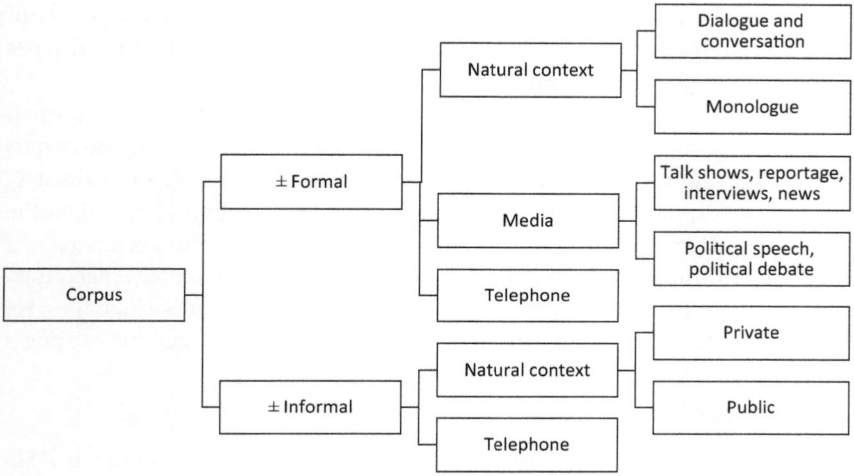

Figure 6.1. Corpus design

Table 6.1. Distribution of words in the Corpus (sum of words from all the corpora used, depending on the type of text)

Type		***Sub_type***	**No. of texts**	**No. of words (tokens)**[2]
Corpus ± Formal	Natural context	Dialogue and conversation	48	26800
		Monologue	51	77400
	Media	Talk shows, reportage, interviews, news	48	50200
		Political speech, political debate	15	92600
	Telephone		23	15400
	Total		185	262400
Corpus ± Informal	Natural context	Private	34	25100
		Public	23	15300
	Telephone		7	6000
	Total		64	46400

2 The words in each corpus were counted using a Python 3.8 script developed especially for this purpose. We would like to thank Mr. Gaël Lejeune, Associate Professor (Maître de conférences) in Computer Science and Linguistics at University Paris-Sorbonne, for his help in generating the cleaned corpus. Any error in data processing is ours.

Quantitatively, we note that the electronic version of our corpus consists of 249 recordings and roughly 308800 words, which are organized into text types according to the above criteria.

Table 6.1 shows that the primary division between formal and informal speech varies considerably. This is because the materials underlying the corpus of work contain texts of various lengths and genres. Containing approximately 262,400 words, the ± Formal Corpus is approximately 5.6 times larger than the ± Informal Corpus (46,400 words). To lessen the impact of this corpus-related limitation, in the quantitative analyses we conducted, the data have been normalized by performing frequency calculations per 10,000 words. Therefore, we will refer to the relative frequency of the investigated DMs in each sub-corpus.

3. Methodology

The AntConc software was used to automatically extract the examined DMs from each corpus, along with a context of roughly 250 left-to-right characters.

Figure 6.2. Identification of occurrences using the AntConc software

Each occurrence was then carefully reviewed to exclude instances that did not meet the criteria for DM. Consequently, we have excluded those occurrences that represent genuine requests by means of which the interlocutor is asked whether s/he knows, sees, or understands something. From the total number of identified occurrences, 194 were classified as DMs.

In example (1) below, the term in bold indicates a case of a lexical verb, and in example (2), we have a case of DM.

Example (1) is part of a conversation between two young students (A and B) from the Republic of Moldova and a University professor (C), the author of the recording. The discussion occurs during the break between classes in a lecture hall.

(1) A: ci faci ↑ vrei sî mergi acasî ↑ în uichend ?
B: <L î: da cred cî vinerea viitoari> = ↓
A: = am vinerea viitoari . io + nu ştiu m-aş duce_acuma + ori vineri dupî ore + ori sâmbătî dimineaţa ↑+ tu de_obicei cu ci te duci ?
[…]
A: = da: unele + da: io: mă gândeam să _ mă duc cu maşîna da' **ştii** ce taxî au introdus + acuma ?
B: nu::? *(mirată)*
A: şî: vinieta şî taxî di poluar' şî cred_că c_am să mă duc cu autobuzu' dar nu ştiu la ci orî ?
B: cu AFTOBUSU (*râde sugerând pronunţia cuvântului ca în limba rusă*) este şi de dimineaţî şi la două_ jumate. (CLRVA II, 222)
'A: How are you? Do you want to go home for the weekend?
B: Yes, maybe next Friday.
A: Ah, next Friday. I don't know what to do. I could go either after classes on Friday or on Saturday morning. What form of transport do you usually use?
[…]
A: Yeah, some of them. But I was thinking of going by car. **Do you know** what new fees they've implemented?
B: No? (surprised)'

We can see that in example (1), *ştii* ('you know', second person singular) can be replaced by 'to have knowledge of', and its omission would alter the sentence content and the grammatical structure of the utterance. Conversely, in the following example, *ştii* 'you know" has lost its referential meaning; hence this form does not provide conceptual content to the utterance; it only marks the call to the interlocutor's attention.

(2) A: =ştii cî erau la un moment dat felicitările alea ↑ î: nu ştiu dacă le-ai prins tu. c-un băieţel şi c-o fetiţî. fetiţ_avea un trandafir ↑ şi băieţelu` era aşa cu: cu pălăriuţî ↑ şi mergeau ei ↑ di mânî. am zis poati totuşi=
B: =nu cred că-mi mai amintesc. da` ↑ ai putea să-i faci [aşa: ↑
A: da. ştii?]
B: o poză şî lui.
A: mă gândeam s-o fac alb negru ↓ da` uiti ↑ cu tipa asta aşa ↑ „cred că am cucerit-o" ↓ **ştii ?** (CLRVA II, 220-221)

‘A: You know, there were these greeting cards at some point, I don’t know if you remember them, with a little boy and a girl on them. The girl was holding a rose and the boy was wearing a hat, they were holding hands. I thought maybe=’
B: =I don’t think I remember. But you could take [like this
A: Yes, you know?]
B: a picture of him.
A: I was thinking of making it black and white, but look, with this girl like that, “I guess I won her over”, **you know**?’

The sequence is part of a spontaneous conversation between two young women on their break at the library. The two protagonists in A’s story are her little son and a young girl. The image of the two children reminds the mother of a greeting card that inspires her to imagine a dialogue between the two children. The fictive utterance of the little boy is followed by the DM *ştii* ‘you know’, which highlights this discursive unit. The interlocutor, B, interrupts at this point (laughing), demonstrating her understanding that *ştii* (‘you know’) is not a specific question but rather a phatic expression used by the interlocutor to keep her attention and to request her agreement.

4. Results

4.1. Distribution and Frequency

We start the quantitative analysis by presenting the frequency of the examined DMs in the material under investigation. We identified 194 DMs, representing 0.062 % of the 308,800 words in the corpus. In other words, such a DM occurs approximately once every 1591 words. The frequency of each DM is statistically analysed in Table 6.2, which includes the number of instances for each marker (absolute frequency) and the proportion of frequencies for each DM to the overall number of instances (relative frequency, presented as a percentage).

Table 6.2. The absolute frequency and relative frequency of discourse markers in the corpora

DM	Absolute frequency (no.)	Relative frequency (%)
Ştii	107	55 %
Ştiţi	24	12 %
Vezi	12	6 %
Vedeţi	29	15 %
Înţelegi	11	6 %
Înţelegeţi	11	6 %
Total	194	100 %

The results of our investigation are graphically summarized in Figure 6.3:

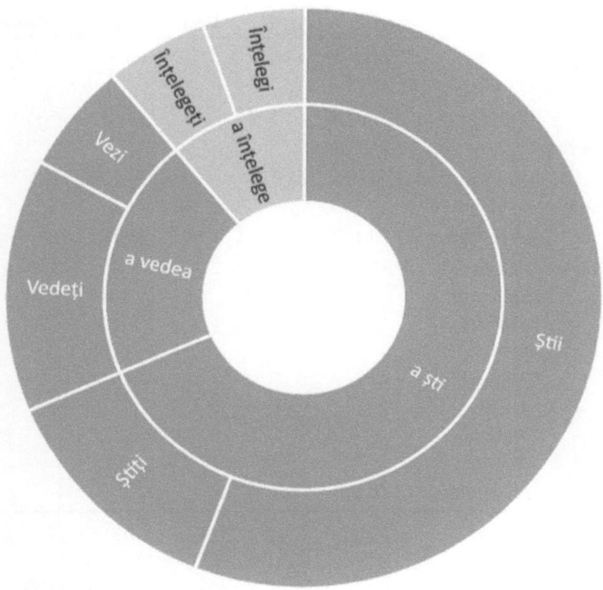

Figure 6.3. Frequency of discourse markers in the corpora

Figure 6.3 provides an overview of the frequency of each DM in proportion to the overall number of DMs identified in our corpora. First, we note an uneven distribution of the analysed DMs. As can be noticed, at one extreme, there is the pair of DMs *ştii, ştiţi* 'you know', accounting for about three-quarters of the 194 reported occurrences. At the other extreme we find the DMs *înţelegi, înţelegeţi* 'you understand', which account for 12 % of all identified DMs. These findings only corroborate earlier research, which revealed high pragmatic productivity in the case of DMs coming from the verb *a şti* 'to know' and a low presence of DMs arising from *a înţelege* 'to understand' (Biriş, 2013 and 2014).

As mentioned above, our study aimed to determine the impact of contextual variables on the frequency of DMs in spoken Romanian. For this reason, our analysis of the frequency of DMs was complemented with a quantitative study of the relationship between DMs and the type of discourse in which they are used. Table 6.3 displays the findings. The absolute frequency and relative frequency per 10,000 words (in parentheses) for each marker within the eight determined sub-corpora are shown.

Table 6.3. Distribution of discourse markers according to text type (relative frequency per 10,000 words in brackets)

			Ştii	*Ştiţi*	*Vezi*	*Vedeţi*	*Înţelegi*	*Înţelegeţi*
± Informal corpora	*Natural context*	*Familial/ Private*	*39 (15,5)*	*3 (1,1)*	*6 (2,3)*	-	*4 (1,5)*	-
		Public	*25 (16,3)*	*1 (0,6)*	*2 (1,3)*	-	*1 (0,6)*	*1(0,6)*
	Telephone		*14 (23,3)*	-	-	-	-	-
± Formal corpora	*Natural context*	*Dialogue and conversation*	*8 (2,9)*	*6 (2,2)*	-	*5 (1,8)*	-	*4 (1,4)*
		Monologue	*1 (0,1)*	*3 (0,3)*	*2 (0,2)*	*17 (2,1)*	-	*1 (0,1)*
	Media	*Talk shows, reportage, interviews, news*	*19 (3,7)*	*3 (0,5)*	*2 (0,3)*	-	*6 (1,1)*	*3 (0,5)*
		Political speech, political debate	-	*5 (0,5)*	-	*7 (0,7)*	-	*1 (0,1)*
		Telephone	*1 (0,6)*	*3 (1,9)*	-	-	-	*1 (0,6)*

Out of the 46,400 words in the ± Informal Corpora, we can see that there are 96 instances of the examined DMs, with a relative frequency of 0.2 %. Figure 6.4 illustrates the progressively declining number of DMs in a formal context.

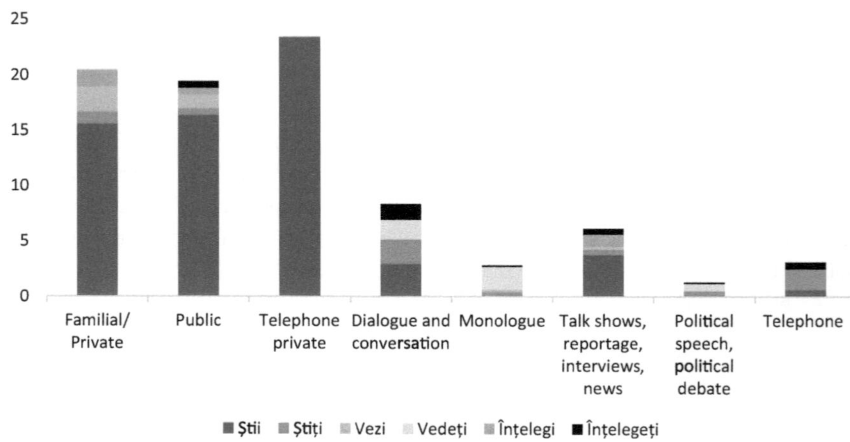

Figure 6.4. Distribution of discourse markers according to text type

Figure 6.4 displays a noticeable difference in the number of DMs employed depending on the context. We see a much higher average score in the informal context than in the formal context (20.6 DMs per 10,000 words vs. 3.7 DMs per 10,000 words). In the Informal Telephone sub-corpus, the speakers employ a higher number of DMs, reaching a total of 14 DMs, or 23.3 per 10,000 words. However, this difference is insignificant when compared to the other categories (Family/Private and Public) in the ±Informal Corpora. However, these statistics must be examined with caution, as small corpora can influence the accuracy of the results. We can see that seven of the 14 occurrences of DMs in the Informal Telephone Sub-corpus appear in Small talk on the phone, a conversation between mother and daughter. These seven occurrences had a significant impact on the frequency calculation, as this sub-corpus has the smallest size (6000 words). Let us look at an excerpt from this conversation:

(3) B: < $_{I}$ da' cel mai bine mai dă un telefon şi spune-i să ROAge o: vecină↓ dacă-i aşa aglomeraţie↓ să roage o vecină# pentru o oră# <$_{J}$ să-ţi dea voie să faci cu ea un pic în bucătărie>

A: îhî↓

B: (xxx) < să se poată concentra dacă e aşa aglomeraţie şi aşa şi asta> # **ştii**↓

A: < $_{J}$ mda↓>

B: vezi şi tu:# fâceţi# undeVA poate le trimete pe ALEA # O ORĂ↓

A: păi nu MĂ↓ nu mă↓ că că cică sînt venite de prin băicoi↓ de nu ştiu pe unde naiba↓de prin toată ţara#

B: ei: doar nu le-o ţine pe capu tău acolo să faci engleză↓

A: ei: na↓ (rîsete) #

B: păi # numa' de engleză nu ţi-ar arde↓

A: da mă: ↑săraca: ↓ce milă mi-era↓ era distrusă↓# zicea că şi-a făcut analizele acum un an jumate # şi: au trimis-o şi la ginecologie că n-au găsit-o în regulă şi AIA: aşa: **ştii**↓ din principiu↓ femeie < $_{F}$ da' nu-i bătrână MAMĂ↓ are cincizeci şi unu de ani↑ >

B: a↓

A: DA↓ e TÎ: nără↓ nu nu bătrână să zici că:- i BABĂ↓

B: păi dacă eu am patruştrei↓

A: păi DA↓ nu e bătrână↓ EU ce zic↓ # DA: şi_a zis că AŞA din principiu de ţărancă proastă ce e↑ n-a vrut să meargă la ginecologie↓ **ştii #** ↓şi uite că tocmai acum are cancer că de atunci până acum îi curgea cică puroi ↓ ((sunete ce exprimă dezgustul)) DA↓ # şi acum < $_{R}$ am înţeles > ⊥că cică v:omită sâ:nge: ↓ # î: îi e afectat totu înăuntru↓ nu mai poate să stea↓ şi are # are momente↓ (IVRLA, 183).

'B: but the best thing to do is to make another phone call and tell her to ask a neighbour, if she is so busy, to ask a neighbour to help you for an hour in the kitchen.

A: huh

B: to be able to focus in case she is so busy and so, **you know**

A: yeah

B: you will see, do it somewhere, maybe she will send them for an hour.
A: Well, no, I don't know, it seems they come from Băicoi, from I don't know where the hell, all over the country.
B: ah, she won't ask you to teach them English there.
A: ah, no (laughter)
B: well, you won't be in the mood for teaching English.
A: yeah, poor thing, I was so sorry for her; she was devastated, she had her tests done a year and a half ago and they also sent her to see a gynecologist because they didn't find her results right and she, you know, from principle, woman, but not old, mother, she is fifty-one years old.
B: I see.
A: Yes, she's young, not old, so to speak.
B: well, if I'm forty-three
A: well, yes, she's not old, that's what I am saying, YES: idiot, she didn't want to go to gynecology, you know, and look now she has cancer, from then until now pus has been flowing (sounds expressing disgust). Yes, and now, as I understood, that she is vomiting blood, everything inside her is affected, she can no longer sit.'

Both participants in the conversation used the DM *știi* 'you know', A four times, and B three times. The DMs occur within larger interventions. It seems that the speaker is not willing to give up the floor but seeks to get signals from the interlocutor that s/he is still paying attention. When speaking on the phone, unlike in face-to-face conversations, the speaker is unable to observe the other person's non-linguistic reactions; thus, s/he employs a number of phatic expressions to make sure the other person is still attentive. Besides all this, the frequent occurrence of DM in this particular conversation can be attributed to certain verbal tics of the speakers, their emotional state at the respective moments or certain speech habits.

If we examine the texts within the ±Formal Corpora, we can also observe that DMs are much more frequent in spontaneous texts with a lower degree of elaboration. Additionally, we note that broadcasted political debates include the fewest DMs. We consider this result predictable in argumentative interactions since the participants are expected not to employ these DMs that promote closeness between the speakers.

Depending on the context, we notice a clear difference in how specific DMs are used. A first DM that stands out in this regard is *vedeți* ('you see', second person plural) (2.1 occurrences per 10,000 words in the Monological Interaction Sub-corpus vs. 0 occurrences in the Informal Corpora). The 29 occurrences of *vedeți* 'you see' are distributed among three different text types: 17 occurrences in formal monologic interactions (of which one is repeated), five occurrences in formal dialogic interaction, and seven occurrences in televised political debate, respectively. The DM *vedeți* 'you see' seems to be stratified, with the rate of use declining as the level of formality of the verbal interaction decreases.

The DM *înțelegeți* 'you understand' is recorded at lower frequencies than the previous ones. *Înțelegeți* ('you understand', second person plural) is used in conversations with a medium level of formality. We also note that *înțelegi/înțelegeți* ('you understand') is usually used in dialogue situations, as opposed to the DMs *vezi/vedeți* ('you see'), which appear quite frequently in monologue interactions.

Also interesting is the case of the DM *înțelegi* ('you understand', second person singular) (1.5 occurrences per 10,000 words in the Family Sub-corpus, 0.6 in the Public Sub-corpus, 1.1 occurrences in the Media Sub-corpus and no occurrences in any other sub-corpus). Within the ±Informal Corpora, the occurrences of *înțelegi* ('you understand') are distributed in two texts representing spontaneous conversations between students. Three of the four occurrences belong to the same female speaker, who describes a nightmare. Three occurrences of *înțelegi* ('you understand') appear in an ironical speech from the show *În gura presei*, presented by Mircea Badea. Here, the journalist imitates the 'ghetto language'. Three other occurrences of *înțelegi* ('you understand') in the Media Sub-corpus also belong to the same speaker, a radio show moderator. Two of these occurrences represent a repetition of the DM. The passage is part of the opening of a radio program, representing the conversation between the program's moderators. The initial lines, where the informal greeting *neața* ('mornin'') also occurs, set a casual tone to the conversation. Other DMs specific to informal speech are also present in this excerpt: *știi* and *auzi* ('you know' and 'you hear').

(4) D. 'Neața, neața, 'neața
W. ''neața 'neața.
D. S-a făcut nouă și vreo zece minuțele. Iată-ne din nou aceiași (…)
W. Ce facem azi?
D. Ce facem, ce facem? (…) Să vedem acu' că ne-am trezit.
W. Așa. Să-ți spun de maimuțele alea.
D. Maimuțe?
W. Ce-au făcut? Le-au conectat la electro (…) 320 de volți (…) pe una din maimuțe.
D. Așa.
W. La cealaltă cred 60 sau 80. Cea cu 320 de Volți și-a mișcat brațul (…) aaa în prima etapă (…)
D. Daaa (…) deci avea un joystick în mână (…) înțelegi.
W. (…)
D. **Înțelegi?** Maimuța era ghidată din creier și din joystick.
W. Și a reușit să facă interactivitate cu jocul acela (…) care-l avea în fața ei
(…)

D. Bine (…) s-a folosit şi sistemul acela cu mâncare. Dacă reuşea o mişcare se dădea de mâncare. Un fel de (…) Pavlov ştii (…) telekinezia asta.
W. Auzi (…) şi sistemul ăsta (…) şi sistemul ăsta (…) înseamnă că îl vom folosi la oameni ca să (…) cu handicap (…) şi aşa mai departe (…)
D. Mai încolo, da.
(b)
W. Cioară?
D. Da, măăă. În Germania. Să nu fim iar acuzaţi. [râde]. Ei, ofiţerii i-au pus mai întâi mâncare pentru pisici. Au vrut s-o prindă cu mâncare pentru pisici. Nimic. I-au dat grăunţe. Nimic. Până la urmă (…) un poliţist mai (…) cu rădăcini în Ardeal, a zis: Auzi, ia daţi-i la cioară nişte schnaps.
W. Da.
D. A venit cioara, a băut, s-a îmbătat pe loc, a căzut şi au prins-o.
W. Zău.
D. A început cioara să zboare în zig-zag (…) **Înţelegi?** (…)[imită avion] (…) crrr (…) crrr (…) crrr (…) hîc (…) (Corpus Pop I, 79)
D. 'Morning, 'morning, 'morning,
W. 'morning, 'morning,
D. It's about ten minutes past nine. Here we are again (…)
W. What are we doing today?
D. What are we doing, what are we doing? (…) Let's see now that we woke up.
W. So, let me tell you about those monkeys.
D. Monkeys?
W. What did they do? They connected them to electro (…) 320 volts (…) on one of the monkeys.
D. OK.
W. I think 60 or 80 for the other one. The one with 320 Volts moved its arm (…) in the first stage (…)
D. Yes (…) so it had a joystick in its hand (…) you understand?
W. (…)
D. **You understand?** The monkey was guided by the brain and the joystick.
W. And it managed to make interactivity with that game (…) that was in front of it (…)
D. Well (…) that system with food was also used. If a move was successful, food was given. A kind of (…) Pavlov, you know (…) this telekinesis.
W. Listen (…) and this system (…) and this system (…) means that we will use it on people to (…) with disabilities (…) and so on (.. .)
D. Later on, yes.
(b)
W. The crow?
D. Yes, man. In Germany. In order to avoid being accused [laughs]. Well, the officers first gave it cat food. They wanted to catch it with cat food. Nothing. They gave it grains. Nothing. Finally (…) a policeman (…) with roots in Transylvania, said: Listen, give it some schnapps.

W. Yes.
D. The crow came, drank, got drunk on the spot, fell and they caught it.
W. Really?
D. The crow began to fly zigzag (…) **you understand?** (…)[imitates an airplane] (…) crrr (…) crrr (…) crrr (…) hic (…)'

Finally, we observed that the DM *știi* 'you know' records maximum frequencies of use in both registers. *Știi* 'you know' is frequently used in informal texts as well as formal texts that mimic informal speech (media speech). Thus, *știi* 'you know' registers 81.2 % of the total occurrences of DMs in the ± Informal Corpus and 29.5 % of the total occurrences in the ± Formal Corpus, i.e., high frequencies in both registers in Romanian. These results confirm that different types of text favor different DMs. On one hand, we have the DM *vedeți* 'you see', with a high frequent occurrence in argumentative speech (especially political or religious speech). A possible explanation could be the argumentative function of this DM, used to reaffirm the speaker's opinion in order to convince the interlocutor. This observation is consistent with the results of Détrie (2010: 758) regarding the French DM *tu vois* 'you see': "dire tu vois, c'est donc aussi tenter de faire voir autrui, d'attirer son attention sur ce que le locuteur aimerait qu'il voie". On the other hand, we have the DM *înțelegi* ('you understand') used, in our corpus, only in informal co(n)text. We stated that despite the basic meaning of the lexical verb, by using the DM *înțelegi* ('you understand') the speaker does not question the listener's ability to understand the message or his communicative competence (see Timoci, 2021:160). However, as noticed by Biriș (2013: 39) the DMs from *a înțelege* ('to understand') are well integrated in the statement and their removal from the context could compromise the dialogue's overall meaning. This milder desemanticization in the case of DM *înțelegi, înțelegeți* ('you understand') can explain the fact that the speaker exercises caution in using them in a formal context.

4.2. Position in a Turn Unit

The discourse markers analysed here were commonly referred to as phatic signals that grab and hold the listener's interest. Thus, in order to determine whether turn-medial is their prototypical position or if they appear in turn-final position as turn-yielding devices, we considered it convenient to analyse their position within a turn unit.

For this section of the study, from the entire corpus, we selected only the texts that involve dialogue or conversation, leaving out of the analysis the monologue encounters such as conferences, sermons, or pleadings. After excluding the monologue texts, the corpus presents 106 occurrences of *știi* ('you know', second person singular), 21 occurrences of *știți* ('you know', second person plural), ten occurrences of *vezi* ('you see', second person singular), 12 of *vedeți* ('you see', second person plural), eight occurrences of *înțelegi* ('you understand' second person singular)[3] and ten occurrence of the form *înțelegeți* ('you understand', second person plural), respectively.

Table 6.4. Position in a turn unit

DM	Turn-initial		Turn-medial		Turn-final		Independent	
	No.	%	No.	%	No.	%	No.	%
Știi	4/106	4 %	77 /106	73 %	24/106	22 %	1/106	1 %
Știți	2/21	10 %	15/21	71 %	4/21	19 %	0	0 %
Vezi	3/10	30 %	3/10	30 %	1/10	10 %	3/10	30 %
Vedeți	4/12	33 %	6/12	50 %	1/12	8 %	1/12	8 %
Înțelegi	0	0 %	7/8	88 %	1/8	13 %	0	0 %
Înțelegeți	0	0 %	7/10	70 %	3/10	30 %	0	0 %

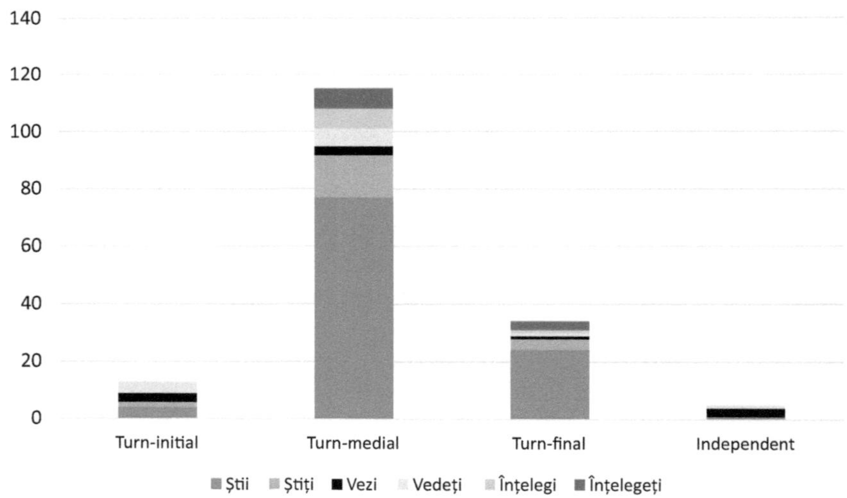

Figure 6.5. Position in a turn-unit

3 We also excluded the three occurrences of *înțelegi* 'you understand' identified in the show *În gura presei*.

As shown in Figure 6.5, the DMs examined here can occupy various places within a turn unit. However, with a relatively high frequency for each marker and an overall average of 69 %, we find that DMs do occur most frequently in the medial position. This means that, in the majority of cases, the occurrence of a DM with an interrogative intonation does not require a prompt answer from the listener. This finding confirms the hypothesis of the role of phatic signals of these DMs, which differ from questions through which the speaker requests a concrete answer from the listener.

Of the 106 occurrences of *ştii* 'you know', only four are in turn-initial position and 77 in turn-medial position. Furthermore, none of the occurrences appears in absolute initial position: such interventions include, in the first positions of the syntagmatic strings, other DMs that precede the occurrence of *ştii* 'you know': *pai, cam aşa↓*. Twenty-four occurrences (about 22 %) appear in turn-final position. We found only one example where *ştiţi* ('you know', second person plural) occurs in the absolute initial position of the intervention (the example illustrated under (6)). Given this small proportion, we consider this a rare use.

(5) EB: <F când au dat PENsii de lux↑ [şi astăzi avem o problemă. F>
CA: deci domnule↓ domnu'::] prim-ministru↓ ++ [dumneavoastră↑
EB: <F Au dat] agenţii guvernamentale cu SUtele↑ şi eu le-am tăiat. Asta fac eu. F>
CA: <F dumneavoastră vorbiţi acum↓ vorbiţi acum <MARC cu mine MARC>F>.
LN: **Ştiţi**↓ campania electorală <MARC s-a încheiat↓ MARC>//
EB: Nu. (CLRVA II, 407).
'EB: when they gave luxury PENSIONS [today we still have a problem.
CA: so, Sir, Sir, prime minister, [you
EB: They gave] government agencies by the hundreds and I cut them. That's what I do.
CA: you talk now, you talk now with me.
LN: **You know**, the election campaign is over.
EB: No.'

Of the three pairs of DMs analysed based on our corpus, the DMs *vezi, vedeţi* 'you see' tend to be placed in turn-initial position. A possible explanation could be that these DMs have an argumentative role, pointing to the speaker's subsequent explanation.[4] As pointed out by Andersen (2007, 21) regarding the French equivalent *tu vois, vous voyez* ('you see'), these DM have an explanatory nature.

4 The six DMs we study here are more common in dialogic exchanges. We do observe, however, that *vedeţi* 'you see' is quite frequent in religious discourse, lectures and political speech, which may be explained by its role in highlighting or emphasizing the upcoming assertion

(6) OP: Nu↓ nu sunt nervoasă. Pentru corectitudine↓ a spus astăzi premieru' că va continua restructurarea agenţiilor guvernamentale. Şi vroiam [să-l întrebăm <F în această seară pe domnu' ŞeiTAN cum se va întâmpla F>.
VV: Corectitudinea cui doamnă? Stimată doamnă↓] aţi spus că am timp să termin.
OP: Vă rog.
VV: **Vedeţi↓** de-aia nu ne înţelegem. Nu tre' să ne smulgem cuvintele din gura altuia. Dumneavoastră↑ la mine după TREIzeci de secunde brusc deveniţi nervoasă↓ nu ştiu din ce motiv.
LN: Vă ascultăm.
OP: Vă rog. (CLRVA II, 442).
'OP: No, I'm not angry. For fairness, the prime minister said today that he will continue the restructuring of government agencies. And this evening we wanted [to ask Mr. Şeitan how this will happen.
VV: Whose fairness Madam? Dear Madam↓] you said I have time to finish.
OP: Please.
VV: **You see,** that's why we don't understand each other. We must not interrupt. Thirty seconds into my conversation and you get annoyed. I don't know why.
LN: We hear you.
OP: Please.'

On the other side, the pair *înţelegi*, *înţelegeţi* 'you understand' frequently emerges at the end of a verbal act or turn unit since most of the time, the speaker is waiting to receive an explicit confirmation from the interlocutor. Consider the following:

(7) A: oricum el <J face (xxx)>
B: CĂ? <F CE face> el noaptea. CE FAce. uite↓ m-a m-a-ntrebat şi adina că nu-i venea să creadă. <J adina **mă-nţelegi**>.
A: păi acu:ma::
B: ((oftează)) aCUm? [...]
A: el aseară
B: aşa↓ (IVLRA, 60)
'A: anyway he does
B: What? What does he do at night. What does he do? look↓ Adina also asked me, because she couldn't believe it. Adina, **do you understand me**?
A: well, now
B: ((sighs)) now? [...]
A: last night
B: so'

These data allow us to assume a more advanced fixation of the DM coming from the verb *a înţelege* 'to understand' in the dialogic context and explain the occurrence of DMs arising from *a vedea* 'to see' within monologic interactions.

5. Concluding Remarks

This study intended to investigate the usage of three pairs of discourse markers in formal and informal spoken Romanian. To accomplish the study's goal, we examined the frequency and distribution of these DMs in eight sub-corpora (informal private, informal public, telephone exchange between family members or friends, formal dialogue in a natural context, formal monologue in a natural context, media, political debate, and telephone exchange in a formal context).

The finding of this research revealed that the number of DMs differs according to the level of formality of the interaction. Our study also showed a complex relationship between the use of specific DMs and specific type of discourse. In addition to the expected fact that second person singular DMs dominate in texts with a lower degree of formality, while second person plural DMs predominate in texts with a higher degree of formality, we could also observe that different text types tend to promote the presence of particular DMs. Thus, the theory that certain DMs are associated with particular speech patterns is supported.

Another research question we tried to address here was the DMs position within a turn unit. We have seen that these DMs frequently take up a turn-medial position. However, we could notice some variations that are worth noting: for instance, the DMs derived from *a înțelege* 'to understand' are used in turn-medial and turn-final positions, while the DMs derived from *a vedea* 'to see' can occur even in turn-initial position, preparing the listener for information of particular importance. The DMs *vezi/vedeți* 'you see' appear to have the highest positional freedom, which could be explained by the higher degree of *desemanticization* in their case. As previous research has indicated, the degree of desemanticization could also determine the degree of DM mobility.

References

Andersen, H. L. (2007). Marqueurs discursifs propositionnels. *Langue française*, 154, 2, 13–28.

Biriș, G. (2013). Verbe de cogniție cu potential de pragmaticalizare. In L. Botoșineanu & O. Ichim et al. (eds.), *Tradiție/inovație – identitate/alteritate: paradigme în evoluția limbii și culturii române*. Editura Universității „Alexandru Ioan Cuza". https://www.diacronia.ro/ro/indexing/details/V2523/pdf

Biriș, G. (2014). Pragmaticalizarea verblui *a ști*. In R. Zafiu & A. Dragomirescu et al. (eds.), *Limba Română: Diacronie și sincronie în stilul limbii române* (vol. 2). Editura Universității din București. https://www.diacronia.ro/ro/indexing/details/V1138/pdf

Cresti, E. (2004). *The C-ORAL-ROM CORPUS. A multilingual resource of spontaneous speech for romance languages*. https://www.academia.edu/1065013/The_C_ORAL_ROM_CORPUS_A_Multilingual_Resource_of_Spontaneous_Speech_for_Romance_Languages.

Détrie, C. (2010). De voir à tu vois / vous voyez: fonction sémantico-énonciative et postures énonciatives construites par ces particules interpersonnelles. Congrès Mondial de Linguistique Française - CMLF, pp. 755-766.

Timoci, C. (2021). *Pragmatica verbului în limba română vorbită actuală*. Unpublished PhD dissertation. Universitatea „Alexandru Ioan Cuza" din Iași. Doctoral Supervisor: Prof. Luminița Hoarță Cărăușu, PhD.

Corpora

CLRVA I = Cărăușu, L. (coord.) (2005). *Corpus de limbă română vorbită actuală*. Editura Tehnică, Științifică și Didactică Cermi.

CLRVA II = Cărăușu, L. (coord.) (2013). *Corpus de limbă română vorbită actuală nedialectală,* Editura Universității. "Alexandru Ioan Cuza".

Corpus Pop I = Pop, L. (ed.) (2004). *Verba Volant. Recherche sur l'oral*. Echinox.

Corpus Pop II = Pop, L. (ed.) (2010). *Où va la communication? (Comunicarea, încotro?)*. Echinox.

Corpus Pop IV = Pop, L., Duma, M., & Pușcalău, C. (eds.) (2011). *Façons de parler.ro*. Echinox.

IVLRA = Ionescu-Ruxăndoiu, L. (coord.) (2002). *Interacțiunea verbală în limba română actuală. Corpus (selectiv), Schiță și tipologie*. Editura Universității București.

IV II = Ionescu-Ruxăndoiu, L. (coord.) (2007). *Interacțiunea verbală. Aspecte teoretice și aplicative. Corpus*. Editura Universității din București.

Anna de Marco, Emanuela Paone

7 Discourse Markers in Complaints and Apologies: A Comparison between Native and Non-Native Speakers of Italian

Abstract: The present study analyses the uses and functions of discursive markers (DMs) in complaints and apologies performed by learners of Italian as L2 and native speakers of Italian engaged in dyadic interactions. Oral data were elicited through prototypical scenarios, where the context and the relationship between the interlocutors were variable. The comparison between learners and natives highlighted some differences both in the use and in the variety of DMs. In general, native speakers exploited the DMs' polyfunctionality when performing the speech acts, combining them with politeness strategies, to strengthen or attenuate the illocutionary force or to guide the interlocutor in the interpretation of the message. This made their expressions more effective and appropriate to the context and the interlocutor. On the other hand, even the most advanced learners did not draw upon similar strategies. Despite using a discrete variety of DMs, they showed less variability in DM usage depending on contextual variables. In some cases, this resulted in expressions that were too emphatic or impositive and less appropriate when addressing a distant interlocutor or a superior. The outcome of this study could offer useful information for language teaching.

Keywords: discourse markers, speech acts, language learning

1. Introduction

The aim of this paper is to analyse the uses and functions of discursive markers (DMs) in complaints and apologies performed by learners of Italian L2 and native Italian speakers engaged in dyadic interactions.[1]

In recent years, there has been a growing interest towards DMs in language acquisition and teaching. These markers are deemed crucial for the effectiveness of oral communication, since, as we know, they contribute to turn management, to the organization and structuring of speech and to establish micro-relationships between the expressed content and the shared knowledge. Additionally, they

1 The paper is the result of the joint work of the two authors; particularly, Anna De Marco is responsible for Sections 1, 2, 4.1 and 5.1; Emanuela Paone is responsible for Sections 3, 4.2, 5.2 and 6.

activate inferential functions guiding the interlocutor in the interpretation of the message. In the context of complaints and apologies, where L2 learners often exhibit inadequacies on the pragmatic level compared to natives, DMs could play a crucial role. However, there is a lack of data or studies in the literature regarding this specific aspect, at least within the limits of our knowledge, except for a recent study we conducted on the use of DMs in complaints, which, however, focused on exclusively written and one-way data. Our goal is therefore to analyse, from a qualitative point of view, the functions performed by the DMSs in the realization of these acts and during the negotiation between the interlocutors in oral interactions. We will compare a sample of L2 learners with native speakers of Italian.

The paper is structured as follows: Section 2 outlines the theoretical framework, focusing on the speech acts under observation and reporting evidence from previous studies in Second Language Acquisition (SLA) that highlights learners' difficulties in performing those acts; a description of our study, the methods and materials is provided in Section 3; results will be reported in Section 4 and discussed in Section 5. Finally, in Section 6 we draw conclusions and implications for language teaching and learning.

2. Theoretical Framework

2.1. Complaints

Complaints are expressive speech acts by which the speaker expresses a negative judgment regarding a given event or situation (see also Nuzzo, 2007:107). They can be accompanied by a request for solution/ repair (directive component).

As noted by Murphy and Neu (1996) and others, a complaint can be defined as a 'speech act set' combining different speech acts to form a complete speech act. Four possible moves can be identified (Murphy & Neu, 1996): 1. initiation and explanation of purpose; 2. complaint; 3 justification; 4. request.

Complaints can vary in intensity in relation to the damage suffered and the relationships between interlocutors. Prosodic variations can also play a significant role in the perception of (im)politeness by the hearer (Paone, 2020, 2021).

Acquisitional and contrastive studies have reported that L2 learners tend to exhibit aggressiveness (Murphy & Neu, 1996) and are less effective compared to native speakers (Trosborg, 1995; Nuzzo, 2007) in performing this speech act.

Concerning the role of DMs in complaints, a recent study (De Marco & Paone, in preparation) based on data from written discourse completion tasks found that A1–A2 learners of Italian as L2 used a more limited variety of DM functions and types compared to B1–B2 learners and native speakers (e.g. DMs with mainly interactional functions related to the request for attention, like *mi scusi* 'excuse me', and as politeness strategies, like *per favore* 'please'). More advanced learners showed a balanced use of DMs intensifying (e.g. *veramente, davvero* 'really') and mitigating (*magari* 'perhaps') the expressive and directive components of the act.

2.2. Apologies

Apologies are expressive and post-event acts, signalling the fact that a certain type of event has already taken place, i.e. a violation of a social norm has been committed (Blum-Kulka & Olshtain, 1984: 206). Apologies imply loss of face for the speaker and support for the hearer.

Five possible strategies can be identified for making an apology (see Cohen & Olshtain, 1981: 119–125): 1. An expression of apology, 2. Acknowledgment of responsibility, 3. An explanation or account, 4. An offer of repair, 5. A promise of non-recurrence. Learners have difficulty in adapting apologies to the level of familiarity of the interlocutors (Cohen et al., 1986).

According to Nuzzo (2007), native speakers of Italian use a wide range of conventionalized formulas to convey an apology. The most frequent expressions in her corpus were *scusa(mi)* and *(mi) scusi* 'excuse me', followed by *mi dispiace* 'I'm sorry'. The author also reported that social distance did not seem to affect the realization of apologies, except for the use of internal modifiers; indeed, in high social distance contexts, her informants employed a higher number of intensifiers, in order to stress their regret for the offense.

Cross-cultural studies and Second Language Acquisition (SLA) research on apologizing (Blum-Kulka et al., 1989) reported that the variation of social distance and power between participants influenced participants' choices of apology strategies and that 'the relative weight of these factors was subject both to situational and cultural variation' (Walker, 2017: 30). In Cohen, Olshtain and Rosenstein (1986), the level of familiarity of the interlocutors 'appeared to influence NNS and NS responses differently: namely, NS apologies to strangers were intensified more than apologies to friends, which was not the case with learner responses'. Among the possible explanations advanced by the authors was the hypothesis that the learners might not yet have gained the ability to vary the intensity of their apologies in accordance with contextual variables. A recent work on the expression of apologies in learners of Italian as L2 confirmed this hypothesis even at a prosodic level: unlike native speakers, learners were not able to vary the 'tone' of the apologies in accordance with contextual variables (see De Marco & Paone, 2022).

Regarding the role of DMs in expressing apologies, no study has explored this aspect so far, to the best of our knowledge (but see Businaro, 2002). However, a recent work by Ghezzi and Molinelli (2019) highlighted the polyfunctionality of forms derived from the Italian lemma *scusi* 'excuse me', including the use of conventionalised formulas and pragmatic markers like *scusa/mi scusi* 'sorry', 'excuse me' to convey both polite and (im)polite messages.

3. The Study

In the light of the theoretical framework we discussed in Section 2, we assume that the use of DMs may be crucial in the realization of complaints and apologies, allowing the speakers to guide the interlocutors in the interpretation of the message and the negotiation of the act. In this sense, our hypothesis is that learners of Italian, independently from their language proficiency, may draw upon a limited range of DMs' functions, resulting in less effectiveness and appropriateness, compared to native speakers.

3.1. Method and Materials

3.1.1. Participants

L2 international students attending Italian courses at University of Calabria (hereinafter, It-L2) and 6 speakers from Calabria, South Italy (It-L1) participated in the study. The It-L2 group came from different countries and had different levels of language proficiency (see Table 7.1).

Table 7.1. Sociolinguistic information about the participants

	Learners of Italian (It-L2)	**Native speakers (It-L1)**
N°	12	6
Country	Iran, Kurdistan, India, Pakistan, Egypt, Brazil, Ecuador, Peru, Mexico, Spain.	Italy (Calabria, South Italy)
Proficiency level	A1–A2 (6 students); B1–B2 (6 students)	---
Age range	19–34	19–34
Length of residence (LOR)	From 3 months to 3 years	---
Occupation	Students at University of Calabria	University students and young professionals

3.1.2. Data Collection Procedure

Oral data were collected through role-plays. Prototypical scenarios (adapted from Nuzzo, 2007; De Marco & Paone, 2019; Paone, 2020; De Marco & Paone, in press) were used to elicit the linguistic acts under investigation, however, the context and the relationship between the interlocutors were variable (see Table 7.2). By equal-intimate, we mean a symmetrical relationship (equal) in which the interlocutors already know each other (see also Gesuato, 2015). Within this label we include different degrees of knowledge ranging from a minimal level, such as between student and professor, to a high level of familiarity, such as between brothers / sisters. By equal-distant, we intend instead a symmetrical relationship in which, however, the interlocutor is a stranger; by superior-intimate, we mean an asymmetrical relationship in which, however, there is a minimum level of knowledge between the interlocutors.

Furthermore, in all scenarios the negative event that arouses the complaint or the apology is non-verbal, that is, it is triggered by extra-linguistic events (Businaro, 2002).

The interactions are symmetric, that is It-L2-It-L2 dyads and It-L1-It-L1 dyads; they have been recorded by means of a professional audio recorder. Along with the complaints and apologies, participants also made other dialogues focused on other speech acts (requests and refusals). Each subject repeated the same scenario twice: the first time in the role of the person complaining, the second time, recorded weeks later, in the role of the addressee of the complaint with a different person.

Table 7.2. Scenarios eliciting complaints and apologies

	Equal- intimate interlocutor	**Equal- distant interlocutor**	**Superior- intimate interlocutor**
Complaints	[COM_S1] Mess in the kitchen (with a roommate)	[COM_S3] Queue at the post office (with a stranger)	[COM_S4] Wrong evaluation (with a professor)
	[COM_S2] Loud music (with a neighbour)		
Apologies	[APO_S1] Torn dress (with a family member)	[APO_S3] Accident in the park (with a stranger for accidentally damaging his / her shirt / blouse)	[APO_S4] Late at an appointment (with a professor)
	[APO_S2] Lost notes (with a fellow student)		

Our corpus consisted of: 96 role-plays performed by It-L2 group (48 per level of proficiency); 48 role-plays performed by It-L1 group. Each role-play lasted from 1 to 5 minutes.

3.1.3. Approach to Analysis

Our study is based on the analysis of the functions rather than the forms, that is we adopted an onomasiological approach rather thana semasiological one. Following the taxonomy proposed by Bazzanella, 1995, 2006; Bazzanella & Borreguero Zuloaga, 2011; Sansò, 2020, we distinguished three types of functions: the interactional function, the metatextual function and the cognitive function. The qualitative analysis aims to identify the functions of the DMs in the realization of the two speech acts and their negotiation between the two interlocutors.

4. Results

4.1. DMs in Complaints

4.1.1. The It-L2 Group

The qualitative analysis of It-L2 group's interactions highlighted the use of DMs as part of the sociopragmatic and pragmalinguistic strategies adopted by the learners to perform the act. We will report some excerpts from the role-plays[2] that are representative of some frequent uses in our corpus. In fragment (1), the speaker A complains to a roommate for leaving the kitchen dirty; we can notice the use of interjections like *mamma mia!* and adverbs like *davvero* 'really' (*è davvero sporco*, 'it's really dirty') that intensifies the expressive component of the complaint. The subsequent use of *guarda* 'look' orients and focuses the interlocutor's attention on the negative event that stimulated the speaker's reaction (*Guarda questo è davvero sporco*, 'Look at this! It's really dirty'). The use of *NO!* and *ma* 'but' in the last turn indicates an interactional conflict by countering the reasons presented by the interlocutor with a repair request (*ma devi pulire questo!* 'but you have to clean up all this!').

2 We acknowledge that the translation of DMs from Italian to English is challenging due to the lack of equivalence of some DMs in the two languages. Also, we would like to underline that many It-L2 productions are characterized by the presence of lexical, morphosyntactic and pragmatic errors, consequently the English translations will reflect some of these errors as well.

(1) **COM_S1_Mess in the kitchen** (with a roommate). Level: B1–B2
A: Mamma mia! Mamma mia! Questo è sporchissimo! E caffè! Non c'è caffè! Caffè! O mamma mia! Caffè!
M: Buon giorno Angie
A: Buon giorno
M: cosa fai?
A: *Davvero* buon giorno? Guarda / Guarda questo / è *davvero* SPORCO!
M: Ma ieri io ho avuto una festa con i miei amici [ee]
A: NO! Ma devi devi pulire questo!
'A: Oh my god! Oh my god! This is so dirty! And the coffee! There's no coffee! Coffee! Oh my god! Coffee!
M: Good morning, Angie
A: Good morning
M: What are you doing?
A: *Really* good morning? Look! Look at this! it's *really* DIRTY!
M: But I had a party with my friends yesterday
A: NO! But you have to clean this up!'

In examples (2) and (3) the complaint is addressed to a neighbour for the loud music coming from his/her apartment in the middle of the night. In (2), we can observe the use of additional DMs that direct the interlocutor's attention on the negative consequences of his/her behaviour (e.g. *ti dico* in *Mi arrabbio assai, ti dico ah* 'I get very angry, I tell you, ah') or as rhetorical expedients to verify that the message has been understood (e.g. *hai capito*? in *All'una si dorme, hai capito?* 'At one a.m everyone is sleeping, do you understand?').

In (3), the pragma-dyad *scusa ma/scusami ma* 'excuse me but' is used to introduce the complaint or to respond to the arguments of the interlocutor. As Ghezzi and Molinelli (2019) and Fedriani and Molinelli (2019) pointed out, these pragma-dyads are often used to introduce a face-threatening act, such as a criticism, an accusation, a conflicting point of view. *Scusa* is used to mitigate or pretend to mitigate a criticism, while *ma* signals a contrast on the interactional level due to the interlocutor's behaviour as in *Escusa, ma abito qua vicino e sento la musica* 'Excuse me but I live nearby and I hear the music' and to counter the arguments of the interlocutor (*scusami ma queste non sono ore per questa musica* 'sorry but it's not time to listen to this music').

(2) **COM_S2_Loud music** (with a neighbour). Levels: Ad. B1–B2; Ag. A1–A2
Ad: Salve Ag., *per favore* bassa la musica voglio dormire non riesco con questo casino che hai nella casa, ma cosa state combinando dentro?
Ag: salve estamo festeggiando per favore signore è solo una riunione di amici
Ad: *ma* non potevate farle al bar? All'una si dorme *hai capito?* Io l'ho aspettato mezzanotte e *ecco* si finiscono *ecco* si vanno, *per favore* bassate la musica o mi arrabbio assai oh, *ti dico ah*

'Ad: *Please* turn down the music I want to sleep I can't with this noise you have in the house, but what are you doing inside?
Ag: Hi we're celebrating please sir it's just a meeting among friends
Ad: But couldn't you have it at the bar? At one o'clock everyone is sleeping, *do you understand*? I waited for midnight and *now* they end they go, *please* turn down the music or I get very angry oh, I tell you ah'

(3) **COM_S2_Loud_music** (with a neighbour). Levels: B1–B2
L: *Escusa*, ma abito qua vicino e sento la musica e mi dispiace dirlo ma è troppo alta. *Per favore* la puoi abbassare un po'?
D: oh *escusami escusami* ma la musica non è alta, è abbastanza bassa
L: no no no, scusami ma queste non sono ore per questa musica
D: forse la tua età è un'età…come dire…non so come si dice, mamma mia… forse tua
L: stai dicendo che sono vecchia? (ride)
'L: *Sorry*, but I live nearby and I hear the music and I'm sorry to say it but it's too loud. Could you *please* turn it down a little?
D: Oh *sorry sorry* but the music isn't loud, it's low enough
L: No no no, sorry but this is not the time for this music
D: maybe your age is an age … how to say … I don't know what they say, mamma mia … maybe yours
L: Are you saying I'm old? (laughs)'

In fragment (4), the speaker complains to a stranger who does not respect the queue at the post office. In this example, we can notice the presence of another pragma-dyad, *ho capito ma*/*ho capito però* 'I understand but' / 'I know, but', recurring in the negotiation phases of the act, to respond to the justifications given by the recipient of the complaint: *ho capito* is used to recognize or pretend to partially recognize the reasons of the other, *ma*/*però* 'but / however' marks a conflict on an interactional level and reiterates the complainer's motivations, possibly appealing to the violated social norm (e.g. *Ho capito ma questo non va bene per tutte queste persone che sono qua* 'I understand but this is not good for all these people who are here').

(4) **COM_S3_Queue at the post office.** Levels: A1–A2
Agu.: *scusi* signore sto aspettando qua nella fila e tu entrato prima di me e questo no va bene
Adi: ah scusa non l'ho visto lei scusami
Agu: *ok ho capito ma*…. Per favore signore
Adi: sì sì sì, chiedo scusa davvero non l'ho visto lei, nemmeno la fila… ma se si può adesso ormai sono qui, si può entrare prima di lei
Agu: *scusi* signore mi *scusi* questo non è possibile *per favore* torna all'inizio della fila
Adi: ma davvero solo un minuto di fare questa cosa

Agu.: *Ho capito ma* questo non va bene per tutte queste persone che sono qua quindi *per favore* signore all'inizio della fila
'Agu: *Sorry* sir I'm waiting here in the line and you get in before me and this is not good
Adi: Sorry, I didn't see you, sorry
Agu: ok *I understand but*.... Please sir
Adi: Yes yes yes, I'm sorry I really didn't see you, not even the queue ... but if I can, now I'm here, can I enter before you
Agu: *Excuse me* sir *excuse me* this is not possible *please* go back to the beginning of the line
Adi: But really just a minute in order to do this thing
Agu: *I understand* but this is not good for all these people who are here so *please* sir go at the beginning of the line'

Finally in example (5), the speaker complains to a professor who made a mistake in evaluating a written exam. We can see the use of DMs that reinforce (e.g. *davvero* 'really') and mitigate (e.g. *mi sembra* 'it seems to me') the explicit accusation, (*lei ha sbagliato* 'you made a mistake'). The subsequent use of *non lo so* 'I don't know', mitigates the request for repair (*non lo so se lei può darmi questo voto* 'I don't know if you can give me this grade').

(5) **COM-S4_Wrong evaluation** (with a professor). Level:B1–B2
Ad: [...] vorrei parlare riguardo al mio voto dell'esame che lei m'ha messo 28 *ma* la verità che io ho studiato tantissimo per questo esame e *davvero mi sembra* che lei ha sbagliato di darmi 30 e lode perché davvero prof io meritavo secondo me trenta e lode *non lo so* se lei può darmi questo voto
'Ad: I would like to talk about my grade of the exam that you gave me 28 *but* the truth is that I studied a lot for this exam and *it really seems to me* that you made a mistake in giving me 28 because really prof I deserved in my opinion 30 cum laude *I don't know* if you can give me this grade'

4.1.2. The It-L1 Group

The use of DMs as part of pragmatic and politeness strategies to convey the act by the It-L1 group is similar to It-L2 group's, even though a broader variety of DMs enriches It-L1 speakers' complaints. In example (6), with the roommate, we may notice the use of DMs that signal a contrast such as *non è tutto ok* 'everything is not ok', *però* 'but', whereas the dyad *scusa ma* 'excuse me but' introduces the complainer's criticism and disapproval towards the interlocutor (*scusa ma avresti potuto pulire* 'excuse me but you could have cleaned up'). *Scusa* in this last example is used with a mock politeness value (see Ghezzi & Molinelli, 2019), triggering 'an impoliteness understanding that does not match the surface form or semantics of the utterance or the symbolic meaning of the behaviour' (Culpeper, 2011: 17).

(6) **COM_S1_Mess in the kitchen** (with a roommate).

E: Ciao, Federì, tutto ok?

M: *non è tutto ok* / perché la cucina fa vomitare // Fa VOMITARE / se non ci sei entrata vai a vedere perché è uno schifo / *ora* io non pretendo che dobbiamo vivere nella reggia perché siamo studenti / *mò figurati* se sto lì attaccata alla cosa / *però* / non c'è un piatto pulito, non c'è un cucchiaino pulito, non c'è una cacchio di tazzina e non me la posso *nemmeno* andare a lavare perché non c'è caffè. *Scusa, ma* ieri avresti anche potuto ripulire!

'E: Hi, Federì, everything okay?

M: *it's not all right* / because the kitchen makes me feel sick // It makes me FEEL SICK / if you didn't go in go and see why it's disgusting / *now* I don't expect to live in a royal palace because we are students / *but* / there isn't even one clean plate, there isn't a clean teaspoon, there isn't even one bloody cup and I can't *even* go wash it because there is no coffee. *Sorry*, but you could have at least cleaned up yesterday!'

In example (7), where the addressee is the neighbour, the use of *ma* signals, again, a contrast with the behaviour of the interlocutor. Furthermore, we can also notice the use of the reformulation marker *cioè* 'that is', to better explain the reasons for the protest, and of *insomma* 'for heaven's sake!', to intensify the expressive component of the complaint, conveying, on the prosodic level, irritation and annoyance. *Insomma* is also used in a subsequent turn with a different function: to urge, together with *dai* 'come on!', a remedial action on the part of the interlocutor, strengthening the request for repair.

(7) **COM_S2_Loud music** (with a neighbour)

MIC: *Beh*, Buonasera, *maaa* abbiamo intenzione di andare avanti per molto con questa storia?

E: Ah *ma* dice per la musica?

MIC: *Eh no!* Per che cos'altro, secondo lei? *Cioè* Sono già le due e mezza del mattino, *insomma* E voi continuate a sparare musica ad alto volume [...] *ma* vi rendete conto che sono le due?

E: Va bene, abbassiamo un po'

MIC: *Eh!* sarebbe anche il caso, *insomma, dai*, su

'MIC: *Well, but* are we going to go on with this for a long time?

E: ah *but* are you talking about the music (do you refer to the music)?

MIC: *Eh no*! What else, in your opinion? *That is*, it is already half past two in the morning, (*for heaven's sake*) come on And you go on playing loud music [...] *but* do you realize that it is two o'clock?

E: Okay, we'll turn it down a bit

MIC: *Eh*! it would be about time, *for heaven's sake, come on*, come on'

(8) **COM_S2_Loud music** (with a neighbour)

M: Ragazze, ciao sono Mari, vi devo supplicare di abbassare la musica perché è l'una e non riusciamo *proprio* a chiudere occhio stanno *proprio* rimbombando *pure* i vetri delle finestre lo sapete che la mattina ci svegliamo all'alba, *ma-* ci abbiamo provato a dormire *ma* è impossibile è anche martedì sera

E: No guarda è il compleanno di Michela per questo stiamo facendo festa, dai, un'altra mezz'oretta e chiudiamo tutto

M: *E lo so però* è anche martedì sera, *voglio dire*, fosse sabato, *figurati*, pure fino alle 5 *però* siamo in un condominio...

'M: Girls, hello, it's Mari, I must beg you to turn the music down because it's one o'clock and we *just* can't sleep, even the windows are *literally* rumbling, you know that in the morning we wake up at dawn, *but-* we have tried to go to sleep but it is impossible it is also Tuesday evening

E: No, look, it's Michela's birthday that's why we're celebrating, come on, another half hour and we'll close everything

M: *And I know but* it's also Tuesday evening, *I mean*, if it was Saturday, *no problem*, even until 5 *but* we are in a condominium...'

(9) **COM_S3_Queue at the post office** (with a stranger)

MIC: EE *mi Scusi, scusi,* mi avrebbe preso il posto. C'ero...ero già in attesa io Ero immediatamente avanti a lei e lei mi ha *praticamente* scavalcato e si è fregata il mio posto

E: Scusi eh io però io non l'ho vista, sto aspettando da un bel po'

MIC: *Ho capito* signora *ma* pure io stavo aspettando qui in fila

E: Le giuro che io proprio non l'ho vista

MIC: *Mah* Faccia *un po'* lei, *insomma*, Non è *manco* giusto, *insomma*, che lei prende e si infila in questo modo

'MIC: EE *Excuse me, excuse me*, you took my place. I was there ... I was already waiting

I was just ahead of you and you *practically* stepped over me and stole my turn

E: Excuse me, but I didn't see you, I've been waiting for quite a while

MIC: *I understand* ma'am but I was also waiting here in line

E: I swear to you that I didn't see you

MIC: *But really*, it's not *even* fair, *for heaven's sake*, that you sneak in this way'

In extract (8), where the addressee is, again, a neighbour, we can see the use of *proprio* that intensifies the severity of the negative event, and the presence of other DMs that support the negotiation of the complaint, such as the dyad *E lo so, ma* 'and I know however', similar to *Ho capito ma* 'I understood but', also present in fragment (9), where the interlocutor is a stranger. In this example (9) there is a balanced use of DMs that mitigate the accusation (*mi ha praticamente scavalcato* 'you practically stepped over me') and DMs that reinforce the illocutionary force of the complaint (e.g. *Non è manco giusto, insomma* 'Well, that's not fair, for heaven's sake').

In examples (10) and (11), where the addressee is a superior, that is a professor, we can notice several DMs used with different functions. In (10) markers as *un po'* 'a little', *mi sembra* 'it seems to me' attenuate the explicit accusation, whereas *magari* 'perhaps' mitigates the request for repair. We may also notice the presence of other DMs that reveal some difficulties in turn planning and structuring: reformulators (e.g. *cioè* 'that is') and fillers (e.g. *niente*, similar to the English 'well', *insomma* in the sentence *riguardando pure insomma i punteggi*). In this sense, we may hypothesize that the speaker feels uncomfortable and a little clumsy while accusing the professor of making a mistake in the grade assignment.

In (11), we can observe how the use of *quindi* 'so, then' contributes on a metatextual and cognitive level to the effectiveness of the arguments that anticipate the request for repair.

(10) **COM_S4_Wrong evaluation** (with a professor)

F: Salve professore, niente, ho visto che lei praticamente aveva--- ho visto il risultato insomma dello scritto, ho ricontrollato pure la mia brutta e riguardando pure insomma i punteggi mi sembra che sia stato un po' cioè non mi torna, mi sembra che lei mi abbia dato qualche punto in meno / non è che potremmo magari riguardare insieme il compito e vedere di risolvere magari i miei dubbi, insomma.

'F: Hi professor, well I saw that you practically had --- I saw the result in short, I also double-checked my draft and looking at the scores as well, it seems to me that it was a bit, that is, it doesn't add up, it seems to me that you gave me a few points less / couldn't we maybe look at the exam paper together and see to maybe solve my doubts, that's all.'

(11) **COM_S4_Wrong evaluation** (with a professor)

M: Professoressa buongiorno, sono Rossi, ho fatto l'esame con lei la settimana scorsa, lo scritto

E: Sì mi ricordo mi dica

M: *ascolti*, io ho controllato on line l'esito dell'esame, che è risultato 27 su 30, *quindi* come voto 27 per tre errori // *solo che* quando sono andata a vedere la traccia c'erano **solo** le correzioni per 2 esercizi come se gli altri risultassero tutti corretti, *quindi* mi aspettavo un 28 su 30, a meno che non ci sia effettivamente un errore su un terzo esercizio *però effettivamente* risulta tutto corretto tranne 2. *Quindi* volevo *insomma* capire come mai.

'M: Professor good morning, I am Rossi, I took the exam with you last week, the writing

E: Yes I remember tell me

M: *Well*, I checked online the result of the exam, which was 27 out of 30, *so* 27 as a score for three errors // *only that* when I went to see the track there were only corrections for 2 exercises as if the others were all correct, *so* I was expecting a 28 out of 30, unless there is actually an error on a third exercise *but actually* everything is correct except for 2. *So* I wanted to understand why.'

4.2. DMs in Apologies

4.2.1. The It-L2 Group

Just as in complaints, DMs perform different functions in conveying the apology and during the negotiation of the act. For example, in extract (12) the speaker apologizes to her sister for damaging a borrowed dress; the use of *non lo so* 'I don't know', after the offended party's request for explanations, functions as a face-saving device: the speaker does not admit her responsibility explicitly, but simply expresses regret for the damage caused (*mi dispiace, non lo so* 'sorry, I don't know'). The subsequent use of *lo so* 'I know' by the same speaker functions as a face-saving device as well, but in the opposite direction, i.e. oriented towards the interlocutor, in order to restore social harmony, legitimizing the offended party's request for repair (*deberia comprarme uno nuovo* 'You should buy me a new one').

(12) **APO_S1_Torn dress** (with a family member). Levels: M (A1–A2) & J (B1–B2)
M: AH! Il mio vestito favorito! Qué pasa?
J: Oh, Marta, mi dispiace, *non lo so.* Sono andata a una festa ieri e quando sono ritornata a casa ho visto che il tuo vestito è strappato.
M: ma io penso che tu deberia comprarme uno nuovo
J: **sì, lo so** mi dispiace. Se vuoi domani possiamo andare a Cosenza e vieni con me e ti compro un altro
'M: AH! My favorite dress! Qué pasa?
J: Oh, Marta, I'm sorry, *I don't know.* I went to a party yesterday and when I got home I saw that your dress was torn.
M: but I think you should buy me a new one
J: **yes, I know** I'm sorry. If you want tomorrow we can go to Cosenza and you'll come with me and I'll buy you another one'

In example (13), again in a context characterized by a high degree of intimacy among the interlocutors, we can notice the use of *dai* to exhort the acceptance of the apology *(mi devi scusare, dai* 'you have to excuse me, come on').

(13) **APO_S1_Torn dress** (with a family member). Levels: B1–B2
G: – Mi piaceva, mi piaceva tantissimo!
A: – Te lo faccio sistemare
G: – No, non si può
A: – Mi devi scusare, *dai*
'G: – I liked it, I liked it very much!
A: – I'll have it fixed
G: – No, it's impossible
A: – You have to forgive me, **come on**'

Moving on to example (14), where the speaker apologizes to a university mate for losing her notes, we notice the use of *non lo so* 'I don't know', and *lo so* 'I know', with functions similar to those described above and the use of *magari* 'maybe' to suggest a possible remedy (*magari possiamo chiedere ai nostri colleghi* 'maybe we can ask our colleagues').

(14) APO_S2_Lost notes (with a university mate). Levels: B1–B2

A: ciao cara.ehm Per questo volevo parlare…Gli appunti che tu mi hai prestato l'altra volta…. credo che ho perso nella biblioteca, non lo so dove
N: come li hai persi?
A: *non so*. Credo che ho dimenticato in qualsiasi parte
N: Armando, come facciamo? Quella era l'unica copia, non avevo fatto le fotocopie… La settimana prossima c'è l'esame!
A: *e lo so* mi dispiace. *Magari* possiamo chiederlo ai nostri colleghi
'A: hello dear. ehm This is why I wanted to talk… The notes you lent me the other time…. I think I lost in the library, I don't know where
N: how did you lose them?
A: *I don't know*. I think I left them somewhere
N: Armando, what can we do? That was the only copy, I hadn't made any photocopies… The exam is next week!
To: *and I know* I'm sorry. *Maybe* we can ask our colleagues'

In extract (15), where the speaker apologizes to a stranger for accidentally staining her shirt with ice-cream, we note the use of DMs such *davvero* that intensify the illocutionary force of the apology (*scusami davvero davvero* 'sorry, really') and of DMs that urge the interlocutor to accept the offer of repair, such as *dai signora* 'come on madam', which is probably inadequate in this context.

(15) APO_S3_Accident in the park (with a stranger). Levels: B1–B2.

G: ah! scusa mi dispiace scusami scusami *davvero davvero* cosa posso fare per scusarmi? […]
G: – E la porto alla lavanderia
A: – Non hai nemmeno i soldi per comprarla, no no no
G: – Sì, ce l'ho, *dai* signora
A: – E devo andare io a portarlo, riportarlo, no no no
G: – Ma signora senti per favore, che non l'ho fatto a a a, non l'ho fatto perché volevo, non l'ho fatto
'G: ah! I'm sorry I'm sorry I'm *really* sorry *really* what can I do to apologize?
[…]
G: – And I'll take it to the laundry
A: – You don't even have the money to buy it, no no no
G: – Yes, I do, *come on* lady
A: – And I have to go and take it, take it back, no no no
G: – But madam listen please, that I did not aaa, I didn't do it because I wanted to, I did not'

In extract (16), where a student apologizes to a professor for being late for an appointment, the speaker uses *un po'* 'a bit', to attenuate the seriousness of the negative event (*credo che arriverò un po' in ritardo* 'I think I'll be a bit late'), also projecting the event into the future (while in fact it has already happened since he is already late). In the final turn, the use of DMss is strategic for the negotiation of the act and also for the safeguard of the speaker's face: *sì, ho capito* 'yes, I understand' are used to recognize and legitimize the arguments of the interlocutor, *però* 'however' is used with demarcative functions to introduce a remedial action (*dieci minuti e arrivo* 'ten minutes and I will be there'), attenuated by the use of *diciamo* 'let's say' as a mechanism of modulation that reduces the speaker's responsibility with respect to the promise just made, also calling into question the interlocutor.

(16) APO-S4_ Late for an appointment (with a professor). Levels: B1–B2-

A: salve professore. Chiedo scusa eh ho avuto un problema eh con la casa con la famiglia, credo che arriverò **un po'** in ritardo…

N: e ma quanto in ritardo, Armando? Io la sto aspettando da almeno un quarto d'ora. Sono venuta apposta all'università per fare ricevimento […] E la sto aspettando da più di un quarto d'ora ormai

A: *sì, ho capito però diciamo* dieci minuti e arrivo

'A: hi professor. I apologize eh I had a problem eh with the house with the family, I think I'll be **a bit** late …

N: and how late, Armando? I've been waiting for you for at least a quarter of an hour. I've come especially for our meeting [… [And I've been waiting for you for more than a quarter of an hour now

A: *yes, I understand but let's say* ten minutes and I'll be there'

4.2.2. The It-L1 Group

Let's now look at the productions of Italian-speaking speakers. In general, in addition to the functions observed in the productions of learners, we can note other functions that underlie different strategies in the realization of the act. In extract (17), with a family member, the use of *senti* 'listen' (pronounced more slowly and followed by a short pause and a sigh) directs the interlocutor's attention to what the speaker is about to communicate, conveying through her tone of voice that she is about to say something unpleasant. We may also note the strategic use of DMs that introduce the act gradually: *allora* 'well' that signals the turn taking and also the introduction of the topic, (*non è stata colpa mia* 'it was not my fault'), focusing the attention of the interlocutor firstly on the fact that the speaker is not responsible for the negative event (face-saving device); the use of *però* 'but/however', introduces instead the expression of regret, emphasizing the contrast between the absence of responsibility and the emotional state of the speaker. After the offer of repair, we finally note the use of *dai* 'come on', to reinforce the request for forgiveness.

(17) APO_S1_Torn dress (with a family member)

MR: EH…*senti*, ti devo dire una cosa
N: che cosa?
MR: *Allora*…non è stata colpa mia
N: che cosa?
MR: *però* mi dispiace da morire. *Praticamente* a quel cacchio di locale c'erano le sedie con…i cosi di paglia, si è agganciato il vestito, si è fatto uno strappo lungo la cucitura […] Se per te va bene, domani andiamo al centro commerciale e ti scegli quello che vuoi. […] *Dai, dai*, mi perdoni? Mi perdoni?
'MR: EH… *listen*, I have to tell you something
N: what?
MR: *Well*… it wasn't my fault
N: what?
MR: *but* I'm so sorry. *Basically* at that fucking club there were chairs with … the straw things, the dress was hooked, it got torn along the seam […] If that's okay with you, tomorrow we'll go to the mall and you'll choose what you want. […] *Come on, come on*, will you forgive me? Do you forgive me?'

In example 18, the DM *però* 'but/however' emphasizes the contrast between the negative event (*ho perso i tuoi appunti* 'I lost your notes') and the speaker's lack of intentionality (*non so come sia potuto accadere* 'I don't know how this could have happened'). The use of *purtroppo* 'unfortunately' and *terribilmente* 'terribly', respectively, emphasize the speaker's regret and her sense of guilt for what happened. Finally, we note the use of *non lo so* 'I don't know', already found in It-L2 productions as a face-saving device on the part of the speaker.

(18) APO_S2_Lost notes (with a university mate)

M: Prima che me la chiedi, è meglio che te lo dica io direttamente. *Allora* / ee/ Non so come sia potuto accadere/ *però*/ ho perso i tuoi appunti.
E: Stai scherzando?
M: No *purtroppo* li ho persi non riesco a trovarli ehm ti avrei chiamato io // praticamente adesso // ee per trovare insieme una soluzione qualsiasi cioè io ti aiuto, dimmi tu quello che posso fare perché mi sento già *terribilmente* in colpa per quello che è successo […] Non riesco a trovarli *NON SO* // *Guarda*, farò tutto io, ti passo miei appunti […] *Dai* a domani, ti giuro che mi impegno
'M: Before you ask me, I'd better tell you directly. *So* / ee / I don't know how it could have happened / *but* / I lost your notes.
E: Are you kidding?
M: No *unfortunately* I lost them I can't find them ehm I would have called you // practically now // and and to find together some solution that is I will help you, tell me what I can do because I already feel *terribly* guilty for what

happened [...] I can't find them *I DON'T KNOW* // *Look*, I'll do everything, I'll pass you my notes [...] *See you* tomorrow, I swear I'll do my best'

In example (19), with a stranger, we notice instead the use of DMs that emphasize the lack of intentionality such as *proprio* (*non me ne sono proprio accorta* 'I didn't really notice it'), or the expression of regret, such as *veramente* 'really, truly' in *mi dispiace da morire, veramente* 'I'm very sorry, really'. Quite interesting is the use of *tutt'al più* 'if anything' to introduce and at the same time circumscribe the offer of remedy, as if to say 'at most I can pay for the laundry'.

(19) APO_S4_Accident in the park (with a stranger).
N: scusi, signorina, faccia attenzione, mi ha sporcato di gelato
R: oddio *mi scusi*, non me ne sono *proprio* accorta. Ma l'ho sporcata assai?
E: eh *guardi*, tutta la camicetta si è sporcata, poi è gelato al cioccolato, questo non uscirà più..
R: mi dispiace tantissimo, *allora* intanto le do un fazzoletto così almeno, mi dispiace da morire, ma non verr-
E: questa è una camicetta di seta, non so se l'ha notato...
R: io *tutt'al più* le posso dire che se la porta in lavanderia mi posso occupare io del conto, di pagarla, mi dispiace da morire, *veramente*.
'N: excuse me, miss, be careful, you stained my shirt with ice-cream.
A: oh my god, *sorry*, I didn't *really* notice. But did I smear it a lot?
E: eh *look*, the whole blouse got dirty, then it's chocolate ice-cream, this will never come out ..
A: I'm very sorry, *so* in the meantime I'll give you a handkerchief like that at least, I'm so sorry, but it won't come
E: this is a silk blouse, I don't know if you noticed it ...
A: *At the most* I can tell you that if you take it to the laundry I can take care of the bill, to pay you, I am so sorry, *really*'

Finally, in example 20, with the professor, the use of *ma* 'but' introduces a contrast between the expression of regret (*sono mortificata* 'I am ashamed') and the account of the circumstances that led the apologizer to violate the social norm (*mi hanno messo in una situazione in cui veramente non avrei potuto neanche alzare il telefono* 'they put me in a situation where I really couldn't even pick up the phone'); here, the use of the adverb *veramente*, with the meaning of 'as a matter of fact', emphasizes the speaker's lack of intentionality, whereas the adverb *sicuramente* 'definitely/certainly', is aimed at reinforcing the promise of not recurrence ('definitely, it will not happen again').

(20) APO_S5_Late at an appointment (with a professor)
M: Io, ripeto, sono mortificata, *ma* mi hanno messo in una situazione in cui *veramente* non avrei potuto neanche alzare il telefono o mandarle il messaggio. [...] *sicuramente* non si ripeterà

'M: Again, I am mortified, *but* they put me in a situation where I *really* couldn't even pick up the phone or send you a message. [...] *Surely* it won't happen again'

5. Discussion

5.1. Complaints

In relation to the complaints, our analysis highlighted the strategic use of DMs in performing the act. To summarize our results, we can illustrate the different functions expressed by DMs in It-L2 and It-L1 productions:

- *Introducing the act.* Both in the Ita-L1 and Ita-L2 productions, we found the presence of the dyad *scusa ma/mi scusi ma* ('excuse me, but' and its formal equivalent in Italian) used to introduce the threatening act, in which *scusa/ scusi* is often used with a mock politeness value (see Ghezzi & Molinelli, 2019), whereas ma marks a contrast on the interactional level (Fedriani & Molinelli, 2019).
- *Intensifying the expressive component of the complaint.* Learners used interjections like *ah, oh, mamma mia* in informal contexts, whereas natives used expressions such as: *insomma!* 'for God's sake!', *mah!* 'Ugh!' *manco, nemmeno* 'not even', etc.
- *Stressing the interlocutor's blame.* The It-L2 group employed expressions like *davvero* 'really', while natives used *proprio* 'just', *pure, anche* 'also'.
- *Mitigating the accusation.* Both groups employed *mi sembra* 'it seems to me'; natives also used 'un po' 'a little/a bit'.
- *Intensifying the directive component of the complaint.* The It-L2 group did not use DMs with this function, whereas in It-L1's productions we found the use of *insomma, dai* to intensify the request of repair. Interestingly, in Ita-L1 productions, *insomma* is used to reinforce both the expressive and directive component of the complaint.
- *Mitigating the directive component of the complaint.* To mitigate the request of repair, the It-L2 group drew upon politeness formulas such as *per favore* 'please', while natives used a great variety of formulas such as *per favore, cortesemente, per cortesia, gentilmente* 'kindly' and other DMs like *magari* 'perhaps/maybe', *un po'* 'a little/a bit'.
- *Negotiating the act.* Learners used dyads like *lo so, però, ho capito, ma/però* 'I know but', 'I understand but', to respond to the justifications given by the addressee of the complaint, whereas natives employed similar and other DMs like *vabbè ho capito ma/però'* 'well, I understand but/however', *comunque sia/ comunque vada* 'however/whatever it is / however it goes'.

- *Supporting the act.* In support of the act, we found DMs with consequential-inferential functions, such as *quindi* 'therefore' (used by both groups) and DMs with reformulation functions as *cioè* 'that is', *voglio dire* 'I mean' used by the Ita-L1 group only. The Ita-L2 group used rhetorical devices to make sure that the message has been received by the addressee: *hai capito?* 'you understood?', a function that is absent from the natives' production. Finally, we found the use of DMs as focalizers aiming at orienting the interlocutor's attention to a specific aspect or to warn him/her about the negative consequences of his/her behaviour, e.g. *ecco* 'here', *ti dico* 'I tell you', *guarda* 'look', in the case of learners, *ascolti* 'listen', *(ma) guarda* '(but) look' in natives.

From this overview and from the examples discussed in Section 4.1, a greater variety of DMs can be noticed in the Ita-L1 productions than in those of the learners.

5.2. Apologies

As for the prevailing functions of DMs in apologies, we can summarize as follows:

- *Intensifying the expressive component of the apology/the expression of regret.* The Ita-L2 group used *veramente, davvero* 'really', whereas natives also employed other DMs like *terribilmente* 'terribly', *purtroppo* 'unfortunately'.
- *Acknowledging the responsibility/fault and intensifying the expression of guilt.* Learners did not use any DM with these functions, while natives used expressions like *perfettamente* 'perfectly', *terribilmente* 'terribly'.
- *Highlighting the lack of responsibility/expression of self-deficiency (face-saving devices).* This function is absent in It-L2's productions, whereas in It-L1's is entrusted to DMs like *proprio, veramente* with the meaning of 'as a matter of fact, really'.
- *Negotiating the act.* The DMs also play a key role in the negotiation of the act and as mechanisms for safeguarding the speaker's face but also as support for the face of the interlocutor. These functions are present both in the productions of learners and Italian speakers and are entrusted to DMs as *non lo so* 'I don't know' and *lo so/capisco/ho capito* 'I know', 'I understand'.
- *Enhancing the textual coherence of the explanation or the account.* Both groups used DMs with logical-argumentative functions, such as *ma/però* 'but/however', *quindi* 'therefore'. Natives also used *allora* 'so/then' with an inferential-consequential value.
- *Encouraging the interlocutor to accept the apology or the offer of repair.* These functions represent the directive component of apology. Both groups used exhortative expressions like *dai* 'come on' but in different contexts: It-L1

employed this DM to address an equal-intimate interlocutor (e.g. a family member), whereas It-L2 also used it in more formal contexts, where the interlocutor was a stranger.

- *Introducing the offer of repair.* Learners and natives used *magari* 'maybe', 'perhaps' to suggest a possible solution/an offer of repair. The It-L1 group also employed *tutt'al più* 'if anything' and *comunque sia* 'whatever goes' to introduce the offer.
- *Intensifying the illocutionary force of the promise of non- recurrence.* This function, which represents the commissive component of apology, is absent in learners' productions, whereas, in those of natives, it was expressed by DMs like *sicuramente* 'surely/definitely'.

6. Conclusions and Future Research

In conclusion, our analysis highlighted the strategic role of DMs in expressing complaints and apologies and in negotiating these acts between the interlocutors.

The comparison between learners and native speakers revealed differences in both the use and the variety of DMs. In general, native speakers exploited the DMs' polyfunctionality in performing the speech actscombination, combining them with politeness strategies to strengthen or attenuate the illocutionary force and guide the interlocutor's interpretation, resulting in a greater effectiveness and appropriateness to the context and the interlocutor. On the other hand, even the most advanced learners did not draw upon similar strategies. Despite using a diverse range of DMs, they exhibited lessvariability depending on contextual variables, occasionally appearing too emphatic or impositive and less appropriate when addressing a distant interlocutor or a superior.

The findings of this study could have an interesting impact on language teachers. It is advisable to teach DMs in relation to the pragmatic functions they perform in the realization of complex and delicate acts such as apologies and complaints. Moreover, specific attention should be given to the contextual and sociolinguistic variables influencing the choice of one DMs over another (e.g. the informal *dai* 'come on') to foster an effective and appropriate use of DMs in oral interactions.

In our future work, we will carry out a quantitative analysis of DMs' frequency and variety in relation to proficiency levels and contextual and sociolinguistic variables. Further analyses are also needed to clarify the role of prosody in conveying DMs' pragmatic functions in apologies and complaints, as, very often, the same form may convey different meanings, depending on its prosodic realizations (as in the case of *insomma,* see Solsona Martínez, 2015).

References

Bazzanella, C. (1995). I segnali discorsivi. In L. Renzi, G. Salvi & A. Cardinaletti. (a cura di), *Grande grammatica italiana di consultazione* (vol. III, pp. 225–257). Il Mulino.

Bazzanella, C. (2006). Discourse markers in italian: Towards a 'compositional' meaning. In K. Fischer (ed.), *Approaches to discourse particles* (pp. 449–464). Elsevier.

Bazzanella, C. & Borreguero Zuloaga M. (2011). 'Allora' e 'entonces': problemi teorici e dati empirici. In E. Khachaturyan (ed.), *Discourse markers in Romance languages* (vol. 3, pp. 7–45). Oslo Studies in Language, 1.

Blum-Kulka, S. & Olshtain, E. (1984). Requests and apologies: A Cross-Cultural Study of Speech Act Realization Patterns (CCSARP). *Applied Linguistics* 5/3, 196–213.

Blum--Kulka, S., House, J., & Kasper, G. (Eds.). (1989). *Cross--cultural pragmatics: requests and apologies*. Ablex Publishing Corporation.

Businaro, B. (2002). Lo Scusarsi tra Convenzione e Conversazione. *Studi Italiani di Linguistica Teorica e Applicata* 31/3, 471–502.

Cohen, A. D. & Olshtain, E. (1981). Developing a measure of sociocultural competence. The case of apology. *Language Learning* 31/1, 113–134. https://doi.org/10.1111/j.1467-1770.1981.tb01375.x.

Cohen, A. D., Olshtain, E., & Rosenstein, D. S. (1986). Advanced EFL apologies: What remains to be learned?. *International Journal of the Sociology of Language* 62/6, 51–74.

Culpeper J.(2011), *Impoliteness, Using Language to cause Offence*, Cambridge University Press.

De Marco, A. & Paone, E. (2019). *Bellissimo B2-C1*. Libro Studente, Corso di Italiano per Stranieri. ELI.

De Marco, A. & Paone, E. (2022). Pitch range variations in L2 Italian learners and native speakers apologies. In S. Gesuato, G. Salvato, E. & Castello, E. (eds.) *Pragmatic aspects of L2 communication: From awareness through description to assessment* (pp. 226–249). Cambridge Scholar Publishing.

De Marco, A. & Paone, E. (2022). The effects of explicit instruction on the use of discourse markers in Italian as L2. *Studi Italiani di Linguistica Teorica e Applicata* (SILTA), 3, 668-689

De Marco, A. & Paone, E. (in preparation), "'Io aspettavo in fila per due ore. Adesso è il mio turno quindi'. L'uso dei segnali discorsivi nella realizzazione delle proteste in italiano L2".

Fedriani, C. & Molinelli, P. (2019). Italian ma 'but' in deverbal pragmatic markers: Forms, functions, and productivity of a pragma-dyad. *Cuadernos de Filología Italiana* 26, 29–56. https://doi.org/10.5209/cfit.62864.

Gesuato, S. (2015). Criteria for the identification of moves: The case of written offers. In S. Gesuato, F. Bianchi, & W. Cheng (eds.), *Teaching, learning and investigating pragmatics: Principles, methods and practices* (pp. 323–361). Cambridge Scholars Publishing.

Ghezzi, C. & Molinelli, P. (2019). Italian scusa from politeness to mock politeness. *Journal of Pragmatics* 142, 245–257. https://doi.org/10.1016/j.pragma.2018.10.018.

Murphy, B. & Neu, J. (1996). My grade's too low: The speech act set of complaining. In S. M. Gass & J. Neu (eds.), *Speech Acts across cultures: Challenges to communication in second language* (pp. 191–216). Mouton de Gruyer.

Nuzzo, E. (2007). *Imparare a Fare Cose con le Parole. Richieste, Proteste, Scuse in Italiano Lingua Seconda*. Guerra.

Paone, E. (2020). Sull'Adeguatezza Prosodica nelle Proteste in Italiano L2: Uno Studio Percettivo. In A. De Meo & F. Dovetto (eds.), *La Comunicazione Parlata/Spoken Communication 2018* (Vol. 2, pp. 203–222). Aracne.

Paone, E. (2021). 'Yo Arrabbiata Perché La Cocina È Sporca e Niente Caffè': Aggressività e Cortesia Percepita nelle Proteste di Apprendenti di Italiano L2. In S. Caruana, K. Chircop, Ph. Gauci & M. Pace (eds.), *Politiche e Pratiche per l'Educazione Linguistica, il Multilinguismo e La Comunicazione Interculturale* (pp. 93–103). Edizioni Ca' Foscari.

Sansò, A. (2020). *I segnali discorsivi*. Carocci.

Solsona Martínez, C. (2015). Los marcadores discursivos en la pragmagramática del italiano/L2 para hispano hablantes: el caso de "insomma". In D. Serrano Dolader, M. Porroche Ballesteros & M. A. Martín Zorraquino (eds.), *Aspectos de la subjetividad en el lenguaje* (pp. 249–272). Institución Fernando el Católico.

Trosborg, A. (1995). *Interlanguage pragmatics. Requests, complaints and apologies*. Mouton de Gruyter.

Walker, T. (2017). Politeness norms: A pilot study on the accomplishment of apologies by learners of Italian. *EuroAmerican Journal of Applied Linguistics and Languages* E-Journal 4/2, 28–48. https://doi.org/10.21283/2376905X.7.95.

III Corpus-Based Approaches to Discourse Markers

Rogelio Nazar, Irene Renau, Hernán Robledo

8 Dismark and Text·a·Gram: Automatic Identification and Categorization of Discourse Markers in Texts

Abstract: We present a methodology for the compilation of a taxonomy of discourse markers (DMs) using a parallel corpus. We first identify the DMs in the corpus, and then classify them according to a clustering algorithm. We avoid all types of explicit linguistic knowledge to facilitate future replication of the method, as this will allow us to amplify the multilingual taxonomy. With this technique, we obtain an extensive taxonomy of DMs with these units aligned by categories (additive connectives, contrastive connectives, digression markers, among many others) and language (Catalan, English, French, German and Spanish). We also present our first tasks of an ongoing dictionary project of DMs, made from scratch using this taxonomy, with the following phases: 1. Extracting DMs from corpus; 2. Clustering DMs; 3. Labelling the clusters; 4. Populating the taxonomy with new DMs. We obtained 619 candidates for Spanish, 733 for English, 556 for French, 677 for German, and 312 for Catalan. Manual evaluation revealed 95 % precision in all languages except German, which resulted in 84 % precision. Results are displayed online in http://www.tecling.com/dismark. Concerning the dictionary project, the taxonomy of DMs obtained with the previous method is being used as the core lemma list for a Multilingual Dictionary of Discourse Markers. The dictionary is unidirectional, with Spanish as the target language, and each entry includes information about the type of DM, its function, punctuation, corpus examples, equivalents in the other 4 languages, etc. https://www.lexonomy.eu/#/dismark

Keywords: discourse markers, taxonomy, parallel corpus, dictionary

1. Introduction

In this chapter, we present a method for automatic extraction and detection of discourse markers (DMs) in corpora. We first describe Dismark[1], the project to extract DMs using parallel corpora. Parallel corpora allow to locate a target unit in a corpus and then search for its translation in parallel texts in other languages. Due to the fact that all functional texts contain DMs, one can expect to find most of the DMs if corpora are large enough. This process allows to expand the initial

1 http://www.tecling.com/dismark

set of DMs and obtain a larger number of units directly from texts. We then explain how we label these units using a handcrafted taxonomy of DMs. Finally, we present Text·a·Gram[2], one of the applications of the method. Text·a·Gram is a software to automatically detect and mark discursive features of texts, such as DMs, referents, deixis, and others. In particular, it highlights each DM in a text, indicating the type of DM in each case, and provides a summary of the number of DMs per category.

Text·a·Gram was initially created as a pedagogical software for the bachelor in Linguistics at the Pontificia Universidad Católica de Valparaíso. However, it is evolving to being also used for other related applications: Estilector (Nazar & Renau, 2023), an automated writing assistant, and the *Dismark Multilingual Dictionary of Discourse Markers* (Renau & Nazar, 2022), an online resource, also with pedagogical purposes. The specific goal of the present study is to evaluate Text·a·Gram's accuracy to detect DMs in texts. Automatic feedback of the number and type of DMs in a text is useful for a variety of tasks, including writing assistance or genre identification.

After this introduction, in Section 2 we provide a theoretical description of DMs, especially of those features that affect the computational treatment of DMs. In Section 3, we give an account of the Dismark project and the main tasks for DMs' extraction and classification. In Section 4, we describe the Text·a·Gram project and explain the results of the software evaluation. Finally, in Section 5 we offer some conclusions and future lines of development of the present study.

2. Theoretical Framework

DMs are linguistic units with specialized functions related to the argumentative, informative, or interactional organization of discourse (Martín Zorraquino & Portolés, 1999; Borreguero & Loureda, 2013). They form a functional-pragmatic category, rather than a formal, morphosyntactic class (Hansen, 1998a, 1998b; Fraser, 1999; Schourup, 1999; Martín Zorraquino & Portolés, 1999; Aijmer, 2002; Cortés & Camacho, 2005; Fischer, 2006, 2014; Stede, 2012; Rae & Asale, 2009; Borreguero & Loureda, 2013; Crible & Zufferey, 2015; Loureda & Rudka, 2020). DMs are, thus, usually observed as a scalar and dynamic phenomenon, with prototypical members showing the central characteristics of the class, and peripheral members showing less distinctive features (Jucker & Ziv, 1998; Jucker, 2002; Pons, 2006; Lutzky, 2012; Rezvani et al., 2012; Fischer, 2014; Borreguero,

2 http://www.tecling.com/textagram

2015). The DMs' class, then, is organized in a flexible continuum (Pons, 1998, 2006; Bazzanella, 2006; Fraser, 2006; Hansen, 2006), rather than in a discrete, well-defined cluster. As will be shown in Section 3, this gray area between a prototypical DM, such as *por lo tanto* 'hence', and a peripheral member, such as *y así* 'and then', correlates with the success in automatic assignment of the 'DM' label to an expression in a given text.

If we focus on the most prototypical concept of DM, it is possible to distinguish some salient features. Prototypical DMs do not hold semantic content, that is, they do not change the meaning of a sentence (Martín Zorraquino & Portolés, 1999; Moder & Martinovic-Zic, 2004). What changes, though, is the meaning of discourse, since these units fulfill functions in the processing of coherence, cohesion, adequacy, and efficacy of discourse (Blakemore, 1987; Fraser, 1990; Montolío, 2001; Bazzanella, 2006; Maschler & Schiffrin, 2015). Many DMs are also multifunctional, that is, they can fulfill different pragmatic functions in the discourse depending on the context (Schiffrin, 1987; Wierzbicka, 2003; Aijmer et al., 2006; Fischer, 2006; Fraser, 2006).

Additionally, prototypical DMs are not part of a sentence. Thus, they do not have a syntactic function at the sentence level –even when most of them are adverbs, conjunctions, or prepositions. For that reason, they have a considerable degree of autonomy, which can vary from one unit to another –e.g., *bueno* 'well' can appear in a turn of speech with total independence, as a whole statement, while *por el contrario* 'on the contrary' is less autonomous. Similarly, most DMs do not have a fixed position and can appear before, in the middle or after a sentence. In written texts, these aspects related to syntactic independence can be observed in the use of punctuation marks, which are often used to separate the DM from the previous and/or following sentence in the text –in these cases, they are called parenthetical markers (Rouchota, 1998; Montolío, 1998; Cuenca, 2001). This feature is relevant for the automatic detection of DMs in corpus, as it helps to disambiguate with respect to homonymous words or expressions (Robledo & Nazar, 2018; Nazar, 2021; Robledo, 2021; Robledo & Nazar, 2023). E.g., *con este fin,* literally 'with this purpose', is usually used without punctuation signs, as in *una tarea con este fin* 'a task with this purpose', however, when used as DM, 'to this end', it tends to be separated with a comma from the rest of the sentence, as in *Con este fin, proponen crear un programa específico* 'To this end, they propose to create a specific program'.

Another usual feature of DMs is that they have only one form (Martín Zorraquino, 1998, 2010, 2011; Portolés, 2001; Martín Zorraquino & Portolés, 1999), as they belong to the already mentioned invariable parts of speech (Pavón, 1999). DMs, thus, could be the result of a gradual process of lexicalization and grammaticalization (Lehmann, 1985; Traugott, 1995; Elvira, 2009; Mendívil, 2009; Degand & Simon-Vandenbergen, 2011; Onodera, 2011; Heine, 2013; Degand & Evers-Vermeul, 2015; Heine & Kaltenböck, 2021). In lexicalization, a certain expression is no longer analysed compositionally. E.g., *sin embargo* no longer means 'without an impediment' but 'however'. In grammaticalization, the part of speech of one or more lexical units changes and evolves from more to less referential meanings (Garachana, 1998, 2014; Company, 2004), e.g., in the previous example, the preposition *sin* 'without' and the noun *embargo* 'impediment' are grammaticalized as a whole expression with a different part of speech: adverb. This phenomenon can also be observed as a pragmaticalization process, as units change their pragmatic-discursive function (Erman & Kotsinas, 1993; Aijmer, 1997, 2002; Dostie, 2004, 2009; Günthner & Mutz, 2004; Frank-Job, 2006; Claridge & Arnovick 2010; Blas Arroyo, 2011; Degand & Evers-Vermeul, 2015).

As already stated, this invariability is not a discrete characteristic in DMs, but a continuum. Thus, some particles or expressions can be considered DMs although they are not fully lexicalized, but show instead a tendency to fixation (Casado Velarde, 1993; Martín Zorraquino & Portolés, 1999; Montolío, 2001; Briz et al., 2008; Martín Zorraquino, 2010; Calsamiglia & Tusón, 2012; Polanco, 2014; Cornillie & Gras, 2015). Examples of semi-fixed DMs are *con todo / aun con todo / con todo y con eso* 'in spite (of)', *es más / aún es más* 'what is more' or *por el contrario / antes por el contrario* 'on the contrary'. These can be considered independent DMs (Martín Zorraquino & Portolés, 1999) or variations of the same DM. Variation in DMs is a problem for automatic detection because it multiplies the forms in which the same DM can be observed in context and makes more difficult the task of identifying them as the same unit, or the same type of DM.

Together with all the already mentioned problematic aspects, a major issue related to DMs is their categorization and classification (Fischer, 2006; Loureda & Acín, 2010; Campillos & González, 2014; Borreguero, 2015; Maschler & Schiffrin, 2015; Fedriani & Sansò, 2017; Ranger, 2018; Furkó, 2020). In Spanish, there are several categorizations (Casado Velarde, 1993; Fuentes Rodríguez, 1996, 2009; Montolío, 2001; Calsamiglia & Tusón, 2012; Holgado Lage, 2017). There are also dictionaries of Spanish DMs (Santos Río, 2003; Briz et al., 2008), although they are not explicit categorizations. For the purposes of the Dismark project, though, the most suitable option is Martín Zorraquino and Portolés (1999)'s classification, because it is presented as a taxonomy. These authors classify DMs into five large groups according to various discursive functions: (i) information structurers (for example, *first of all, finally*), (ii) connectors (*therefore, however*), (iii) reformulators (*that is, better said*), (iv) argumentative operators (*in fact, in particular*) and (v) conversational markers (*well, you know*).

3. The Dismark Project

Dismark is a project for automatic extraction and categorization of DMs in several languages. It is also devoted to the development of applications for writing assistance and other tools in which DMs are involved. We use a series of algorithms for DMs induction from a parallel corpus, and we then classify them using Martín Zorraquino and Portolés (1999)'s taxonomy. After this, the classification is used to recursively identify and classify further units –a detailed description of the full process can be found in Nazar (2021). At the current state of the project, Dismark includes a taxonomy in English, Spanish, French, German, and Catalan, as well as a software for the detection and classification of DMs. Further developments of the project involve adding more languages to the taxonomy, and more units per language, among other aspects.

Parallel corpora have been previously used for different tasks related to functions and uses of DMs in different languages (Versley, 2010; Zhou et al., 2012; Hajlaoui & Popescu-Belis, 2013; Laali & Kosseim, 2014; Ramón, 2015; Hidey & McKeown, 2016; Bourgonje et al., 2017; Crible et al., 2019). However, all of them use additional linguistic resources, such as DMs lexicons, manual annotation, or syntactic rules. Along with this, they mainly study connectors, a subcategory of DMs. Other studies have also applied the back-translation technique to study aspects of the meaning or senses of specific discourse connectives in different languages (Prasad et al., 2010; Versley, 2010; Meyer et al., 2011; Popescu-Belis et al., 2012; Cartoni et al., 2013; Laali & Kosseim, 2014). As in the previous case, however, these studies also focus only on the identification of certain translation equivalences of previously defined DMs. The use of parallel corpora as input for the extraction and organization of a taxonomy of DMs of a given language is a methodological innovation of the Dismark project. In addition to the extraction of categories, the most valuable result is the exhaustive inventory of DMs that the method provides.

3.1. Method

We used the OPUS Corpus (Tiedemann, 2016), a parallel corpus which provides sets of corpora in various domains and genres, aligned at the sentence level, in TMX format, a standard in the use of translation memories (Savourel, 2005). Each pair of languages (the ones we used for the project) is around 3.5 billion tokens, distributed in around 30 corpora for each language. So far, in this project we have used the following language pairs: Spanish-English, French-English, German-English and Spanish-Catalan. The number of words per language exceeds one billion tokens in most cases.

The procedure for the extraction and classification of DMs is divided into four steps, described below.

1. *Extraction of DMs from corpora.* The first step consists of separating all DMs from the rest of the units of each target language. For this purpose, the algorithm first filters between lexical and functional units, based on the characteristic distribution of the latter in the corpus. DMs show a uniform distribution in the corpus and collocate with a large set of other words, so these words are not very informative, that is, their distributional behaviour does not usually predict the occurrence of other units. In contrast, a lexical item will occur alongside a more restricted set of units. E.g., the word *technology* often co-occurs with specific lexical items such as *research, development, information,* etc. (Figure 8.1). In contrast, the DM *after all* does not hold any informative distributional behaviour, as it co-occurs mainly with other functional units, such as *this, because* or *about* (Figure 8.2). Hence, the co-occurrence profiles are different and, in the first case, the area under the curve is larger in relative terms (i.e., ignoring absolute frequency).

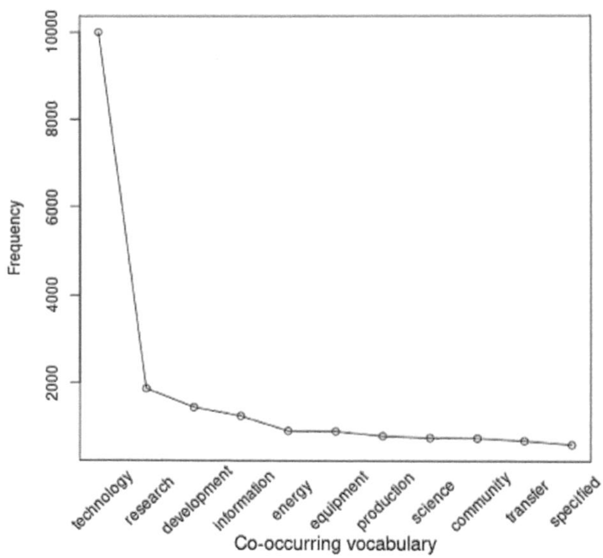

Figure 8.1. Shape of the co-occurrence frequency curve of the unit technology

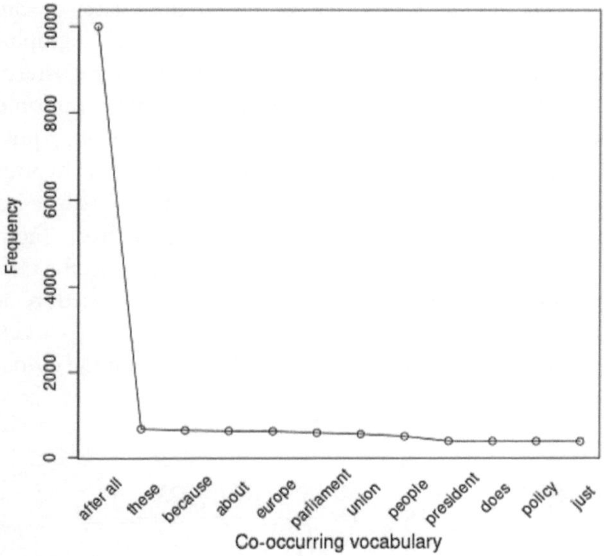

Figure 8.2. *Shape of the co-occurrence frequency curve of the English DM after all*

To capture this property, we define a coefficient (1), where x is a DM candidate; R_x the set of co-occurring units; *m(x)* the set of contexts of x and $R_{x,i}$ is the frequency of the unit at position i in the list of most frequent units in those contexts (in our experiments, $n = 20$). At one extreme, this coefficient yields a very low value for function words such as articles, conjunctions, prepositions, etc. At the opposite extreme are the more specialized vocabulary units. The cut-off value of this continuum between lexical (*L*) and functional (*F*) categories is given by an arbitrary parameter k (2).

$$I(x) = \frac{\log_2 \sum_{i=1}^{n} R_{x,i}}{\log_2 |m(x)|} \tag{1}$$

$$C(x) = \begin{cases} L, I(x) > k \\ F, otherwise \end{cases} \tag{2}$$

2. *Clustering DMs per similarity.* The second step consists of clustering the obtained DMs according to their similarity. For this task, a graph-based clustering algorithm is designed. As a similarity measure for clustering the DMs extracted in the previous step, this algorithm uses the common equivalence of DMs in a second language, hence the use of the parallel corpus. The parallel corpus is used as a 'semantic mirror'. For example, it is hypothesized that the English DMs *however* and *nevertheless* are similar because both have *sin embargo* as equivalents in Spanish. We obtain these cross-linguistic equivalences in the parallel corpus and then use them to find the corresponding intra-linguistic similarities, e.g., we repeat the same procedure and find out that *sin embargo* and *no obstante* are Spanish equivalents. To find these equivalences we apply an association coefficient (3) based on the co-occurrence of the elements in the aligned segments.

$$A\left(DM_{x,i}, DM_{y,j}\right) = \frac{f\left(DM_{x,i}, DM_{y,j}\right)}{\sqrt{f\left(DM_{x,i}\right)}\sqrt{f\left(DM_{y,j}\right)}} \tag{3}$$

With this coefficient we establish the probability that the DM i of language X is equivalent to the DM j of language Y. Once the list of cross-linguistically aligned DM pairs is obtained, the clustering process begins to obtain the intra-linguistic similarities. For each pair in this set, we check if either of the two has been present in a previously examined pair. E.g., if *por esa razón* is found in a previous pair, it can be assumed that *for that reason,* which is found in a new pair, is similar to all DMs that have already been clustered. Hence, the new DM *for that reason* is added to the already formed cluster.

3. *Labelling DMs per category.* The previous step results in an indeterminate number of clusters of DMs in each language, although at this point the system only identifies them with arbitrary numerical codes. Thus, the third stage of the method consists of assigning a category to each of the obtained clusters. For this, as already explained, we used the taxonomy of DMs by Martín Zorraquino and Portolés (1999), which contains some examples linked to each category. This allows the clusters to be automatically labelled according to these categories, because each cluster should contain these examples as part of the group. Specifically, this was achieved by calculating the intersection (4) between these examples (E) and the members of each cluster (DMC).

$$O\left(E_p, DMC_q\right) = \frac{\left|\vec{E}_p \cap \overrightarrow{DMC_q}\right|}{\left|\vec{E}_p\right|} \tag{4}$$

4. *Identification of new DMs and population of the taxonomy.* Once a basic taxonomy of DMs has been formed in step 3, it is used to classify new DMs recursively. Given a candidate DM, it is first classified by language and then the unit follows the steps 1, 2, and 3 already described. For all tasks, the same parallel corpus is used. If the candidate is a true DM, its category will be indicated by the parallel corpus. For example, a Spanish candidate such as *de la misma manera* will have English elements such as *in the same way*, *likewise*, *similarly*, etc., as equivalents according to the parallel corpus. As these equivalents are already registered in the English part of the taxonomy, it is then concluded that the candidate *de la misma manera* is a correct DM (as in step 1) and belongs to the same category (as in step 3).

3.2. Current State of the Project

At this moment, the multilingual taxonomy of DMs that is being built contains 2,897 elements in total: 619 in Spanish, 733 in English, 556 in French, 677 in German and 312 in Catalan. These units are divided into 70 functional categories.

We evaluated the precision of the procedure for all languages involved. For that purpose, we reviewed all DMs contained in the taxonomy and counted the number of cases of the following three cases:

(a) An extracted element was not a DMs, e.g., *cambio* 'change' (a mistake for *en cambio* 'instead').
(b) An extracted multi-word candidate was not correctly segmented and, then, it was not a correct DM, e.g., *aun en* 'even in'.
(c) The extracted element was a DM and it was correctly segmented but it was not correctly classified in a category, e.g., labeling a counter-argumentative DM as an additive DM.

According to this evaluation, precision was 95 % average in all languages except German, where we found 84 % of true positives, mostly due to problems with segmentation.

Table 8.1 shows an example of one of the clusters, labeled with the category of counter-argumentative connectors, that is, those DMs used to express an argument which is opposed to another previous argument, according to Martín Zorraquino and Portolés (1999)'s taxonomy.

Table 8.1. Example of one of the clusters corresponding to the category of counter-argumentative connectors

Language	DMs
English	*all the same; although; and yet; but; but still; despite all; despite the fact that; despite these; despite this; even if; even so; even though; however; in spite of all; in spite of the fact; nevertheless; nonetheless; that being said; that said; though; while; yet*
Spanish	*a cambio; ahora bien; al contrario; aparte de eso; a pesar de ello; a pesar de eso; a pesar de esto; a pesar de todo; aun así; aun cuando; aun en; aunque; bien que; con todo; de cualquier forma; de cualquier modo; de todas formas; de todas maneras; de todos modos; dicho esto; en cambio; en lugar de eso; en vez de eso; incluso aunque; no obstante; pero; pero aun así; pese a ello; pese a todo; por el contrario; si bien; sin embargo; todo lo contrario; y sin embargo*
French	*cependant; et pourtant; mais encore; mais toujours; malgré cela; malgré tout; même ainsi; même si; néanmoins; pourtant; toutefois*
German	*aber immer noch; aber nicht; aber trotzdem; allerdings; auch wenn; auftreten müssen; dachte; dennoch; jedoch; obwohl; selbst wenn; sogar; trotzdem; trotz der tatsache; trotz dieser; trotz dieses*
Catalan	*al contrari; ans al contrari; ben al contrari; de qualsevol manera; de tota manera; de totes formes; de totes maneres; en comptes d'això; en lloc d'això; i no obstant això; malgrat això; no obstant; pel contrari; però tot i així; tanmateix; tot el contrari; tot i així; tot i això*

Table 8.1 shows a variety of units that, in a wide percentage, match the existing classifications of DMs. We can also observe some errors, such *aun en* 'even in' for Spanish, in which the algorithm failed to correctly separate the DM from the rest of the text. We also find expressions that are not usually classified as a DM, such as *y sin embargo* 'and nevertheless', but we do not consider this an error, but an example of the flexibility of the concept of DM that we described in Section 2: these two particles (*y* 'and' and *sin embargo* 'nevertheless') are found together very frequently and the algorithm considers them as merged in a single unit: indeed, in this case, we observe that the function of the conjunction *y* is subsumed by the DM *sin embargo* and becomes a spurious particle, although it is frequent to find it because probably the authors want to emphasize the link between two ideas. The aspects related to variation in DMs are currently being studied by Hernán Robledo in the Fondecyt Postdoctoral Project No. 3230617.

This, among other aspects, proves that the method is not only useful for applications, but also as empirical evidence to support theory. In addition, we find DMs that have not been registered in the literature, as the variant *a pesar de esto*, which is not found in the extensive catalog by Santos Río (2003). This shows potential for the method to be applied to the enlargement of existing classifications in each language, but also for specialized corpora that could include less widespread, more genre-specific units that are often missing from generic classifications.

4. The Text·a·Gram Project

Text·a·Gram is a software for automatically detecting, marking, and categorizing reference, deixis, modalization, and DMs in a given text. At the moment, it only works with Spanish, but we are gradually expanding it for the rest of the languages. Currently, only the detection of DMs is available on the languages of the Dismark project, and in this section we will deal only with the part of software devoted to DMs.

Text·a·Gram is powered by the Dismark database. Hence, it will evolve together with it, as more DMs are added to the list, following the iterative process shown in Section 3. So far, Text·a·Gram does not include any additional procedure to disambiguate an expression in the analysed text, as it only uses the list of Dismark's DMs. For example, it does not use any rule for detecting parenthetic DMs, which are found more frequently between punctuation signs (see Section 2). The software works in a web interface and allows the user to paste a text, and then displays the same text with the DM candidates highlighted in colour (one colour per category). It also shows the name of each category next to the DM and offers a list of tables with a summary of the type and number of DMs that were used in that text. This helps the user to automatically analyse DMs in a text for different applications, e.g., writing assistance, discourse analysis, translation, etc.

Figure 8.3 shows an example of a fragment analysed by Text·a·Gram, in which three DM candidates were correctly identified and labeled per category. The figure also shows an example of an incorrect case (*en ese caso* 'in that case') which here is not used as a DM but rather as an anaphora.

Es posible que, por temor a los iraníes, los gobiernos árabes se vean empujados a aproximarse a Estados Unidos, país que detestan, e **incluso [Conector aditivo]** que descubran intereses comunes con Israel. **Ahora bien [Conector contraargumentativo]**, **en ese caso [Operador de concreción]**, su divorcio de la opinión pública de sus países puede llegar a ser explosivo. Habrá tentaciones de guerra santa, no contra los infieles y los cruzados, sino contra todos los herejes o supuestos herejes en los diversos campos musulmanes enfrentados.

Figure 8.3. A fragment of text analysed by Text·a·Gram

We evaluated precision and recall of Text·a·Gram, comparing the software's performance against human judgment. We analysed 20 journalistic texts, specifically, editorials and opinion pieces, as these are argumentative genres which are supposed to contain a high number of DMs. Two evaluators annotated the same 20 texts –one evaluator was a member of the Dismark team, and the other one was an external evaluator which had been trained in the same type of annotation. The evaluation task consisted of reading each text marked by Text·a·Gram and indicating correct and incorrect marks (for precision), together with the cases that were not detected by the software (for recall).

In total, the evaluators marked 307 decisions (correct, incorrect, absent) and had disagreement in 27 cases (8.8 %). This percentage, which is relatively low, is due to the non-discrete nature of DMs, that can be semi-fixed expressions and give reasons to classify them as DMs or as adverbs or conjunctions with a function in the sentence level. As discussed in section 2, DMs are at different stages in the processes of grammaticalization and lexicalization, and this fact makes their empirical identification difficult. To solve these discrepancies, a third evaluator (member of the Dismark team) was used to break ties. Results of the evaluation are shown in Table 8.2.

Table 8.2. Results of the evaluation of Text·a·Gram

	N	%
True positives (correct Text·a·Gram marks)	212	74.38
False positives (incorrect Text·a·Gram marks)	73	25.61
False negatives (DMs not detected by Text·a·Gram)	22	7.16
Total Text·a·Gram marks	**285**	
Total marks	**307**	

Results show that the software could accurately detect and classify 74.38 % of the DM candidates, and covered almost all of them in the text, leaving only 7.16 % undetected. Errors of detection are due to ambiguous forms (expressions or words that can have other functions different from DMs) and to the flexible nature of these particles. This problem derives from the fact that, as we explained in Section 2, DMs form a class defined by functional criteria, in which their members come from different parts of speech. For example, the software lacks precision in cases such as *también* 'also', because it is frequently used as an adverb in the sentence level, e.g., in 'las *también* multicentenarias raíces' 'the also multicentennial roots', in which the particle has a clear syntactic function as adverb. It seems that Text·a·Gram underperforms especially with one-word DMs, such as the cited *también, igualmente* 'similarly', etc., since they are more likely to be ambiguous. Other errors are due to the fact that, as said at the beginning of Section 4, Text·a·Gram does not have specific rules for identifying parenthetic units. E.g., in '*Esto es* una paradoja extraordinaria' '*This is* an extraordinary paradox', the software incorrectly indicates *esto es* as the reformulator DM 'that is', when it is really a pronoun and a verb. The exclusion of rule-based methods is made on purpose because it allows flexibility regarding language, genres, and other variables. One may attempt to increase precision by adding supplementary rules per language or genre –as has been done in other studies (Robledo & Nazar, 2018; Robledo, 2021; Robledo & Nazar, 2023)–, but it is challenging to do so without harming flexibility and recall. The inclusion of rules regarding punctuation signs or other aspects associated with applications of Dismark to specific genres could be tasks for the future.

5. Conclusions and Future Work

In this chapter, we gave an account of the current state of the Dismark project, devoted to detection and classification of DMs from corpora. We also described Text·a·Gram, a ready-to-use tool which marks DMs in a given text and classifies them for the user. Both projects are inter-connected and perform well enough to be used for plenty of applications, including language teaching, writing assistance, or translation. They can also be used as software for helping linguists to find empirical evidence of the use of DMs in real texts and eventually contribute, with usage data, to increase the inventories of DMs classified in the different theoretical categories, some of them mentioned in Section 2. For future work, we contemplate to continue populating the Dismark taxonomy with more units and improve Text·a·Gram precision. A new version of this software will soon be offering the user the possibility to process a large set of documents at the same time in order to compute statistics of the distribution of DMs and other elements. As said in Section 1, both projects are also connected to Estilector (Nazar & Renau, 2023) and with the *Dismark Multilingual Dictionary of Discourse Markers* (Renau & Nazar, 2022), two resources for language learning and writing assistance currently in progress. We plan to continue developing these tools and improving the inter-connection between the different software.

Acknowledgments

We thank ANID (Government of Chile) for funding the third author through the Fondecyt Postdoctoral Project No. 3230617. We also thank the reviewers for their comments.

References

Aijmer, K. (1997). Epistemic modality as a discourse phenomenon – a Swedish-English cross-language perspective. In U. Fries, V. Müller & P. Schneider (eds.), *From Ælfric to the New York Times: Studies in English corpus linguistics* (pp. 215–226). Rodopi.

Aijmer, K. (2002). *English discourse particles: Evidence from a corpus*. John Benjamins.

Aijmer, K., Foolen, A., & Simon-Vandenbergen, A.-M. (2006). Pragmatic markers in translation: A methodological proposal. In K. Fischer (ed.), *Approaches to Discourse Particles* (pp. 101–114). Elsevier.

Bazzanella, C. (2006). Discourse markers in Italian: Towards a 'compositional' meaning. In K. Fischer (ed.), *Approaches to discourse particles* (pp. 449–464). Elsevier.

Blakemore, D. (1987). *Semantic constraints on relevance*. Blackwell.

Blas Arroyo, J. L. (2011). From politeness to discourse marking: The process of pragmaticalization of *muy bien* in vernacular Spanish. *Journal of Pragmatics* 43/3, 855–874.

Borreguero, M. (2015). A vueltas con los marcadores del discurso: de nuevo sobre su delimitación y sus funciones. In A. Ferrari, L. Lala & R. Stojmenova (eds.), *Testualità: Fondamenti, unità, relazioni. Textualité: Fondements, unités, relations. Textualidad: Fundamentos, unidades, relaciones* (pp. 151–170). Franco Cesati.

Borreguero, M. & Loureda, Ó. (2013). Los marcadores del discurso: ¿un capítulo inexistente de la NGLE? *LEA. Lingüística Española Actual* 35/2, 181–210.

Bourgonje, P., Grishina, Y., & Stede, M. (2017). Toward a bilingual lexical database on connectives: Exploiting a German/Italian parallel corpus. In *Proceedings of the Fourth Italian Conference on Computational Linguistics (CLiC-it 2017)* (pp. 53–58). Rome, Italy.

Briz, A., Pons, S., & Portolés, J. (coords.) (2008). *Diccionario de partículas discursivas del español* [on line]. http://www.dpde.es

Calsamiglia, H. & Tusón, A. (2012). *Las cosas del decir: manual de análisis del discurso* (3a. ed.). Ariel.

Campillos, L. & González, P. (2014). Oral production of discourse markers by intermediate learners of Spanish: A corpus perspective. In J. Romero-Trillo (ed.), *Yearbook of corpus linguistics and pragmatics 2014. New empirical and theoretical paradigms* (pp. 239–259). Springer.

Cartoni, B., Zufferey, S., & Meyer, T. (2013). Annotating the meaning of discourse connectives by looking at their translation: The translation-spotting technique. *Dialogue & Discourse*, 4/2, 65–86.

Casado Velarde, M. (1993). *Introducción a la gramática del texto del español.* Arco/Libros.

Claridge, C. & Arnovick, L. (2010). Pragmaticalisation and discursivisation. In A. H. Jucker & I. Taavitsainen (eds.), *Historical pragmatics* (pp. 165–192). De Gruyter Mouton.

Company, C. (2004). ¿Gramaticalización o desgramaticalización? Reanálisis y subjetivación de verbos como marcadores discursivos en la historia del español. *Revista de Filología Española* 84/1, 29–66.

Cornillie, B. & Gras, P. (2015). On the interactional dimension of evidentials: The case of the Spanish evidential discourse markers. *Discourse Studies* 17(2), 141–161.

Cortés, L. M. & Camacho, M. M. (2005). *Unidades de segmentación y marcadores del discurso: elementos esenciales en el procesamiento discursivo oral.* Arco/Libros.

Crible, L., Abuczki, Á., Burkšaitienė, N., Furkó, P., Nedoluzhko, A., Rackevičienė, S., Oleškevičienė, G. V. & Zikánová, Š. (2019). Functions and translations of discourse markers in TED Talks: A parallel corpus study of underspecification in five languages. *Journal of Pragmatics* 142, 139–155.

Crible, L. & Zufferey, S. (2015). Using a unified taxonomy to annotate discourse markers in speech and writing. In H. Bunt (ed.), *Proceedings of the 11th Joint ACL-ISO Workshop on Interoperable Semantic Annotation* (isa-11) (pp. 14–22). London, UK.

Cuenca, M. J. (2001). Los conectores parentéticos como categoría gramatical. *LEA. Lingüística Española Actual* 23/2, 211–236.

Degand, L. & Evers-Vermeul, J. (2015). Grammaticalization or pragmaticalization of discourse markers? More than a terminological issue. *Journal of Historical Pragmatics* 16/1, 59–85.

Degand, L. & Simon-Vandenbergen, A. M. (2011). Introduction: Grammaticalization and (inter) subjectification of discourse markers. *Linguistics* 49/2, 287–294.

Dostie, G. (2004). *Pragmaticalisation et marqueurs discursifs: Analyse sémantique et traitement lexicographique.* De Boeck & Larcier.

Dostie, G. (2009). Discourse markers and regional variation in French: A lexico-semantic approach. In K. Beeching, N. Armstrong & F. Gadet (eds.), *Sociolinguistic variation in contemporary French* (pp. 201–214). John Benjamins.

Elvira, J. (2009). *Evolución lingüística y cambio sintáctico*. Peter Lang.

Erman, B. & Kotsinas, U.-B. (1993). Pragmaticalization: The case of *ba'* and *you know'*. In J. Falk, K. Jonasson, G. Melchers & B. Nilsson (eds.), *Studier i Modern Språkvetenskap* (Vol. 10, pp. 76–93). Almqvist & Wiksell.

Fedriani, C. & Sansò, A. (2017). Pragmatic markers, discourse markers and modal particles: What do we know and where do we go from here? In C. Fedriani & A. Sansò (eds.), *Pragmatic markers, discourse markers and modal particles. New perspectives* (pp. 1–33). John Benjamins.

Fischer, K. (2006). Towards an understanding of the spectrum of approaches to discourse particles: Introduction to the volume. In K. Fischer (ed.), *Approaches to discourse particles* (pp. 1–20). Elsevier.

Fischer, K. (2014). Discourse markers. In K. Schneider & K. Barron (eds.), *Pragmatics of discourse* (pp. 271–294). De Gruyter Mouton.

Frank-Job, B. (2006). A dynamic-interactional approach to discourse markers. In K. Fischer (ed.), *Approaches to discourse particles* (pp. 395–413). Elsevier.

Fraser, B. (1990). An approach to discourse markers. *Journal of Pragmatics* 14/3, 383–395.

Fraser, B. (1999). What are discourse markers? *Journal of Pragmatics* 31, 931–952.

Fraser, B. (2006). Towards a theory of discourse markers. In K. Fischer (ed.), *Approaches to discourse particles* (pp. 189–204). Elsevier.

Fuentes Rodríguez, C. (1996). *La sintaxis de los relacionantes supraoracionales*. Arco/Libros.

Fuentes Rodríguez, C. (2009). *Diccionario de conectores y operadores del español*. Arco/Libros.

Furkó, B. P. (2020). *Discourse markers and beyond: Descriptive and critical perspectives on discourse-pragmatic devices across genres and languages*. Palgrave Macmillan.

Garachana, M. (1998). La evolución de los conectores contraargumentativos: la gramaticalización de *no obstante* y *sin embargo*. In M. A. Martín Zorraquino & E. Montolío (eds.), *Los marcadores del discurso. Teoría y análisis* (pp. 193–212). Arco/Libros.

Garachana, M. (2014). Gramática e historia textual en la evolución de los marcadores discursivos. El caso de *no obstante*. *Rilce. Revista de Filología Hispánica* 30/3, 959–984.

Günthner, S. & Mutz, K. (2004). Grammaticalization vs. pragmaticalization? The development of pragmatic markers in German and Italian. In W. Bisang, N. Himmelmann & B. Wiemer, B. (eds.), *What makes grammaticalization? A look from its fringes and its components* (pp. 77–107). Mouton de Gruyter.

Hajlaoui, N. & Popescu-Belis, A. (2013). Assessing the accuracy of discourse connective translations: Validation of an automatic metric. In *Proceedings of the international conference on intelligent text processing and computational linguistics* (pp. 236–247). Springer.

Hansen, M.-B. M. (1998a). *The function of discourse particles: A study with special reference to spoken standard French*. John Benjamins.

Hansen, M.-B. M. (1998b). The semantic status of discourse markers. *Lingua* 104, 235–260.

Hansen, M.-B. M. (2006). A dynamic polysemy approach to the lexical semantics of discourse markers (with an exemplary analysis of French *toujours*). In K. Fischer (ed.), *Approaches to discourse particles* (pp. 21–41). Elsevier.

Heine, B. (2013). On discourse markers: Grammaticalization, pragmaticalization, or something else? *Linguistics* 51/6, 1205–1247.

Heine, B. & Kaltenböck, G. (2021). From clause to discourse marker: On the development of comment clauses. *Language Sciences* 87, 1–16.

Hidey, C. & McKeown, K. (2016). Identifying causal relations using parallel Wikipedia articles. In *Proceedings of the 54th annual meeting of the association for computational linguistics (Volume I: Long papers)* (pp. 1424–1433). Association for Computational Linguistics.

Holgado Lage, A. (2017). *Diccionario de marcadores discursivos para estudiantes de español como segunda lengua*. Peter Lang.

Jucker, A. H. (2002). Discourse markers in Early Modern English. In R. Watts & P. Trudgill (eds.), *Alternative Histories of English* (pp. 210–230). Routledge.

Jucker, A. H. & Ziv, Y. (1998). Discourse markers: Introduction. In A. H. Jucker & Y. Ziv (eds.), *Discourse markers: Descriptions and theory* (pp. 1–12). John Benjamins.

Laali, M. & Kosseim, L. (2014). Inducing discourse connectives from parallel texts. In *Proceedings of COLING 2014, the 25th International Conference on Computational Linguistics: Technical Papers* (pp. 610–619). Dublin, Ireland.

Lehmann, C. (1985). Grammaticalization: Synchronic variation and diachronic change. *Lingua e Stile* 20/3, 303–318.

Loureda, Ó. & Acín, E. (2010) *Los estudios sobre marcadores del discurso en español hoy*. Arco/Libros.

Loureda, Ó. & Rudka, M. (2020). Prólogo. In Ó. Loureda, M. Rudka & G. Parodi (coords.), *Marcadores del discurso y lingüística contrastiva en las lenguas románicas* (pp. 9–16). Iberoamericana/Vervuert.

Lutzky, U. (2012). *Discourse markers in Early Modern English*. John Benjamins.

Martín Zorraquino, M. A. (1998). Los marcadores del discurso desde el punto de vista gramatical. In M. A. Martín Zorraquino & E. Montolío (eds.), *Los marcadores del discurso. Teoría y análisis* (pp. 19–53). Arco/libros.

Martín Zorraquino, M. A. (2010). Los marcadores del discurso y su morfología. In Ó. Loureda & E. Acín (coords.), *Los estudios sobre marcadores del discurso en español, hoy* (pp. 93–181). Arco/Libros.

Martín Zorraquino, M. A. (2011). El tratamiento de los marcadores del discurso en la *Nueva gramática de la lengua española* (*NGLE*) de la Real Academia Española. In J. J. de Bustos, R. Cano, E. Méndez & A. López Serena (coords.), *Sintaxis y análisis del discurso hablado en español: homenaje a Antonio Narbona* (vol. II, pp. 843–864). Secretariado de Publicaciones de la Universidad de Sevilla.

Martín Zorraquino, M. A. & Portolés, J. (1999). Los marcadores del discurso. In I. Bosque & V. Demonte (dirs.), *Gramática descriptiva de la lengua española* (vol. 3, pp. 4051–4213). Espasa Calpe.

Maschler, Y. & Schiffrin, D. (2015). Discourse markers: Language, meaning, and context. In D. Tannen, H. E. Hamilton & D. Schiffrin (eds.), *The handbook of discourse analysis* (2nd ed., pp. 189–221). John Wiley & Sons.

Mendívil, J. L. (2009). Palabras con estructura externa. In E. de Miguel (ed.), *Panorama de lexicología* (pp. 83–112). Ariel.

Meyer, T., Roze, C., Cartoni, B., Danlos, L., Zufferey, S., & Popescu-Belis, A. (2011). Disambiguating discourse connectives using parallel corpora: Senses vs. translations. In *CorpLing2011, Proceedings of the sixth corpus linguistics conference* (pp. 104–105). Birmingham, UK.

Moder, C. L. & Martinovic-Zic, A. (2004). *Discourse across languages and cultures*. John Benjamins.

Montolío, E. (1998). La teoría de la relevancia y el estudio de los marcadores discursivos. In M. A. Martín Zorraquino & E. Montolío (coords.), *Los marcadores del discurso: teoría y análisis* (pp. 93–119). Arco/Libros.

Montolío, E. (2001). *Conectores de la lengua escrita. Contraargumentativos, consecutivos, aditivos y organizadores de la información*. Ariel.

Nazar, R. (2021). Inducción automática de una taxonomía multilingüe de marcadores discursivos: primeros resultados en castellano, inglés, francés, alemán y catalán. *Procesamiento del Lenguaje Natural* 67, 127–138.

Nazar, R. & Renau, I. (2023). Estilector: un sistema de evaluación automática de la escritura académica en castellano. *Perspectiva Educacional,* 62/2, 37–59.

Onodera, N. O. (2011). The grammaticalization of discourse markers. In H. Narrog & B. Heine (eds.), *The Oxford Handbook of Grammaticalization* (pp. 614–624). Oxford University Press.

Pavón, M. V. (1999). Clases de partículas: preposición, conjunción y adverbio. In I. Bosque & V. Demonte (dirs.), *Gramática descriptiva de la lengua española* (Vol. 1, pp. 565–655). Espasa Calpe.

Polanco, F. (2014). Variación funcional y polisemia en la descripción de marcadores conversacionales en español peninsular: el caso de "vaya". *Revista Española de Lingüística* 44/2, 131–164.

Pons, S. (1998). *Conexión y conectores: estudio de su relación en el registro informal de la lengua.* Anejo XXVII de *Cuadernos de Filología.* Universidad de Valencia.

Pons, S. (2006). A functional approach to the study of discourse markers. In K. Fischer (ed.), *Approaches to discourse particles* (pp. 77–99). Elsevier.

Popescu-Belis, A., Meyer, T., Liyanapathirana, J., Cartoni, B., & Zufferey, S. (2012). Discourse-level annotation over Europarl for machine translation: Connectives and pronouns. In *Proceedings of the eighth international conference on Language Resources and Evaluation (LREC'12)* (pp. 2716–2720). European Language Resources Association.

Portolés, J. (2001). *Marcadores del discurso.* Ariel.

Prasad, R., Joshi, A. & Webber, B. (2010). Realization of discourse relations by other means: Alternative lexicalizations. In *Proceedings of the 23rd International Conference on Computational Linguistics (COLING 2010)* (Posters Volume, pp. 1023–1031). Chinese Information Processing Society of China.

Real Academia Española [RAE] & Asociación de Academias de la Lengua Española [ASALE]. (2009). *Nueva gramática de la lengua española.* Espasa.

Ramón, N. (2015). The English discourse particle 'oh' in Spanish translations: Evidence from a parallel corpus. *Procedia–Social and Behavioral Sciences* 173, 337–342.

Ranger, G. (2018). *Discourse markers: An enunciative approach.* Springer.

Renau, I. & Nazar, R. (2022). Towards a multilingual dictionary of discourse markers. In A. Klosa-Kückelhaus, S. Engelberg, C. Möhrs & P. Storjohann (eds.), *Dictionaries and society. Proceedings of the XX EURALEX international congress* (pp. 262–272). IDS-Verlag.

Rezvani, S. A., Abdullah, A. N., Mukundan, J., & Tannacito, D. J. (2012). Discourse connectors: An overview of the history, definition and classification of the term. *World Applied Sciences Journal* 19/11, 1659–1673.

Robledo, H. (2021). *Categorización de los marcadores del discurso del español: una propuesta inductiva guiada por corpus paralelo.* PhD thesis, Pontificia Universidad Católica de Valparaíso, Valparaíso. https://catalogo.pucv.cl/cgi-bin/koha/opac-detail.pl?biblionumber=434483

Robledo, H. & Nazar, R. (2018). Clasificación automatizada de marcadores discursivos. *Procesamiento del Lenguaje Natural* 61, 109–116.

Robledo, H. & Nazar, R. (2023). A proposal for the inductive categorisation of parenthetical discourse markers in Spanish using parallel corpora. *International Journal of Corpus Linguistics* 28/4, 500–527.

Rouchota, V. (1998). Procedural meaning and parenthetical discourse markers. In A. Jucker & Y. Ziv (eds.), *Discourse markers: Description and theory* (pp. 97–126). John Benjamins.

Santos Río, L. (2003). *Diccionario de partículas.* Luso-española de ediciones.

Savourel, Y. (2005). *TMX 1.4 g specification.* Localization Industry Standards Association (LISA). http://www.gala-global.org/oscarStandards/tmx/tmx14b.html.

Schiffrin, D. (1987). *Discourse markers.* Cambridge University Press.

Schourup, L. C. (1999). Discourse markers. *Lingua* 107/(3–4), 227–265.

Stede, M. (2012). Discourse processing. *Synthesis Lectures on Human Language Technologies* 4/3, 1–165.

Tiedemann, J. (2016). OPUS – Parallel corpora for everyone. In *Proceedings of the 19th annual conference of the European Association of Machine Translation (EAMT): Projects/Products* (p. 384). Riga, Latvia.

Traugott, E. C. (1995). The role of the development of discourse markers in a theory of grammaticalization. In *12th international conference on Historical Linguistics.* Manchester: The University of Manchester.

Versley, Y. (2010). Discovery of ambiguous and unambiguous discourse connectives via annotation projection. In *Proceedings of the workshop on Annotation and Exploitation of Parallel Corpora (AEPC)* (pp. 83–92). Tartu, Estonia.

Wierzbicka, A. (2003). *Cross-cultural pragmatics: The semantics of human interaction.* Mouton de Gruyter.

Zhou, L., Gao, W., Li, B., Wei, Z., & Wong, K.-F. (2012). Cross-lingual identification of ambiguous discourse connectives for resource-poor language. In *Proceedings of the 24th international conference on Computational Linguistics (COLING 2012): Posters* (pp. 1409–1418). Mumbai, India.

Bianca Maria Alecu

9 Digital Discourse Markers in Romanian Forum Communication: The Case of *welp*, *TBH (to be honest)* and *TBF (to be fair)*

Abstract: Previous studies have shown that mediated online interaction may be analysed using models of unmediated verbal interaction developed by pragmatics and conversation analysis. This study is concerned with computer-mediated communication (CMC) in the case of the Romanian subreddit r/Romania, part of the well-known international forum Reddit. We aim to investigate the forms and functions of discourse markers occurring in forum interactions. Our study focuses on three English borrowings that occur in Romanian forum conversations: *welp* (< eng. *well*), TBH (*to be honest*) and TBF (*to be fair*). We apply Crible and Degand's 2019 model of annotating discourse markers using the two dimensions of domains and functions. Our main objective is to describe the discursive functions of these markers in CMC. A secondary objective is to analyse the interaction between English borrowings and code-switching sequences in the case of discourse markers. We finally propose the term *digital discourse markers* to describe the specificity of our object of study.

Keywords: discourse markers, pragmatics, computer-mediated communication, online interaction

1. Introduction

Computer-mediated communication and discourse have been the topic of multidisciplinary research since the early 1990s. In the last decade there have been multiple pragmatics and discourse handbooks dedicated to online communication, digital communication, technologically-mediated interaction or social media (see S. Herring, D. Stein, T. Virtanen (eds.), 2013; Ch. Hoffmann, W. Bublitz (eds.), 2017, among others). What may be called *internet linguistics* (Crystal, 2006, 2011; McCulloch, 2020) is a scientific research area concerned with issues like: linguistic variation across internet modes, platforms, applications and devices, synchronous vs. asynchronous online interaction, internet generations (McCulloch, 2020) and their employment of linguistic and multimodal strategies, context in the digital environment (see the notion of context-collapse elaborated by Marwick & boyd, 2011), multiple online selves, speech acts on social networking sites (SNS, boyd & Ellison, 2007), and so on. Multiple theoretical models have been proposed for analysing online communication in the last three decades. One of the earliest and most used conceptual frameworks for explaining online communication practices is modelling online communication based on theories developed for face-to-face interaction like, for instance, the theory of relevance (Yus, 2011). Other models are inherently interdisciplinary and take into account the multimodality of the online medium, which cannot be analysed from a linguistics-only point of view (Herring, 2018). Another very popular framework for online communication is based on the scripturality vs. orality continuum (Carter, 2004: 175; Crystal, 2006, 2011), especially relevant for stylistic or linguistic variation studies.

Forum interaction has been less studied than its synchronous counterparts such as chat or instant messaging (Arendholz, 2017). Forums are usually associated with a first-era of online interaction also known as pre-web, taking place between 1983 and 1993, according to Herring (2018; see also O'Reilly, 2012). Forum and e-mail communication have been historically some of the first peer-to-peer technologically mediated communication. While e-mail typically facilitates one-to-one (formal) interactions, forums are usually an example of a one-to-many or many-to-many interaction.

Reddit data has been used for statistical purposes in linguistic, psychological and other studies (Proferes et al., 2021). Because of the emergence of new technological affordances, online corpora have appeared as an innovative solution to observing real, contemporary language in action. However, Reddit data has not only been used for quantitative analysis, since a lot of research in pragmatics, conversation analysis or discourse analysis is based on case studies of Reddit communities. These studies involve selecting content from threads as prototypical examples of interaction in qualitative analyses (see, for instance, Dynel & Poppi, 2019).

2. Theoretical Background

2.1. Computer-Mediated Communication and Discourse

Computer-mediated communication is a term proposed by Susan Herring (1996, 2018, among others) in order to describe any human-to-human interaction via an intelligent machine, part of a network of devices. Recently, with the advent of smartphones, the term has been used to refer to any technological device that can be used for communication, from laptops and tablets to the afore-mentioned smartphones. Computer-mediated discourse is the theoretical counterpart of CMC: 'the communication produced when human beings interact with one another by transmitting messages via networked or mobile computers, where computers are defined broadly to include any digital communication device' (Herring & Androutsopoulos, 2015: 127)[1].

2.2. Forum Communication

Forums (or fora, if we relate the term to its Latin etymon) are a digital space of conversation and interaction between people who share common interests or, as Arendholz (2017: 127) puts it, 'platforms of communication for self-selected participants who collect, categorize and offer contents relevant for other members, thereby shaping their very own communicative environment both topically as well as interpersonally'. Historically, forums have emerged as message boards and chain e-mails (mailing lists) were being developed in the early 1990s as hybrids of mass-communication and interpersonal communication. One of the first ancestors of present forums is Usenet, a network of host-computers that required users to connect through a special program called *newsreader*. Currently, forums are widely available and do not require special additional programs in order for anyone to read, post and comment in their respective communities. One of the largest and most successful forums is Reddit, an American-based service that hosts more than 100,000 active subreddits or communities (Reddit, 2023), i.e. groups of people organised around common interests. The number of individual users of Reddit is also very high, with more than 70 million daily active users worldwide (Reddit, 2023).

Forums have some general features that constitute their specificity in the online medium. Briefly, forums are characterized by (see also Arendholz, 2017):

- a large number of participants who contribute to discussions as original posters (OP) or commenters;
- discursive and social power imbalance between normal users and moderators, who have the option of banning others from participating (silencing them, essentially) or by excluding them altogether from the community;

---

1 For the purposes of this paper, we do not distinguish between communication, discourse and text, although we are aware of the terminological issues in conversation analysis, discourse analysis, pragmatics and textual studies. We will follow the understanding of discourse as presented by Susan Herring and Jannis Androutsopoulos (2013) for the online environment. However, in our opinion, CMC is focused on the *process* of conversation (and can be the object of conversation analysis), while CMD refers to discourse as a *result* of conversation, so, in other words, discourse as a collaborative product of online interactants.

- polylogues that are thematically organized, in which members are self-selected 'speakers' (participants) that submit written accounts in the forms of comments;
- the monotopicality of threads or even communities; in the case of threads, the conversation theme is established by the original post (the 'topic' in emic terms); off-topic behaviour is reprimanded by the community;
- multiple unwritten social, pragmatic and linguistic conventions that regulate the community as a community of practice. Examples of these norms are: the appropriate length of a comment before it becomes TL; DR (*Too long; didn't read*) relating to the topic and general atmosphere of the conversation (humorous / non-humorous), engaging in verbal play or phantasy-scenarios, using graphical conventions to mark tone of voice (McCulloch, 2020) or pragmatic information (Heath, 2018). This can be seen in the use of random capitals to suggest the imitation of another person's voice or behaviours (postulating a discursive persona, in Goffmanian terms), simultaneously marking one's stance[2].

Previous studies of forums are relatively scarce compared to the interest gained by chat communication, social media or social networking sites such as Twitter (Zappavigna, 2012, 2017) and, recently, smartphone communication (Yus, 2021). However, interesting applications of theoretical models developed by pragmatics, conversation analysis or discourse analysis may be read in Baym's (1997) study of a soap-opera forum from an interpersonal perspective, Kasunic and Kaufman's (2018) analysis of abrasive humour on Reddit, Vepsäläinen's (2022) conversation analytic approach to advice-seeking on Reddit and others.

2.3. Discourse Markers

Discourse markers (DMs) have been the topic of numerous studies and theoretical debates. The seminal study of Schiffrin (1987)[3] situates discourse markers at the intersection of interpersonal meaning and discursive action. These elements of discourse in interaction constitute a homogenous group from a functional point of view, albeit a formally diverse one (see Guțu Romalo (coord.) 2008).

2 Random capitalization might be a pervasive trans-linguistic convention, having been documented so far, to our knowledge, in English (McCulloch, 2020; Heath, 2018) and Romanian (Alecu, 2022).

3 We note that both discourse markers and computer-mediated communication have been developed as new research areas around the early 1990s, currently spanning three decades of on-going scientific inquiries.

Discourse markers are sequences that 'bracket units of talk (Schiffrin, 1987: 35)[4] and may be seen in relation to pragmatic markers (for a comprehensive overview of this relation, see Ştefănescu, 2007). The primary discursive function of DMs consists in marking the speaker's attitude towards the message and, in some cases, towards their interlocutor.

As pragmatic units, discourse markers are syntactically optional, have no impact on the truth-condition of a sentence, are highly grammaticalized and fulfil a discursive purpose. Their interpretation in interaction is contextual and requires knowledge of their procedural meaning (see also Zafiu, 1989).

Our paper is concerned with the functioning of three discursive patterns that are pervasive in the community, namely *welp, TBH (to be honest)* and *TBF (to be fair)*. We believe these are employed as digital discourse markers in forum interaction (see also Section 4.4). Thus, we rely on several assumptions: on the one hand, the use of these patterns is not random, but subject to unwritten community linguistic and social norms. Therefore, they can be seen as discourse markers that are conventionalized inside a community of discourse. On the other hand, we need to extend the definition of discourse markes to include abbreviated forms in written digital communication and to exclude the prosodic dimension of traditional definitions of discourse markers.

3. Data and Method

3.1. Data

3.1.1. Corpus Gathering from Reddit

Reddit hosts multiple communities, called subreddits (abbreviated: *subs*), which are thematically organized. The subjects of such communities might be general, such as r/Memes, r/politics, r/History, or particular, e.g. r/Aww, dedicated to posting pictures or videos of cute animals, r/AskMeAnything, dedicated to a

4 Schiffrin (1987: 317) highlights the fact that the 'communicative force' of DMs is in part due to their context of use; however, their linguistic properties are also relevant for their interpretation. Her seminal model defines five planes of discourse or 'talk', which will later be a resource for Crible and Degand's (2019) model. Schiffrin's dimensions of DMs are: the ideational structure of discourse (linking logical propositions), the action structure (linking speech acts), the information structure (organizing background knowledge), the exchange structure (regulating turn-taking strategies) and the participation framework (communication speakers' perception of each other and their relations in discourse).

type of verbal play in which the original poster is subjected to questions from the audience of commentators.

We used data from the subreddit r/Romania, created in 2008 as a space for the Romanian users of the platform. Currently, the community has over 418.000 members, ranking among the top 1 % of the largest communities of Reddit. The 'About' section of the community reads: 'Romania, a country famous for its beautiful landscapes, rich history and awesome people. This is our little Romanian corner of Reddit!'. The topics of discussion are diverse and usually concern Romanian day-to-day life, internal and external politics, history or popular culture (movies, TV shows, celebrities). Among the most interesting conversational forms are advice-seeking posts, humorous banter and verbal play, fantasy-scenarios and conversational narratives.

Reddit is an example of a nested forum (see Arendholz, 2017), which means that contributions to the conversation are hierarchically organized (see Figure 9.1).

We manually extracted 30 occurrences of the DMs in question, 10 for each of the emerging discourse marker. Our examples occur both in posts and comments. Our research is essentially an exploratory one, hence the relatively small size of our corpus. We are using a personal annotation framework for describing the exact conversational 'place' of the DM, as following:

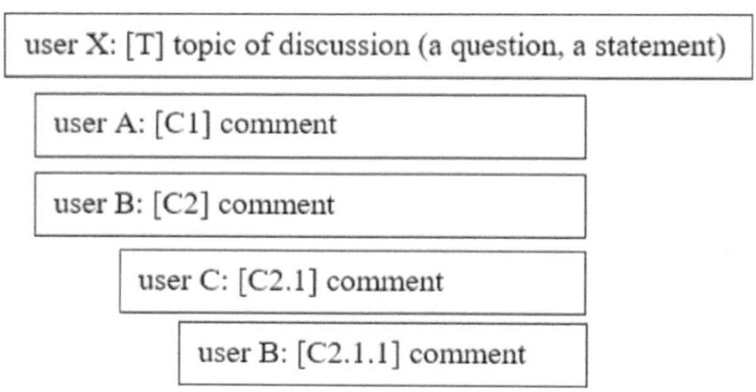

Figure 9.1. Schematic representation of a nested forum (see also Alecu, 2022)

For instance, a DM occurring at the C2.1.1. level may be interpreted taking notice of the fact that user B's contribution is nested within a one-to-one exchange. These 'side-conversations' can be off-topic exchanges, flaming or trolling, although they might be the site for verbal play and banter as well.

3.1.2. *Data Display and Ethics*

We are aware of the difficulties of researching publicly available data in online environments such as social networking sites (SNSs). Studies show that Reddit data is a popular resource for corpora and statistics (Proferes et al., 2021). Qualitative studies usually involve publishing linguistic data (texts produces by users). However, the terms and conditions of Reddit include a statement on the public and searchable nature of user-generated objects (texts, videos, images). The research community has not reached an agreement on how to handle data extraction and analysis from publicly available online environments. For now, researchers are taking case-by-case decisions on how to handle data display in social media research, based on criteria such as: quantitative vs. qualitative research design, topics of discussion, public vs. private interaction, emic vs. etic perspective, etc. There is, however, a consensus regarding the need for researchers to demonstrate awareness of the ethical concerns of their activities. For these reasons, we have taken the supplementary measure of anonymizing all possibly identifying data (pseudonyms, personal information). Moreover, we have not collected data from threads that were discussing sensitive personal topics. This is in line with other measures taken by linguists analysing social media interaction (see, for instance, Vepsäläinen, 2022).

3.2. Annotation Method: Using Crible and Degand's Model (2019)

As mentioned earlier, we are taking comments to be responses in adjacency-pairs. Thus, our 30 occurrences have been annotated taking account of their nature as (a) responses to topic-initiating posts [T], in the larger context of conversation or (b) responses to the previous comment [C], in the minimal context of conversation. Cross-validating the results of two annotators is a further development of our current research.

Crible and Degand's (2019) model proposes the annotation of two layers of pragmatic information: the four domains and fifteen functions of DMs in interaction. Their seminal research is a quantitative analysis of a conversational French corpus including formal and informal interaction, amounting up to 7,545 words (Crible & Degand, 2019: 13). Moreover, DMs have been annotated by both authors, thus validating the application of the model.

Figure 9.2. Summary of Crible and Degand's annotation scheme (2019)

Domains	Functions
Ideational (IDE) – factual meanings Rhetorical (RHE) – ideas, opinions Sequential (SEQ) – structure Interpersonal (INT) – exchange	addition (ADD), alternative (ALT), cause (CAU), concession (CCS), condition (CND), consequence (CSQ), contrast (CTR), hedging (HDG), monitoring (MNT), specification (SPE), temporal (TMP), agreeing (AGR), disagreeing (DIS), topic (TOP), quoting (QUO)

We have annotated our corpus using the following criteria:

- the position of the DM in the utterance: initial, middle, final (see also Schneebeli's 2020 study of *lol* in Youtube comments);
- domain and function, as per the inventory provided by Crible and Degand (2019) and synthesized in Figure 9.2;
- (optional) exchange-related functions such as turn-taking / turn-yielding signals, pragmatic functions (impact on illocutionary force or politeness strategies, etc.);
- (optional) co-occurrence with other DMs, in what Ștefănescu (2011) calls a 'constellation of DMs' in face-to-face conversational narratives.

4. Analysis

4.1. Forms and Functions of *welp*

Welp is a graphical alteration of the adverbial discourse marker *well*. This variation is believed to have a spoken American English origin, with a final phonetic modification rendered graphically. This written modification mirrors a phonetic alteration, more precisely an expiratory excrescent bilabial sound [p], which occurs, *mutatis mutandis*, in the *yep / yup* variations of *yes*, *nope* (< *no*). The online version of Merriam Webster, s.v. *welp* (introduced in 2018), offers two possible explanations for this modification: firstly, an articulatory process of two successive sounds might result in a 'bridge-sound' [p]; secondly, an informal manner of speaking, together with the intention of communicating a relaxed attitude might result in the phonetic alteration of *well*, *yes* and *no*[5]. The first academic

5 Other phonetical explanations have been put forth by J. Sheidlower (apud Kilkenny, 2012), who considers welp an iteration of the excrescent [p] phenomenon, or by B. Zimmer (apud Kilkenny, 2012), for whom abruptly pronouncing *well* leads to a bilabial stop.

mention of *welp* is in Bolinger's (1946) short essay on the afore-mentioned elements. Mair (2020) highlights the fact that, although formally similar to *welp, yep and nope, sup* (< *what's up*?) is the result of a different process (concatenation of two different words, with the elision of the initial sound of the phrase). *Welp* is an instance, along other graphical alterations of text, of a typographical tone of voice (McCulloch, 2020; Heath, 2018).

Welp is an informal graphical alteration of a common English polyfunctional DM, the result of a process of grammaticalization (< adj. *good*). Although this graphical rendering was known in writing before the advent of computer-mediated communication, we believe that it became a digital discourse marker of stance in CMC environments (chat, e-mail, forums). Different online sources[6] have shown that, from an emic perspective, *welp* is associated with surprise, a sense of resignation and finality, great disappointment, nonchalant attitude, acceptance, reluctance, lack of enthusiasm, hopelessness, frustration, and so on. An interesting folk linguistics perspective is mentioned in an article on the online magazine Slate (Kilkenny, 2012): *welp* is 'roughly speaking, a linguistic shrug, which you might imagine as a combination of *well* and a gulp'.

Below are some examples from the corpus, two for each of the initial, middle and final positions in which the DM can be used.

(1) a. [T] Evitarea intrării României în război direct cu Rusia a devenit de azi mai mult improbabilă
[C1] **Welp**, e timpul să-mi iau tălpășița
'[T] Romania cannot avoid going to war with Russia [...]
[C1] **Welp**, it's time for me to get out of here'

b. [T] Voi ce hoarduiți?
[C1] **Welp**, eu mi-am luat o țeapă cu lemn neuscat cum trebuie pus parchet, și 4 ani mai târziu trebuie rașchetat, chituit [...]
'[T] What do you hoard?
[C1] **Welp**, I got tricked into buying some improperly dried wood for the floors, 4 years later I need to sand it, varnish it [...]'

(2) a. [T] Protestul din Piața Victoriei București acum – nu sunt X mii de oameni, dar sunt mai mulți ca alatăieri
[C1] Wow pentru o secundă credeam că se protestează civilizat cu distanțare socială.. până am dat zoom.. **welp** am sperat până în ultima clipă i guess 🤷
'[T] The protest in Victory Square right now – not thousands, but more than yesterday

6 In order to reconstruct an insider's perspective on the use of *welp* in CMC, we consulted Urban Dictionary (urbandictionary.com), a mock-up dictionary of internet slang in which users add definitions and examples of relevant words.

[C1] Wow for a second I thought they were civilised having social distancing... until I zoomed in... **welp** I had hoped to the very last second I guess

b. [T] Povești din Al Doilea Război Mondial
[C1] Când te gandești la perioada aia și la prin ce au trecut nu îți mai vine să zici că o pandemie și o lună de stat închis în casă sunt vremuri de căcat.
[C2] Yep. Citind și amintindu-mi ce povestea și bunica despre viața ei din timpul războiului, fără tata, **welp**, eu trăiesc un vis frumos mereu.
'[T] Stories from World War Two
[C1] When you think about those times and what they went through, you don't feel like saying a pandemic and a month in isolation are shitty times.
[C2] Yep. Reading and reminiscing what grandma used to tell me about her life during the war, without my dad, **welp**, I'm always living in a dream.'

(3) a. [T] AMA Am covid și sunt vaccinat
[C1] Oh fuck, de vreo săptămână am gâtul uscat. **Welp**.
'[T] AMA I got covid and I'm vaccinated.
[C1] Oh fuck, I've been having a sore throat for about a week. **Welp**.'

b. [T] România nu este țara unde dezinformarea omoară cel mai mult.[...]
[C1] Doctor care nu știe chimie de clasa a opta. **Welp**.
'[T] Romania isn't the country in which disinformation is the number one killer [...]
[C1] A doctor who doesn't know 8th grade chemistry. **Welp**.'

A quantitative analysis of the position of *welp* in discourse shows a slight preference for the initial position (half of the occurrences in our sample, 5 out of 10), with 3 middle-occurring DMs and only 2 in the final position (examples 3a and 3b). We highlight the fact that both examples are instances of a graphically isolated *welp*, which might have multiple interpretations. On the one hand, final *welp* might actually be initial-position *welp* of an abandoned structure or an elliptical one (as in *Welp, I am disappointed*). On the other hand, the graphical dimension of CMC is unreliable, being altered in order to compensate for paraverbal (tone of voice) and nonverbal cues (attitude). Having considered these explanations, we believe *welp* in these examples qualifies as a final *welp*. All three positions seem to have conventionalised meanings: initial position of the DM may be a turn-taking signal mimicking face-to-face interaction (see 2a, introducing opinion; 2b, replying to a question); the use of welp in middle position might act as a general sequential DM (it can be replaced by Eng. *and*, or *and so*). The final or isolated position of *welp* might serve as an emphatic stance-taking or turn-yielding element.

Using Crible and Degand's model (2019) we noticed *welp* is used more in the interpersonal domain (6/10 occurrences), with no ideational instance identified. Following the results of our annotation, we consider that the dominant function of *welp* is that of introducing consequence in the rhetorical domain. In (1a), for example, the speaker links the topic of war to his or her personal decision of leaving the country, in the form of a commissive speech act (a promise or a threat). A potential contextual equivalent for *welp* in this case is Fr. *donc*, Eng. *so* or Rom. *deci*, the latter usually introducing consequence. As with any DM, an otherwise logical connector such as Rom. *deci* may receive a more interpersonal meaning in interaction. The same function, although in the interpersonal domain, is fulfilled, in our opinion, by the final-position *welp* (3a, 3b), simultaneously suggesting a turn-yielding usage. We base our interpretation on the fact that there is 'no linguistically expressed consequence', and that any correlation is to be reconstructed by the interlocutor (Crible & Degand, 2019: 26). In this case, welp might be the contextual equivalent of the Fr. *eh bien*, Rom. *ei bine, deci* (in the reading: 'my throat hurts, so < I have covid >', with implicated information inside brackets). However, the conveyed attitude might be that of resignation, disappointment.

In (1b), on the other hand, we consider *welp* to fulfill a specification function in the interpersonal domain, since the marker introduces an answer to a question, while simultenously suggesting a detailed account of the information required, as in the prototypical phrasing *well, let me tell you a story…*, that introduces a conversational narrative. Lastly, *welp* in the middle position might serve as an addition element (2a) or a contrasting element (in 2b, an opposition of scenarios: *my grandmother's past* vs. *my present*).

4.2. Forms and Functions of *TBH (to be honest)*

TBH is the abbreviation of the collocation *to be honest*, which is usually used to introduce opinion. The online version of Oxford English Dictionary, s.v. *TBH*, considers the abbreviation an internet-specific element, with the alternative graphical forms *tbh*. It is a 'colloquial element, originally and chiefly in online and electronic communication' (OED.com), an initialism[7] like many others (LOL = Laughing Out Loud, IMHO = In My Humble Opinion, TL:DR = Too Long; Didn't Read and so on).

From an emic perspective, TBH is used for time efficiency in texting and communication, although it seems to be a rather recent innovation of a certain demographic: 'most commonly used […] among kids and teens' (Urban

7 CMC research had proposed the term 'initialism' to describe abbreviations that are widely used online. Initially, some abbreviations were used in military communication and were subsequently transferred to the online medium (since networked communication was originally a project of the American military scientists).

Dictionary, s.v. *tbh*). According to the same emic source, TBH has been nominalised by conversion, denominating a type of verbal play on social media which is highly conventional: 'a tbh in social media is just giving your honest opinion to someone about them'; 'it's used when a follower tells an account owner to explain to them what they think of them […]. But it must be all 100 % honest'. Some examples of this nominal use are: *Anyone want* ***a tbh****?*; *Who wants* ***a tbh*** *from me?* (Urban Dictionary, s.v. *tbh*). Although we are not concerned with the nominal development of the abbreviation and the special interaction it describes, we highlight its multidimensional use in the online environment.

We have analysed 10 occurrences of TBH, both in abbreviated and phrasal form.

(4) a. [T] Credeți că e dubios să intri în vorbă cu „străine"?
[C1] Uite un sfat [al, sic!] cuiva de vârsta ta (17 ani) ;))) Suntem în aceeași situație **tbh**, de multe ori fac contact vizual cu fetele (să nu vă gândiți ca sunt ceva libidinos care se holbeaza la ea sau ceva de genul), uneori mai primesc și un mic zâmbet […]
'[T] Do you think it's weird to approach strangers (girls)?
[C1] Here's some advice from someone your age (17 yo) ;))) We are in the same situation **tbh**, I usually make eye-contact with girls (don't think I'm a creeper who stares at here or something like that), I sometimes get a smile […]'

b. [T] S-a deschis și pasajul vieții (a picture of a new passageway in Bucharest)
[C1] **to be honest** cred că e prima oară în 32 de ani când ceva se deschide la termenul anunțat
'[T] The new passageway was finally opened
[C1] **to be honest** I think it's the first time in 32 years when something is inaugurated on time'

c. [T] Câți dintre voi trăiți doar din salariu?
[C1] Trăiesc doar din salariu. […] Dacă nu comand nimic pentru casă (accesorii gătit, de ex., nu cred că depășesc 1.500 ron toate cheltuielile, iarna) […] Nu am mașină și nu am rate. I think I am very lucky, **to be honest.**
'[T] How many of you live on just your salary?
[C1] I only live on salary […] If I don't order anything for the house (kitchenware, for instance) I think I spend less than 1500 RON on bills in the winter. […] I don't own a car and I don't have instalments. I think I am very lucky, **to be honest.**'

TBH seems to be equally distributed in our corpus in terms of position, although there is a slight preference for the initial position, regardless of the use of abbreviated or phrasal forms. We believe that the initial position (4b) contributes to the DM's functioning as a turn-taking signal, simultaneously marking the introduction of the speaker's opinion. The middle position (4a) seems to facilitate the marker's function of ameliorating face-threatening acts: the speaker assumes a likeness with the interlocutor, which the latter might find offensive. The DM is thus employed in order to modulate the illocutionary force associated with the imposition of giving advice, risking a patronizing attitude. The co-occurring emoticon serves the same purpose, in our opinion. Lastly, TBH occurs in the final position in a modified context, because of a code-switching sequence. The other final occurrences in the corpus are not similar to this instance: the marker appears at the end of the (Romanian) utterance / contribution. More precisely, in (4c) we observe an inter-sentential code-switching situation, since the majority of the speaker's discourse occurs in Romanian, while the last phrase of his/her contribution is communicated in English (for more on DM and code-switching, see Section 5).

We have noticed a large preference for the interpersonal (7 occurrences) and rhetorical domains (the remaining three examples). This is correlated, in our opinion, with the general functions of introducing opinion, building rapport and marking stance. For instance, building rapport is visible in (4a), in which the speaker tries to establish common ground (see also 'someone your age', 'we are in the same situation tbh') and introduce his personal experience on the matter discussed. In this case, we believe the use of the abbreviated form of the DM acts as a social cue, suggesting that the speaker belongs to the same social group (the Reddit community) as the interlocutor (who solicited the opinion of the group).

In our annotation we have considered TBH to perform mostly the function of hedging in the interpersonal domain. TBH acts as an 'approximation because of politeness or face-threatening material' (Crible & Degand, 2019: 27) in (4a, 4c). Other potential functions are marking agreement in the interpersonal domain or specifying details for stylistic effect in the rhetorical domain (5):

(5) [T] Bani de buzunar făcuți online.
[C1] Fiver, freelancer, odesk [...] cel mai ușor e să cauți români care au echipe făcute și să îi contactezi
[C1.1.] Și cum găsești români cu echipe făcute?
[C1.1.1.] Pe freelancer din ce îmi amintesc poți pune filtru pe țara din care vin ofertele. Eu **to be honest** am căutat nume de useri români care angajau
'[T] Online pocket money.
[C1] Fiver, freelancer, odesk [...] it's easier to search for Romanians who made their own teams and contact them
[C1.1.] And how do I find Romanians with ready-made teams?
[C1.1.1] I **to be honest** have looked for names of Romanian users who were hiring'

We notice the interpositioning of TBH in the phrasal form between the subject and the verb. This is a matrix position for other DM like Rom. *sincer, de exemplu* or Eng. *for instance*. However, the juxtaposition of the Romanian discourse and the English DM acts as a very powerful emphasis, and this is why we think it fulfils a specifying function. It might, however, retain some of its hedging effects, since it modulates a potentially impolite situation (self-praise).

4.3. Forms and Functions of 'TBF' (*to be fair*)

TBF is an initialism which, according to the online version of Cambridge, is used 'on social media and in text messages, when you have considered everything that has an effect on a situation in order to make a fair judgment'. Other emic sources indicate a specialized use of TBF to play the 'devil's advocate' in a conversation, stating one's opinion as opposed to one's interlocutor. Contributors to the Urban Dictionary indicate contextual synonymy with 'honestly' or 'to make things fair'. Moreover, some suggest partial synonymy with its counterpart, TBH. We have found less instances of TBF in online dictionaries of English and internet terms than we have found for TBH.

(6) a. [T] Conflictul Rusia-Ucraina [...] E bizar cât de calmi sunt ei faţă de cei din est care-s mai aproape de front.
[C1] **Tbf**, din 2014 încoace a tot fost low intensity combat in Donetsk şi Luhansk. Oamenii s-au obişnuit cu ideea de război, bănuiesc.
'[T] Russia-Ukraine conflict [...] It's weird to see how calm they [Ukrainians near Odessa] are, compared to the ones in the east, who are much closer to the front.
[C1] **Tbf**, they have been engaged in low intensity combat in Donetsk and Luhansk since 2014. People got used tot the idea of war, I guess.'

b. [T] Voi credeţi că fiecare e pentru el şi că oamenii sunt răi?
[C1] **To be fair**, nu mă aştept la nimic de la nimeni. Totuşi, nu mă opreşte să îi ajut pentru că it seems the right thing to do.
'[T] Do you think that everyone is out for themselves and that people are bad?
[C1] **To be fair**, I don't expect anything from anybody. However, that doesn't stop me from helping out because it seems the right thing to do.'

c. [T] E ok dacă beau 7l de apă pe zi?
[C1] Depinde ce face şi cât de mare eşti. Dacă mergi exagerat de des la baie, în special te trezeşti noaptea, aş merge la un medic. Aş merge la un medic anyway **to be fair** dar nu aş sări direct la concluzii pripite.
'[T] Is it okay to drink 7 l of water per day?
[C1] Depends on what you do and how much you weight. If you wake up often during the night to go to the bathroom, I would see a doctor. I would go to a doctor anyway **to be fair** but I wouldn't jump to conclusions.'

We noticed a wide preference for the initial position of TBF: 8 instances included both abbreviated and phrasal forms in the beginning of the contribution (6a, 6b).

Our corpus does not include any instance of final TBF, although such instances may be found in a larger sample of Romanian forum interaction.

As with the other two DMs, we believe TBF is largely used in the interpersonal domain for multiple functions. The most interesting result we have come across in our analysis is the disagreeing function of TBF (6a). This function relies on establishing an interpersonal relationship with the interlocutor, while simultaneously offering a different take on the topic of conversation. This function is to be annotated only 'when none of the other functions apply' (Crible & Degand, 2019: 28). However, we disagree with this annotation stipulation, because we believe TBF introduces a dissenting opinion with the purpose of attenuating it, so it has, in our opinion, an authentic discursive purpose.

4.4. Summary of Findings. Towards Digital Discourse Markers

The three English borrowings found in Romanian forum communication can fit an expanded definition of discourse markers, considering the fact that they fulfil diverse pragmatic functions, as was shown using Crible and Degand's annotation model. We call for an expanded definition of DMs that takes into account not only spontaneous spoken and written discourse, but also digital discourse and interaction from the point of view of mixed registers and forms. In our view, the digital interaction is a distinct environment for the production and interpretation of DMs. Moreover, an expanded definition of DMs may include forms that are only present in digital discourse, such as abbreviated forms (*tbh, tbf, lol, omg*) or verbal patterns (*cries in, laughs in*, discussed in Alecu, 2022). The main domain in which these elements function is, in our opinion, the interpersonal domain. Their position in the utterance / written contributions is flexible and may be linked to code-switching phenomena (see also Section 5). Leaving aside the prosodical restrictions of DMs because of the written characteristic of CMC, we believe these elements contribute to the structuring and interpretation of the users' discourse. Moreover, all three elements suffered some form of alteration by graphic-phonetic modification (*welp*) or abbreviation (*TBH, TBF*). These elements may perform similar functions to DMs in oral conversational turns, such as turn-taking and turn-yielding indicators. We, therefore, propose an understanding of digital discourse markers (DDMs), as exemplified by the three case studies: DDMs are discursive elements that fulfil pragmatic functions in forum exchanges, regulated by unwritten community norms in the context of complex online environments. They differ from DMs by having an exclusive textual form and by being employed in mediated interaction.

5. *Digital Discourse Markers* in Relation to Code-Switching

Computer-mediated communication has been linked to furthering the prominent function of English as a *lingua franca* in the modern world. What traditional media might have started by lexical borrowings from English on the chance of documentaries, TV-shows or news coverage, the Internet has further developed, by dramatically increasing exposure to mediatic content from across the globe. Reddit is an American-based web service and social networking site which serves as an intercultural space for discussion. However, members of 'national' communities like r/Romania use the national language in interaction (see also the use of the endonym r/Deutschland for the German community of Reddit). Assuming that Reddit is a source of lexical borrowings of DMs from English is a statement that needs to be carefully proved, since communities consistently use national languages in communicating, if the profile of the community is that of a national one. We are, therefore, aware of the fact that the Internet and, possibly, Reddit increases exposure to English (especially American English), but we do not make assumptions regarding the specific source of lexical borrowings in the case of DMs. However, we suggest that initialisms like TBH and TBF have been borrowed through written contact between native and non-native speakers of English.

The most interesting problem of DM borrowings is their relation to code-switching (CS)[8]. We offer below several instances of code-switching co-occuring with DMs:

(7) a. dar dacă tu te-ai înscris la învățământ cu frecvență, **welp**, *that's kinda on you*, job ne-job, în țară sau afară
'but if you enrolled for in-person teaching, welp, that's kinda on you, with or without a job, here or in another country'

b. **Welp**, nu îi greu să iei un numar de telefon [...] Repeat cu 50 de magazine mai mici de pe raza unui oraș. Profit. Oarecum zici că îi o mișcare de marketing dar idk. Dezinformarea îi strong.
'Welp, it's not hard to get a phone number [...] Repeat on 50 smaller stores and you get profit. You might think it's a marketing strategy but idk. Disinformation is strong.'

---

8 English DMs as pragmatic borrowings have been previously discussed by Cojocaru (2020) on a corpus of informal conversations collected from social media and blogs. The items that are discussed by the author occur in spoken Romanian as well (*so, anyway, also, Jesus!*), while we have yet to witness the use of *welp*, *tbf* or *tbh* in face-to-face Romanian conversations.

c. **welp** am sperat până în ultima clipă i guess
'welp I had hoped to the last second i guess'
d. **Tbh**, pentru mine a fost cam a breath of fresh air
'Tbh for me it kinda was a breath of fresh air'
e. Nu am maşină şi nu am rate. I think I am very lucky, **to be honest**
'I don't own a car and I don't have installments. I think I am very lucky, to be honest.'
f. **Tbf**, din 2014 încoace a tot fost low intensity combat
'**Tbf**, they have been engaged in low intensity combat'
g. **To be fair,** există oameni care legitimately want this. Poate tu nu [...]
'**To be fair,** there are people who legitimately want this. Maybe you don't'

Following McCormick (2001), we operate the distinction between conversational code-switching and situational code-switching, the latter essentially being a case of diglossia in face-to-face interaction. Conversational code-switching, on the other hand, occurs due to factors like stylistic effect, personal choices, identity-building strategies or group norms. Other factors for conversational CS mentioned in the literature are generating humour and filling a lexical gap. These are not present in our data, in our opinion, since DMs are part of the basic vocabulary of a native speaker and cannot be subject to a lexical gap. Moreover, humorous effect is not an outcome of any of the examples in our sample. Conversational CS might be similar to discursive CS which, according to Auer (2001), refers to the insertion of an ad-hoc lexical borrowing into the utterance. However, it seems to us that the use of *welp, TBH* and *TBF* is conventionalised inside the Romanian community of Reddit. These DMs are used in an informal manner and are not glossed by the speaker for informative purposes, which might mean that their lexical meaning is shared knowledge. DMs are a functional category which is morphologically varied, and the borrowing of such language-specific pragmatic elements is an interesting case of language variation. We adapt the notion of conversational CS to fit the nature of DMs: lexical borrowings (e.g. *weekend, computer, supermarket*) behave differently, in our opinion, to pragmatic borrowings[9].

There are situations in which the use of a DM triggers intra-sentential code-switching: *welp, that's kinda on you* (7a). This is one of the few instances of proximal code-switching sequence relating to the DDM. A correlative of this is seen in (7d); however, the CS sequence precedes the DM. The most common type, we

9 We note that 19th century and early 20th century Romanian has been highly influenced by French-speaking high society, and several DMs have been borrowed and are still in use today (although sporadically, by certain demographics and professions): *bref, bon, eh bien* (replaced by Rom. *ei bine*).

think, is the distance code-switching sequence, which may or may not be triggered by the DM. A general scheme of this is [English DDM] [Romanian phrase] [English phrase]: ***welp*** *am sperat până în ultima clipă* ***I guess*** (7c), in which *I guess* may act as a DM as well. We notice syntactic CS in (7g) and modifiers (7d). However, DDMs usually occur isolate, and might be associated with other lexical borrowing (7b). Finally, 'constellations' of DMs appear in the case of online interaction as well (see *I guess* in 7c).

6. Conclusions

Digital discourse markers are discursive elements confined to the online environment in which mediated interactions occur. They are similar to discourse markers and can be analysed using already established models for the analysis of face-to-face interaction. English DDMs occur in forum exchanges in Romanian in code-switching situations, which seem to be based on unwritten community norms of forum interaction. Our small-scale pilot-study of digital discourse markers (DDMs) in Romanian forum interactions has found that there are several correlations between their functions and position. The DDM welp is largely used in the initial position, with the purpose of introducing the speaker's opinion, among others. TBH and TBF fulfill several functions in the interpersonal domain, among which hedging (TBH) or signalling disagreement (TBF). However, a larger-scale study must be conducted in order to verify whether there are exact correlations between the position and function of these DDMs. Based on the results of our study, we believe DDMs are as polyfunctional as DMs, regardless of their position in the utterance. Further research is required to establish, among others, the connection between discourse markers and digital discourse markers, and between conversational code-switching and the borrowing of pragmatic elements. For now, we believe the present study confirmed the diversity of DMs in digital interactions and has contributed to our knowledge of Romanian language use in digital environments. We also endorse the possibility that digital discourse markers will become an object of study from several points of view in pragmatics and internet linguistics research.[10]

10 We would like to thank Prof. Rodica Zafiu for her insightful remarks on Romanian online communication and Prof. Maj-Britt Mosegaard Hansen for her observations on the preliminary version of this study, presented at the Discourse Markers in Romance Languages (DISROM 7) International Conference, which took place at the University of Craiova (16th–18th of June 2022).

References

Alecu, B. (2022). Cries in…/laughs in… Pragmatic and discursive functions of emergent linguistic patterns in online Romanian. In I. Nedelcu, I. Paraschiv & A. Vasilescu (coord.), *Orientări actuale în lingvistica teoretică şi aplicată. Actele celui de al XXI-lea Colocviu Internaţional al Departamentului de Lingvistică (Bucureşti, 19–20 noiembrie 2021)* (pp. 379–389). Editura Universităţii din Bucureşti.

Arendholz, J. (2017). Message boards. In Ch. Hoffmann & W. Bublitz (eds.), *Pragmatics of social media* (pp. 125–150). De Gruyter Mouton.

Auer, P. (2001). Code-switching: Discourse models. In R. Mesthrie (ed.), *Concise encyclopedia of sociolinguistics* (pp. 443–447). Elsevier.

Baym, N. (1997). Interpreting soap operas and creating community: Inside an electronic fac culture. In S. Kiesler (ed.), *Culture of the internet* (pp. 103–120). Lawrence Erlbaum.

Bolinger, D. (1946). Thoughts on yep and nope. *American Speech* 21/ 2, 90–95.

boyd, d., Ellison, N. (2007). Social network sites: Definition, history, and scholarship. *Journal of Computer-Mediated Communication* 13/ 11, 210–230.

Carter, R. (2004). *Language and creativity: The art of the common talk.* Routledge.

Cojocaru, V. (2020). English discourse markers in spoken Romanian: Pragmatic borrowings or a code-switching phenomenon?. *RRL* LXV/3, 261–271.

Crible, L. & Degand, L. (2019). Domains and functions: A two-dimensional account of discourse markers. *Discours*, 24. https://doi.org/10.4000/discours.9997

Crystal, D. (2006). *Language and the internet* (2nd ed.). Cambridge University Press.

Crystal, D. (2011). *Internet linguistics: A student guide.* Routledge.

Dynel, M. & Poppi, F. I. M. (2019). *Risum teneatis, amici?*: The socio-pragmatics of RoastMe humour. *Journal of Pragmatics* 139, 1–21.

Guţu Romalo, V. (coord.) (2008). *Gramatica limbii române [GALR]* (2nd ed.), 2nd vol. *Enunţul*. Editura Academiei.

Heath, M. (2018). Orthography in social media: Pragmatic and prosodic interpretations of caps lock. *Proceedings of the Linguistic Society of America* 3/ 55, 1–13.

Herring, S. (ed.) (1996). *Computer-mediated communication. Linguistics, social and cross-cultural perspectives.* John Benjamins.

Herring, S. C. (2018). The co-evolution of computer-mediated communication and computer-mediated discourse analysis. In P. Bou-Franch & B.

Garcés-Conejos Blitvich (eds.), *Analysing digital discourse: New insights and future directions*. Palgrave Macmillan. https://doi.org/10.1007/978-3-319-92663-6_2

Herring, S. & Androutsopoulus, J. (2015). Computer-mediated discourse 2.0. In D. Tannen, H. E. Hamilton & D. Schiffrin (eds.), *The handbook of discourse analysis* (2nd ed., pp. 127–151). Wiley Blackwell.

Herring, S., Stein, D., & Virtanen, T. (eds.) (2013). *Pragmatics of computer-mediated communication*. De Gruyter Mouton.

Hoffmann, Ch. & Bublitz, W. (eds.) (2017). *Pragmatics of social media*. De Gruyter Mouton.

Kasunic, A. & Kaufman, G. (2018). *At least the pizzas you make are hot*: Norms, values, and abrasive humor on the subreddit r/RoastMe. *Proceedings of the Twelfth International AAAI Conference on Web and Social Media*, pp. 161–170.

Kilkenny, K. (2012). Where did the expression *Welp* come from?. https://slate.com/culture/2012/11/welp-slang-term-has-longer-history-than-you-might-think.html. Language Log.

Mair, V. (2020). Welp, sup, yep, nope. https://languagelog.ldc.upenn.edu/nll/?p=47300.

Marwick, A. E. & boyd, d. (2011). I tweet honestly, I tweet passionately: Twitter users, context collapse, and the imagined audience. New Media & Society, 13/1, 114-133. doi:10.1177/1461444810365313.

McCormick, K., M., (2002). Code-switching: Overview. In R. Mesthrie, (ed.), *Concise Encyclopedia of Sociolinguistics*, Elsevier, 447-454.

McCulloch, G. (2020). *Because internet. Understanding how language is changing*. Penguin Random House.

O'Reilly, T. (2012). What is Web 2.0? Design patters and business models for the next generation of software. In M. Mandiberg (ed.), *The social media reader* (pp. 32–52). New York University Press.

Proferes, N. et. al. (2021). Studying Reddit: A systematic overview of disciplines, approaches, methods and ethics. *Social Media + Society* 7/2. https://doi.org/10.1177/20563051211019004

Reddit (2023), Reddit by the Numbers, https://www.redditinc.com/.

Schiffrin, D. (1987). *Discourse markers*. Cambridge University Press.

Schneebeli, C. (2020). Where *lol* is: Function and position of *lol* used as a discourse marker in Youtube comments. *Discours* 27. https://doi.org/10.4000/discours.10900

Ştefănescu, A. (2007). *Conectori pragmatici*. Editura Universității din București.

Ştefănescu, A. (2011). Marcatorii discursivi în naraţiunea conversaţională: un studiu de caz. In L. Dascălu Jinga (coord.), *Româna vorbită actuală (ROVA). Corpus şi studii* (pp. 279–311). Editura Academiei.

Vepsäläinen, H. (2022). Responses to advice-seeking on Reddit that do not give advice. *Journal of Pragmatics* 191, 143–155.

Yus, F. (2011). *Cyberpragmatics: Internet-mediated communication in context.* John Benjamins.

Yus, F. (2021). *Smartphone communication. Interactions in the app ecosystem.* Routledge.

Zafiu, R. (1989). Câteva observaţii asupra conectorilor pragmatici din limba română. *SCL* XL/3, 315–319.

Zappavigna, M. (2012). *Discourse of Twitter and Social Media: How we use language to create affiliation on the Web.* Bloomsbury.

Zappavigna, M. (2017). Twitter. In Ch. Hoffmann & W. Bublitz (eds.), *Pragmatics of social media* (pp. 201–224). De Gruyter Mouton.

Heejung Kim

10 Reformulation Markers, Linguistic Typology and Rhetorical Conventions: The Case of Spanish and Korean

Abstract: In this paper a contrastive study of Reformulation Markers (RMs) between Spanish and Korean has been conducted taking into account linguistic typology (Moreno Cabrera, 2005, 2021) and the contrastive rhetorical features of these two languages (Kaplan, 1966; Hinds, 1987; Clyne, 1994; Connor, 1996, 2008). To carry out this analysis, following a line of previous research in Murillo (2007, 2012), the cases of RMs found in the Spanish and Korean journalistic corpus have been studied. The results obtained from the research showed that the different typological configuration of the given languages (fusional / agglutinative languages) should be considered to explain the number of cases found in the corpus, the lexicalized forms of the markers addressed, and their syntactical relations of RMs in Spanish and Korean. Moreover, with regard to rhetorical traditions of two languages, we could observe as examples the use of the structure of double reformulation, especially the repetition of the Korean markers (*jeuk… jeuk…/ got… got…*), the copulative structure of the marker *got*, denoting Korean culture, and the different discursive values such as definition, denomination, and conclusion in Korean and Spanish RMs.

Keywords: reformulation, linguistic typology, contrastive rhetoric, Spanish, Korean

1. Introduction

In this paper a corpus-driven contrastive study of Reformulation Markers (henceforth referred to as RMs) between Spanish and Korean has been conducted against the backdrop of the typological characteristics of the two languages (Moreno Cabrera, 2005, 2021) and their contrastive rhetorical features (Kaplan, 1966; Hinds, 1987; Clyne, 1994; Connor, 1996, 2008).

Since the establishment of theoretical frameworks for Reformulation and its markers in Indo-European Languages (mainly Romance and Germanic Languages; Gülich & Kotschi, 1983; Roulet, 1987; Rossari, 1994; Hyland, 2005, 2007; Murillo, 2007), RMs have been the subject of several cross-linguistic studies in Spanish and other languages. For example, they have been described in Spanish and Catalan (Cuenca, 2003), Spanish and English (Del Saz, 2003; Murillo, 2007), Spanish and French (Garcés Gómez & García Pérez, 2009), Spanish and Italian (Flores Acuña, 2003), Spanish and Portuguese (Pons & Macário Lopes,

2014), Spanish and German (Robles, 2017), Spanish and Icelandic (García Pérez, 2009), Spanish and Basque (Barandiaran & Casado, 2011), Spanish, English and Catalan (Cuenca & Bach, 2007), and Spanish and Malaysian (Alias, 2018). On the other hand, it should be pointed out that relatively little research has been devoted to RMs in non-Indo-European Languages (Chinese, Japanese, Arabic, Swahili, etc.). Therefore, as with Spanish and Korean RMs, which are the objects of this paper, given that the languages addressed are characterized as having a great disparity of morphological and syntactical features (Section 2.2) and different ways of developing words, phrases, clauses, sentences, paragraphs or texts (Section 2.3), it is necessary to consider their typological characteristics and rhetorical conventions in order to look in more detail at their similitudes and differences.

More concretely, this paper attempts to give considerable insight into the following questions:

(i) Does reformulation exist in Korean?
(ii) Are there any new features of reformulation and its markers in Korean in comparison to Spanish?
(iii) What are the similarities and differences of reformulation and its markers observed in Spanish and Korean corpus data from the perspectives of linguistic typology and contrastive rhetoric?

The present study is organized as follows. The first section explores some previous theoretical backgrounds in relation to reformulation, linguistic typology and rhetorical conventions in Spanish and Korean. The second deals with the corpus and choice of methodology. The third presents the results and discussions of this study. Finally, the fourth section summarizes the conclusion and highlights further implications.

2. Theoretical Framework

2.1. Reformulation and Reformulation Markers (RMs)

Previous works have set out to define the reformulation process. Firstly, drawing on Relevance Theory, Blakemore (1993, 1996) started to consider reformulation as an example of how an expression can be relevant as the interpretation of another with which it holds some resemblance (*interpretative resemblance*). Secondly, according to Cuenca (2003: 1073), reformulation is 'a complex semantic category that ranges from strict paraphrase to other values such as specification, explanation, summary or denomination, and even to non-paraphrastic meanings such as implication, conclusion and contrast'.

With regard to RMs, Murillo (2007, 2012), taking the perspective of Relevance Theory and Discourse study tradition in French, addressed RMs as procedural items that allow interlocutors to achieve a relevant interpretation of the text by assigning referents ('identification', 'specification'), adding background information ('definition', 'denomination'), or making conclusions explicit ('conclusion', 'mathematics operation'), etc. On the other hand, in Hyland's view of the metadiscourse[1] model (2005), RMs serve as 'code glosses' with exemplification markers. They work mainly for providing additional information by explaining or specifying in order to help the interlocutors' understanding.

Finally, in Korean, in Li's (2013) proposal on paraphrase and paraphrasing markers, a paraphrased sentence is defined as 'a sentence that forms a paraphrasal relation, in which the words, phrases, clauses, sentences or texts expressed in different forms with semantic equivalence are connected back and forth around the paraphrase marker' (Li, 2013: 220, our translation). Bearing in mind that research on RMs in Korean is still in its early stages, the term 'reformulation' in this language has not been addressed elsewhere.

Regarding the markers which fulfil the above mentioned process, several items have been considered: *es decir*, *o sea*, *esto es* and *a saber*, and other less grammaticalized elements such as *dicho de otra manera*, *dicho de otra forma*, etc. in Spanish (Portolés, 2016); *that is*, *that is to say*, *in other words*, and *namely*, and less grammaticalized items such as (*to put it*) *another way*, (*to put it*) *simply* in English (Murillo, 2007, 2012); *jeuk*, *got*, *geureonikka* and *malhajamyeon*, and less grammaticalized markers such as *bakkwo malhamyeon* (*to put it another way*), *dasi malhamyeon* (*to put it in a repeated way*), *yoyakhamyeon* (*in summary*), etc. in Korean (Seo, 1995; Li, 2013).

2.2. Typological (Morphological) Characteristics of Spanish and Korean

From the point of view of the morphological typology of languages (Moreno Cabrera, 2005, 2021), there are three groups of languages in the world: (i) fusional languages (most Romance Languages, Russian, Arabic, etc.); (ii) agglutinative languages (Korean, Japanese, Basque, Turkish, Hungarian, etc.); (iii) isolating languages (Chinese, Vietnamese, etc.). With respect to the present research, the marked contrast between Korean and Spanish is that while

1 Reformulation has traditionally been studied as a type of metadiscursive operation in Romance Languages (Gülich & Kotschi, 1983; Roulet, 1987; Rossari, 1994; Briz, 1998; Pons, 2006).

the former language belongs to agglutinative languages, the latter is included in fusional languages, according to their common morphological structures.

The fact that the Korean language has an agglutinative feature means that different affixes or postpositions, such as particles (case particles, auxiliary particles, conjunctive particles) and verbal (connective) endings[2], can be added to the root of the words. These categories, together with conjunctive adverbs, are also considered as discourse markers or connectives in the given language. In other words, while Romance languages may use mainly conjunctions or conjunctive adverbs to express the connection in the discourse, this function in Korean can be carried out through the three classes of words outlined above (Kim, 2021).

Nevertheless, especially important here is that these three syntactic categories have their own scope of connection. In the examples presented below, conjunctive particles such as *-wa* or *-gwa* are used to connect words or noun forms (example 1). Second, verbal connective endings (*-go*, *-animyeon*, etc.) function in linking inflectional verbal forms or clauses (example 3). Finally, conjunctive adverbs (*geuraeseo*, *geureonikka*, *banmyeon*, etc.) connect words, sentences or paragraphs (examples 2, 4) (Yu, 2005: 93, 96):

<u>Between words (or noun forms): conjunctive particles, conjunctive adverbs</u>

(1) Beotkkot**gwa** namu [**gwa**: conjunctive particle]
'Cherry blossoms **and** trees'

(2) Beotkkot, **geurigo** namu [**geurigo**: conjunctive adverb]
'Cherry blossoms, **and** trees'

<u>Between clauses (or inflectional forms): verbal connective endings</u>

(3) Beotkkochi pi**go**, namuga jaranda. [**go**: verbal connective ending]
'Cherry blossoms bloom, **and** trees grow.'

<u>Between sentences: conjunctive adverbs</u>

(4) Bomeneun beotkkochi pigo namuga jaranda. Gyeoul jameul jadeon dongmuldeureun jameseo kkaeeonanda. Eorin aideuldo hakgyoe gagi sijakanda. **Banmyeon**, gyeoureneun kkotgwa namuga sideulgo, nalssiga chuwojigi sijakanda. [**Banmyeon**: conjunctive adverb]
'In spring, cherry blossoms bloom and trees grow. Animals from their winter sleep wake up. Young children also start to go to school. **On the other hand**, in winter, flowers and trees wither, and the weather starts to get colder.'

---

2 The so-called particles (*josa*) in Korean normally refer to the items that are postponed to the nominal forms (nouns, pronouns and numerals), denoting the grammatical relations with other items in the sentence. The verbal endings (*eomi*) mean the inflectional forms postponed to the verb or adjective that carry out the verbal conjugation, in order to express the tense and the verbal mood (but they do not mark the grammatical gender or number like in Romance Languages) (Ihm (ed.), 2001).

In the light of the above examples (1–3), while in English the connective function would be marked mainly with the conjunction *and*, in Korean the same function can be introduced through conjunctive particles, verbal connective endings and conjunctive adverbs. Furthermore, it is also observed that while conjunctive adverbs perform their connective function at all linguistic levels – with the exception of between clauses – (examples 2, 4), the syntactical connective relation of conjunctive particles or verbal connective endings in the sentence is limited to nominal forms (example 1) or clauses (or inflectional verbal forms) (example 3).

2.3. Rhetorical Conventions of Spanish and Korean RMs

In addition to the linguistic typology perspective, this research is also based on the premise of Contrastive Rhetoric in which there are different rhetorical conventions in writing according to a multitude of cultural contexts (Kaplan, 1966; Hinds, 1987; Clyne, 1994; Connor, 1996, 2008). With respect to RMs, as some approaches have already indicated (Cuenca, 2003; Cuenca & Bach, 2007; Murillo, 2007, 2012), their frequency and functions are not only simple matters in different grammars, but also are linked to the rhetorical strategy of each cultural convention[3].

For example, in relation to RMs in academic texts in Spanish and English, Cuenca (2003: 1085) commented that a synthetic and linear style of writing as well as the high use of simple grammatical RMs are expected when constructing texts in English, because English texts are part of a form-oriented culture. But, on the other hand, in the Spanish (Romance) culture, a greater number of RMs with complex variable forms are observed, since the authority is related to a great extent to the variety and complexity of expressions (content-oriented culture). In Catalan, the frequency of markers and the rhetorical style is somewhere between Spanish and English.

Likewise, Cuenca and Bach (2007) studied RMs in research papers of linguistic discipline written by English, Spanish and Catalan authors. The results proved that more simple and grammatically fixed RMs in English are used in comparison with in Catalan and Spanish. Furthermore, their findings also indicated that

---

3 Regarding the meaning and the translation problem of discourse markers, Portolés (2002) has already commented that it should be considered the rhetorical (or discursive) traditions of each language: 'the differences between the systems and norms of two or more languages, the problem of differences in discursive traditions, (…) also the frequency of its use in texts and discourses' (Portolés, 2002: 158).

Spanish and Catalan writers tend to use RMs in order to reduce content previously mentioned, while RMs in English papers are mostly used for expanding previous sequences.

In a similar line to the authors aforementioned, Murillo (2007) demonstrated a sharp contrast in the frequency of RMs in general English and Spanish (797 in English / 2,823 in Spanish examples in her corpus). Moreover, Murillo (2012) investigated the use of RMs in L1 English and Spanish and in L2 English research articles of Business Management, and she observed that L2 research articles seemed to adapt, to a certain extent, to the rhetorical tendencies of the two languages (Murillo, 2012: 84).

As for Korean RM rhetoric conventions, as noted earlier in the Section 2.1, these items have never been examined in detail in the given language. But Li (2013)'s classification of paraphrastic sentences in Korean provides some useful information as to their rhetoric traditions. In his research four types of paraphrastic structures were found (Li, 2013: 229–239): (i) summary, (ii) annotation, (iii) exemplification, and (iv) semantic connection (deduction and induction). Here 'annotation', as its name suggests, refers to adding an explanation of the technical vocabulary used in the previous segment. Four subtypes are distinguished: 'translation of the meaning of words' (reformulating the meaning of a lexical unit presented in the previous segment by other easier to understand lexical units), 'explanation of the metaphorical meaning', 'explicitation through enumeration' and 'explicitation of the reference' (Li, 2013). Interestingly, with the exception of 'summary', these three types of paraphrase have rarely been considered as reformulation in Romance Languages.

On the contrary, with regards to 'annotation' and 'exemplification' functions described in Korean RMs, it should be mentioned that Chinese rhetorical tradition displays a similarity to that of Korean. According to Liu (2020) and Liu and Huang (2021), who carried out a contrastive study of the expository writing styles of Chinese and English, Chinese rhetorical modes in exposition show divergence from English rhetoric, with exemplification and quotation highly recommended. That is to say, Chinese textbooks do not include detailed explications on how to develop a topic sentence or a paragraph, and instead put emphasis on using exemplification (of famous people) and well-known quotations to support their texts.

3. Corpus and Methodology

Following a line of previous research in Murillo (2007, 2012), a corpus-driven contrastive study has been carried out regarding the frequency and functions of the RMs in Spanish and Korean journalistic corpus. For Spanish, the corpus from the years 1997, 2000–2004 in CREA (Corpus de Referencia del Español Actual, https://www.rae.es/banco-de-datos/crea) with 12,314,564 words was utilised. CREA consists of a set of selected texts from diverse sources, prepared by the Real Academia Española (RAE). Its latest version (June 2008) has more than 160,000,000 words of written and oral texts, chronologically covering the years from 1975 to 2004.

For the Korean corpus, the CORPUS SEJONG (National Corpus of South Korea) was employed. The corpus development project was carried out between 1998 and 2007. Its latest version includes a total of 58,062,050 words and has been available since 2013 at the National Institute of Korean Language (https://corpus.korean.go.kr/). For this paper, examples from the journalistic corpus from 2001 to 2003 in SEJONG, which includes 7,284,733 words, have been collected.

The number of words from Spanish and Korean, combined (12,314,564 / 7,284,733 words) forms the ratio of 1.69:1. Owing to the agglutinative features and the lexical composition (**Sino-Korean**[4]) of the Korean language being responsible for far fewer words being used, in order to achieve a more comparable proportion between the two languages, seven novels translated from Korean to Spanish were also observed (Shin, 2011 [2008], *Por favor, cuida de mamá*; Gong, 2012 [2005], *Nuestros tiempos felices*; Park, 2013 [1992], *Memorias de una niña de la guerra*; Hwang, 2014 [2003], *Shim Cheong: la niña vendida*; Hwang, 2015 [2007], *Bari, la princesa abandonada*; Choi, 2016 [1963], *El hombre gris*; and Han, 2017 [2007], *La vegetariana*). Lastly, chi-square tests were realized to determine the study's statistical significance, and the program SPSS was employed in order to handle the large amount of data.

The selected RMs are four items for each language: *es decir*, *o sea*, *esto es* and *a saber* (Spanish), *jeuk*, *got*, *geureonikka* and *malhajamyeon* (Korean). These items have already been considered as RMs in the references addressed in both languages (Murillo, 2007; Portolés, 2016; Seo, 1995; Li, 2013). Searches were not made for non-grammaticalized and complex reformulation markers. In total, 2,698 occurrences of Spanish and 2,144 of Korean RMs were found.

4 On the lexical level, Korean vocabulary has been widely influenced by the Chinese Language. Accordingly, more than 80 % of the vocabulary is Sino-Korean, which strongly maintains logographic characters.

4. Results and Discussions

4.1. Typological Comparisons

Regarding the typological characteristics, as mentioned in Section 2.2, the fundamental difference between Spanish and Korean is their morphological configuration (fusional / agglutinative language). Comparing and developing this aspect is essential, since it may give convincing answers to the number of words that can be included in the corpus of both languages, the frequency of RMs found in the corpus, their lexicalized forms and syntactical connective relations.

Firstly, with respect to the frequency of RMs found in the corpus, as can be seen at the end of section 3, 2,698 cases of Spanish and 2,144 cases of Korean were obtained. Although there is no notable difference in the total number of cases for both languages in comparison with the numbers obtained in Murillo (2007) (see Section 2.3), it seems that a relatively small number of Korean RMs, observed in comparison with those of Spanish, is that because in Korean other connective elements such as verbal connective endings (between verb phrases) or conjunctive particles (between noun phrases) (see Section 2.2) are also used. In fact, according to Ahn (2000: 130–131) and Yu (2005: 98), the most commonly-used connective items in Korean would be verbal connective endings (not conjunctive adverbs), because the connection beyond the level of a sentence in this language is not usually made grammatically explicit.

Secondly, certain differences are observed in the lexicalized forms of the RMs and their semantic-pragmatic features. While three Spanish markers are formed with the copulative structure (***es*** + *decir*, *o* + ***sea***, *esto* + ***es***) – so it is seen even more with an explanatory sense – , the lexicalized forms of Korean RMs such as *jeuk* and *geureonikka* are linked more with a consecutive sense. More specifically, as for the first marker *jeuk*, it is considered as an RM that has its origin in a conjunctive adverb, but it is also used as a verbal connective ending with a consecutive value in modern Korean (Choi, 1983 [1937]; Nam & Ko, 2011 [1985]; Yang 2017). And, in the case of *geureo**nikka***, its verbal connective ending *-nikka* introduces a conclusion and consequence (see also its Japanese counterpart *da**kara*** and its verbal connective ending *-kara*, Matsui, 2002).

Finally, in terms of the syntactical relations of RMs, Spanish reformulators are used more often between phrases (59.3 %, compared to 49.9 % in Korean); but, on the other hand, those of Korean, are much more common between clauses (41.7 %, compared to 34.8 % of Spanish) (see Table 10.1 below):

Table 10.1. Distribution of reformulation markers in Spanish and Korean

	clause + clause	phrase + phrase	clause + phrase	phrase + clause	Total
Spanish	939	1,601	39	119	2,698
	34.8 %	59.3 %	1.4 %	4.4 %	100.0 %
Korean	893	1,070	21	160	2,144
	41.7 %	49.9 %	1.0 %	7.5 %	100.0 %

Likewise, as mentioned in Section 2.2, it has also been shown that each Korean item has a more defined scope of connection than those of Spanish. For example, the marker *got* acts almost exclusively between phrases (81.5 %), while *geureonikka* and *malhajamyeon* are used more between clauses (82.2 %, 70.7 %) (Table 10.3). The RMs of Spanish, on the contrary, differ in the sense that *esto es* and *a saber* are observed more in reformulation between phrases (Table 10.2). Finally, *es decir*, *o sea* and *jeuk* are used more frequently, both between clauses and between phrases (Tables 10.2 and 10.3):

Table 10.2. Distribution of Spanish reformulation markers

	clause + clause	phrase + phrase	clause + phrase	phrase + clause	Total
Es decir	756	1.242	34	92	2,113
	35.8 %	58.8 %	1.1 %	4.4 %	100.0 %
O sea	124	154	11	9	298
	41.6 %	51.7 %	3.7 %	3.0 %	100.0 %
Esto es	51	174	5	12	242
	21.1 %	71.9 %	2.1 %	5.0 %	100.0 %
A saber	8	31	–	6	45
	17.8 %	68.9 %	–	13.3 %	100.0 %

Table 10.3. Distribution of Korean reformulation markers

	clause + clause	phrase + phrase	clause + phrase	phrase + clause	Total
Jeuk	565	690	15	142	1,412
	40.0 %	48.9 %	1.1 %	10.1 %	100.0 %
Got	56	313	3	12	384
	14.6 %	81.5 %	0.8 %	3.1 %	100.0 %
Geureoni-	185	36	2	2	225
kka	82.2 %	16.0 %	0.9 %	0.9 %	100.0 %
Malhaja-	87	31	1	4	123
myeon	70.7 %	25.2 %	0.8 %	3.3 %	100.0 %

4.2. Rhetorical Comparisons

4.2.1. The Structure of Double Reformulation and Some Particular Rhetorical Patterns of the Marker Got

As is known, the basic structure of reformulation is 'reformulated member (A) + reformulation marker (RM) + reformulating member (B)'. Nevertheless, in Li (2013) different forms of paraphrase (reformulation) with Korean RMs are reported, which for the purpose of this paper will be called 'the structure of double reformulation'. The author refers to those constructions in which more than two RMs are used in linked segments. Four types of double reformulation are found (i–iv):

(i) A (a1 + RM 1 + a2) + RM 2 + B;
(ii) A + RM 1 + B (b1 + RM 2 + b2);
(iii) A (a1 + RM 1 + a2) + RM 2 + B (b1 + RM 3 + b2);
(iv) A + RM 1 + B + RM 2 + C

In the corpus, no statistically significant data is observed with reference to double reformulation. Only 3.0 % of the cases were obtained in the Korean corpus, and 1.5 % in the Spanish. Nonetheless, it should be indicated that there are some rhetorical patterns that deserve special attention. Firstly, see the following examples of the structure of double reformulation A (a1 + RM 1 + a2) + RM 2 + B:

(5) Otra sustancia indisolublemente unida a estas muertes es la sangre. Pero, a diferencia de lo que ocurre con el aire, *la sangre*, **es decir**, *una hemorragia*, *no es síntoma indefectible de muerte en el acto.* **O sea**, *que perder sangre implica la muerte, pero a medio plazo* (*Odiseo Revista de Historia*, nº 1, 22/04/2001)
'Another substance inextricably linked to these deaths is blood. But, unlike what happens with air, *blood*, **es decir**, *a hemorrhage, is not an unfailing symptom of death on the spot.* **O sea**, *losing blood implies death, but in the medium term.*'

(6) 북한이 노리는 것은 신년 공동사설에서도 밝힌 것처럼 *핵이라는 수단을 빌려 남과 북*, 즉 *'조선 민족 대 미국'이라는 대결 구도를 만드는 것이다.* 즉 *'민족 공조'라는 말을 빌려 한·미 공조의 틈새를 만들자는 것이다.* (*Weekly Chosun* nº 1758, 2003)
'As stated in the New Year's joint editorial, what North Korea is aiming for is *to create a confrontational structure between the North and the South*, **jeuk**, *the Korean nation versus the United States, by the means of nuclear weapons.* **Jeuk**, *borrowing the term 'national cooperation', the goal is to create a gap between South Korea and the United States.*'

Of special interest is that, as can be seen from the example (6), in the structure of the double reformulation, the two RMs in Korean used can be the same (*jeuk, … jeuk, …*). In other words, unlike in Spanish, in which the immediate repetition of the same lexical elements is not usually recommended in a text, this does not happen in Korean. In this language, repetition is frequently presented with an emphasis value (or with a rhythmic value) and, therefore, the repetition of the same reformulation marker is more frequent than in Spanish[5]. This repetition of the same marker in double reformulation is also observed with the marker *got* in the following examples (7–8):

(7) 지역이 곧 열린 학교이고, 학교는 곧 지역의 한 부분이기 때문에…
'Because the town is ***got*** an open school, and the school is ***got*** a part of the town…'
(*Greenreview*, 41, 2001)

(8) 누구를 미워한다. 그것은 곧 자기자신을 미워하는 것이죠.
누구를 해친다. 그것은 곧 자기 생명을 해친다는 얘기죠.
누구를 제거한다. 그것은 곧 자기 생명을 제거하는 일이죠.
'You hate someone. *That is* ***got*** you hate yourself.
You hurt someone. *That is* **got** you will end up destroying your own life.
You kill someone. *That is* ***got*** you would be killing your own life.' (*Greenreview*, 41, 2001)

In these examples of double reformulation with the marker *got*, the structure is also marked with the repetition of the marker (*got*… *got*… *got*…). Example (7) refers to the pattern *A got B, B got A*, and the example (8) presents *A got A'. B got B'. C got C'*. These structures only appear with *got* and not with any other item observed in this paper. From my observation, this type of structure of repetition, or double reformulation, offers the value of emphasis in Korean, but it also seems related to the initial hypothesis of Kaplan's Contrastive Rhetoric (1966, 1972) in which he described the pattern of explanatory discourse of Eastern languages as an inductive, indirect and non-linear style. In these examples, the development of the theme is not clearly observed between the associated segments.

The following examples are also from the marker *got*, but denote a characteristic of Korean culture. 6 % of all examples of *got* indicate this type of structure in our corpus.

(9) a. 그들의 아픔은 곧 저의 아픔입니다.
'Their pain is ***got*** my pain.' (*Hankyoreh Daily*, 2003, theme: lady / daily life)
b. 네 자식이 곧 내 자식인데…
'Your son is ***got*** my son…' (*Dong-a Daily*, 2003, theme: culture)

5 In terms of repetition as a discursive value, the study of John Hinds should be mentioned (1983). This researcher tried to demonstrate the existence of a Japanese expository writing style that is highly appreciated by speakers of that language, but negatively evaluated by English-speaking audiences. In this paper, repetition is an example as to the contrastive analysis of Spanish and Korean RMs.

c. 현대건설의 부도위기는 곧 국내 건설업의 부도위기 (...)
'The bankruptcy crisis of Hyundai E&C is ***got*** the bankruptcy crisis of the domestic construction industry. (...)' (*Chosun Daily*, 2001, theme: economy)

In examples (9a)–(9c), the expressions of the reformulated member (*their pain, your son, the bankruptcy crisis of Hyundai E&C*) are described as *my pain, my son, the bankruptcy crisis of the domestic construction industry* in the reformulating member, denoting, thus, the collective, inclusive or supportive sense of the speaker. These expressions reveal very important features of Korean culture such as unity, empathy, and responsibility, but often serve to highlight collective opinions more than individual ones.

4.2.2. The Process of Definition and Denomination in RMs in Spanish and Korean

The process of definition and denomination is related to implicatures, in particular, with the implicated premises in Relevance Theory (Sperber & Wilson, 1986, 1995), because through these functions the encyclopaedic (or contextual) value of the reformulated segments is expressed (Murillo, 2007, 2012). The result of the corpus analysis indicates some divergence of these two functions in Spanish and Korean RMs (Table 10.4):

Table 10.4. The cases of definition and denomination of RMs in Spanish and Korean

	Definition		**Denomination**		**Total cases and % of each language**
	Cases	**%**	**Cases**	**%**	
Spanish	262	9.7 %	33	1.2 %	295 / 2,698 (10.9 % / 100 %)
Korean	126	5.9 %	104	4.9 %	230 / 2,144 (10.8 % / 100 %)

As shown in the table, the sum of the two discursive functions (related to the premises) appears with a similar frequency in both languages (Spanish 10.9 % – Korean 10.8 %). However, the definition value in Spanish is displayed with a higher frequency (9.7 %) than in Korean (5.9 %); and that of denomination is observed more in Korean (4.9 %) than in Spanish (1.2 %). See the following examples of definition (10, 11) and denomination (12, 13):

(10) Al Gobierno le preocupa especialmente el *llamado* "efecto estadístico", ***es decir***, que la entrada en la UE de regiones más pobres hará descender la media y varias

regiones españolas quedarán reflejadas en la estadística como artificialmente más ricas. (*La Razón*, 17/06/2003)'The Government is especially concerned about the so-called "statistical effect", ***es decir***, the entry into the EU of poorer regions will lower the average and several Spanish regions will be reflected in the statistics as artificially richer.'

(11) 다모는 '차 심부름을 하는 여자', 즉 관청에서 차를 끓이는 등의 잡무를 담당하는 여성을 말한다. (*Weekly Chosun* nº 1769, 2003)'DAMO is 'the woman who brings tea', ***jeuk*** refers to the woman who was in charge of preparing tea in the city hall.'

(12) Los accidentes laborales cuestan en España cerca del 4 por ciento de la riqueza generada en un año, ***es decir***, de PIB (Producto Interior Bruto), según se desprende de un informe de CCOO, (…). (*Diario de Jerez Digital*, 27/01/2004)
'Occupational accidents in Spain cost about 4 percent of the wealth generated in a year, ***es decir***, of GDP (Gross Domestic Product), according to a CCOO report, (…).'

(13) 파두의 '운명'은 저항이 아니라 수용이다. 파두의 주된 가사인 배신당한 사람, 죽음과 절망을 모두 받아들이는 정서, 갈망을 머금은 포용이 곧 사우다데다. (*Dong-A Daily*, 2003, Theme: culture)'The 'destiny' of Fado is not a resistance, but rather an acceptance. The main lyrics of Fado speak of men being betrayed, of the feeling of death and despair, as well as of the acceptance of a burning desire ***got*** Saudade.'

In this sense, and as pointed out in Cuenca and Bach (2007) (cf. Gülich and Kotschi, 1995), definition is perceived as a semantic 'expansion' of the reformulated segment, while denomination is considered a 'reduction'. Thus, taking into account the results obtained in Table 10.4, it could be argued that Spanish RMs are characterized by expanding the content of the reformulated member, developing ideas or the complexity of reasoning through reformulation (definition). But those of Korean, on the contrary, fundamentally serve to introduce the reduction or condensation of the semantic content of the reformulated member (denomination).

4.2.3. The Process of Conclusion in RMs in Spanish and Korean

With regards to the conclusive function, as mentioned in 4.1, the lexicalized forms of Korean RMs, such as *jeuk* and *geureonikka*, display conclusive and consecutive values. On the contrary, those of Spanish RMs, such as *es decir*, *o sea*, *esto es*, in connection with their lexicalized forms (copulative structure), present more explanatory values. As a result, and as the following table indicates, approximately 5 % of these functions are found more commonly with Korean RMs (34.1 %) than Spanish RMs (29.2 %) (Table 10.5):

Table 10.5. The cases of conclusion in Spanish and Korean

	Conclusion		**Mathematic operations**		**Total cases and % of each language**
	Cases	**%**	**Cases**	**%**	
Spanish	787	29.2 %	158	5.9 %	945 / 2,698 (35.1 % / 100 %)
Korean	732	34.1 %	32	1.5 %	764 / 2,144 (35.6 % / 100 %)

Examples (14) and (15) are cases of conclusion introduced by *es decir* and *jeuk*:

(14) En otro apartado, Del Olmo dice que El Haski utilizaba un sistema de comunicación vía Internet, consistente en facilitar un correo electrónico y una contraseña para abrirlo. Cuando el destinatario lo abre, lee los mensajes en el apartado "grabar" y responde con su mensaje en el apartado "borrador", evitando así el tráfico de mensajes de una cuenta a otra, "***es decir***, no existe correo electrónico entre los comunicantes". (*El País*, 22/12/2004)'In another section, Del Olmo says that El Haski used a communication system via the Internet, consisting of providing an email and a password to open it. When the reciever opens it, she reads the messages in the section "record" and replies with her message in the "draft" section, thus avoiding the traffic of messages from one account to another, "***es decir***, there is no email between the communicators"'.

(15) 연구결과 사람 환자에게는 히포크레틴 수용체의 돌연변이가 없었다. 그러나 환자의 뇌나 척수액 중 히포크레틴이 정상인에 비해 분명히 적다는 것이 밝혀졌다. 즉 인간 환자에게 있어 유전적 이상은 없지만 히포크레틴의 절대량 부족은 역시 문제가 되는 것이다 (*Dong-A Daily*, 2003, Theme: science)
'The results of the study showed that there were no hypocretin receptor mutations in human patients. However, it was found that hypocretin in the brain or the spinal fluid of the patient was clearly lower than that of a normal person. ***jeuk***, there is no genetic abnormality in human patients, but an absolute deficiency of hypocretin is also a problem.'

5. Conclusions

This paper has attempted to study Spanish and Korean reformulation markers from the perspectives of linguistic typology and contrastive rhetoric. The results could provide a useful ground to analyse more reformulation markers in non-Indo-European languages, apart from Korean. The conclusions which can be drawn from this study are the following:

(i) Regarding the typology of languages (Moreno Cabrera, 2005, 2021), the fundamental divergence between Spanish and Korean is their morphological configuration (fusional and agglutinative language). An in-depth comparison and development of these aspects has been essential to analyse the RMs of both languages, in particular to gain convincing insight or explications in terms of the number of cases found in the corpus in the two languages, the lexicalized forms of the markers addressed, and their syntactical connective relations.

(ii) With regard to rhetorical traditions (Kaplan, 1966; Hinds, 1987; Clyne, 1994; Connor, 1996, 2008), Spanish and Korean RMs demonstrate different frequencies and uses in our corpus. As examples, we have been able to observe the use of the structure of double reformulation, especially the repetition of the Korean markers (*jeuk… jeuk…/ got… got…*), the copulative structure of the marker *got,* denoting Korean culture, and the different discursive values such as definition, denomination, and conclusion in Korean and Spanish reformulation markers.

(iii) Based on the Sections 4.2 and 4.3, the definition value in Spanish (9.7 %) is observed with a higher frequency than in Korean (5.9 %), while that of denomination is displayed more in Korean (4.9 %) than in Spanish (1.2 %). Therefore, it is speculated that Spanish RMs are characterized by expanding the content of the reformulated marker, or the complexity of reasoning through reformulation process. In contrast, those of Korean are mainly employed to introduce the condensing or reduction of the semantic content of reformulated member.

(iv) In regard to the conclusive value, approximately 5 % of examples are registered more with Korean RMs (34.1 %) than with Spanish RMs (29.2 %). It seems that the high use of the conclusive functions in Korean RMs relates to their lexicalized forms. On the contrary, Spanish RMs, in connection with the copulative structure in their forms, tend to present more explicatory values.

(v) As for the quantitative and qualitative analysis carried out in the present paper, unlike Murillo (2007), in which a notable difference is observed in terms of the cases of the RMs of Spanish and English (797 occurrences in English / 2,823 occurrences in Spanish), in the RMs of Spanish and Korean the divergence is found more clearly in the qualitative analysis. However, the difference in the total number of Spanish and Korean reformulators is also significant (Spanish: 2,698 cases, Korean: 2,144 cases). Seemingly, the reason being is that in Korean the connection is usually manifested through the verbal connective endings and not with the conjunctive adverbs.

Nevertheless, the results of this study call attention to several topics in need of future investigation. First, it is necessary to continue to expand the list of languages in order to make further linguistic and rhetorical comparisons, and to develop methodological frameworks (with relation to different level of texts such as words, phrases, sentences and paragraphs) for a more complete picture of reformulation as a universal process. For example, we have observed in this study that the Korean RMs are characterized as reducing the segment previously addressed in comparison with the Spanish RMs (Section 4.2.2); however, Cuenca and Bach (2007) concluded that Spanish RMs are mostly used to reduce content previously commented, while those of English serve to expand previous sequences (Section 2.3). In that sense, there remains a need to realize more detailed comparative studies with the concepts finely defined (terms such as expansion, reduction, etc.). Second, there is a necessity to study the origins of RMs in non-European languages with regard to reformulation and other discursive functions in depth; as we have observed, the conclusive value was more frequently found in the lexicalized forms of Korean reformulation markers. Lastly, more genre-driven or cross-disciplinary research of reformulation and its markers are also required.

References

Ahn, J. H. (2000). On the process of grammaticalization of *geureo-* type's connectives in Korean. *Journal of Korean Linguistics* 35, 113–141.

Alias, N. (2018). *Contribución al estudio de las partículas reformuladoras de explicación en español y en malayo actuales. (Con referencia especial a sendos corpus de textos escritos de lenguajes especializados)*. PhD dissertation, Universidad de Zaragoza.

Barandiaran, A. & Casado M. (2011). Marcadores discursivos: calas contrastivas en los reformuladores del español y el euskera. In H. Aschenberg & O. Loureda Lamas (eds.), *Marcadores del discurso: de la descripción a la definición* (pp. 375–395). Iberoamericana/Vervuert.

Blakemore, D. (1993). The relevance of reformulations. *Language and Literature* 2, 101–120.

Blakemore, D. (1996). Are apposition markers discourse markers? *Journal of Linguistics* 32, 325–347.

Briz, A. (1998). *El español coloquial en la conversación*. Ariel.

Choi, H. B. (1983 [1937]). *Korean Grammar*. Chungumsa.

Choi, I. H. (2016 [1963]). *회색인*. Moonji [Spanish Version. *El hombre gris* (2016). Verbum].

Clyne, M. (1994). *Inter-cultural communication at work. Cultural values in discourse*. Cambridge University Press.

Connor, U. (1996). *Contrastive rhetoric*. Cambridge University Press.

Connor, U. (ed.) (2008). *Contrastive rhetoric: Reaching to intercultural rhetoric*. John Benjamins.

Cuenca, M. J. (2003). Two ways to reformulate: A contrastive analysis of reformulation markers. *Journal of Pragmatics* 35, 1069–1093.

Cuenca, M. J. & Bach, C. (2007). Contrasting the form and use of reformulation markers. *Discourse Studies* 9/2, 149–175.

Del Saz, M. M. (2003). *An analysis of English discourse markers of reformulation*. PhD dissertation. Universitat de València, Servei de Publicacions.

Flores Acuña, E. (2003). *Los marcadores de reformulación: análisis aplicado a la traducción español/italiano, de* en fin *y de* hecho. PhD dissertation. Universidad de Málaga.

Garcés Gómez, M. P. & García Pérez, R. (2009). La reformulación del discurso en español en comparación con el francés. Estudio contrastivo de los marcadores de reformulación. In M. P. Garcés Gómez (dir.), *La reformulación del discurso en español en comparación con otras lenguas (catalán, francés, italiano, inglés, alemán e islandés)* (pp. 67–92). Agencia Estatal Boletín Oficial del Estado.

García Pérez, R. (2009). La reformulación del discurso en español en comparación con el islandés. Estudio contrastivo de los marcadores de reformulación. In M. P. Garcés Gómez (dir.), *La reformulación del discurso en español en comparación con otras lenguas (catalán, francés, italiano, inglés, alemán e islandés)* (pp. 203–223). Agencia Estatal Boletín Oficial del Estado.

Gong, J. Y. (2012 [2005]). *우리들의 행복한 시간*. Prunsoop [Spanish Version. H. K. Lee (2012). *Nuestros tiempos felices*. La Esfera de los Libros].

Gülich, E. & Kotschi, T. (1983). Les marqueurs de la reformulation paraphrastique. *Cahiers de Linguistique Française* 5, 305–351.

Gülich, E. & Kotschi, T. (1995). Discourse production in oral communication. In U. M. Quasthoff (ed.), *Aspects of oral communication* (pp. 30–66). Walter de Gruyter.

Han, K. (2017 [2007]). *채식주의자*. Moonji [Spanish Version. Yoon, S. M. (2017). *La vegetariana*. Editorial Rata].

Hinds, J. (1983). Contrastive rhetoric: Japanese and English. *Text-Interdisciplinary Journal for the Study of Discourse* 3/2, 183–196.

Hinds, J. (1987). Reader versus writer responsibility: A new typology. In U. Connor & R. B. Kaplan (eds.), *Writing across languages: Analysis of L2 texts* (pp. 141–152). Addison-Wesley.

Hwang, S. Y. (2014 [2003]). *심청, 연꽃의 길*. Munhakdongne [Spanish Version. Riestra, B. (2014). *Shim Cheong: la niña vendida*. Alianza].

Hwang, S. Y. (2015 [2007]). *바리데기*. Changbi [Spanish Version. Álvaro, F. and L. Alfredo (2015). *Bari, la princesa abandonada*. Alianza].

Hyland, K. (2005). *Metadiscourse*. Continuum.

Hyland, K. (2007). Applying a gloss: Exemplifying and reformulating in academic discourse. *Applied Linguistics* 28, 266–285.

Ihm, H. B., ed. (2001). *Korean Grammar for International Learners*. Yonsei University Press.

Kaplan, R. B. (1966). Cultural thought patterns in intercultural education. *Language Learning* 16, 1–20.

Kaplan, R. B. (1972). *The anatomy of rhetoric: Prolegomena to a functional theory of rhetoric*. The Center for Curriculum Development.

Kim, H. (2021). *Estudio comparativo de los marcadores discursivos de reformulación explicativa en español y en coreano*. PhD dissertation. Universidad Autónoma de Madrid.

Li, H. M. (2013). A study on Korean paraphrasing sentences. *Korean Semantics* 40, 219–248.

Liu, D. (2020). Comparative rhetorical approach to Chinese expository paragraphs. In K. Lloyd, Keith (ed.), *Routledge handbook of comparative world rhetorics* (pp. 206–216). Routledge.

Liu, D. & Huang, J. (2021). Rhetoric construction of chinese expository essays: Implications for EFL composition instruction. *SAGE Open* 11/1, 1–10.

Matsui, T. (2002). Semantics and pragmatics of a Japanese discourse marker *dakara* (*so/ in other words*): A unitary account. *Journal of Pragmatics* 34, 867–891.

Moreno Cabrera, J. C. (2005). *Las lenguas y sus escrituras: tipología, evolución e ideología*. Síntesis.

Moreno Cabrera, J. C. (2021). *La clasificación de las lenguas*. Síntesis.

Murillo, S. (2007). *A Contribution to the pragmalinguistic contrastive study of explicatory reformulative discourse markers in contemporary journalistic written English and Spanish*. PhD dissertation. Universidad de Zaragoza.

Murillo, S. (2012). The use of reformulation markers in business management research articles. An intercultural analysis. *International Journal of Corpus Linguistics* 17/1, 64–90.

Nam, K. & Ko, Y. (2011 [1985]). *Standard Korean Grammar*. Top Press.

Park, W. S. (2013 [1992]). *그 많던 싱아는 누가 다 먹었을까*. Segyesa [Spanish Version. Moro Núñez, L. & Shim S. W. (2013). *Memorias de una niña de la Guerra*. Verbum].

Pons Bordería, S. (2006). A functional approach to the study of discourse markers. In K. Fischer (ed.), *Approaches to discourse particles* (pp. 77–99). Elsevier.

Pons Bordería, S. & Lopes Macário, A. C. (2014). *Ou seja* vs. *O sea*: Formal identity and functional diversity. *Revista de Estudos Linguísticos da Universidade do Porto* 9, 103–128.

Portolés, J. (2002). Marcadores del discurso y traducción. In J. García Palacios & M. T. Fuentes Morán (eds.), *Texto, terminología y traducción* (pp. 145–168). Almar.

Portolés, J. (2016). Los marcadores del discurso. In J. Gutiérrez-Rexach (ed.) *Enciclopedia Lingüística Hispánica* 1 (pp. 689–699). Routledge.

Robles i Sabater, F. (2017). Information structure and grammaticalization: Discourse markers and utterance position in Catalan and German. *Zeitschrift für Katalanistik: Revista d'Estudis Catalans* 30, 185–206.

Rossari, C. (1994). *Les opérations de reformulation*. Peter Lang.

Roulet, E. (1987). Complétude interactive et connecteurs reformulatifs. *Cahiers de Linguistique Française* 8, 111–140.

Seo, J. S. (1995). *Korean grammar*. Hanyang University Press.

Shin, K. S. (2011 [2008]). *엄마를 부탁해*. Changbi Publishers [Spanish Version. A. Echevarría (2011). *Por favor, cuida de mamá*. Grijalbo].

Sperber, D. & Wilson, D. (1995 [1986]). *Relevance: Communication and cognition*. Blackwell.

Yang, Y. (2017). A probe into the translation paradigm of '則' in Korean annotation of Chinese Classics. *Korean Language & Literature* 102, 91–115.

Yu, H. R. (2005). A study on the function of the connective endings. *Grammar Education* 3/3, 87–105.

Fátima Silva, Fátima Oliveira, Ana Sofia Pinto

11 On Discourse Reformulation Markers with the Structure *More + Adverb* in European Portuguese: A Corpus-Based Study

Abstract: Reformulation and its markers have been the subject of extensive investigation in different theoretical frameworks. However, little research has concerned markers consisting of the structure 'more + adverb' except for the description of Spanish and English, or these two languages in contrast (a.o. Saz Rubio, 2007; 2009; Gerhalter, 2018, 2020). The present study aims at: (1) systematising the properties and conditions of use of each marker in EP; (2) comparing the discourse markers of reformulation (DMRs); (3) analysing the role of the discourse domain in their use; and (4) discussing their role in a typology of European Portuguese (EP) discourse markers of reformulation (DMR). For this, we assembled a corpus from available corpora, three written and two oral, representing different discourse genres. For the analysis of each marker and subsequent comparison of the results, we adapted Saz Rubio's (2007) proposal. The results showed a higher frequency of all five discourse markers in the written sub-corpora, with bigger use of *mais precisamente* (more precisely), followed by *mais concretamente* (more concretely), *mais exatamente* (more exactly), *mais propriamente* (more properly), and rather more scarcely of *mais corretamente* (more correctly). Furthermore, the DMRs were distributed along a scale, encompassing discourse values ranging from correction/rectification to precision/concretion.

Keywords: reformulation markers, corpus linguistics, cross-linguistic analysis

1. Introduction[1]

Reformulation, its discourse mechanisms, and linguistic structures have been widely studied in different theoretical and applied perspectives. However, little research has been done on discourse markers with the structure 'more + adverb' in the case of Spanish and English, or their contrast (a.o. Saz Rubio, 2009; Gerhalter, 2020). The most studied are *más precisamente*, *más exactamente*, *más correctamente*, and *more precisely*, *more exactly*, *more accurately*, which

1 This research was supported by Centro de Linguística da Universidade do Porto, under the FCT Funding Programme – UIDB/00022/2020 (Fundação para a Ciência e a Tecnologia) and PhD Grant UI/BD/150975/2021 for Ana Sofia Pinto.

often co-occur with *or* and less with *and*. For European Portuguese (EP), to our knowledge there is no systematic description of the equivalent DMRs.

The present study aims at: (1) systematising the properties and conditions of use of each marker in EP; (2) comparing the five DMRs; (3) analysing the role of the discourse domain in their use; and (4) discussing their role in a typology of European Portuguese (EP) DMRs.

To achieve this, we compiled a corpus by combining three written and two oral corpora, which represent various discourse genres. The corpus was then subjected to both quantitative and qualitative analyses. The annotation scheme adopted in this study is adapted from Saz Rubio's (2007) proposal for the analysis of these markers in English and Spanish.

The structure of the article is as follows. In Section 2, we outline the theoretical framework supporting this study, and we focus on the DMR with the structure *more + adverb* and related studies; in Section 3, we describe the corpus and the methodology; in Section 4, we provide the data analysis; in Section 5, we discuss the results; and finally, in Section 6, we present some concluding remarks.

2. On Discourse Markers of Reformulation with the Structure *More + Adverb*

Generally, reformulation can be characterised as a discourse strategy that enables the speaker to revisit a preceding segment of discourse, rephrasing it with the intent of addressing potential interpretation issues and expressing a certain point of view (a.o., Garcés Gómez, 2008, 2009, 2010; Cuenca & Bach, 2007; Lopes & Carapinha, 2017; Lopes, 2014; Rabatel, 2017). So, it implies the production of a new version of what was said before, by returning to the previous subject, to clarify, synthesize or correct it (cf. Martínez, 2016: 16). In that sense, it corresponds to a process of reinterpretation that ensures textual cohesion and progression—, facilitating communication (cf. Cuenca & Bach, 2007: 149—150). As several authors have already proposed, this can be viewed as a scalar process (Lopes & Carrilho, 2020; Pinto, 2018; Silva & Pinto, 2021), positioned between paraphrasing and rectification, with an intermediate type of clarification.

DMRs are a very frequent mechanism to express reformulation, by signalling the following instruction: interpret what follows as a better formulation of what has just been said (a.o., Lopes, 2014; Pons Bordería & Lopes, 2014).

Like many other discourse markers, DMRs present some specific syntactic, semantic and discourse properties. The first may be described as grammaticalised expressions, consisting of a two-place operator (the source text segment and the rephrased text segment), being a prosodic constituent with a flexible distribution, although the initial position is the most common. As for the discourse properties, we would highlight their procedural meaning, which may be associated with a conceptual meaning (cf. Vassiliadou, 2008), and present different semantic-discourse values. These discourse markers serve as strategies for both auto-reformulation and hetero-reformulation. They may pertain to the propositional content or the structure of the utterance, presenting, in accordance with their function, a movement of expansion, reduction or permutation.

In this study, our focus is on the DMRs with a fixed structure consisting of *more + adverb -ly/mais + adverb – mente*. The adverb is formed from an adjective. So, for example, *exactly* derives from the adjective *exact* and *precisely* from the adjective *precise*. Its meaning is semantically transparent and may be paraphrased by 'speaking more precisely/accurately' (Saz Rubio, 2007: 177).

These markers have primarily been analysed in terms of their syntactic, semantic and discourse properties, and have been assigned a peripheral status in the set of DMRs due to their considerable lower usage compared to other reformulators (a.o. Saz Rubio, 2007, 2009), Gerhalter (2018, 2020). For European Portuguese, *(ou) mais corretamente*, *(ou) mais exatamente*, and *(ou) mais precisamente* are mentioned by Lopes (2016) and Lopes and Carrilho (2020) in the framework of a general typology of EP discourse markers, as non-paraphrastic discourse markers of reformulation (DMRs). *(Mais) concretamente* is in the group of elaborative discourse markers for encoding an "elaboration through specification" (Lopes, 2016: 445). *Mais propriamente* has no place in her typology.

As previously mentioned, there is a lack of descriptions of these DMRs since only a limited number of studies examined them in the scope of DMRs. Gerhalter (2018, 2020), following other authors, indicates 4 main semantic-discourse values of these markers: concretion, concretion-precision, rectification, and explanation. Saz Rubio (2003, 2006, 2007, 2009), on the other hand, categorises *more precisely* and *more exactly* as modification DMR.

Saz Rubio (2007, 2009), who refers to the occurrence of these markers with the disjunctive conjunction, and Gerhalter (2018, 2020), who includes both the disjunctive conjunction *ou* (or) and the copulative conjunction *e* (and), signal their optional nature. Moreover, while the conjunction *ou* expresses an alternative of the content or part of the content of S1, the conjunction *e* conveys the addition of information that is considered more precise or more correct than the one stated in S1. Therefore, commutation between them is not permitted (cf. Gerhalter, 2018).

In our study we will examine five DMR with the structure *mais adverb -mente*. Although the paper does not have contrastive objectives, we consider the following equivalences in their use for approximate translation purposes: *mais concretamente* 'more concretely/precisely', *mais exatamente* 'more exactly/accurately', *mais precisamente* 'more precisely/more concretely/more exactly', *mais propriamente* 'more exactly/properly/appropriately', *mais corretamente* 'more correctly'. The adverbs derive from the adjectives *exato* 'exact', *preciso* 'precise', *concreto* 'concreto', *correto* 'correct', and *próprio* 'proper'.

3. Corpus and Methodology

For this study, we use a corpus comprising five sub-corpora: two oral – *Integrated Reference Corpora for spoken Romance Languages* (C-Oral-Rom[2]) (29h51min) and *Perfil Sociolinguístico da Fala Bracarense* (PSFB[3]) (81h51min) – and three written sub-corpora – *CETEMPúblico*[4] (180 million words), NOW (2012–2019) from the *Corpus do Português*[5] (1.1 billion words), and 122 scientific papers (1 million words) from different fields. The constitution of the corpus was based on two criteria: (i) oral and written modality, (ii) diversity of genres, and discursive domains.

The methodological steps were as follows: (i) selection of the sub-corpora; (ii) extraction of the relevant segments; (iii) definition of the annotation criteria; (iv) annotation by sub-corpora by two annotators, both experts in linguistics, preceded by a random sample annotation to check the level of inter-annotator agreement; (v) analysis of the results for each criterion by sub-corpora; (vi) discussion of the results.

The annotation criteria, adapted from Saz Rubio's proposal (2007), consist of: (i) DMR position; (ii) scope of the reformulation; (iii) contexts of use; and (iv) mode of realization. In terms of methodology, we have opted essentially for

2 *C-Oral-Rom* is a multilingual corpus which consists of spontaneous speech produced by speakers with different sociolinguistic profiles, and is characterised by a differentiated structural organisation, corresponding to various discourse genres (cf. Cresti & Moneglia, 2005: 13).

3 *PSFB* is an open-source corpus of spontaneous speech, consisting of 80 semi-planned face-to-face interviews with speakers of different educational levels and age groups. It is homogeneous as far as genre is concerned, since it is only constituted by interviews, and focuses on the variety of Portuguese spoken in the city of Braga (cf. Marques & Aguiar, 2014.

4 *CETEMPúblico* (Corpus of electronic text extracts MCT/Público) is an open-source corpus of approximately 180 million words in European Portuguese extracted from the newspaper *Público*.

5 The *Corpus do Português* (Portuguese Corpus) was created by Mark Davies and provides billions of words from four varieties of Portuguese.

a qualitative approach of a descriptive nature, complemented by a quantitative analysis for characterising the data from each sub-corpora concerning the five MDRs considered.

4. Results

In this section, we start by providing a global analysis of the corpus and subsequently proceed to a comparative analysis of the sub-corpora based on the previously defined criteria.

4.1. DMRs Distribution by Sub-Corpora

The analysis of Table 11.1, summarising the quantification of occurrences of each DMR in the sub-corpora, provides valuable insights into their occurrence in terms of both modality and discourse domains. It also allows us to observe comparatively the behaviour of each DMR. In this analysis, we considered both the occurrence of the DMR with and without the co-occurrence of the conjunctions *e* and *ou*.

Table 11.1. DMR distribution per sub-corpora

	C-Oral-Rom	PSFB	Scientific papers	Cetempúblico	Corpus do Português[6]
mais concretamente	0	1	8	168	915
e mais concretamente	0	0	1	93	73
ou mais concretamente	0	0	0	29	12
mais corretamente	0	0	0	5	21
e mais corretamente	0	0	0	1	1
ou mais corretamente	0	0	0	26	13
mais exatamente	1	0	0	286	146
e mais exatamente	0	0	0	3	4
ou mais exatamente	0	0	2	62	24
mais precisamente	0	0	12	594	950

(*continued on next page*)

6 For this study, we selected a sample of 1000 randomly selected occurrences of these European Portuguese DMRs.

Table 11.1. Continued

	C-Oral-Rom	PSFB	Scientific papers	Cetempúblico	Corpus do Português[6]
e mais precisamente	0	0	2	32	51
ou mais precisamente	0	0	3	78	32
mais propriamente	0	0	4	26	638
e mais propriamente	0	0	0	7	15
ou mais propriamente	0	0	0	20	35

In total, these DMRs occur 4394 times in the corpus and are distributed as follows, from most to least used: *mais precisamente* (1754 occurrences), followed by *mais concretamente* (1300 occurrences), *mais exatamente* (528 occurrences), *mais corretamente* (67 occurrences).

Concerning their use by the sub-corpora, we observe that these DMRs are almost inexistent in the oral sub-corpora. There is only one occurrence of *mais exatamente* in C-Oral-Rom and one of *mais concretamente* in PSFB, having a reformulation value of rectification and concretion, respectively.

The situation relating to the written sub-corpora is quite different in terms of the number of occurrences of these markers, and it is possible to observe differences in the use of discourse markers in the three sub-corpora (see Figure 11.1).

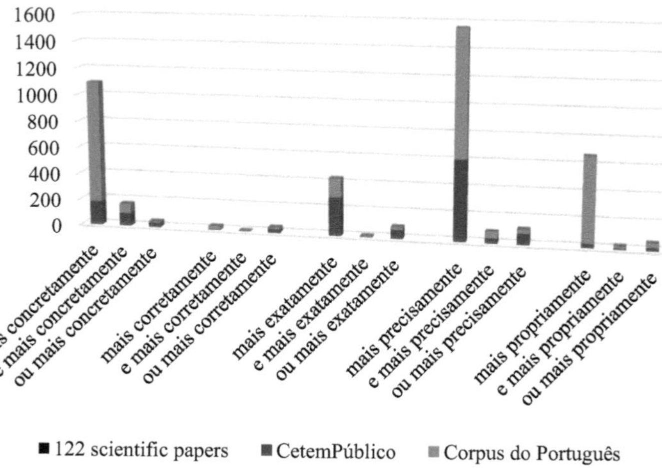

Figure 11.1. Occurrences of the DMR per written sub-corpora

As shown in Figure 11.1, in the sub corpora of scientific articles, the DMRs *mais concretamente* and *mais precisamente* occur mainly, with only two occurrences of *mais exatamente* and none of *mais corretamente*. Opposing to the small number of occurrences in the scientific academic discourse domain, these DMRs are widely used in the journalistic discourse, corresponding to the sub-corpora CETEMPúblico and Corpus do Português. When comparing the distribution of the DMRs in these two sub-corpora, it is observed that the DMRs *mais precisamente* and *mais corretamente* occupy the first and last position in the number of occurrences in both sub-corpora, which present positioning differences regarding the other DMRs:

- CETEMPúblico: *mais precisamente, mais exatamente, mais concretamente, mais propriamente, mais corretamente*;
- Corpus do Português: *mais precisamente, mais concretamente, mais propriamente, mais exatamente, mais corretamente.*

Moreover, we observe that, except for *mais corretamente*, in CETEMPúblico, these DMR have more isolated occurrences than when used with the conjunctions *e* or *ou*. When considering their use with these conjunctions, we note that the markers with higher co-occurrence with the conjunction *e* are *mais concretamente* and *mais precisamente*. In contrast, the least used are *mais exatamente*, *mais corretamente* and *mais propriamente*, respectively. This trend differs when considering the co-occurrence with *ou*, as the marker *mais concretamente* is much less used when compared to *mais corretamente*, *mais exatamente*, and *mais propriamente*, which display a more extensive use.

4.2. DMRs Characterisation

To characterise these DMRs, we consider their distribution, scope of the reformulator, contexts of use, and modes of realisation.

4.2.1. DMRs Position

Regarding their position, the five DMRs can occur in the initial, medial, and final positions. The initial position is dominant, followed by the medial, and then the final position, corresponding, respectively, to the following schemes:

(i) S1 [DMR] S2
(ii) S1 [S2 [DMR] S2]
(iii) S1 [S2 [DMR]]

Examples (1) to (3) illustrate each one of these schemes, respectively.

(1) Estamos, afinal, perante um documentário que se "transfigurou" em ficção. **Mais exatamente**, Mendoza correspondeu a uma encomenda para registar os efeitos devastadores de o tufão Yolanda. (CP-16-11-02 PT)
'This is, after all, a documentary that has been "transfigured" into fiction. **More exactly**, Mendoza was commissioned to record the devastating effects of typhoon Yolanda.'

(2) Não é no entanto a feição geral da filosofia ocidental que teve quase sempre uma má relação com o amor – que, **mais precisamente**, teve quase sempre um encontro falhado com o amor. (SP_02-F-UC-3)
'It is not, however, the general feature of Western philosophy that it has almost always had a bad relationship with love – that, **more precisely**, it has almost always had a failed encounter with love.'

(3) Beloved está traduzido, desde há uns anos, desde 1989, **mais exatamente**. (CETEMPúblico,par=ext1473261-clt-93b-1)
'Beloved has been translated for a few years now, since 1989, **more exactly**.'

In (1), the DMR *mais exatamente* occurs in the initial position (scheme i), introducing S2 ('Mendonza correspondeu a uma encomenda para registar os efeitos devastadores do tufão Yolanda') with the instruction that what follows (S2) should be interpreted as a new and more exact formulation of S1. In (2), S2 is introduced by the relative pronoun – *que* (that) – and followed by the DMR *mais precisamente*, inserted into the reformulated segment – *que teve quase sempre um encontro falhado com o amor*. In (3), the DMR *mais exactamente* occurs in the final position, after S2, considering it a more exact version of S1 relevant segment – 'desde há uns anos'.

The DMRs may optionally occur with the coordinative conjunctions *e* and *ou*, becoming integral parts of the DMR, at least with the DMRs under analysis. Therefore, we may consider a variant of scheme i. to include their co-occurrence (scheme iv), which is not possible when the DMR is in the medial and final position.

(iv) S1 [ou/e DMR] S2

Examples (4) and (5) exemplify this scheme, in which the DMR precedes the conjunction and introduces S2. In (4), The DMR instructs that the S2 serves as an alternative to the relevant part of S2 to which it refers. In (5), using the DMR with the conjunction *e* allows for the interpretation that S2 precises S1 by defining it.

(4) Dos doze hóspedes de Laura Rei os suspeitos ficam assim reduzidos aos que estavam na pensão na tarde da sua morte **ou mais propriamente** ao grupo dos sonos trocados. (CP – 18-08-04 PT)

Of the twelve guests of Laura Rei, the suspects are thus reduced to those who were in the pension on the afternoon of her death **or more properly/more accurately** to the group of swapped sleepers. (CP – 18-08-04 EN)

(5) As atualizações **e mais concretamente** a frequência com que os updates são lançados, ou não, pode ser uma questão importante na escolha de um smartphone. (CP – 19-06-23 PT)
'Updates and **more specifically** the frequency with which updates are released, or not, can be an important issue when choosing a smartphone.'

4.2.2. Scope of the Reformulator

We also identified the scope of the reformulator by determining the syntactic structures of S1 subject to reformulation. For this purpose, we identified six linguistic structures: W – word, NP – noun phrase, PP – prepositional phrase, QNP – quantificational noun phrase, VP – verb phrase and U – utterances.

Table 11.2 summarises the results of this analysis, presenting the identified structures that occur with all the DMRs under study.

Table 11.2. Scope of the reformulator

MDR	**Scope**					
	W	**NP**	**PP**	**QNP**	**VP**	**U**
mais concretamente	Π	Π	Π	Π	Π	Π
mais corretamente	Π	Π	Π	Π	Π	Π
mais exatamente	Π	Π	Π	Π	Π	Π
mais precisamente	Π	Π	Π	Π	Π	Π
mais propriamente	Π	Π	Π	Π	Π	Π

Examples (6) to (12) exemplify each of these structures.

(6) Ahhh… O que seria de Marrocos sem camelos, **ou mais corretamente**, dromedários? Não foi difícil cruzarmo-nos com os "cavalos do deserto" (CP-18-11-29 PT)
'Ahhh… What would Morocco be without camels, **or more correctly**, dromedaries? It wasn't difficult to cross paths with the "desert horses".'

(7) O horário dominical, **ou, mais concretamente,** o regime de funcionamento dos hipermercados ao domingo, permanece ainda como a grande «questão crítica». (CETEMPúblico, par=ext410713-eco-96a-2)
'Sunday opening hours, **or more precisely**, the opening hours of hypermarkets on Sundays, still remains the great "critical issue".'

(8) Nessa noite da maior celebração mundial do cinema – **ou, mais exatamente**, do maior espetáculo mundial a propósito do cinema – que foi apresentada como de homenagem ao género musical, passou-se algo grosseiro, injusto e triste….(CP-17-03-25 PT)
'On that evening of the world's greatest celebration of cinema – **or, more accurately**, the world's greatest show about cinema – which was presented as a tribute to the musical genre, something crass, unfair, and sad happened.'

(9) E se fizéssemos um referendo sobre a Europa? **Ou, mais precisamente**, 27 referendos. (CP-17-03-09 PT)
'What if we had one referendum on Europe? **Or, more precisely**, 27 referendums.'

(10) S. diz que quem ler "os e-mails (…), dificilmente e honestamente encontrará (**mais exatamente**, não encontrará) fundamento sério para as suspeitas aventadas." (CP-19-02-16 PT)
'S. says that whoever reads "the e-mails (…), will hardly and honestly find (**more exactly**, will not find) any serious basis for the suspicions raised." '

(11) Que fazer com os refugiados? **Ou mais precisamente**: como abordar, politicamente, a questão dos refugiados? (CP-17-09-30 PT)
'What to do with refugees? **Or more precisely**: how should we approach the refugee issue politically?'

In (6), the scope of the reformulator is the word *camelos*, which is reformulated by *dromedários*, considered a more correct or accurate term, instead of the general class, camel. This kind of reformulation usually occurs within a lexical relation of hypernymy. In (7), the reformulation's scope is the NP *o horário dominical*, which is reformulated by the NP *o regime de funcionamento dos hipermercados ao domingo*. The DMR used with *ou* provides an alternative to the previous formulation to precise it. The scope of the reformulator in (8) is the PP *da maior celebração mundial do cinema*, which is reformulated in S2 *do maior espectáculo mundial a propósito do cinema*, by a PP introduced by the DMR *ou, mais exatamente*. In turn, (9) features a QNP as the scope of the reformulator: S2 – *27 referendos* – is introduced by *ou mais precisamente* and reformulates S1, corresponding to *um referendo*. In (10), a VP – *encontrará* – constitutes the scope of the reformulator and is reformulated by its negative counterpart – *não encontrará*, introduced by the DMR, S2 is introduced by *ou mais precisamente* and reformulates S1, which corresponds to *um referendo*. Finally, the scope of the reformulator may be a complete utterance as seen in (11), where S1 is an interrogative sentence (*Que fazer com os refugiados?*) reformulated also as an interrogative sentence (*como abordar, politicamente, a questão dos refugiados?*) by means of the DMR *mais precisamente* preceded by *ou*.

Although a full quantitative analysis of the corpus has not been conducted yet, its qualitative analysis, of which these examples are a sample, allows us to draw the following conclusions regarding the scope of the reformulator: (i) there is a higher occurrence with NP, PP, and QNP structures; and (ii) S1 and S2 typically have the same syntactic structure (e.g., N-N, PP-PP, QNP-QNP).

4.2.3. *Contexts of Use of DMRs*

The delimitation of the contexts of use of these markers is an essential criterion for their characterisation. It stemmed from analysing a random sample of each sub-corpora and the existing literature for its study in Spanish and English (cf. Saz Rubio, 2007, 2009; Gerhalter, 2018, 2020).

These contexts of use represent the semantic-discursive functionality signalled by the DMRs when used independently or in conjunction with *e* or *ou*. We have provisionally defined nine contexts, as outlined in Table 11.3.

Table 11.3. Contexts of use in which the DMR operates

Contexts of use	**DMR**				
	(ou/e) mais corretamente	**(ou/e) mais precisamente**	**(ou/e) mais exatamente**	**(ou/e) mais concretamente**	**(ou/e) mais propriamente**
S2 rectifies any imprecise, inexact, or erroneous information	Π	Π	Π	Π	Π
S2 precises numbers and quantities	Π	Π	Π	Π	Π
S2 replaces a more general concept, location, or date by a more specific one	Π	Π	Π	Π	Π
S2 introduces new information regarding S1	Π	Π	Π	Π	Π
One element of S2 contrasts with one element of S1	Π	Π	Π	Π	Π
S2 explicitly negates S1	X	Π	X	X	Π
The scope of the reformulation in S2 is all S1, expressing speaker's attitude	Π	Π	Π	Π	Π
S2 clarifies or explains S1	X	Π	Π	Π	Π
S2 invalidates S1 (or part of S1)	Π	X	X	X	Π

Although the DMRs under analysis operate in most contexts, we observed some specificities related to the conceptual content of these discourse markers. So, *mais corretamente* and *mais propriamente* allow for an invalidation of S1. However, unlike *mais propriamente*, *mais corretamente* is excluded from contexts in which S2 specifies or clarifies S1. Besides, only two DMRs allow for explicit negation of S1: *mais precisamente* and *mais propriamente.*

Examples (12)–(20) display each of these contexts of use.

(12) Em Nova Iorque, **mais exatamente** na Times Square, onde milhares de pessoas festejam a entrada do novo, serão colocados, em torno de a praça, dezenas de camiões do lixo carregados de areia… (CP – 16-12-31 PT)
'In New York, **more exactly** in Times Square, where thousands of people celebrate the arrival of the new year, dozens of rubbish trucks full of sand will be placed around the square.'

(13) Ao todo, a Alta Autoridade iniciou quase três mil processos desde a sua entrada em funcionamento, **mais concretamente** 2.963 processos. (par=ext408914-soc-92b-2)
'In all, the High Authority has initiated almost three thousand cases since it came into operation, **more concretely** 2,963 cases.'

(14) Diz-se que Olivença foi fundada por templários espanhóis (**mais correctamente**, por templários leoneses… o que é importante, pois a Espanha não existia). (CP-18-02-21 PT)
'It is said that Olivenza was founded by Spanish Templars (**more correctly**, by Leonese Templars… which is important, as Spain did not exist).'

(15) Estamos, afinal, perante um documentário que se "transfigurou" em ficção. **Mais exatamente**, Mendoza correspondeu a uma encomenda para registar os efeitos devastadores do tufão Yolanda. (16-11-02 PT)
'This is, after all, a documentary that has been "transfigured" into fiction. **More exactly**, Mendoza was commissioned to record the devastating effects of Typhoon Yolanda.'

(16) Esta disciplina oscila entre ser um tempo em que os professores arengam as turmas sobre o bom comportamento (**ou mais propriamente** sobre a falta dele) (CP – 19-03-16 PT)
'This subject oscillates between being a time when teachers harangue classes on good behaviour (**or more properly** on the lack of it).'

(17) S. diz que quem ler "os e-mails (…), encontrará (**mais exatamente**, não encontrará) fundamento sério para as suspeitas aventadas." (CP-19-02-16 PT)
'S. says that whoever reads "the e-mails (…), will find (**more exactly**, will not find) any serious basis for the suspicions raised." '

(18) Estes dados tudo sugerem que, até que tivessem uma palavra, é provável que os nossos ancestrais nunca tivessem visto o azul – **ou, mais precisamente**, provavelmente viam-no como o fazemos actualmente, mas nunca o perceberam (CP-18-04-09 PT)

'This data suggests everything that, until they had a word, it is likely that our ancestors never saw blue – **or, more accurately**, probably saw it as we do today, but never understood it.'

(19) Em resumo, o aproveitamento político é aquilo que um homem quiser. **Ou mais precisamente** em Portugal o aproveitamento político é aquilo que certos homens quiserem. (CP-17-07-30 PT)
'In short, political advantage is whatever a man wants. **Or, more precisely**, in Portugal, political advantage is whatever certain men want.'

(20) O espectáculo dos carros que andam na água, dos barcos que andam em terra, **ou mais correctamente** dos veículos que planam em ambas estas superfícies, ficou, no entanto, muito prejudicado. (CETEMPúblico par=ext369911-des-93a-1)
'The show of cars on the water, boats on land, **or more correctly**, vehicles gliding on both surfaces, was, however, greatly impaired.'

In (12), the speaker in S2 refers to a specific location out of several that are part of the location mentioned in S1, providing more exact information to the interlocutor. In (13), S2 offers a precise number, contrasting with the indefinite value of S1 due to the presence of the adverb *quase*. In (14), S2 brings the specific value to which the percentage in S1 refers. In (14), part of S2 *templários leoneses* specifies a general concept from S1 *templários espanhóis*, through the rectifying feature present in DMR *mais correctamente*. This context of use often involves concepts in a hyperonymy relation. As for (15), S2, headed by the DMR 'mais exatamente', provides a clearer explanation of S1 by adding more concrete information, considered more precise than S1. In (16), a segment of S2 – *sobre a falta dele* – rectifies a segment of S1 – *sobre o bom comportamento,* by inserting a contrasting element, typically involving words in an antonymic relation. In (17), S1 and S2 present the same verb in different forms (positive/negative). In other words, S2, through the negation of the verb, corrects S1, nullifying it. Regarding (18), S2 does not give more precise or exact information, but reflects the speaker's point of view, patent in the use of modal constructions. In (19), S1 presents the concept *aproveitamento político* in a generalized scope and *um homem* as equivalent to *any man*. Through S2, these general concepts are clarified. That is, the concept *aproveitamento político* is particularised through the addition of *em Portugal* and the quantificational noun phrase *um homem* is reformulated by *certos homens*, transitioning from a universal quantification to existential quantification. Finally, in (20), S2 invalidates S1, justifying the use of the DMR *mais corretamente*, since this is the DMR whose compositional meaning is closest to invalidation or correction. Once S1 is invalidated, S2 becomes the only relevant segment for interpreting the utterance, highlighting the hierarchy between the segments involved in the reformulation process.

4.2.4. *Mode of Realisation*

Concerning the mode of realization of these DMRs, as shown in Section 4.2.1., they can be used independently or in combination with the conjunctions *and* and *or*.

This preference is more easily understood when we consider the basic function of these connectors occurring with DMRs and it contributes, at least partially, to their distinction.

Our data show that, in EP, the five DMRs considered admit co-occurrence with these two conjunctions, showing, however, differences at the level of their occurrence and their expression with the different markers. In fact, we observe that although both conjunctions occur with all DMRs, the DMRs *mais corretamente* 'more correctly', *mais propriamente* 'more properly' and *mais exatamente* 'more exactly' occur more often with the conjunction *ou* 'or' while *mais concretamente* 'more concretely' and *mais precisamente* 'more precisely' more often with the conjunction *e* 'and'.

As for English and Spanish (cf. Saz Rubio and Gerhalter), the co-occurrence of the disjunctive conjunction *ou*, signals that S1 or part of S1 are reformulated by S2, which should be understood as an alternative expressing it in a more correct, proper, exact, precise, or concrete manner. Let us look at (21) and (22).

(21) Durante a primeira meia hora do espectáculo, o ritmo da peça é, deste modo, o de <u>uma pequena ópera</u> **ou mais exactamente**, <u>uma oratória</u>. (CETEMPÙblico, par= ext736430-clt-93b-1)
'During the first half hour of the performance, the rhythm of the play is that of <u>a small opera</u>, **or more exactly**, <u>an oratorio.</u>'

(22) É estranho ver <u>uma região</u>, **ou mais corretamente** <u>um pequeno punhado de produtores dessa região</u>, pretenderem negar o estilo que tornou famosa essa região (…).
'It is strange to see a region, or more correctly a small handful of producers from that region, claiming to deny the style that made that region famous.'

In (22), *ou, mais exactamente*, gives the instruction that S2 – *uma oratória* – is an alternative formulation to S1 – *uma pequena ópera*. This procedimental meaning of reformulation adds to the conceptual meaning of the DMR: 'in a more exact way'. In (22), the alternative presented with the DMR mais *corretamente* can be paraphrased by 'or said in a more correct manner'.

In both cases, this means that there is the idea of an alternative introduced by *or* to which a rectification feature is associated. Still, the instruction given by the two markers is different. In fact, the rectification in (21) relates to the possibility of saying S1 more accurately, which corresponds to an exercise in precision, not necessarily better. In (22), the alternative presented implies the invalidation of S1, being S2 necessarily a better formulation, which adds a stronger feature of correction.

Nevertheless, *ou* is optional in both contexts and can be elided without compromising the propositional truth, as we may see in (21'). But it should also be noted that the contexts in which occurs *ou* may not commute with the conjunction *e*, as (21") shows.

(21') ΠDurante a primeira meia hora do espectáculo, o ritmo da peça é, deste modo, o de uma pequena ópera, **mais exactamente**, uma oratória.
'During the first half hour of the performance, the rhythm of the play is that of a small opera, **more exactly**, an oratorio.'

(21") *Durante a primeira meia hora do espectáculo, o ritmo da peça é, deste modo, o de uma pequena ópera, **e mais exactamente**, uma oratória.
'During the first half hour of the performance, the rhythm of the play is that of a small opera, **and more exactly**, an oratorio.'

The explanation for the non-commutability lies in the information instruction produced by the conjunctions, since *e* gives the instruction that S2 should be understood as an addition relative to S1 and not an alternative, as can be seen in (23) and (24), where S2 is understood as a formulation that adds information to S1 to concretize it, specify it, which is indicated by the DMR *more concretely*.

(23) Fazendo mostra da convicção com que o Executivo português assumiu a integração comunitária **e, mais concretamente**, a União Económica e Monetária (UEM), Braga de Macedo quis reforçar a ideia de que «Portugal não precisou de Maastricht para apostar na UEM». (CETEMPúblico, par=ext1319273-pol-92a-2)
'Demonstrating the conviction with which the Portuguese government has embraced Community integration **and, more specifically/concretly**, Economic and Monetary Union (EMU), Mr Braga de Macedo stressed that "Portugal did not need Maastricht to take part in EMU".'

(24) Quanto maior for o número de pessoas informadas sobre o que fazer em caso de emergência médica, **e mais concretamente** em caso de paragem cardiorrespiratória, mais vidas podem ser salvas. (CP-19-05-26 PT)
'The more people are informed about what to do in the event of a medical emergency, **and more specifically** in the event of cardiac arrest, the more lives can be saved.'

The procedimental meaning of reformulation adds to the conceptual meaning of the DMR: 'in a more precise, exact, concrete way + new formulation, mostly of concretion and precision. It cannot occur independently of this DMR, as (24') shows. Its occurrence with the conjunction *ou* does not convey that information, and the consideration of S2 as an alternative to S1 alters its interpretation.

(24') ? Quanto maior for o número de pessoas informadas sobre o que fazer em caso de emergência médica, **ou mais concretamente** em caso de paragem cardiorrespiratória, mais vidas podem ser salvas. (CP-19-05-26 PT)
'The more people are informed about what to do in the event of a medical emergency, **or more concretely** in the event of cardiac arrest, the more lives can be saved.'

5. Discussion

The results obtained in analysing these discourse markers considering distribution, reformulator's focus, contexts of use, and mode of realisation allow us to outline some properties that characterise them. Furthermore, they offer some clues to their status in a typology of discourse markers of reformulation, enhancing our understanding of the similarities and specificities of their uses and values.

Considering the corpus analysed, we verify that this is a set of DMRs with an almost inexistent use in spoken language, exhibiting a distinct behaviour in writing according to the domain. Its use is very scarce in the scientific article genre, occurring mainly in the journalistic discourse. The greater tendency of these markers to occur in writing is also confirmed by in other studies (Gerhalter, 2020), supporting the hypothesis that these are more extended forms than those typically used in oral communication. A previous study of DMR with the same oral Portuguese sub-corpora (Silva & Pinto, 2021) has shown that the most used markers in EP are *quer dizer*, *isto é* and *ou seja*. Additionally, refer to Duarte and Marques (2019) for insights intothe metadiscursive uses of verb *dizer* in oral corpora.

In related studies, attention has been focused on the interpretation of markers such as *more exactly/more accurately/más exatamente* and *more precisely/más precisamente* as reformulators. Because we consider the five may encode the instruction that S2 or part of S2 constitutes a new formulation of S1 or part of S2 to make it more accurate, more precise, more appropriate, or correct, we opted for also analysing *mais concretamente* 'more concretely', *mais propriamente* 'more properly/more exactly' and *mais corretamente* 'more correctly', besides *mais exatamente* 'more exactly' and *mais precisamente* 'more precisely'.

The relation between these DMRs may be better understood when we test their commutation possibilities in context, such as in (25). In this example, we can assign a value closer to precision/concretion than correction/rectification, as the possibilities of commutation with other DMRs with the same structure.

(25) Lembraram que a taxa de abstenção tinha sido quase 70%, **mais exatamente**, 68.64%. Por isso, os valores avançados por Marcelo estavam inflacionados. (19-05-31 PT)

'They noticed that the abstention rate had been almost 70%, **more exactly**, 68.64%. Therefore, the figures advanced by Marcelo were inflated.'

(25') ΠLembraram que a taxa de abstenção tinha sido quase 70%, **mais precisamente**, 68.64%. Por isso, os valores avançados por Marcelo estavam inflacionados.
'They noticed that the abstention rate had been almost 70%, **more precisely**, 68.64%. Therefore, the figures advanced by Marcelo were inflated.'

(25") *Lembraram que a taxa de abstenção tinha sido quase 70%, **mais corretamente**, 68.64%. Por isso, os valores avançados por Marcelo estavam inflacionados.
'They noticed that the abstention rate had been almost 70%, **more correctly**, 68.64%. Therefore, the figures advanced by Marcelo were inflated.'

(25"') Π Lembraram que a taxa de abstenção tinha sido quase 70%, **mais concretamente**, 68.64%. Por isso, os valores avançados por Marcelo estavam inflacionados.
'They noticed that the abstention rate had been almost 70%, **more concretely**, 68.64%. Therefore, the figures advanced by Marcelo were inflated.'

In fact, it is possible to establish a scale of these DMRs considering two basic values associated with them: precision and rectification. Figure 11.2 represents this scale.

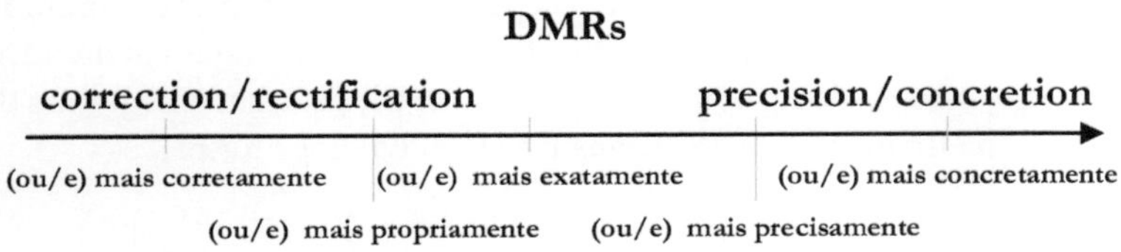

Figure 11.2. Distribution of the DMs by discourse value

(Ou/e) mais precisamente is the DMR that presents the highest number of occurrences in the corpora, and its most common value is that of concretion-precision, although it may also occur in contexts of rectification. *(Ou/e) mais precisamente* can rarely replace *mais corretamente* and can more easily commute with *mais exatamente*. The DMRs *mais precisamente* and *mais exatamente* can be integrated into the DMRs of modification (cf. Saz Rubio: S2 is presented as a conceptually modified alternative of S1). In contrast, *mais corretamente* presents a value of rectification, which consists in the reinterpretation and replacement of S1, totally or partially, by a more correct formulation (cf. Saz Rubio – DMR reassessment). *(Ou/e) mais corre(c)tamente* is always rectificative. *(Ou/e) mais exatamente* can clarify, precise or also correct, and is very frequent in quantificational contexts, specification of meaning, contrast, and explicit negation. *(Ou) mais propriamente* is closer to *mais corretamente* regarding its corrective value,

as well as of *(ou/e) mais exatamente* for sharing its precision value. *(Ou/e) mais concretamente* is closer to *mais precisamente* and presents a value of concretion or specification. *Mais concretamente* is the least frequent when combined with *ou* and the most frequent when combined with *e*. This can justify the fact that it appears mostly with precision/concretion value instead of rectification.

6. Concluding Remarks

The description of the DMRs with the structure 'mais + adverb – mente' contributes to a better understanding of how the DMRs under analysis function in terms of their syntactic, semantic, and discourse properties. The results allow us to conclude that, except for *mais corretamente* (more correctly) these DMRs present traits of semantic polyfunctionality, that, depending on the context of use, allow them to express values ranging from correctness to precision. These notions of polyfunctionality and scalarity contribute to a better description and distinction of these DMRs but also to the wider group of discourse markers signalling reformulation.

Our next steps are continuing the corpus analysis to provide a more fine-grained analysis of the corpus, comparing their use with the values of the adverbs when used isolatedly, doing a statistical analysis of the data, and integrating these markers in the framework of an exhaustive DMR typology for EP.

References

Cresti, E., & Moneglia, M. (Eds.). (2005). *C-ORAL-ROM: integrated reference corpora for spoken romance languages*. John Benjamins Publishing.

Cuenca, M.-J. & Bach, C. (2007). Contrasting the form and use of reformulation markers. *Discourse Studies* 2/9, 149–175.

Duarte, I. D. & Marques, M. A. (2019). Expressions métadiscursives comprenant le verbe portugais *dizer*. *Studii de lingvistică* 9/2, 113–130.

Garcés Gómez, M. P. (2008). *La organización del discurso: marcadores de ordenación y de reformulación*. Iberoamericana.

Garcés Gomez (ed.) (2009). *La reformulación del discurso en español en comparación con otras lenguas: (catalán, francés, italiano, inglés, alemán e islandés)*. Universidad Carlos III de Madrid.

Garcés Gomez, M. P. (2010). Marcadores de corrección y rectificación en los textos escritos. *Revista de Investigación Lingüística* 13/1, 87–105.

Gerhalter, K. (2018). Innovación y analogía en la creación de los marcadores de reformulación más exactamente y más precisamente. *Estudios Humanísticos. Filología* 40, 163–190.

Gerhalter, K. (2020). *Paradigmas y polifuncionalidad. Estudio diacrónico de preciso/precisamente, justo/justamente, exacto/exactamente y cabal/cabalmente.* De Gruyter.

Lopes, A. C. (2014). Contributo para o estudo sincrónico dos marcadores discursivos 'quer dizer', 'ou seja' e 'isto é' no português europeu contemporâneo. *Diacrítica*, 28/1, 33–50.

Lopes, A. C. (2016). Discourse Markers. In W. L. Wetzels, J. Costa & S. Menuzzi (eds.). *The Handbook of Portuguese Linguistics* (pp. 441–456). Wiley Blackwell.

Lopes, A. C. & Carapinha, C. (2017). Por outras palavras e digamos: marcadores de reformulação? *Revista Galega de Filoloxía* 18, 115–131.

Lopes, A. C. & Carrilho, E. (2020). Discurso e marcadores discursivos. In Raposo, E. P., Nascimento, M. F. B., Mota, M. A., Segura, L. & Mendes, A. (Orgs.) *Gramática do Português*, Vol. III, pp. 2667-2698. Fundação Calouste Gulbenkian.

Marques, M. A.& Aguiar, M. (2014). Usos de portanto no falar bracarense. In Veloso, J. Moreno, A., Silva, F., Falé, I. & Pereira, I. *XXIX Encontro Nacional da Associação Portuguesa de Linguística (Coimbra, 2013). Textos Selecionados*, pp. 321-331. APL.Martínez, F. P. (2016). Marcadores del discurso y contextos funcionales: la reformulación como construcción discursiva. *Onomázein Revista Semestral de Linguística, Filologia y Traducción* 34, 14–35.

Pinto, A. S. (2018). *Marcadores de reformulação parafrásticos no género artigo científico*. MA dissertation. FLUP.

Pons Bordería, S. & Lopes, A. C. M. L. (2014). Ou seja vs. o sea: Formal identity and functional diversity. *Linguística. Revista de Estudos Linguísticos da Universidade do Porto* 9, 103–128.

Rabatel, A. (2017). Frontières Supra-Catégorielles, Catégorielles, Infra-et-Trans-Catégorielles de la Reformulation. *Analele Universității din Craiova. Seria Științe Filologice. Limbi și Literaturi Romanice* 1, 65–103.

Saz Rubio, M. M. del. (2003). *An analysis of English discourse markers of reformulation*. PhD dissertation. Universitat de Valencia.

Saz Rubio, M. M. del. (2006). An overview of Spanish discourse markers of reformulation. *Odisea: Revista de Estudios Ingleses* 7, 89–102.

Saz Rubio, M. M. del. (2007). *English discourse markers of reformulation.* Peter Lang.

Saz Rubio, M. M. del. (2009). La reformulación del discurso en español en comparación con el inglés. Un estudio contrastivo de los marcadores de modificación en inglés y en castellano. In M. P. Garcés Gomez (ed.), *La reformulación del discurso en español en comparación con otras lenguas: (catalán, francés, italiano, inglés, alemán e islandés)*. Universidad Carlos III de Madrid.

Silva, F. & Pinto, A. S. (2021). O marcador de reformulação quer dizer no discurso oral: funções semântico-discursivas e questões de género. In D. Ablali, M. Gonçalves & F. Silva (eds.), *Reformuler, une question de genres? / Reformular, uma questão de géneros?* (pp. 141–164). Editora Humus.

Vassiliadou, H. (2008). Quand les voies de la reformulation se croisent pour mieux se séparer: à savoir, autrement dit, c'est-à-dire, en d'autres termes. In M.-C. Le Bot, M. Schuwer & Richard E. (eds.), *La reformulation. Marqueurs linguistiques et stratégies énonciatives* (pp. 35–50). PUR.

Anna de Marco, Mariagrazia Palumbo

12 Interactional Discourse Markers in a Corpus of Italian Migrants in Munich

Abstract: The present study focuses on the use of interactional discourse markers (DMs) in the context of Italian migration varieties. Data are analysed in two generations of Italian migrants living in Munich. The research aims to explore how the use of interactional DMs varies in terms of their functional space across generations. Results indicate a gradual loss of the functional space of DMs lost in the first generation while in the second generation is partly stable and partly replaced by German DMs. From the second generation onwards, the functions of DMs undergo a process of restructuration or are replaced by German DMs, as in the case of *also* that covers the function of *allora* as turn taking.

Keywords: interactional markers, Italian migration, language contact, migrant generations

1. Introduction[1]

The research aim of this paper is to verify how the use of the interactional DMs, both in terms of their functional space and forms, varies across two generations of Italian migrants in Germany.

DMs constitute a topic of significant theoretical interest, with studies focusing on their use in various types of discourse including language of the media, and interactive contexts, linguistic contact settings, language acquisition and foreign language learning.

Research on DMs – regardless of the specific field of investigation – faces initial challenges in defining them from a descriptive-functional perspective. These elements are not immediately assigned to a grammatical category and serve several functions simultaneously, acting as connecting elements at all levels, explaining the interpersonal dimension, serving as means of discursive planning or clarifying cognitive processes. Therefore, the functional identification of the DMs in a given context often results from the core meaning of the single DM and various parameters such as the surrounding speech unit (contextual parameters) and the discursive situation, the relationship between the interlocutors and the

1 Although the paper is a joint work of the two authors, the first author is responsible for Sections 1, 2, 3, 4 and the second author is responsible for Sections 5, 6 and 7.

communicative purposes of the interaction within which the DMs are used (cf. Romero Trillo, 2018; Redeker, 2006).

As emphasizedin a recent work (De Marco & Palumbo, 2022), DMs have an intriguing character. They are marked by some contrasting forces: one the one hand, their polyfunctionality makes them more difficult to acquire, and less amenable to transfer from one language to another. On the other hand, their pervasiveness in conversation and their independence from propositional content makes them easy to acquire and to transfer into contact contexts (Matras, 1998). Investigating DMs in contact varieties is motivated by these specific features: wn in previous research has demonstrated that DMs belong to the linguistic structures used to foster the process of (reciprocal) comprehension of the message and the management of the interaction. They fall into the category of linguistic structures that allow speaker to place the utterance in the right perspective, considering the listener's expectations and potential reactions to it (Matras, 1998: 85).

As Sansò (2020: 109) has underlined, DMs in contact context are typically chosen based on the speakers' preferences for linguistic codes, i.e. they use DMs belonging to one of the languages present in their linguistic space. This could represent one of the initial steps towards the creation of a mixed variety, either involving the fusion of linguistic systems or the pragmatic dominance of one language for communicative functions outside the group of emigrants (Scaglione, 2003: 46) depending on social factors or the linguistic systems in contact. However, researches are still investigating the driving force that lead to the adoption of DMs from one system to the other. Our article aligns with this line of research.

Our paper is organized as follows: 1. Introduction. 2. DMs in a migration context; 3. Interactional DMs; 4. Aims and theoretical framework; 5. Methodology and participants; 6. Data discussion; 7. Conclusion.

2. DMs in a Migration Context

Migration linguistics is a relatively recent but productive area of study, with the primary goal of analysing the dynamics of linguistic contact in a migratory context (Krefeld, 2004; De Marco & Palumbo, 2015). The use of DMs in migratory varieties has gained increasing interest only in recent years, although earlier research underscored the importance of studying DMs in language contact situations (Haugen, 1953; Poplack, 1980). Research has often correlated the use of DMs, along with other linguistic dynamics in contact situation, to social factors such as the generation of speakers, the level of education and the linguistic pressure of L2 (Clyne, 2003: 215; Krefeld 2004) but also with issues related to the perception of identity with reference to language use (De Fina, 2007; De Marco & Palumbo, 2015).

While languages come into contact for various reasons, migration languages become endangered under the pressure of the host standard language or of a dominant language fulfilling a specific communicative function (Fishman, 2001).

As for DMs in a bilingual context, they are perceived as a distinct category and are often transferred when used with a DM function but are not when used with a propositional meaning (Maschler, 1997). The functional and formal similarity of DMs in some languages leads to transfer processes as happens with the German *also* and the Italian *allora* 'then' (De Marco, 2017). Concerning generational variation, Clyne (2003: 225–233) considering the German/Hungarian/Dutch and Croatian community in Australia states that English discourse markers are transferred especially by later generation groups, such as second generation. It has also been shown that in the second generation of speakers metadiscursive DMs undergo a progressive reduction of forms and functions (De Marco & Palumbo, 2022).

Maschler (1997) argues that the conversation among speakers in contact situations is a privileged ground from which to observe the DMs: they seem to be perceived as a distinct category and are therefore often expressed in a different language. Depending on the linguistic systems of the contact languages, the DMs having a lexical or deictic value are more sensitive to code-switching or mixing because they are often placed in a peripheral position of sentences or clauses, where these phenomena generally occur (Myers-Scotton, 1993). Another reason, as shown in De Marco (2018), has to do with the fact that the functions external to the propositional content such as turn taking, reformulation, and fillers, are more sensitive to the shift from one language to another.

3. Interactional DMs

The interactional function mainly pertains to the communicative situation and the interaction between the speaker and hearer, encompassing aspects such as turn-taking, agreement, confirming attention, acknowledgment, etc.. More specifically, DMs serve to mark the conversational moves of the interlocutors. On the speakers' side, they function as as turn-taking, phatic, checking comprehension and modulation devices (e.g. *sì, sì sì* 'yes', *certo* 'sure', *direi* 'I would say', *per me* 'for me', *si può dire* 'one can say', *dunque* 'therefore'). On the addressee's side, they function as listener responses and reactive tokens (e.g. *allora* 'well', *ma* 'but', *scusa* 'excuse me', *insomma* 'in conclusion').

In the following examples, the DM *dunque* is used as turn taking (1) and the DM *quindi* is used as turn leaving:

(1) P: Ah, ho capito. E come erano organizzate le lezioni?
I: *Dunque* cinque, cinque giorni alla settimana, un'ora e mezza della conversazione, e un'ora e mezza di grammatica
'I: Oh, I see. And how were the lessons organized?
P: *well*, five, five days a week, an hour and a half of conversation, and an hour and a half of grammar' (Nigoević, Sučić, 2011)

(2) N: e pratichi: altri sport oltre all'atletica/ o solo l'atletica?
NN: no no solo la corsa(.) solo l'atletica ↓ tempo fa un po' di calcio però: / diciamo che ormai> non avendo più la possibilità di diventare un: < non lo so un giocatore professionista
N: Un calciatore
NN: eh un calciatore proprio come Del Piero↑magari (ride) e quindi no/ proprio mi sono preoccupato più-per ↑/no ma poi l'atletica è un modo uno stile di vita/ *quindi:/*
'N: do you practice other sports besides athletics, or only athletics?
NN: No no only running(.) only athletics ↓ I used to play soccer a bit: /let's say that by now> not having the possibility anymore to become a: <I do not know a professional player
N: a soccer player?
NN: eh a soccer player just like Del Piero↑ may be (laughs) and so no/I wish or therefore no I never minded any longer for ↑ no but after all athletics is a way of life *so::/*' (De Marco, 2016)

In the process of interaction, agreement plays a crucial role as a conversational move, confirming an ongoing process of negotiation of meaning among the interactants. The most widely used DMs in Italian, that cover various functions, are *sì* and *no* (Borreguero & Ferroni, 2020) appearing early in the process of language acquisition (see Jafrancesco, 2015 for L2 Italian DMs).

Interactional DMs are highly sensitive to the axes of variation including age, social group, individual differences, geographical area, used medium, language phase, etc. (Bazzanella, 2006; Sansò 2020). Therefore, they present particularly interesting aspects to investigate in the context of migration contact.

4. Aims and Theoretical Framework

The study will focus on the following research questions: 1. How does the use of interactional DMs in terms of their functional space varies across generations? 2. Can we identify the forces driving the changes occurring from one generation to the other?

The analysis aims to identify the most frequent functions, the number of DM types and tokens for each group. Data are investigated using an onomasiological approach, examining he functions DMs entail in conversation.

The functions found in the corpus are summarized in table 12.1, adapted on the taxonomy presented in Bazzanella (2006), Borreguero et al. (2017) and Sansò (2020).

Table 12.1. Interactional functions (Bazzanella, 2006; Borreguero & De Marco, 2021: 131; Sansò, 2020)

Functions	Subfunctions
Control (Speaker)	Turn taking, keeping and leaving the floor: *Sì* 'yes', *no* 'no', *cioè* 'that is'
	Request for confirmation/ attention: *Vero?* 'really?', *no?* 'no?', *capito?* 'do you understand?'
	Agreement or disagreement: *Sì* 'yes', *d'accordo* 'all right', *no* 'no'
	Mitigation and intensification (modulation devices): *Diciamo* 'well', *non so* 'I don't know', *per quanto ho capito* 'as far as I understood', *così* 'thus'
	Fatism: *Ma sai* 'but you know'
Contact (Listener)	Acknowledgment: *ah ok* 'ah ok', *sì* 'yes', *no* 'no'
Reaction (Speaker alternation)	Reactive response: *Nah* 'no', *ma* 'but'

Depending on the sociocultural, educational and linguistic variables, mentionedin par. 2, it is possible to assume that the number of DMs types with an interactional function slowly decreases across generations and that they are gradually replaced by German DMs.

5. Methodology and Participants

A corpus of approximately 13 hours of audio recordings have been elicited through description tasks and semi-structured interviews based on the following topics: migration, family, identity, job, Italian politics and tasks like picture descriptions.

The interviews of an average length of 30 minutes were conducted with 15 informants representing two generations of Calabrian migrants living in

Munich[2]. Interactions are transcribed following the Conversational Analysis annotation.

Table 12.2 shows that most of the informants reside in an Italian speaking context engage in endogamic marriages, and predominantly use Italian language in their private lives. While the first-generation informants have studied in Italy, the second generation studied in Germany. However, both generations work in Germany and use the host language in their professional lives.

Table 12.2. The informants

	Job	**Endogamous/ exogamous marriage**
1st generation		
1.EF66IA	Retired	Endogamous marriage
2.EM66IA	Restaurant owner	Endogamous marriage
3.EF40IA	Teacher	Exogamous marriage
4.EF67IA	Housewife	Endogamous marriage
5.EM77IA	Worker	Endogamous marriage
6.EF54IA	Waiter	Endogamous marriage
7.EM57IA	Worker	Endogamous marriage
8. EM42IA	Worker	Endogamous marriage
2nd generation		
1.EF42IIB	Assistant	Endogamous marriage
2.EM37IIA	Restaurant owner	Endogamous marriage
3.EM10IIA	Student	-
4.EF42IIA	Salesperson	Endogamous marriage
5.EF37IIA	Editor	Endogamous marriage
6.EF33IIA	Assistant	Endogamous marriage

2 In analogy with other migration corpora, informants are indicated using letters and number descriptive of those sociological features shaping migration contact: the first letter, E, means 'emigrant', the second one indicates the sex, male or female, the number is the age of the informant, the Roman number indicates informants' generation. The last letter is used to identify informants who have the same features, i.e. same age, sex and generation (for instance EF42IIA and EF42IIB). Interactions are transcribed following the Conversational Analysis annotation.

6. Data Discussion

6.1. Quantitative Data

Regarding quantitative data, we calculated the number of DMs over the total number of words and the number of DMs with the interactional function over the total number of DMs (Table 12.3). The most notable difference between the two generations is the change in the number of tokens and types. Thetoken number of DMs declines from the first to the second generation but the relative frequency of DMs and of interactional signals, i.e. the percentage over the total number of words and the percentage over the total number of DMs, increase in the second generation. However, differences are minimal, likely influenced by the sample size.

Table 12.3. Percentages of interactional DMs

	Total number of words	Discourse markers tokens	Interactional DMs tokens
1st generation	**18803**	587	**176**
Relative frequencies		3.12 %	**30 %**
2nd generation	**6448**	264	**104**
Relative frequencies		4.1 %	**40 %**

Observing the number of types in Table 12.4, the second generation shows a decrease compared to the first generation, inversely proportional to the frequency of the tokens. This aligns with the hypotheses that the second generation still uses a greater number of tokens than the first one since the informants need to implement certain functions (which we will see in detail later) to control the conversation function, while the number of types decreases due to their integration into the host country's social context (work, education) and the lack of sufficient input in L1 outside the family.

Table 12.4. Number of discourse marker types in the two generations

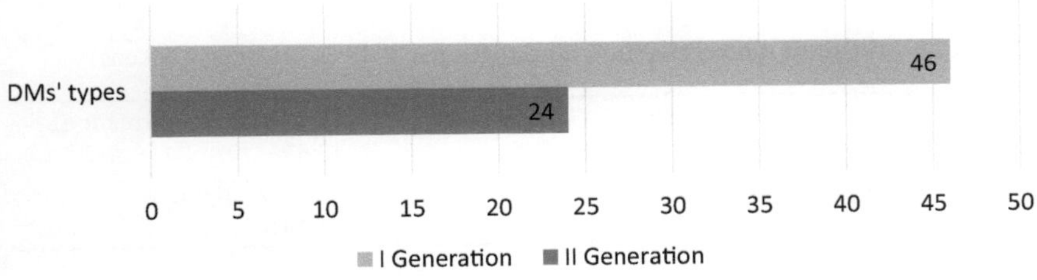

To have a better understanding of how the data change between the two generations, we can have a look at the functions and see which of the functions are the most represented in the two groups of informants.

To understand the data changes between the two generations, Figure 12.1 showcases the most frequent functions. Functions remain relatively stable between generations, with turn-taking, agreement and request for confirmation being the most frequent, particularly in the first generation. Furthermore, the second generation uses DMs more frequently for intensification and reactive response.

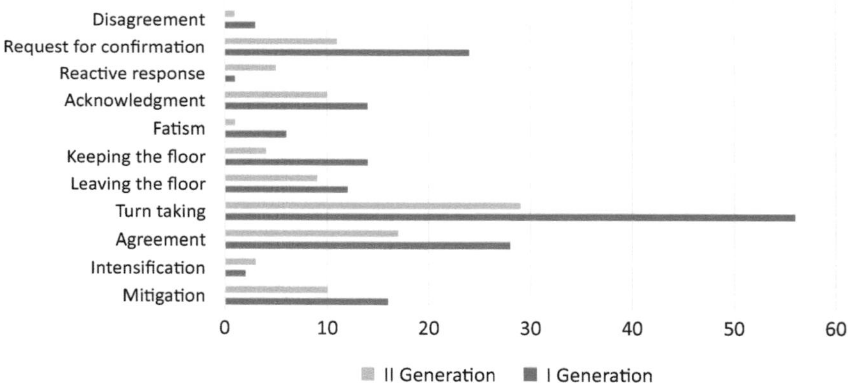

Figure 12.1. Interactional functions conveyed by DMs in both generations

Table 12.5 provides detailed percentages for the most represented functions, that are slightly less represented but still frequent in the first (request for confirmation) and in the second generation (acknowledgment). The following sections will describe the most representative functions in the two groups of speakers with examples from the corpus.

Table 12.5. The most represented functions throughout the generations (Tokens)

1st generation	**Turn taking** **30.9 %**	**Agreement** **15 %**	Request for confirmation 13.6 %
2nd generation	**Turn taking** **25.6 %**	**Agreement** **16 %**	Acknowledgment 9.6 %

6.2. Qualitative Data

If we look at the types (Figure 12.2) we notice that the second generation maintains more types for the turn taking function compared to the other functions, maybe due to the fact that this function fulfills the speakers' need to control the flow of conversation (Borreguero & De Marco, 2021). The phonetically light forms *ma* 'but', *sì* 'yes', *no* 'no' are the most stable types in the two generations.

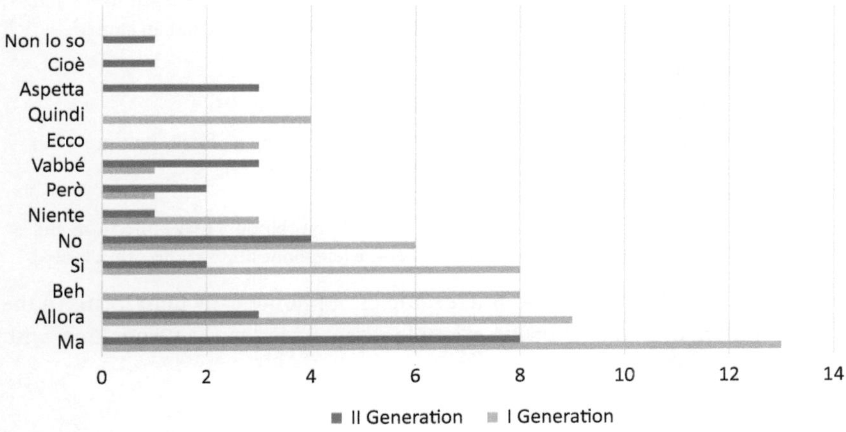

Figure 12.2. DMs with turn-taking function

The examples below show the use of the discourse marker *ma* 'but' as turn taking:

1st generation

(3) I: ah e che facevate nelle discoteche?
EM661A: *ma* io // aiutavo in un cucina!
'I: ah and what were you doing in discos?
EM661A: *but* I // was helping in the kitchen!'

2nd generation

(3) I: Kindergeld / questa m'interessa cos'è?
EM40IIA: *Ma* l'aiuto dello stato no? Per le mamme per le famiglie danno un tot per ogni bambino fino al…fino al…quattro anni tre anni
'I: Kindergeld / It is interesting. What is it?
EM40IIA: *But* the help of the Government? For the mothers and the families, they give a certain amount for each child up to four three years.'

In the following examples, another phonetically light form, *sì*, is used as turn taking:

1st **generation**

(5) I: Però è molto buono che parlano due lingue §
EM42IA: *Sì sì* / quello che vorrei / che purtroppo non sono riuscito e speriamo che lo faranno loro da grandi/ è / fare qualche corso di italiano
'I: But it is good that they speak two languages §
EM42IA: *Yes yes* / what I wish / that unfortunately I haven't managed to do and hopefully they will do it when they grow up /is/ attending some Italian course'

2nd **generation**

(6) I: Puoi ripetere non ho capito
EF33IIA: *Sì*↑ Allora faccio assistente di medico? tiro sangue, faccio punture e mh poi faccio anche davanti i conti mh , telefono e tutte cose varie
'I: Can you repeat I don't understand
EF33IIA: *Yes* ↑ So I work as a medical assistant. I draw blood, I make injections and mh then I also do the accounts mh, answer the telephone and various other tasks'

In our corpus, it is quite easy to find examples of phonetically light forms in the 1st generation, as in the following example where *no* is used as turn taking, with an overlapping of turn:

1st **generation**

(7) EM661A: Per riprendermi alla vita di che fanno giù ci vogliono anni io
I: no ma non credo che ti adatteresti perché [
EM661A: [*no no* non mi sarei -non è possibile adattarmi là sotto no non no
'EM661A: It takes years to get used to their (Calabrian) way of life
I: no but I don't think you would adapt because [
EM661A: [*no no* I wouldn't be – it is not possible for me to adapt down there no no no'

2nd **generation**

(8) I: ok ah ah dialetto?
EF42IIB: il calabrese
I: ma lo parli?
EF42IIB: sì
I: e con i ragazzi
EF42IIB: *no* -sì con i ragazzi lo parlo quando mi fanno mi fanno incazzare (risate) allora parlo il calabrese (risate)
'I: ok ah ah dialect?
EF42IIB: Calabrian

I: but do you speak it?
EF42IIB: yes
I: and with the kids?
EF42IIB: *no* -yes I speak Calabrian with the kids when they make me angry (laughter) then I speak Calabrian (laughter)'

Besides, as shown in Figure 12.2, the most frequent Italian DMs – as *allora* – are also used in our corpus:

1st generation

(9) I: Senti essere emigrata italiana qui è stato facile o no?
E1F40A: *allora* mi ricordo benissimo che ho passato i primi quattro cinque mesi piangendo perché le reazioni dei tedeschi nei miei confronti <che ancora non parlavo bene la lingua> erano veramente devastanti
'I: Do you feel that being an Italian immigrant here was easy or not?
E1F40A: *well,* I remember very well that I spent the first four five months crying because the reactions of the Germans towards me < since I did not speak the language well> were really devastating'

2nd generation

(10) I: e in famiglia che lingua parlate coi bambini?
EF42IIB: *allora* mio marito parla l'italiano con loro io invece parlo il tedesco
'I: and in the family what language do you speak with the children?
EF42IIB: *then* my husband speaks Italian with them, while I speak German'

Another well balanced function across generations is agreement, 15 % in the first generation and 16 % in the second one (see Table 12.5). This datum in not surprising considering that agreement is

> one of the most frequent conversational moves, both in formal and informal interactions, and it has proved to be one of the best indicators of linguistic competence in a foreign language as it requires comprehending what has been said by the conversational partner and overtly expressing both comprehension and solidarity with the content of the previous utterance (Borreguero, 2019: 1).

First generation informants use the most common agreement DMs in Italian, *sì*, (Bazzanella, 1995, 2006; Borreguero, 2019), while in the second generation the number of types decreases and is restricted to phonetically light forms such as *sì* 'yes', *no* 'no'.

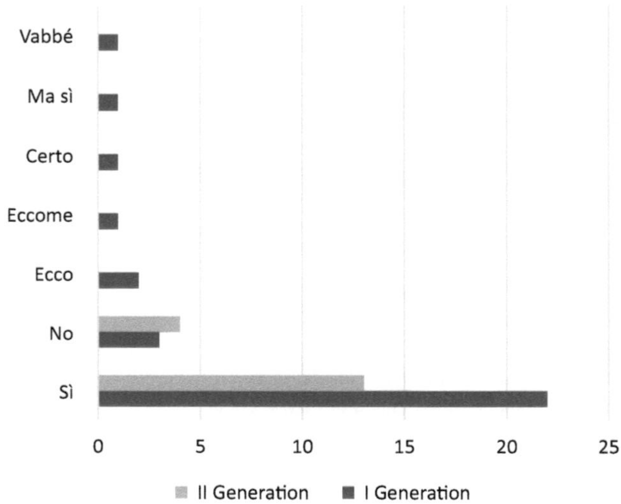

Figure 12.3. DMs with agreement function

In the following examples, *sì* is used in both generations to accomplish the agreement function. Both the examples show that the use of this DM is necessary to keep the interaction going.

1st **generation**

(11) I: italiani ↑
EM42IA: Certo *sì* stiamo parlando in Italia
'I: Italians?
EM42IA: Sure *yes* we are talking about Italy'

2nd **generation**

(12) EF41IIA: ehm vendo prodotti chimici
I: mm interessante
EF41IIA: *sì*
'EF41IIA: I sell chemical products
I: mm interesting
EF41IIA: *yes*'

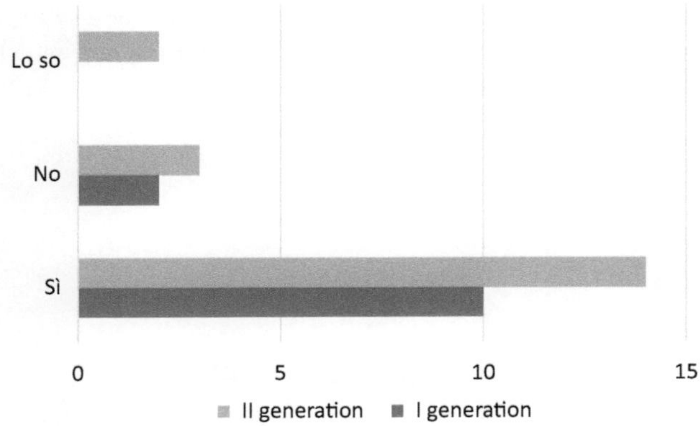

Figure 12.4. DMs with acknowledgment function

The second generation acknowledgment function shows one more type and several tokens more than the first generation. The opposite occurs in the case of the request for confirmation, where the first generation shows more tokens and one more type. Most of the tokens are again expressed by phonetically light forms (see Figure 12.5).

One of the reasons why acknowledgment and turn taking functions persist in the second generation has to do with the tendency of DMs to be more frequent in the left periphery of the utterance (Degand, 2014: 152) as an expression of subjectivity, representing the speaker's point of view. In this sense, perhaps these functions placed in the initial position may represent the primary communicative need of second generation speakers.

1st generation

(13) EM57IA: e là è fallito, è chiuso
I: ah!
EM57IA: *sì sì*
'EM57IA There he is gone bankrupt, he closed
I: ah!
EM57IA: *yes yes*'

2nd generation

(14) I: [Ah si dove?
EF33IIA: [sì sì Per due anni (2) dopo da la scuola facevo anche un altro corso / / alla scuola stesso
'I: [Ah yes where?
EF33IIA: [yes yes For two (2) years after school I also took another course / / at the same school'

As shown in Table 12.5, the first generation displays a wide use of request for confirmation functions, realized through the question tag *no?*, which is maintained in the second generation (see Figure 12.5):

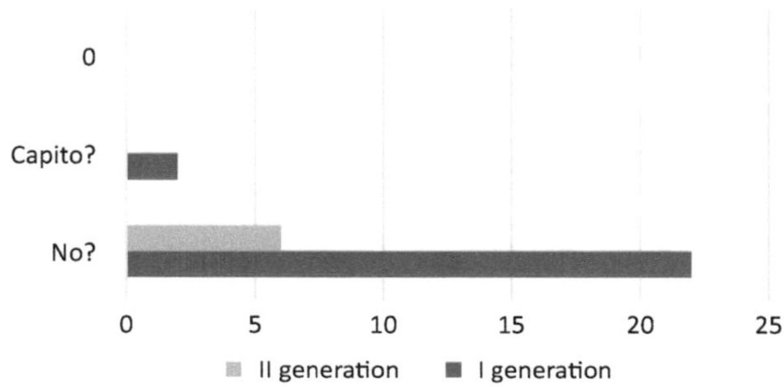

Figure 12.5. DMs with request for confirmation function

1st generation

(15) IE1M77A: (…) noi facevamo risparmiare anche questo portavamo una persona sicura, noi l'accudivamo noi e di conseguenza anche le ditte stavano più tranquille *no?* Perché il capo quando aveva qualcosa da dire veniva da te
'IE1M77A: (…) we made them save money also this we brought a honest person, we took care of it and consequently the companies were also calmer, *right*? Because when the boss had something to say, he came to you'

2nd generation

(16) I: Kindergeld questa m'interessa cos'è?
EM40IIA: Ma l'aiuto dello stato *no?* Per le mamme per le famiglie danno un tot per ogni bambino fino al…fino al…quattro anni tre anni
'I: Kindergeld this is interesting what is it?
EM40IIA: But the help of the Government, *right*? For the mothers and the families, they give a certain amount for each child up to four three years'

These last three functions (agreement, acknowledgment and turn taking) not only do not undergo the second generation loss of types (see Table 12.4) but instead display a higher numbers of types. These may depend on the fact that signalling agreement, acknowledgment and request for confirmation are key functions to encourage reciprocal interaction (Borreguero, 2019).

Both the first and second generation displays some atypical use of Italian DMs. In the first example we observe a use of *magari* as turn holding and *cioè*, as turn taking. In both cases, they do not display their typical functions, namely the epistemic one and the introducer of an exemplification one respectively (De Marco

& Palumbo, 2022). This tendency to incorporate a greater number of functions in the same signal (see Figures 12.2–13.5, the DMs *sì* and *no*) is a consequence of the gradual loss of types, especially in the second generation.

1st generation

(17) EF66IA: sono un ma … po' certe volte sono gentili certe volte sono aggressivi.. e il clima un pochettino // perché in Italia è meglio c'è il sole *magari* qua sempre pioggia ma negli anni 70 era più brutto ancora però nevicava di più, adesso non è. è tutta cambiata
'EF66IA: they are but … sometimes they are kind sometimes they are aggressive .. and the climate a little bit // because in Italy it's better it's sunny *maybe* here it's always raining but in the 70's it was even worse but it used to snow more, now it is not. everything has changed'

2nd generation

(18)
I: E' un po' pesantuccio / ma vorresti cambiarlo questo lavoro?
EM40IIA: no
I: Ti piace?
EM40IIA: *cioè* ehm si vorrei vorrei per i miei figli e per la famiglia però se dovrei fare un altro lavoro non lo farei no / mi piace.
'I: It's a bit boring / but would you like to change this job?
EM40IIA: no
I: Do you like it?
EM40IIA: *that is,* um yes I would like for my children and for the family but if I had to do another job I would not do it no / I like it.'

Besides, it is possible to observe a gradual emerging of German DMs in the second generation:

2nd generation: turn taking

(19) E1F40A: questo è il Referatt Mark?
E2M10A: *ja aber* anche io ho fatto ich habe ein… zwei comma funf
'E1F40A: Is this the Referatt Mark?
E2M10A: *yes but* I did it I have one… two comma five'

7. Conclusions

Our first research question dealt with the use of interactional DMs in terms of intergenerational variation, extending a previous study on metadiscursive DMs in a similar corpus (De Marco & Palumbo, 2022).

From a quantitative perspective, interactional functions remain relatively stable across generations, similar to the metadiscursive ones (see De Marco

& Palumbo, 2022). Both interactional and metadiscursiveDM types gradually decrease in the second generation. Thee first generation presents a higher number of interactional and metadiscursive DM types due to a greater exposition to the input, i.e. to the Italian language input. In the second generation, interactional functions are realized by a lower number of DMs types and a higher number of tokens, with the exception of the functions necessary to encourage reciprocal interaction (acknowledgment and turn taking). This type reduction leads to greater accumulation of functions in the same type, as seen in the case of *sì*, or a restructuring of the inventory of form-function relations, as with th types *magari* and *cioè* gaining non-typical functions (see examples 17 and 18). Compared to the previous study, cited above, the metadiscursive function shows a similar picture: although the functions are stable, there is a general decrease in the number of types and tokens. This contrasts with interactional DMs, where there is an increase in the number of tokens in the second generation.

The loss of interactional types in the second generation could be ascribed, on the one hand, to a lack of exposition to the first language, and on the other hand, to the nature of DMs: they are external to the propositional content, not necessary to its meaning and not easy to perceive in daily conversation, which makes them prone to being lost.

Furthermore, in bothgenerations, the most stable interactional functions in terms of tokens are turn taking, agreement, acknowledgment and request for confirmation, i.e. the function most widely used in Italian and most linked to the interaction management. In both generations, the system of DMs undergoes a process of change fostered both by the switch to German DMs and the non-typical use of Italian DMs.

Our second research question addressed the driving forces leading to the construction of a DM system in migration. In accordance with the findings of previous research, the driving forces that contribute to changes across generations come from both language-contact structures and social factors. The differences between the two generations are mainly related to their distinct sociocultural background: the first generation displays a higher competence in L1 leading to a higher number of DM types than the second generation. The second generation maintains functions that are strictly linked to the conversation management, such as agreement, acknowledgment, turn taking and request for confirmation. Despite their endogamous marriage, they display a higher linguistic competence in the language of migration due to their education and well-rooted professional life in the host country.

An important driving force in leading the linguistic change in migration contact is the structure of the language. As previous research has pointed out, functional similarities between some structures of the language foster the change as in the case of the Italian *allora* and the German *also* (De Marco, 2017). Moreover, phonetically light forms also tend to be maintained as our data show for the DMs *sì, ma, no*, which are the most stable across the generations.

Since DMs are elements belonging to the linguistic domain of discourse, whose value is determined by the dynamics of conversation, it is difficult to analyse them without considering other factors such as prosodic cues, and negotiation of meaning which can be detected at various levels of the discourse chain. Therefore, in future research, it will be useful to include a control group, i.e. a comparison with a corpus of Italian speakers, and to consider a greater number of informants, including the third generation, along with a more balanced numbers of informants for all three generations. These factors could certainly enhance our understanding of the dynamics that takes place in migration contexts.

References

Bazzanella, C. (1995). *I segnali discorsivi*. In L. Renzi, G. Salvi & A. Cardinaletti (eds.). *Grande grammatica italiana di consultazione* (pp. 225–257). Il Mulino.

Bazzanella, C. (2006). Discourse markers in italian: Towards a 'compositional' meaning. In K. Fischer (ed.), *Approaches to discourse particles* (pp. 449–464). Elsevier.

Borreguero Zuloaga, M., Pernas Izquierdo, P., Gillani, E. (2017). Metadiscursive functions and discourse markers in L2 Italian. In A. P. Loureiro, C. Carapinha, C. Plag (coords.), *Marcadores discursivos e(m) tradução* (pp. 16-57). Coimbra.

Borreguero Zuloaga, M. (2019). Expressing agreement in L2 Italian. Strategies and discourse markers in Spanish learners. In M. V. Calvi, E. Landone & I. Bello (a cura di), *Cognitive insights in discourse markers in second language acquisition* (pp. 195–226). Peter Lang.

Borreguero Zuloaga, M. & De Marco, A. (2021). The role of immersion and non-immersion contexts in l2 acquisition: A study based on the analysis of interactional discourse markers. *Corpus Pragmatics, International Journal of Corpus Linguistics and Pragmatics* 5, 121–151.

Borreguero Zuloaga, M. & Ferroni, R. (2020). Lo sviluppo della competenza interazionale in italiano LS: l'espressione dell'accordo in apprendenti ispanofoni e lusofoni. *Italiano LinguaDue* 1. https://doi.org/10.13130/2037-3597/13745

Clyne, M. (2003). *Dynamics of language contact. English and immigrant languages*. Cambridge University Press.

De Fina, A. (2007). Parlando di mangiare: l'identità come costruzione interazionale. In A. Ciliberti (a cura di), *La costruzione interazionale di identità: repertori linguistici e pratiche discorsive degli italiani in Australia* (pp. 68–89). Franco Angeli.

Degand, L. (2014). 'So very fast very fast then' Discourse markers at left and right periphery in spoken French. In K. Beeching, U. Detges, (eds.). *Discourse Functions at the Left and Right Periphery: crosslinguistic Investigations of Language Use and Language Change.* (pp. 151-178), Brill.

De Marco, A. (2016). The use of discourse markers in L2 Italian: A preliminary investigation of acoustic cues. *Language, Interaction and Acquisition* 7/1. https://doi.org/10.1075/lia.7.1.03dem

De Marco, A. (2017). I segnali discorsivi nel parlato di emigrati italiani in Germania. *Rassegna Italiana di Linguistica applicata* 1, 69–89.

De Marco, A. & Palumbo, M. (2015). Derive fonetiche e percezioni identitarie: il caso dell'emigrazione italiana a Monaco. *Rassegna Italiana di Linguistica applicata* 2–3, 177–194.

De Marco, A., (2018). I segnali discorsivi nel contatto linguistico: il caso di allora. In M. W. Bruno et alii (a cura di), *Linguistica e filosofia del linguaggio. Studi in onore di Daniele Gambarara*. Mimesis.

De Marco, A. & Palumbo, M. (2022). Metadiscoursive markers in the context of Italian migration: an intergenerational perspective. *Cuadernos de filología italiana*, 107–124.

Fishman J. A. (2001). *Can Threatened Languages be Saved?*. Multilingual Matters.

Haugen, E. (1953). *The Norwegian Language in America: A study in Bilingual behaviour.* University of Pennsylvania Press.

Jafrancesco, E. (2015). L'acquisizione dei segnali discorsivi in italiano L1. *Italiano Lingua Due*, 1. https://doi.org/10.13130/2037-3597/5010

Krefeld, T. (2004). *Einführung in die Migrationslinguistik. Von der Germania italiana in die Romania multipla*. Gunter Narr Verlag.

Maschler, Y. (1997). *Discourse markers at frame Shis in Israeli Hebrew talk-in-interaction.* Pragmatics 7/2, 183–211.

Matras, Y. (1998). Utterance modifiers and universal grammatical of borrowing. *Linguistics* 36/2, 282–331.

Myers-Scotton, C. (1993). Common and uncommon ground: Social and structural factors in codeswitching. *Language in Society*, 22(4), 475–503. https://doi.org/10.1017/S0047404500017449

Nigoević, M. & Sučić, P. (2011). Competenza pragmatica in italiano L2: l'uso dei segnali discorsivi da parte di apprendenti croati. *Italiano Lingua Due* 2. https://doi.org/10.13130/2037-3597/1917

Poplack, S. (1980). Sometimes I'll start a sentence in English, Y TERMINO EN ESPAÑOL. *Linguistic* 18 7/8, 581–618.

Redeker, G. (2006). Discourse markers as attentional cues at discourse transitions. In K. Fischer (ed.), *Approaches to discourse particles* (pp. 339–348). Elsevier.

Romero-Trillo, J. (2018). Prosodic modeling and position analysis of pragmatic markers in English conversation. *Corpus Linguistics and Linguistic Theory* 14/1, 169–195. https://doi.org/10.1515/cllt-2014-0026.

Sansò, A. (2020). *I segnali discorsivi*. Carocci.

Scaglione, S. (2003). Segnali discorsivi allogeni nelle varietà di emigrazione: you know, and, so, well nell'italiano di San Francisco. In A. De Fina, F. Bizzoni (a cura di), *Italiano e italiani fuori d'Italia* (pp. 45–67). Guerra.

Alice Ionescu

13 Discourse Markers *si vous voulez* in French and *dacă vreți* in Romanian: A Comparative Analysis

Abstract: This chapter undertakes a comparative analysis of French discourse marker *si vous voulez* 'if you want' and its Romanian equivalent *dacă vreți* 'if you want', both introducing sequences of speech which are presented as virtual. The questions we tried to answer were: What semantic features allowed the emergence of this new use? What are the semantic and discursive mechanisms that allowed the evolution of the unit from the status of metadiscursive commentary to the status of metadiscursive marker? Was it in both cases an internal evolution or is the Romanian marker a calque/the result of an evolution favored by language contact/borrowing? Our research will focus on the following issues: theoretical concepts concerning the discursive-pragmatic functions of the sequences *si vous voulez* and *dacă vreți*; some descriptive aspects of the use of these two discourse markers, based on the study of their occurrences in various corpuses; a hypothesis concerning the process of pragmaticalisation of the subordinate clause *si vous voulez* (*if you want, if you will*) in French. The supporting corpus for our research consisted of literary and journalistic texts coming from three different sources.

Keywords: (meta)discursive marker, French, Romanian, grammaticalization, pragmatics

1. Introduction

In this chapter, we will look at a series of metadiscursive uses of modal incises *si vous voulez*, in French and *dacă vreți*, in Romanian, in contexts such as:

(1) – Comment appelles-tu, par exemple, un fil de cuivre roulé en spirale ?
– Mais… hé bien, c'est un fil de cuivre roulé en spirale, voilà tout.
– Je te demande le nom scientifique, qui m'échappe.
– Un solénoïde, **si vous voulez**. (G. Bernanos, *La joie*)
'– What do you call, for example, a copper wire rolled up in a spiral?
– But… well, it's a copper wire wound in a spiral, that's all.
– I ask you for the scientific name, which escapes me.
– A solenoid, **if you will**.'

(2) Ce qui est naturel, c'est le microbe. Le reste, la santé, l'intégrité, la pureté, **si vous voulez**, c'est un effet de la volonté et d'une volonté qui ne doit jamais s'arrêter. (A. Camus, *La Peste*)
'What is natural is the microbe. The rest, health, integrity, purity, **if you like**, is an effect of the will and of a will that must never stop.'

(3) À partir de là, ça n'était pas grand-chose, **si vous voulez**, mais c'étaient la joie et l'amour.
(J. Giono, *Que ma joie demeure*)
'From there, it wasn't much, **if you will**, but it was joy and love.'

(4) Dar inflaţia are două cauze principale, cauza principală a fost şi cea care a surprins, **dacă vreţi**, cea legată de creşterea preţurilor la gaze şi la energie. (https://cugetliber.ro/stiri-politica-administratie-radu-oprea-plafonarea-nu-este-intotdeauna-o-solutie-daca-nu-e-bine-gandita-poate-duce-la-penurie-454310)
'But inflation has two main causes, the main cause was also the one that surprised, **if you want**, the one related to the increase in gas and energy prices.'

(5) Înţelegeţi, aceasta a devenit pasiunea, sau, **dacă vreţi**, nebunia mea. Să smulg măştile de sticlă. (O. Paler, *Viaţa pe un peron*)
'You see, this has become my passion, or, **if you will**, my obssession: to tear off the glass masks.'

(6) Cultele religioase nu sunt instituţii de stat sau ale statului. Sunt organizaţii publice de drept privat asemănătoare cu universităţile, dacă vreţi. (http://confluente.ro/stelian_gombos_1434955777.html)
'Religious cults are not state institutions. They are public organisations under private law like universities, **if you will**.'

It appears clearly, in the examples above, that the bolded groups are morphologically fixed units, coming from parenthetical clauses formed with the modal verbs *vouloir*, in (classical) French, and *a vrea*, in (modern) Romanian. These constructions, made of the conditional conjunction *si/ dacă* and a modal verb in the 2nd person of the present indicative have a particular semanticism, making it clear that the saying is only potential and that the advanced utterance (P) will only be effective if the interlocutor validates it. From a pragmatic point of view, the use of such markers signals the opening of a virtual dialogue space, where a negotiation of P is possible. And from a dialogic point of view, it is part of the strategies developed by the speaker in order to prevent the refusal of a way of saying (also see Authier-Revuz, 1995).

2. State of the Art

In French, the marker *si vous voulez* is considered a grammaticalised unit (or pragmaticalised, in the sense of Dostie 2004) and has been the subject of several recent works (Schnedecker, 2016; Ciry, 2017; Banegas-Saorìn &Ciry, 2018; Beeching, 2018).

On the other hand, the expression *dacă vreţi* 'if you want' has not yet been studied by Romanian specialists. We hypothesize that its discursive use, quite common in certain genres, the fixed character of the sequence in the examined contexts and the instructions it carries show that it is indeed a (meta)discursive marker, most probably a semantic copy of the French marker.

It seemed therefore interesting to verify this hypothesis by analysing their pragmatic functioning (metadiscursive) on various types of corpora (French, Romanian, bilingual and parallel) to see what the common points and the possible divergent points are.

As for French, the discursive marker *si vous voulez* 'if you want' has been studied by Ciry, 2017, who established that it belongs to a paradigm of DM in *Si* + Pronoun subject +Verb: *si on veut (bien)* 'if one wants', *si tu veux* 'if you want', *si l'on peut dire* 'if we can say', *si je peux (le) dire* 'if I can say (it)', *si j'ose dire* 'if I dare say', etc. and pointed to its multifunctional and multidimensional character. In their work, Mercedes Banegas Saorín and Guillaume Ciry (2018) propose a contrastive approach between Spanish and French based on a description of the strategies implemented when a speaker uses the French discursive marker *si vous voulez* 'if you want'. Indeed, the meaning of this French discursive marker will not be the same depending on whether it occupies the initial, middle, or final position in the host utterance. In fact, the place plays a decisive role in maintaining the semes at the origin of these pragmaticalised constructions.

In Romanian, the marker *dacă vreți* is part of a shorter paradigm of metadiscursive comments (*dacă vrei* 'if you want', *dacă se poate spune așa* 'if we can say so') that have been studied only within the framework of some general studies on grammaticalization. It is used in a neat register, both in writing and orally, its use revealing a bookish and even precious style.

3. Research Objectives

First, we propose to describe the path of pragmaticalisation for each marker, then to compare their syntax, their semantics and their metadiscursive functioning, to see what the points of convergence and divergence at each level are, in the two Romance languages. Through this research, we also propose to verify the hypothesis of exolingual influence in the case of the Romanian marker, more precisely to see whether it is an internal evolution or a calque.

The structure of the paper runs as follows: first, we present the state of the art and the objectives of our research; then, we follow with a theoretical framework for metadiscourse and some recent studies on the French marker *si vous voulez*; afterwards, we describe the methodology and corpora used to support our assumptions, along with a corpus analysis of the markers *si vous voulez* and *dacă vreti* aiming at illustrating their functions with examples taken from French and Romanian corpora; finally, we focus on the analysis of parallel corpora and translations from French to Romanian.

The aim of our work will therefore be threefold:

- For the French marker: to take stock of the observations on its syntactic and discursive behaviour, as made in recent relevant works such as Ciry, 2017 and 2020 (to what extent the position of the French DM in the utterance is related to the attitude of the speaker?) and Banegas-Saorín and Ciry, 2018, and the discursive functions it assumes.
- For the Romanian marker: to establish, on the one hand, its degree of pragmaticalisation and de-semanticisation, which is also related to its place in the host utterance;
- To check the points of convergence and divergence in the syntactic and semantic features and in the pragmatic functions of the two markers.

The corpus which supports our analysis is made up, for French, of samples of written literary texts, from the Frantext online database (about 300 occurrences) and, for Romanian, of examples collected by the author using Google online search engine, including about a hundred occurrences of the marker extracted from Romanian grammars and dictionaries, as well as from texts of different types: literary works, political speeches, parliamentary speeches, press conferences, newspaper articles, etc.

To these corpora we added a bilingual corpus made up of French literary works from the 19th and 20th centuries and their official translations into Romanian, a parallel corpus of texts of European legislation (EUR-Lex), and other written examples from various sources provided by online plurilingual dictionaries (www.linguee.com, www.reverso.net).

4. Theoretical Framework

Utterance (or the process of putting words into discourse) is a complex linguistic and cognitive operation that has drawn the attention of linguists and discourse analysts in recent decades. It is often accompanied by metadiscursive comments or reflexive loops (Authier-Revuz, 1995) which are interventions the subject feels necessary in order to explain himself or to adjust his utterance and which are the sign of an enunciative duplication. They occur as result of a change of the enunciative perspective on the matter, followed by of an intervention of the speaker (through a metadiscursive commentary, an incise or a marker) meant to prevent the situation where his point of view is misjudged or contested by the interlocutor.

As for the metadiscursive markers, they are defined as a series of lexical units or syntagms, having a lower or a higher degree of grammaticalization, whose main function is to indicate the organization of the utterance which hosts them, as well as to signal the questioning of a certain element or part of it and whose general purpose is to ensure the acceptability of the message. The metalinguistic activities they indicate represent an inseparable dimension of the functioning of language. These markers may refer to different manifestations of the reflexivity of natural languages, manifested by 'non-coincidences of saying', whether it is expressions relating to the use of language (metalinguistic, in a strict sense), to the utterance (meta-enunciatives) or to the discourse itself (metadiscursive).

As for the markers which are the subject of our study, it should be noted first that their use is not characteristic of monologous discourse, but that it falls within the framework of a verbal interaction in which they have a function oriented simultaneously towards the message and towards the interlocutor, in a broader context of 'inter-subject regulation', as defined by Culioli (1991: 92). It appears to us that the French marker *si vous voulez* and its Romanian correspondent *dacă vreţi* function, in certain contexts, as cognitive and discursive instruments in the negotiation of the meaning between the two poles of communication. At the same time, they point to the fact that the speaker seeks adherence to his discourse, in accordance with Grice's principle of cooperation.

In our study, we shall focus more on the mechanisms at play in the use of these discourse markers than on the strict operation of putting words into discourse, of lexical choice, or metadiscursive commentary.

In some dialogues, faced with the possibility that the interlocutor's viewpoint may not be the same as his, the speaker develops strategies aimed at thwarting this risk, by preventing a refusal of a way of saying. J. Authier-Revuz states that:

> In a way, it is considered like a threat, that of the potential refusal by the interlocutor to co-state, to assume his participation as receiver in the fact from the enunciation of an element X, that non-coincidence appears, represented by the enunciator, in various strategies aimed at thwarting it. (1995: 181)

4.1 French Metadiscursive Marker *si vous voulez*: Morphosyntactic Status, Origin, Pragmatic Uses and Values

The phrase made up of the conditional *si* 'if' and the verb *vouloir* 'want' conjugated in the present indicative expressed originally, on a referential level, outside of their pragmatic or conversational use, the will of the subject of enunciation / of the addressee (Banegas Saorín & Ciry, 2018).

Furthermore, the conjunction *si* presents the utterance 'as conditional, depending on the will of the audience' (Authier-Revuz, 1995: 193), the fact that the statement is only potential and will only be effective if the interlocutor wants it/ if he validates it. *Si*, in Culiolian terminology, is thus a 'tool of bifurcation' which 'marks the construction of a domain of possible values, that is to say (*p*, *p'*)'. The linguistic use and the metalinguistic use of the expression *si vous voulez* 'if you will' coexist in usage and it is difficult to distinguish between them, should we consider strictly syntactic criteria. Indeed, we see that both types of usage are characterized by the split middle position and that they are preceded by the disjunctive conjunction *ou* 'or':

(7) Montons sur un des points élevés des Vosges, ou, **si vous voulez**, au Jura. Tournons le dos aux Alpes. (Jules Michelet, *Tableau de la France*, 1833) [linguistic use]
'Let's climb to one of the high points of the Vosges, or, **if you prefer**, the Jura. Let's turn our back on the Alps.'

(8) La sensibilité est cette faculté, ce pouvoir, cet effet de notre organisation, ou**, si vous voulez**, cette propriété de notre être en vertu de laquelle nous recevons des impressions de beaucoup d'espèces, et nous en avons la conscience. (Destutt de Tracy, *Eléments d'idéologie*, 1803) [metalinguistic use]
'Sensibility is that faculty, that power, that effect of our organization, or, **if you like**, that property of our being by virtue of which we receive impressions from many kinds, and we are conscious of them.'

We must therefore look at other criteria to distinguish propositional use from discursive use. At this point, we consider it useful to discuss the properties of discursive markers (DM), as formulated by Dostie and Pusch (2007):

- they do not contribute to the propositional content of the statement, and therefore their presence or absence does not modify the truth value of the statements to which they are attached.
- they tend to form independent prosodic units, so they are usually outside the structure of the sentence.
- they are syntactically optional, that is to say that, in cases where they are attached to an utterance, their absence does not result in ungrammaticality.
- they play a role beyond the sentence, and they come under the macro-syntax of discourse (Blanche-Benveniste, 1997).

Without pretending to trace here the full path of grammaticalisation of the sequence *si vous voulez*, we will nevertheless present a few constructions testifying to a stage preceding the current use of the marker:

(9) Mais, en définitif, cette organisation n'est faite que pour amener de bons résultats ; elle n'est préférable à l'anarchie (**entendez, si vous voulez,** l'indépendance

naturelle), que par les maux qu'elle évite et les biens qu'elle procure ; on ne doit juger de son degré de perfection que par les effets qu'elle produit. (Destutt de Tracy, *Commentaire sur l'Esprit des Lois de Montesquieu*, 1807, p. 219)
'But, ultimately, this organization is only made to bring about good results; it is preferable to anarchy (**understand, if you will,** natural independence), only by the evils which it avoids and the goods which it procures; one should only judge of its degree of perfection by the effects it produces.'

(10) Appelez, **si vous voulez**, ces hommes illuminés ; je serai tout à fait d'accord avec vous, pourvu que vous prononciez le nom sérieusement. (Joseph de Maistre, *Les Soirées de Saint-Pétersbourg ou Entretiens sur le gouvernement temporel de la Providence* : t. 2, 1821)
'You may call, **if you want**, these men enlightened; I will totally agree with you, as long as you take the name seriously.'

(11) Et puis **appelez cela, si vous voulez,** monarchie, république ou socialisme. Les hommes qui viendront, soulevant ce manteau pompeux, verront que sous le nom menteur gisait une chose pourrie. (G. Clémenceau, *L'Iniquité*, 1899)
'And then **call it, if you like**, monarchy, republic or socialism. The men who will come after us, by lifting this pompous coat, will see that under the liar's name lay a rotten thing.'

(12) On allègue l'usage : la raison et la justice, **disons** la logique **si vous voulez**, doivent être au-dessus de l'usage, tenir compte de l'infirmité morale du contractant qui se laisse prendre au piège, et avoir l'esprit qu'il n'a pas aujourd'hui. (ibidem)
'We allege usage: reason and justice, **let's say** logic **if you like**, must be above usage, and take into account the moral infirmity of the contracting party who lets itself be trapped, and have the spirit that it doesn't have now.'

We see in the examples above that the phrase *si vous voulez* is part of a classic conditional construction, being the subordinate depending on a governing verb in the present imperative (verb of speech or of cognitive experience). Gradually, the complete conditional structure became an elliptical construction, the main clause no longer being necessary for the audience to understand the message.

4.2. The Position of *si vous voulez* in the Sentence

Although our work relies on the analysis of the pragmatic functions of the two DM, these functions cannot be fully and rigorously described if we do not consider also the positions they may assume in the sentence, in relation with the different degrees of pragmaticalisation of the markers.

The marker *si vous voulez* appears mainly in the middle position, sometimes preceded by a conjunction like *ou* 'or' or *et* 'and', more rarely by *et même* 'or even'. Sometimes we can find it at the end, like in example (1) above.

(13) Je me trouve heureuse d'être seule, pourquoi changerais-je ma vie, égoïste **si vous voulez,** contre les caprices d'un maître ? (Balzac, *La Peau de chagrin*)
'I find myself happy to be alone, why would I change my life, selfish **if you will**, against the whims of a master?'

(14) Nous ne disputerions pas aujourd'hui : car c'est, à mon avis, très-bien, très-justement, et même, **si vous voulez,** très-philosophiquement fait d'établir comme dogme national, que tout fléau du ciel est un châtiment : et quelle société humaine n'a pas cru cela ? (Pompéry, *La morale naturelle et la religion de l'humanité*)
'We should not argue today: for it is, in my opinion, very well, very just, and even, **if you like**, very philosophically done to establish as a national dogma, that every scourge of heaven is a punishment: and what human society has not believed this?'

The DM *si vous voulez* can assume multiple pragmatic functions, such as:

– it provides a label, an explanation, or a designation:

(16) L'homme ici a des élans et des insouciances, un acharnement au travail et tout à coup une lassitude qui surprennent l'étranger. Cela paraît inné en lui. Il a l'air de vivre et agir par inspiration. C'est la mobilité apportée du désert. **Si vous voulez,** la goutte de sang arabe en chacun de nous. (Joseph de Pesquidoux, *Le Livre de raison* : t. 3)
'The men here have impulses and carelessness, a determination to work and suddenly a weariness which surprises the foreigner. It seems innate in them. They seem to live and act by inspiration. It is the nomadism brought from the desert. The drop of Arab blood in all of us **if you will**.'

(17) Je suis revenu de ces fantaisies qui absorbent trop de temps et de moyens. Je n'ai plus qu'un goût dominant ou, **si vous voulez,** une manie ; celle-là ne me quittera pas, car elle n'a rien de chimérique, et ne donne pas de grands embarras pour un vain but. (Senancour, *Obermann*)
'I let go those fantasies which take too much time and resources. I only have one desire or, **if you like**, one mania; this one will not leave me, for it has nothing chimerical about it, and does not cause great trouble for a vain purpose.'

– it expresses an approximation:

(18) Pour obtenir cet effet, suivez-moi, j'invente un personnage de romancier, que je pose en figure centrale; et le sujet du livre, **si vous voulez,** c'est précisément la lutte entre ce que lui offre la réalité et ce que, lui, prétend en faire. (André Gide, *Les Faux-monnayeurs*)
'To obtain this effect, you should follow me, I shall invent a novelist character, whom I'll pose as the central figure; and the subject of the book, **if you will**, is precisely the struggle between what reality offers him and what he claims to do with it.'

(19) […] ; pas tout à fait une robe de mariée :une robe de jardin, **si vous voulez,** assez théâtre, d'un blanc foncé, crémeux. (Roger Martin du Gard, *Les Thibault : La Belle saison*)

'Not quite a wedding dress: a garden dress, **if you will**, quite theatrical, pale white, creamy.'

- from the interlocutor's point of view, it seems that the speaker leaves him/her with the choice to accept or not what s/he has just said:

(20) Robespierre est moins coupable, responsable, laissons ces mots, il est moins actif que Marie-Antoinette et les Polignac. Je vais plus loin, si un Danton, un Marat sont des apaches, Robespierre n'en est pas un et Versailles est plein d'apaches. Un médiocre, **si vous voulez,** mais dans une maison bien gérée il eût été à son rang un serviteur suffisant. (Barrès, Maurice, *Mes Cahiers* : t. 5 : 1906–1907)
'Robespierre is less guilty, responsible, let's leave these words, he is less active than Marie-Antoinette and the Polignac. I go further, if a Danton, a Marat are Apache, Robespierre is not one and Versailles is full of Apaches. A mediocre, **if you will,** but in a well-run house he would have been an acceptable servant in his rank.'

Banegas Saorín and Ciry (2018) point out that in this type of uses *si vous voulez* may be replaced by *si vous préférez* 'if you prefer':

> It is again in this position that in searching for the adequate term, the speaking subject leaves his saying suspended on the will of the interlocutor, this "willing of the other" being however taken in charge by the speaker himself. In this case, in fact, the speaker who uses the DM proposes, in the open interstitial space, an overbidding in the capture (or overcapture) based on what he thinks of what the co-speaker might prefer. (2018 : 41)

(21) Je ne vous loue pas mes services, je vous les donne. Je serai votre secrétaire par dilettantisme, par amour de l'art, **si vous voulez,** parce que je suis désœuvré et que je m'ennuie. (M. Dekobra, *La Madone des sleepings*)
'I do not rent you my services, I give them to you. I'll be your secretary out of dilettantism, out of love of art, **if you like**, because I'm idle and bored.'

The same authors note that there is another type of use, more radical, where *si vous voulez* can evolve towards a correction of capture or recapture:

(22) – Vous êtes drôle, dit-il.
- Drôle, non! Prudente, **si vous voulez**. On n'est pas sur terre pour se martyriser mutuellement, jouer aux bons esclaves… (example of Banegas Saorín & Ciry, 2018)
'- You are funny, he said.
- Funny, no! Cautious, **if you will**. We are not on earth to mutually martyr each other, to play good slaves…'

When followed by par *mais P 'but P'*, the marker *si vous voulez* expresses a concessive movement:

(23) Ces pensées et ces sentiments sont petits et bas, **si vous voulez, mais** ce qui est petit et bas est déjà meilleur que ce qui n'est pas. (Maeterlinck, Maurice, *La Vie des abeilles*)

'These thoughts and feelings are small and low, **if you will**, but what is small and low is already better than what is not.'

(24) La Berma dans Phèdre, dans le Cid, ce n'est qu'une actrice **si vous voulez**, mais vous savez, je ne crois pas beaucoup à la "hiérarchie" des arts ; (M. Proust, *À la recherche du temps perdu. 1, 2, 3. Du côté de chez Swann*)
'The great Berma playing Phèdre, in Le Cid, is only an actress **if you like**, but you know, I don't really believe in the "hierarchy" of the arts'

4.3. The Romanian Metadiscursive Marker *dacă vreți*: Morphosyntactic Status, Origin, Pragmatic Uses and Values

In Romanian, *dacă vreți* is part of a short paradigm of metadiscursive comments (*dacă vrei, dacă se poate spune așa*) that have only been studied within the framework of some general research on grammaticalization. It is used in a neat register, both in writing and orally, its use revealing a bookish and even precious style.

It has been recently used as a metadiscursive marker, resulting from the pragmaticalisation of the hypothetical sentence *dacă vreti,* under the influence or by copying a Roman metadiscursive marker (French *si vous voulez*, Spanish *si quieren*, or Italian *se vuole, se non le dispiace*).

In the following, we will use the theoretical framework provided by studies on grammaticalisation/ pragmaticalisation (Dostie, 2004; Hopper & Traugott, 2003; Marchello-Nizia, 2006) to trace the pragmaticalisation path of this expression. Thus, three levels of passage are distinguished by Dostie: when a unit passes from the lexical zone to the grammatical zone, it is a process of grammaticalization; when a unit moves from the lexical or grammatical zone to the pragmatic zone, it is a process of grammaticalization, it is important, in order to understand a marker, to grasp the mechanisms of its appearance as a marker (as described by Hopper & Traugott, 2003): decategorisation, paradigmatisation, persistence, semantic demotivation and superimposition. Indeed, the emergence of the new pragmatic unit coexists or even interacts with its first function.

In contemporary Romanian, the form *dacă vreti* functions at the same time in the lexical zone and in the pragmatic zone – a new use which has taken place in diachrony, probably under the influence of French and possibly reinforced in the last thirty years by the influence of DM in spoken English, which has become dominant in Romanian. It can express:

- an actual condition:

(25) **Dacă vreți** gaz, găsiți ruble.
'**If you want** gas, find rubles.'

- a hypothesis / possibility:

(26) **Dacă vreti** cafea, trebuie să v-o plătiți singuri.
'**If you want** coffee, you must pay for it yourself.'

(27) **Dacă vreți** să vedeți cel mai trist exemplar de lup, mergeți la Zoo Băneasa!
'**If you want** to see the saddest specimen of a wolf, go to Băneasa Zoo!'

- an offer made to the interlocutor:

(28) **Dacă vreți**, vă arăt în câteva clipe.
'**If you want**, I'll show you in a moment.'

- a metadiscursive comment on the choice of a term or a label:

(29) „Platonic" este proiectul meu de suflet… este, **dacă vreți**, caracterizarea mea muzicală, proiecția sufletului, a gândirii și a minții mele în muzică.
http://www.zilesinopti.ro/articole/1873/interviu-cu-nicu-patoi
'"Platonic" is my soul project… it is, **if you like**, my musical characterization, the projection of my soul and my mind into music.'

The places the metadiscursive marker *dacă vreți* can occupy in the sentence are not very relevant for its interpretation: still, according to its position (at the beginning of the utterance, at the end, on the middle) the marker will assume different pragmatic functions. For instance, when placed at the beginning of a sentence, it suggests a label, a designation:

(30) Într-adevăr, timpul, **sau dacă vreți** putem să-i spunem și răbdare, e combustibilul cel mai important al *Recorder*-ului și asta ne dă un avantaj important. Nu avem fascinația *breaking-news*-ului, dar avem și noi fascinațiile noastre.
(https://dilemaveche.ro/sectiune/tema-saptamanii/articol/timpul-sau-daca-vreti-putem-sa-i-spunem-si-rabdare-e-combustibilul-cel-mai-important-al-recorder-ului-interviu-cu-cristian-delcea-redactor-sef-si-co-fondator-recorder)
'Indeed, time, or **if you want/prefer**, we can call it patience, is *Recorder*'s most important fuel and that gives us an important advantage. We don't have the fascination of the breaking news, but we have our fascinations.'

or it serves to ask the interlocutor to accept a formulation or a judgment:

(31) În România, gândirea juridică, formată în universități, în practica judiciară sau în cadrul autorităților publice pune accentul pe metodele de interpretare a normelor, nu pe știința elaborării acestora. Este, **dacă vreți**, efectul unui tipar cultural românesc: descriem ce fac alții mai bine decât concepem noi înșine. (https://pressone.ro/de-ce-avem-atatea-legi-neclare-si-imprecise)
'In Romania, legal thinking, formed in universities, in judicial practice or within public authorities, emphasizes the methods of interpreting the rules, not the science of their elaboration. It is, **if you will**, the effect of a Romanian cultural pattern: we describe what others do better than we ourselves conceive.'

(32) „Există un activism, **sau** hiper-activism**, dacă vreți**, uneori, în justiție, pe temele justiției. E o remanență aici din anii 2017–2018, atunci au fost niște lucruri pe muchie, destul de grave, și pe undeva justificată această reacție". (Interview of Mr. Predoiu, Minister of Justice:adev.ro/r79m4t)
'There is an activism, **or** hyper-activism, **if you want**, sometimes in justice, on the themes of justice. There is a remnant here from the years 2017–2018, when there were some things on the edge, quite serious, and somewhere this reaction was justified.'

Placed in the middle of the sentence, the marker *dacă vreți* opens a mental space for a condition or a hypothesis, by interrupting the linearity of the speech. The mental space it opens is more interstitial than in the final position, either because the speaker seeks to attenuate a statement that is too bold, or because s/he is not entirely satisfied with his/her formulation. In this configuration, the speaker strategically aims to divert the attention of the co-speaker not to lose face and so that the communication can continue under acceptable conditions. (see also Banegas Saorín & Ciry, 2018)

(33) Dar inflația are două cauze principale, cauza principală a fost și cea care a surprins, **dacă vreți**, cea legată de creșterea prețurilor la gaze și la energie. Atunci a fost un moment important în care s-ar fi putut interveni rapid cu o plafonare, astfel încât să nu crească inflația.
(https://cugetliber.ro/stiri-politica-administratie-radu-oprea-plafonarea-nu-este-intotdeauna-o-solutie-daca-nu-e-bine-gandita-poate-duce-la-penurie-454310)
'But inflation has two main causes, the main cause was also the one that surprised, **if you like**, the one related to the increase in gas and energy prices. Then it was an important moment when we could have intervened quickly with a ceiling, so that inflation would not increase.'

(34) Aseară, însă, adică în joia din săptămâna Floriilor ortodoxe sau, **dacă vreți**, în Joia Mare la catolici, am văzut sferturi de miel, trase în pungă, și la Lidl. https://www.timisoarastiri.ro/au-bagat-miel-si-la-lidl-vreti-sa-stiti-costa-un-sfert/
'Last night, however, that is, on the Thursday before the Orthodox Palm Sunday or, **if you want**, Maundy Thursday for the Catholics, I saw lamb quarters, packed in bags, also at Lidl's.'

By using the DM, the speaker appears to ask his/her interlocutor to accept a formulation, a way of saying or a remark. The function of the marker is to convey an expression, a wording, or a judgment:

(35) Înțelegeți, aceasta a devenit pasiunea, sau, **dacă vreți**, nebunia mea. Să smulg măștile de sticla. Lumea e plină de măști de sticlă. Te uiți și nu le vezi. (O. Paler, *Lumea pe un peron*)
'You see, this has become my passion, or **if you will**, my obsession. To tear off the glass masks. The world is full of glass masks. You look at people and you don't see them.'

(36) Eram un fel de Sisif, **dacă vreţi**, care-şi arunca singur stânca pe coasta muntelui odată ajuns sus. (ibidem)
'I was a kind of Sisyphus, **if you will**, who threw his rock down the side of the mountain once he reached the top.'

(37) (…) pustiul este mai rău decât frica, sau, **dacă vreţi**, o altfel de frică. (ibidem)
'the wilderness is worse than fear, or, **if you like**, it's a different kind of fear.'

In final position, the marker *dacă vreţi* opens a mental space for the condition in which the co-speaker enters by capture (according to Banegas Saorìn & Ciry, 2018). The interlocutor has (the illusion of) the choice to validate or not the saying, whether it is coinciding or not with his own view:

(38) Cultele religioase nu sunt instituţii de stat sau ale statului. Sunt organizaţii publice de drept privat asemănătoare cu universităţile, **dacă vreţi**. Sunt localizate mai degrabă în zona societăţii civile. (http://confluente.ro/stelian_gombos_1434955777.html)
'Religious cults are not state institutions. They are public organisations under private law like universities, **if you will**. They are located rather in civil society.'

(39) Aş mai specifica că acest proiect de act normativ a fost lucrat atât cu structurile asociative ale autorităţilor locale, ca fiind unul dintre principalii beneficiari ai acestei ordonanţe de urgenţă, ca şi autoritate contractantă, cât şi cu partea de specialitate, antreprenori, a firmelor de construcţii cu structurile, **dacă vreţi**, reprezentative ale lor.
https://gov.ro/ro/guvernul/sedinte-guvern/briefing-de-presa-la-finalul-sedintei-de-guvern-sustinut-de-ministrul-dezvoltarii-attila-zoltan-cseke-ministrul-culturii-lucian-roma-canu-i-purtatorul-de-cuvant-al-guvernului-dan-carbunaru
'I would also add that this draft of normative act was written both with the associative structures of the local authorities, as one of the main beneficiaries of this emergency ordinance, as a contracted authority, and with the specialized part, the contractors, the construction companies, with their representative structures, **if you will**.'

4.4. A Partial Conclusion

In our opinion, the metadiscursive marker *dacă vreti* 'if you want' has a social role, in the sense that its use is a form of courtesy or deference towards the interlocutor and a cognitive role, in the sense that it is linked to the negotiation of meaning between the two poles communication. Positive politeness can indeed be described as 'the desire to be approved of'. If the speaker is addressing the positive side of his interlocutor, the latter will feel less threatened by the statement put forward. We would like to point out that other researchers, such as Beeching (2002), also interpreted discourse markers within the framework of politeness theory. She made a distinction between discursive markers that fulfill a 'referential' job and those that fulfill an 'interactional' job. In our opinion, markers such as *si vous voulez* and *dacă vreți* indicate that the speaker is searching for the appropriate word(s) or expression(s) and asks for the interlocutor's approval about them.

(40) Este, **dacă vreți**, un dar de suflet, un nou-născut, un copil de suflet, pentru mine și ceilalți din jurul meu, indiferent că mi-au fost copii, rude, inamici, prieteni, vecini, consăteni, colegi, amici sau simpatizanți, dușmani sau adversari, interesați sau indiferenți. (http://confluente.ro/geo_stroe_1481591446.html)
'It is, **if you like**, a gift of the soul, a newborn, a soul child, for me and the others around me, regardless of whether they were my children, relatives, enemies, friends, neighbors, fellow citizens, colleagues, friends or sympathizers, enemies or adversaries, interested or indifferent.'

(41) Teologul convertește la credința în Dumnezeu, pe când politicianul este obligat să practice, **dacă vreți**, o „convertire" la democrație.
'The theologist converts to faith in God, while the politician is obliged to practice, **if you will**, a "conversion" to democracy.'

5. A Contrastive Perspective

In this section of our paper, we shall analyse some translations of the French marker *si vous voulez* in Romanian, using a corpus formed of original literary texts and their official translations into Romanian[1]. The literary texts belong to French 19th century novelist Honoré de Balzac, whose works have been translated in Romanian during the second half of the 20th century. This corpus has provided us with two different translations of *si vous voulez*: *dacă vreți* and *cu alte cuvinte,* both metadiscursive markers in contemporary Romanian.

(42) Depuis le dimanche où Mlle de Watteville avait reçu ce regard, ou, **si vous voulez**, ce baptême de feu, magnifique expression de Napoléon qui peut servir à l'amour, elle mena chaudement l'affaire du belvédère. (Balzac, *Albert Savarus,* 1842)
Din duminica în care Dra de Watteville primise acea privire sau, **dacă vreti**, acel botez al focului, după magnifica expresie a lui Napoleon, aplicabilă si în dragoste, ea conduse energic afacerea cu foișorul. (Balzac, *Comedia umană*, vol. 2, *Albert Savarus*, p. 39)
'From the Sunday when Mademoiselle de Watteville had received this look, or, **if you like**, this baptism of fire, a magnificent expression of Napoleon's which can be of use to love, she passionately conducted the construction of the belvedere.'

1 The translations into English belong to the author of the paper.

(43) La lionne est due à la fameuse chanson d'Alfred de Musset : Avez-vous vu dans Barcelone… C'est ma maîtresse et ma lionne : il y a eu fusion, ou, **si vous voulez,** confusion entre les deux termes et les deux idées dominantes. (Balzac, *Albert Savarus*, 1842)
Lionne se datorează faimoaselor versuri ale lui Alfred de Musset : Avez-vous vu dans Barcelone… C'est ma maitresse et ma lionne : a avut loc o fuziune, sau, **dacă vreți**, o confuzie între cei doi termeni si între cele două idei desemnate. (Balzac, *Comedia umană*, vol. 2, *Albert Savarus*, p. 22)
'The term lionne is due to the famous song by Alfred de Musset: *Avez-vous vu dans Barcelone… C'est ma maitresse et ma lionne*: there has been a fusion, or, if you like, a confusion between the two terms and the two dominant ideas.' (Balzac, A. Savarus, 1842)

(44) Francesca était bien l'Italienne classique, et telle que l'imagination veut, fait ou rêve, **si vous voulez,** les Italiennes.
Francesca era într-adevăr italianca tipică, sau, **cu alte cuvinte**, era așa cum o vrea, o visează sau o creează imaginatia pe italiancă. (Balzac, *Comedia umană*, vol 2, *Albert Savarus*, p. 39)
'Francesca was indeed the classic Italian woman, or she was like as the imagination wants, makes or dreams, if you will, of Italian women.'

The analysis of parallel corpora provided by online dictionaries Linguee and Reverso (French and Romanian, Romanian and French) testifies to the low degree of recognition of the metadiscursive value of the marker by the translators or the translating machines. Besides the correct equivalent of *si vous voulez (dacă vreți)* we find in two of the Romanian versions a literal translation of *si vous voulez* as a modal 'boulique' verb (*dacă doriți).*

(45) Reverso: Fr-Ro
C'est une forme différente d'entreprise pour une économie nouvelle. C'est une forme, **si vous voulez**, d'altruisme écologique – quelque chose dans cette ligne-là.
Este un fel diferit de întreprindere pentru o nouă economie. Este o formă, **dacă vreți**, de altruism ecologic – poate ceva de genul ăsta. (Transcribed talks)
'It is a different form of business for a new economy. It's a form, **if you will**, of ecological altruism – something along those lines.'

(46) Reverso: Ro-Fr
BAA: Da. Ceea ce face cu adevărat este să descopere. Creează hiper-legături, **dacă vreți**, între imagini. Și realizează asta bazându-se pe conținutul imaginilor. (TED talks)
BAA: Oui. Ce que le logiciel fait, c'est découvrir. Il crée des hyperliens, **si vous voulez**, entre les images. Et il le fait en se fondant sur le contenu des images
'BAA: Yes. What this is really doing is discovering. It's creating hyperlinks, **if you will**, between images.'

(47) La communauté Minecraft est devenue complètement dingue de ce projet, et Ben est instantanément devenu une célébrité médiatique. En en effet, pour pas mal de personnes, faire ce "pèlerinage" NAND2Tetris, **si vous voulez**, s'est transformé en une expérience qui a changé leur vie.
Comunitatea Minecraft s-a bucurat foarte mult de acest proiect, și Ben a devenit instantaneu o celebritate mass-media. Și într-adevăr, pentru câțiva oameni, acest pelerinaj NAND2Tetris, **dacă vreți,** s-a transformat într-o experiență care le-a schimbat viața.
'The Minecraft community went crazy over this project, and Ben instantly became a media celebrity. Indeed, for quite a few people, doing this NAND2Tetris "pilgrimage", **if you will**, has turned into a life-changing experience.'

(48) Et les faire s'équilibrer toutes au milieu est cette notion de compassion. Qui doit être là, **si vous voulez**, à nos racines. Cette idée de compassion nous arrive parce que nous sommes faits à l'image de Dieu. (Transcribed talks)
Echilibrând toate astea, obții noțiunea de compasiune. Ea trebuie să fie acolo, **dacă doriți**, la rădăcinile noastre. Găsim în noi ideea de compasiune pentru că suntem făcuți după chipul lui Dumnezeu.
'And balancing them all in the middle is this notion of compassion. Who needs to be there, **if you will**, at our roots. This idea of compassion comes to us because we are made in the image of God.'

(49) Nous voyons le résultat, les traces, **si vous voulez,** des bacilles de Pasteur que l'on a enrôlés pour sculpter le désert en des environnements habitables.
Vedem rezultatele, urmele, **dacă doriți,** ale Bacillus pasteurii fiind valorificate pentru sculptarea deșertului formând aceste medii locuibile.
'We see the result, the traces, **if you will**, of Pasteur's bacilli that have been enlisted to sculpt the desert into habitable environments.'

6. Conclusion

In French, *si vous voulez*, as some other discourse markers containing the verb *vouloir*, is very old and therefore well established in metadiscursive use, as G. Ciry points out in his thesis (2017). In Romanian, the DM *dacă vreți* is attested much later and we believe that it began to be used with a metadiscursive value under the influence of French. In our view, it is a metadiscursive marker, which functions as an attenuator of a statement or as a mark of hesitation in the choice of a label, a denomination, or a comment on the choice of a linguistic unit.

We also thought it would be interesting to check the hypothesis of Banegas Saorìn and Ciry (2018) concerning the relationship between the position the marker occupies in the sentence and the pragmatic function it assumes in the speech. At the beginning of the sentence, the two markers, in French as in Romanian, are mainly used in argumentative contexts: they open a space of capture – or of seduction – of the interlocutor which allows the speaker to advance his/her – often controversial – opinion. In the middle position, the discursive markers *si vous voulez* et *dacă vreți* continue to open a mental space of the condition by interrupting the linearity of the discourse. The mental space is then more interstitial than in the final position, either because the speaker seeks to attenuate a statement that is too daring, or because s/he is not entirely satisfied with his/her formulation/statement. In this configuration, the speaker strategically aims to divert the attention of the co-speaker so as not to lose face and so that the communication can continue under acceptable conditions (also see Banegas Saorìn & Ciry, 2018). In final position, these discursive markers open a mental space of the condition that the co-speaker is attracted to enter. S/he then has the choice to validate or not the utterance, whether the statement coincides with his/her own view or opinion or not.

The analysis of the bilingual and parallel corpora shows that there is a great similarity in the use of the two markers, which leads us to conclude that we find the same linguistic attitude in the two languages, the same concern to affirm a point of view. There is therefore an invariant in the two languages being compared.

References

Authier-Revuz, J. (1995). *Ces mots qui ne vont pas de soi. Boucles réflexives et non-coïncidences du dire*. Larousse.

Banegas Saorín, M. & Ciry, G. (2018). *Si vous voulez* et ses équivalents en espagnol. *Pragmalingüística* 1, 34–51. https://revistas.uca.es/index.php/pragma/article/view/2428

Beeching, Kate. (2002). *Gender, politeness and pragmatic particles in French*. John Benjamins Publishing Company.

Beeching, K. (2018). Metacommenting in English and French. A variational pragmatics approach. In K. Beeching, C. Ghezzi & P. Molinelli (eds.), *Positioning the self and others: Linguistic perspectives* (pp. 127–153). Pragmatics & Beyond New Series, 292.

Blanche-Benveniste, C. (1997). La notion de variation syntaxique dans la langue parlée. *Langue française*, 19–29.

Ciry, G. (2017). Analyse multidimensionnelle du marqueur discursif *si vous voulez* et de ses variantes en français contemporain. In G. Dostie & F. Lefeuvre. (dir.), *Lexique, grammaire, discours. Les marqueurs discursifs* (pp. 453–469). Honoré Champion.

Ciry, G. (2020). *Analyse multidimensionnelle des marqueurs discursifs commençant par* si. PhD dissertation. Université polytechnique Hauts-de-France, Ecole doctorale Sciences de l'Homme et de la Société (ED SHS473).

Culioli, A. (1991). *Pour une linguistique de l'énonciation*, tome 1. Ophrys.

Dostie, G. (2004). *Pragmaticalisation et marqueurs discursifs. Analyse sémantique et traitement lexicographique*. De Boeck, Duculot.

Dostie, G. & Pusch, C. D. (2007). Présentation. Les marqueurs discursifs. Sens et variation. *Langue française* 2/154, 3–12. Armand Colin.

Hopper, J. & Traugott, E. (2003). *Grammaticalization*. Cambridge University Press.

Marchello-Nizia, C. (2006). *Grammaticalisation et changement linguistique*. Duculot

Schnedecker, C. (2016). *Si tu veux/Si vous voulez*: caractéristiques syntaxiques et fonctions sémantico-pragmatiques des hypothétiques en *si* portant sur le dire. *Journal of French Language Studies*, 1–18. Cambridge University Press.

Louise Behe

14 *Même* Discourse Marker? A Study of Its Argumentative Uses

Abstract: In this chapter we will analyse the 'argumentative' uses of French *même*. The aim is to show that the adverb can be classified as a discourse marker. After a brief presentation of our theorical positions, we will object to certain examples in which *même* do not seem to behave as a discourse marker. Using the Semantic Blocks Theory, we will show that these uses differ based on how the meaning of the connected contents is constructed. We will propose an analysis of these uses of *même* and we will see that after all they meet the criteria allowing *même* to be considered as a discourse marker. In this perspective, we will also question the origin and the nature of the 'unexpectedness' introduced by the argumentative uses of *même*.

Keywords: discourse markers, même, argumentative semantics, unexpectedness

1. Introduction[1]

This paper intends to discuss whether the adverb *même* belongs to the discourse markers category. French *même* has various uses, as we can see in the examples below:

(1) J'habite dans le centre **même** de Paris.
'I live in the **very** center of Paris.'

(2) Nous vivons dans la **même** rue.
'We live on the **same** street.'

(3) Pierre a lavé la cuisine, la salle à manger, le salon : il a **même** lavé la salle de bain
'Pierre cleaned the kitchen, the dining room, the living room: he **even** cleaned the bathroom.'

We will not study the postpositive uses – as seen in (1) – or anaphoric uses – as seen in (2) – analysed by Culioli (2002) or Kleiber (2005), but rather the uses like (3), that we will call *argumentative*, described by Anscombre (1973).

Let us clarify, first of all, what we mean by 'discourse marker'. As Degand, Cornillie and Pietrandrea (2013) points out, discourse markers are a complex

1 I would like to thank my anonymous reviewers for their thoughtful and very helpful comments and advice on the first version of this paper. I am also very grateful to Lily Ruban for helping me translating it.

category; not only because of the proliferation of terminological questions and disagreements (they are sometimes referred to as textual connectors, discourse particles, pragmatic markers, etc.), but also because few definitions reach a consensus. According to the argumentative semantics approach, as well as discourse markers studies such as the founding works of Blakemore (1992, 2002), Fraser (1999), Hansen (1997, 2006), or Schourup (1999), we will consider three essential criteria – without any ambition, obviously, to redefine the category of discourse markers.

First, we will admit that discourse markers connect linguistic contents (Blakemore, 1992; Hansen, 1997). Moreover, and as Blakemore (1988), Fraser (1999), Schourup (1999), and Hansen (1997: 161) point out 'discourse markers do not contribute to the propositional content of their host unit [...] and [they] function as instructions from the speaker to the hearer'. Since we adopt the ascriptivist approach of argumentative semantics[2], we will go a step further and consider that discourse markers must not contribute to the argumentative content of their host unit. Thus, discourse markers must be optional, and the relationship they signal must be pre-existing: 'if a DM is omitted, the relationship it signals is still available to the hearer, though no longer explicitly cued' (Schourup, 1999: 231).

A few studies about *même* have been conducted in the field of argumentative semantics, such as Anscombre (1973), Anscombre and Ducrot (1983), Ducrot et al. (1980). These studies provided a description of how our uses of *même* operate, with an emphasis on their fundamentally argumentative dimension. But within argumentative semantics, positions differ as to the analysis of *même*. The description proposed by Anscombre (1973) does not allow us to classify *même* among discourse markers since it intervenes, according to him, on the argumentative content, adding by its mere presence a presupposed content to the utterance. On the contrary, we believe that *même* could be a discourse marker since it connects contents that have a prior relationship, inscribed into language. After a brief presentation of our theorical positions and our analysis of *même*, we will demonstrate that the adverb effectively belongs to the discourse markers category. This will allow us to confirm a general hypothesis about the 'unexpectedness' of its argumentative uses, which we believe results from a change in meaning.

---

2 See Anscombre and Ducrot (1983), Carel (2011, 2023), Behe, Carel, Denuc and Machado (2021).

For our written corpus we analysed two French novels from the 20th century: *Les mémoires d'Hadrien* written by Marguerite Yourcenar (1974), and *La Peste* written by Albert Camus (1947) which will be noted as (MY) and (AC). We also chose to use an oral corpus, composed of two interviews (ESLO_ENT_1001, and ESLO_ENT_1002), of an hour each, between linguists and French native speakers from Orléans, and recorded as part of the construction of the ESLO corpus by the University of Orléans and CNRS since 2014. For the sake of concision, we will only present a reduced selection of utterances in this paper.

2. *Même* and Unexpectedness

The uses of même that we propose to analyse are based on what many studies consider to be the 'grading' phenomena (Fauconnier, 1976), and that we will consider through the prism of *unexpectedness*. First, let us explain this choice of unexpectedness, which is central to our analysis. It is true that if we take an example such as (4):

(4) Cet immeuble est grand, **même** immense
'This building is big, it's **even** huge.'

one might think that what distinguishes the two adjectives compared by *même* is on a quantitative level: the second would possess the property of 'dimension' to a greater degree than the first. *Même* would only be comparing two states of a quantitative scale existing in the world. However, as Ducrot (1996) already pointed out, the concept of a single scale of 'dimension', on which all sizes would figure, makes it incomprehensible that we cannot state (5) whereas (6) is acceptable:

(5) Pierre est moyennement grand, il est **même** grand.
'Pierre is moderately tall, he's **even** tall.'

(6) Pierre est moyennement grand, il est **même** petit.
'Pierre is moderately tall, he's **even** small.'

Moreover, considering example (3):

(3) Pierre a lavé la cuisine, la salle à manger, le salon : il a **même** lavé la salle de bain.
'Pierre cleaned the kitchen, the dining room, the living room: he **even** cleaned the bathroom.'

it is difficult to understand which property would be raised to a higher degree by *Pierre a lavé la salle de bain*. It is possible to imagine that the number of cleaned rooms is raised to a higher degree, or that the 'cleanliness' of the house is raised to a higher degree – thus accepting that there are degrees of cleanliness.

But in doing so, it seems that we miss an obvious interpretation of the utterance (3) which is that the bathroom is a room that *normally* Pierre would not clean – what *normally* means has yet to be defined.

According to Anscombre et Ducrot, we must see in these uses of *même* the comparison of arguments of different strength, to assert more strongly a given conclusion. In (3), the compared arguments would be 'Pierre cleaned the kitchen', 'Pierre cleaned the dining room', "Pierre cleaned the living room' and 'Pierre cleaned the bathroom'; and the conclusion could be 'Pierre is involved in household chores' or 'Pierre is a great host'.

But the notion of 'better argument' or 'better proof' is problematic and based on a 'non-argumentative graduality' (Ducrot, 1996: 194). For, co-oriented towards Pierre's involvement in household chores, *laver la salle de bain* et *laver le salon* can both be followed by the conclusions 'Pierre is involved in household chores', 'Pierre is very involved in household chores', or 'Pierre is extremely involved in household chores', there is no linguistic manifestation of this difference of argumentative strength. Presenting arguments on an argumentative scale is only an illusion: it simply reproduces, metaphorically, a quantitative difference. This brings us back to our initial problem.

In the end, in an utterance such as (3):

(3) Pierre a lavé la cuisine, la salle à manger, le salon : il a **même** lavé la salle de bain
'Pierre cleaned the kitchen, the dining room, the living room: he **even** cleaned the bathroom.'

what *même* seems to signal is not that Pierre cleaned more rooms than expected or that the fact that he cleaned the bathroom is a better argument than the fact that he cleaned the other rooms for the conclusion 'Pierre is involved in household chores'. What *même* seems to signal in (3) is that it is unexpected that Pierre cleaned the bathroom. This unexpectedness – let's quickly point it out – is not the one found in Fillmore (1965) whose limits have been shown by Anscombre (1973). This unexpectedness is rather the one that we find in Culioli (2002), emerging from a 'force d'entraînement' which would be neutralized by the use of *même*. Indeed, regarding utterances such as (7), (8), (9) and (10):

(7) Même en marchant vite, il vous faudra quand **même** une bonne heure.
'Even if you walk fast, it will **still** take you an hour.'

(8) C'est une machine très maniable, très efficace, **même** en terrain accidenté.
'It's a very handy machine, very efficient, **even** on a rough terrain.'

(9) C'est un légume savoureux, **même** au naturel
'It's a good vegetable, **even** unseasoned.'

(10) S'il pleut, je n'irai pas à la fête, mais **même** s'il fait beau, je n'irai pas
'If it rains, I won't go to the party, but **even** if the weather is nice, I won't go.'

Culioli (2002) states that:

> All these statements have the same kind of relation: one qualifies an event (speed, type of ground, cooking, weather), all notions which concern the *force d'entraînement* on the course of things: normally, a fast walk is more efficient than a slow walk (in this case, of course), a rough terrain hinders a good functioning, this vegetable, unseasoned, has no flavor, the good weather encourages to go out. However, each time, the addition with *même*, thanks to *même*, eliminates the differential force. (2002: 23)

According to Culioli, the unexpectedness of the utterances modified by *même* is thus constructed by the confrontation of a norm and an effective situation. To highlight the fact that this norm and its contradiction are sometimes inscribed in the lexicon itself, we will use the Semantic Block Theory.

3. The Semantic Blocks Theory

3.1. Argumentative Chainings and Argumentative Templates

Developed by Marion Carel, from the framework of Jean-Claude Anscombre's and Oswald Ducrot's' theory of *Argumentation dans la Langue*, the Semantic Blocks Theory postulates that 'any utterance can be reformulated into argumentative chainings attached to the templates they materialize' (Carel, 2019). Argumentative chainings are sequences formed by two grammatical propositions linked by a connector such as *pourtant* (however) – these sequences are called transgressive – or a connector such as *donc* (therefore) – these sequences are called normative. For example, in the utterance (11):

(11) Pierre est capable.
'Pierre is capable.'

according to SBT, an argumentative chaining 'Si ce n'est pas difficile alors Pierre comprendra' 'If it's not difficult, Pierre will understand' is evoked. This chaining formulates a pattern, called argumentative template, which is written [NEG DIFFICILE DC COMPREND] (NEG DIFFICULT TF UNDERSTANDS). The conventional notation DC (TF in the translation) reminds us that the chainings formulating the template will be normative. Argumentative templates are often – but not always – contained in the meaning of words. For instance, in (11), the expressed template belongs to the meaning of *capable*. Similarly, in the utterance (12):

(12) C'était simple et pourtant Pierre n'a rien compris.
'It was simple, yet Pierre didn't understand anything.'

an argumentative chaining such as 'C'était simple pourtant Pierre n'a rien compris' (It was simple, yet Pierre didn't understand anything) is evoked. This chaining formulates a template [NEG DIFFICILE PT NEG COMPRENDRE] (NEG DIFFICULT HW NEG UNDERSTAND). In this case, the template belongs to the meaning of *stupid*, and the notation PT in the template (HW in their translation) reminds us that the chainings formulating the template will be transgressive. Any kind of argumentative negation in the chainings (whether it is *not/ne...pas* or, *few/peu*[3]) will be noted as NEG in the formulated template.

As Carel (1995) points out: 'It is assumed that every rule has exceptions as well as cases of regular application and that it can therefore be considered either from the point of view of its regularities, or from that of its exceptions.'. This is what the binary model of normativity and transgressivity allows us to do: with SBT, the 'contradiction of the norm' is no longer considered as an exception, but as a linguistic possibility, inscribed in the lexicon.

3.2. The Transposition

The templates formulated by the chainings expressed in (11) and (12) belong to the same semantic block. A semantic block is a unit composed of four argumentative templates, which share the same segments and maintain various relations. Since they share the two segments DIFFICULT and UNDERSTANDS and what varies is only connectors and negation, the templates formulated in (11) and (12) therefore belong to the block of 'difficulty and understanding' as follows:

difficult HW understand *intelligent*	NEG difficult HW NEG understand *stupid*
difficult TF NEG understand *not particularly intelligent*	NEG difficult TF understand *capable*

Amongst the possible relations within the semantic block, one will attract our attention in this study: the transposition relation. Within the same block, it is said that two templates have a transposition relation when the former is normative and the latter transgressive, and that one of the templates – but not the other – has a negation in its first segment. Carel (2014: 395) notes that 'the transposition of two templates is a "favorable" condition [...] for the possibility of linking by *même* the terms that express them'.

In the block above, [DIFFICULT TF NEG UNDERSTANDS] and [NEG DIFFICULT HW NEG UNDERSTANDS] have a transposition relation. Same goes for [NEG DIFFICULT TF UNDERSTANDS] and [DIFFICULT HW UNDERSTANDS]. And indeed,

3 See Ducrot (2005) for an analysis of the relation of *peu* to negation.

it is possible to link by *même* the words that contain the transposed templates in their signification: respectively *not particularly intelligent* and *stupid* and *capable* and *intelligent*.

4. Our Analysis of *Même*

SBT, like the *Argumentation dans la langue* theory, is an ascriptivist theory. The contents are not considered as descriptive or informative, but as argumentative. Therefore, we will admit that *même*, no matter its type of use, never intervenes on the propositional content of the statements. Instead, as we mentioned earlier, we will observe its behaviour in relation to the argumentative content of the utterances in which it occurs.

We believe that *même* always signals a particular change in meaning within a semantic block. In other words, *même* does not compare different quantities, different degrees of quality, different strengths of arguments, but contents that express different meanings. These contents express argumentative templates that belong to the same semantic block and have a particular relation: the relation of transposition. And the feeling of unexpectedness originates from this transposition relation, from the confrontation of a content expressing normative chaining and template, with a content expressing its transposed transgressive chaining and template. If we take an utterance such as (13):

(13) Oui c'est possible d'y aller en métro, c'est **même** facile
'Yes, it is possible to go there by metro, it's **even** easy.'

the two expressions *possible* and *facile* express respectively two chainings with transposed templates:

(13a) Si on fait des efforts alors on réussira
'If we make efforts then we will succeed.'

that formulates the template [EFFORTS DC RÉUSSITE] (EFFORTS TF SUCCESS), contained in the meaning of *possible,* and

(13b) On réussira sans efforts
'We will succeed without effort.'

that formulates the template [NEG EFFORTS PT RÉUSSITE] (NEG EFFORTS HW SUCCESS), contained in the meaning of *facile.* This relationship of transposition maintained by the templates exists prior to the introduction of *même* in (13), since it is inscribed into the language, as *facile* and *possible* belong to the following semantic block:

[efforts HW NEG success] *difficile* *difficult*	[NEG efforts HW success] *facile* *easy*
[efforts TF success] *possible* *not difficult*	[NEG efforts TF NEG success] *pas facile* *not easy*

Thus, their relation remains in the modified utterance (13'):

(13') Oui c'est possible d'y aller en métro, c'est facile
'Yes, it is possible to go there by metro, it's easy'

which expresses the same chainings, formulating the same templates.

This description of *même* allows us to classify it as a discourse marker. Indeed, in an utterance such as (13), *même* satisfies the three necessary criteria to belong to the class of discourse markers: it connects contents; these contents maintain a particular relationship which is pre-existing and survives the removal of *même*; and the presence of the adverb does not modify the propositional or argumentative contents of the discourse.

The same thing can be observed in these utterances:

(14) Le petit rentier déclara tout net qu'il ne s'intéressait pas au cœur et que **même** le cœur était le dernier de ses soucis. (AC)
'The little annuitant declared outright that he was not interested in the heart and **even** that the heart was the least of his worries.'

The expression *il ne s'intéressait pas au cœur* formulates the chaining (14a) and the expression *le cœur était le dernier de ses soucis* formulates the chaining (14b):

(14a) Le cœur ne lui était pas présenté comme important donc il n'y prêtait pas attention
'The heart was not presented as important to him therefore he didn't pay attention to it'

(14b) Si le cœur lui était présenté comme important, il n'y accorderait aucune attention pour autant
'While the heart was presented to him as important, he didn't pay attention to it'

(14a) formulates the template [NEG X PRÉSENTÉ COMME IMPORTANT À Y DC NEG Y PRÊTER ATTENTION À X] (NEG X PRESENTED AS IMPORTANT TO Y TF NEG Y PAY ATTENTION TO X), and (14b) formulates [X PRÉSENTÉ COMME IMPORTANT À Y PT NEG Y PRÊTER ATTENTION À X] (X PRESENTED AS IMPORTANT TO Y HW NEG Y PAY ATTENTION TO X).

These templates have a transposition relation and belong to the following semantic block:

[x presented as important to y HW NEG y pay attention to x] *x est le dernier de ses soucis* *x is the least of his worries*	[NEG x presented as important to y HW y pay attention to x] *curieux*[4] *curious*
[x presented as important to y TF y pay attention to x] *à l'écoute* *attentive*	[NEG x presented as important to y TF NEG y pay attention to x] *ne s'intéresse pas à x* *doesn't care about x*

(15) A l'intérieur des limites infranchissables dont je parlais tout a l'heure, je puis défendre ma position pied à pied, et **même** regagner quelques pouces du terrain perdu. (MY)
'Within the impassable limits I mentioned earlier, I can defend my position foot to foot, and **even** regain a few inches of lost ground.'

Défendre ma position expresses a chaining such as (15a) and *regagner quelques pouces du terrain perdu* expresses a chaining such as (15b):

(15a) C'est sa position donc il se bat pour elle
'It's his position so he fights for it'
(15b) Bien que ce ne soit pas sa position il se bat pour elle
'Although it's not his position he fights for it'

(15a) formulates the template [x ÊTRE LA POSITION DE Y DC Y SE BATTRE POUR X] (X IS Y'S POSITION TF Y FIGHT FOR X), and (15b) the transposed template [NEG X ÊTRE LA POSITION DE Y PT Y SE BATTRE POUR X] (NEG X IS Y'S POSITION HW Y FIGHT FOR X). These templates belong to the following block:

4 It is sometimes better to add in the aspects the denominations x and y. These x and y are to be found in the chainings but not necessarily in the words of the lexicon. That's what happens in the case of *curieux* and *à l'écoute*, as it seems that the terms already presuppose these x and y. Indeed, one is generally *à l'écoute de* something and *curieux (à propos) de* something. This 'something' appears systematically when we try to paraphrase an utterance such as 'Y est curieux'.

[x is y's position HW NEG y fight for x] *ne pas défendre/se rendre* *not defend/surrender*	[NEG x is y's position HW y fight for x] *regagner/attaquer* *win back/attack*
[x is y's position TF y fight for x] *défendre* *defend*	[NEG x is y's position TF NEG y fight for x] *ne pas attaquer* *not attack*

As Ducrot (2001) points out, several hypotheses justify the choice of which templates belong to the meaning of words in the lexicon. We will focus on the negation hypothesis: if an expression contains in its meaning a template [(NEG) X DC Y], the negation of this expression will contain in its meaning the template [(NEG) X PT NEG Y]; on the other hand, if an expression contains in its meaning a template [(NEG) X PT Y], the negation of this expression will contain in its meaning the template [(NEG) X DC NEG Y]. This is what justifies our choice of the template contained in the meaning of *regagner du terrain*. Indeed, it seems to us that to *regagner* is to attack in response. Thus, this expression can be the antonym of 'not attacking', which we believe expresses the idea of 'not fighting for a position that is not its own'. In the same way, it seems to us that 'not to defend' is 'to have a position for which, however, one does not fight', and that *défendre* thus expresses, according to the hypothesis of Ducrot (2001), the idea 'to have a position and therefore to fight for it'.

Based on the analysis of these examples, *même* can be classified as a discourse marker. Indeed, it satisfies the criteria mentioned earlier, namely connectivity, as *même* always connects a normative content to its transposed transgressive content; optionality, as *même* can be removed from examples (13), (14), and (15) without causing the loss of the transposition relation between the chainings and templates expressed by the contents it connects; and the absence of impact on the propositional or argumentative content of the statements.

5. Is *Même* Really a Discourse Marker?

5.1. Problematic Examples

If the analysis of our previous examples seems to allow *même* to be classified as a discourse marker, how can we explain that in some cases its removal leads to the loss of unexpectedness? Let us observe example (3), (7), (8), and (9) again:

(3) Pierre a lavé la cuisine, la salle à manger, le salon : il a **même** lavé la salle de bain.

'Pierre cleaned the kitchen, the dining room, the living room: he **even** cleaned the bathroom.'

(7) Même en marchant vite, il vous faudra quand **même** une bonne heure.
'Even if you walk fast, it will **still** take you an hour.'

(8) C'est une machine très maniable, très efficace, **même** en terrain accidenté.
'It's a very handy machine, very efficient, **even** on a rough terrain.'

(9) C'est un légume savoureux, **même** au naturel.
'It's a good vegetable, **even** unseasoned.'

It seems indeed that the unexpectedness disappears from these examples when we remove *même*. But how to explain it? Could there be a difference between these uses, in which *même* seems to be indispensable to the unexpectedness, and those that we previously analysed? Could *même* only behave – and only in some particular cases – as a discourse marker, without being one? Could it have, in some cases, an impact on the argumentative content?

We shall see that the Semantic Blocks Theory allows us to identify a structural difference between two ways of constructing argumentative meaning in the utterances, that will explain the feeling of loss of unexpectedness in examples (3), (7), (8), and (9).

5.2. An Essential Difference: Interpretation and Decoding

A fundamental and determining point in this study of the argumentative use of *même* is the importance of the intertwining of words in discourse: SBT postulates that if the argumentative content of an utterance can sometimes result from the presence of a single word, the intertwining of words, their linking, also makes it possible to produce argumentative chainings. Language itself, through its combinatorial activity, has the capacity to construct argumentative chainings. Chainings can thus be constructed in two ways, and we hypothesize that it is in this variation that the difference between our examples lies.

Indeed, the uses of *même* previously analysed in examples (13), (14), and (15) all appear within utterances whose argumentative chainings were **decoded**. Let us explain this term. An argumentative chaining will be said to be decoded if it is expressed by the meaning of a single expression in the utterance. This is what we have observed in our examples (13), (14), and (15), in which, respectively, *possible* and *facile*, *le cœur ne l'intéressait pas* and *le cœur était le dernier de ses soucis*, and *défendre sa position*, and *regagner du terrain* each express one argumentative chaining.

The second possibility is the argumentative interpretation. We will say that a chaining is **argumentatively interpreted** 'when no term is materially there to express its meaning, and to allow the chaining to be attached to a template'

(Carel, 2019), and that the chaining is therefore constructed from the intertwining of words in the discourse. Such a case can be observed in the utterance (16):

(16) Pierre a lavé la salle de bain.
'Pierre cleaned the bathroom.'

in which no term seems to fully express its meaning. In this case, the reader or interlocutor needs to try to argumentatively interpret the expressed chaining, and the template it formulates. A possible choice for (16), is to interpret the utterance as expressing the argumentative chaining (16a)

(16a) C'est laver la salle de bain pourtant Pierre l'a fait
'It's cleaning the bathroom, yet Pierre did it'

which can be attached to the argumentative template [DIFFICILE PT FAIRE] (DIFFICULT HW DO). However – and this is the main difference between argumentative interpretation and decoding – it is possible to interpret (16) as expressing other chainings and argumentative templates, since no term fully expresses its meaning.

In our examples (13), (14), and (15), in which *même* functions as a discourse marker, it connects decodable contents. On the other hand, in examples (3), (7), (8), and (9), it seems that *même* connects contents of which the expressed chainings must be argumentatively interpreted.

6. Hypotheses and Verification

We can henceforth formulate several hypotheses. First, we hypothesize that every argumentative use of *même* signals that the connected contents formulate chainings and templates that observe a transposition relation. Secondly, we hypothesize that in these uses, *même* satisfies the required criteria to belong to the class of discourse markers. Finally, we hypothesize that the feeling of loss of unexpectedness originates from the phenomenon of argumentative interpretation.

Amongst the uses that seem to stop us from classifying *même* as a discourse marker, we can distinguish two cases that correspond to two types of construction: *p même q* and *même q*. First of all, let us observe the case of the type *même q*. We will see that they satisfy two of our criteria to belong to the class of discourse markers.

In an utterance like (17):

(17) **Même** la légère satisfaction d'écrire nous fut refusée. (AC)
'**Even** the slight satisfaction of writing was denied to us.'

the removal of *même* would indeed lead to the impression that the unexpectedness is lost. However, in this kind of examples, we can see, in accordance with our hypothesis, that *même* connects two contents: an implicit one, on its left, and an explicit one, on its right. And these contents maintain a transposition relation. On its left, a first content, implicit, formulates a template such as [DANGEREUX DC INTERDIT] (DANGEROUS TF FORBIDDEN) and on its right, a second one, explicit, expresses a chaining such as 'C'était une légère satisfaction pourtant elle nous était refusée' (It was a slight satisfaction, yet we were denied it), which formulates the transposed template [NEG DANGEREUX PT INTERDIT] (NEG DANGEROUS HW FORBIDDEN).

(18) **Même** en province, le système de recrutement causa vers cette époque des émeutes sérieuses.
(MY)
'**Even** outside the capital, the recruitment system caused serious riots around this time.'

Here, *même* still connects two contents, one implicitly formulating the template [NEG DOCILE DC REBELLION] (NEG OBEDIENT TF REBELLION) and the other explicitly constructing a chaining such as 'C'est la province pourtant il y a eu des émeutes' (It was outside the capital yet there were riots), formulates the template [DOCILE PT REBELLION] (OBEDIENT HW REBELLION).

(19) RL2 : quand ils arrivent **même** à six ans ils ont déjà eu un parcours tellement chaotique
(ESLO2_ENT_1002)
'RL2: when they arrive **even** at six years old they have already had such a chaotic journey'

même connects two contents here, one implicit, which formulates a template [ÂGÉ DC PARCOURS DIFFICILE] (OLD TF DIFFICULT JOURNEY) and the other, explicit, which constructs a chaining such as 'Ils ont six ans pourtant ils ont un parcours chaotique' (They are six years old, yet they have had a chaotic journey), formulating the transposed template [NEG ÂGÉ PT PARCOURS DIFFICILE] (NEG OLD HW DIFFICULT JOURNEY).

In these examples, as well as in the previous ones, *même* connects argumentative contents that it does not modify in any way. It thus satisfies two of our criteria for belonging to the class of discourse markers – connectivity and the absence of impact on the propositional or argumentative content of the statements – and validates our first hypothesis. But can we really consider it as optional? Would the argumentative chainings and templates formulated by the contents it connects still have a transposition relation if we remove *même* from our examples?

In the cases that seem to stop us from classifying *même* among the discourse markers, and as we previously evoked, the reader needs to **interpret** what are the argumentative chainings expressed, and which templates they formulate. Let us observe example (3) again:

(3) Pierre a lavé la cuisine, la salle à manger, le salon : il a **même** lavé la salle de bain.
'Pierre cleaned the kitchen, the dining room, the living room: he **even** cleaned the bathroom.'

In this example, *même* compares two chainings: on the left, *Pierre a lavé la cuisine, la salle a manger, le salon*, constructs a chaining such as 'C'est laver la cuisine, la salle à manger, le salon, donc Pierre l'a fait' 'It's cleaning the kitchen, the dining room, the living room, so Pierre did it.' and on the right *Il a lavé la salle de bain* constructs a chaining such as 'C'est laver la salle de bain pourtant Pierre l'a fait' 'It's cleaning the bathroom, yet Pierre did it.'. Let's see what happens, beside the loss of unexpectedness, if we remove *même* from this utterance.

Let us observe the contents (21) and (22), from the modified utterance (20). They could respectively express the chainings (21a), or (21b), and (22a) or (22b):

(20) Pierre a lavé la cuisine, la salle à manger, le salon : il a lavé la salle de bain.
'Pierre cleaned the kitchen, the dining room, the living room: he cleaned the bathroom.'
(21) Pierre a lavé la cuisine, la salle à manger, le salon
(21a) C'est laver la cuisine, la salle à manger, le salon, pourtant Pierre l'a fait.
'It's cleaning the kitchen, the dining room, the living room, yet Pierre did it.'
(21b) C'est laver la cuisine, la salle à manger, le salon, donc Pierre l'a fait.
'It's cleaning the kitchen, the dining room, the living room, so Pierre did it.'
(22) Pierre a lavé la salle de bain.
(22a) C'est laver la salle de bain pourtant Pierre l'a fait.
'It's cleaning the bathroom, yet Pierre did it.'
(22b) C'est laver la salle de bain donc Pierre l'a fait.
'It's cleaning the bathroom, so Pierre did it.'

(21a) and (22a) can be understood as formulating the transgressive template [DIFFICILE PT FAIRE] (DIFFICULT HW DO). Similarly, (21b) and (22b) can be understood as formulating the transgressive template [NEG DIFFICILE DC FAIRE] (NEG DIFFICULT TF DO).

In (3) *la salle de bain* is obviously presented as a room that is 'difficult to clean', in comparison with the kitchen, the dining room, and the living room, that are presented as 'not difficult to clean'. Thus, *Pierre a lavé la salle de bain* could only – and we insist on that – construct a transgressive chaining, that formulates the template [DIFFICULT HW DO][5]. But if we remove *même* from the utterance, it seems that this interpretation is no longer the only one possible.

5 Because it is inscribed in language that if something is difficult, we can only do it despite the difficulty, not thanks to its difficulty.

Therefore, we can formulate the following hypothesis as to the use of *même* when it modifies utterances that need to be argumentatively interpreted: insofar as it is mainly an indicator of a relation of transposition between the contents it connects, the use of *même* is intended to give a clue as to the interpretation of the contents. This would explain why the unexpectedness seems to disappear when *même* is removed from the utterance: because *même* is no longer here to clue the transposition relation. Let us explain this hypothesis; as Schourup (1999) underlined, 'while DMs are typically said to "display" or 'reflect' existing propositional connections rather than creating them [...] they are also commonly said to 'reinforce', or 'clue' the interpretation intended by the speaker' (1999: 232).

Thus, connecting contents by means of using *même* could be a way for the speaker to indicate that these contents express chainings formulating transposed templates. In (3), linking the contents with *même* would help the reader choose between the possible chainings by indicating that *Pierre a lavé la salle de bain* expresses the transgressive chaining (21a) and the template it formulates. *De facto*, this would also indicate that *Pierre a lavé la cuisine, la salle a manger, le salon* must be interpreted as expressing the transposed normative chaining (22b) and the template it formulates. Hence, *même* would fulfill an essential role of discourse markers: 'guiding the hearer toward a particular interpretation and simultaneously ruling out unintended interpretations' (Schourup 1999: 231–232).

Thus, the reader of (3) cannot choose to argumentatively interpret the content *Pierre a lavé la salle de bain* as presenting the bathroom as a room that is easy to clean. On the contrary, the reader of (20) could choose this interpretation. Correspondingly, the reader of (3) cannot choose to argumentatively interpret the content *Pierre a lavé la cuisine, la salle à manger, le salon* as presenting these rooms as difficult to clean, which the reader of (20) could choose to do.

(3) Pierre a lavé la cuisine, la salle à manger, le salon : il a **même** lavé la salle de bain.
'Pierre cleaned the kitchen, the dining room, the living room: he **even** cleaned the bathroom.'

(20) Pierre a lavé la cuisine, la salle à manger, le salon : il a lavé la salle de bain.
'Pierre cleaned the kitchen, the dining room, the living room: he cleaned the bathroom.'

Même would thus indicate, in these uses, which chainings and templates are formulated by the linked contents, which is, since the contents must be argumentatively interpreted – and are, in the case of *p même q* both explicit – particularly useful. Moreover, as Rossari (2000) and Hansen (2006) point out:

> It is often said that a defining property of discourse markers is their optionality, i.e., it should be possible to remove a marker without fundamentally changing the meaning of

> its host utterance [...] In many cases, this does appear to be correct. But as pointed out by Rossari (2000: 32), it is not invariably the case: some markers can never be deleted without radically altering the range of possible interpretations of the discourse. (Hansen, 2006: 26).

It seems that in the uses of *même* that we studied; it is not totally impossible for the reader to choose the interpretations that satisfy the transposition relation if we delete *même* – especially in cases like *même q*. This is because the transposition relation is inscribed into the language and therefore exists 'as a potentiality'. However, if we remove *même*, this relation is no longer marked, and the speaker may miss it by choosing to interpret the argumentative expressions of the contents differently. And we believe that it is because of this suppression of the explicit marking of the transposition relation that the sensation of loss of unexpectedness occurs.

For instance, if we consider utterance (23):

(23) Il en était de ma convoitise du pouvoir comme de celle de l'amour, qui empêche l'amant de manger, de dormir, de penser, et **même** d'aimer, tant que certains rites n'ont pas été accomplis.
(MY)
'My lust for power was like the one for love, which prevents the lover from eating, sleeping, thinking, and **even** loving, until certain rites have been performed.'

we believe that it expresses two argumentative chainings:

(23a) C'est manger, dormir, et penser donc il ne peut pas le faire
'It is eating, sleeping, and thinking so he cannot do it.'
(23b) C'est aimer pourtant il ne peut pas le faire
'It is loving, yet he cannot do it.'

which are respectively understood as formulating the template [NEG ESSENTIEL DC NEG FAIRE] (NEG ESSENTIAL TF NEG DO IT) and the transposed template [ESSENTIEL PT NEG FAIRE] (ESSENTIAL HW NEG DO IT). If we delete *même* from (23), chances are that most readers will not interpret *manger, dormir, et penser* as 'non-essential'. Yet, this interpretation still effectively exists as a potentiality. The removal of *même* only leads to an alteration of 'the range of possible interpretation', not its disappearance. Thus, it does not invalidate our hypothesis as to whether *même* belongs to the discourse markers category.

It is worth noting that the presence of *même* does not solve all the difficulties introduced by the argumentative interpretation, especially in examples where it might be difficult to find the meaning of the terms of the discourse. Let us observe (24):

(24) RL2 : moi je les ai jamais non plus poussées quoi j'ai jamais eu je leur ai jamais mis la pression euh
même leur père hein euh (ESLO2_ENT_1002)
'RL2: I never pushed them either, I never got I never put pressure on them hm
even their father, eh hm'

In this last example, taken from our oral corpus, two chainings are expressed:

(24a) C'est moi donc je ne les ai pas poussées
'It's me so I didn't push them.'
(24b) C'est leur père pourtant il ne les a pas poussées
'It's their father yet he didn't push them.'

In this case, the presence of *moi* and *leur père* offers a multitude of possible interpretations, each assuming a certain position in relation to the stereotypical roles or personal temper, personality traits of the father and mother. For example, we could state that they respectively formulate the transposed templates [NEG ANXIOUS TF NEG PUT UNDER PRESSURE] and [ANXIOUS HW NEG PUT UNDER PRESSURE] but also [NEG AMBITIOUS TF NEG PUT UNDER PRESSURE] and [AMBITIOUS HW NEG PUT UNDER PRESSURE]. Either way, the presence of *même* forces us to choose chainings and templates that have a transposition relation.

7. Conclusion

In its argumentative uses, *même* does not modify the propositional or argumentative content of the discourse in which it appears. It is regularly found in initial position of the utterances, and it connects contents that observe a particular relation, inscribed into the language: the transposition relation. It thus seems to satisfy all the criteria that we retained as essential for belonging to the discourse markers category. However, we noticed that, when we remove *même* from some examples, the unexpectedness, seemingly inherent to the transposition relation, sometimes disappeared too. The Semantic Block Theory, and the dualism it introduces between decoding and argumentative interpretation, has however allowed us to explain this disappearance. It seems to us that the transposition relation is always present 'as a potentiality', but that in certain cases – when it is necessary to interpret argumentatively the chainings and templates expressed by the connected contents – it can pass unnoticed by the interlocutor or the reader, who must often choose between several possible interpretations. It is due to this phenomenon that we believe the sensation of loss of unexpectedness when reading certain examples arises: once *même* is removed from the statement, the reader is no longer forced to interpret the chainings and templates expressed by the contents as having a transposition relation.

This does not invalidate our hypothesis as to whether *même* belongs to the discourse markers category. Indeed, and as Rossari (2000) and Hansen (2006) have pointed out, some markers, precisely because they might impact the range of possible interpretations of a discourse, cannot be deleted without altering this range of possibilities. We believe that this is the case of *même*, which indicates by its presence which interpretations are possible and which are not. Thus, Semantic Blocks Theory has allowed us to abandon the description of *même* as adding 'comments' or 'presuppositions' to the utterances in which it appears. It has also allowed us to validate our hypothesis, even though it seemed to suffer from a heavy contradiction; and in the end *même*, in its argumentative uses, does seem to belong to the discourse markers category.

References

Anscombre, J.-C. (1973). Même le roi de France est sage. *Communications* 20, Le sociologique et le linguistique, 40–82.

Anscombre, J.-C. & Ducrot, O. (1983). *L'argumentation dans la langue*. ED. Mardaga.

Behe, L., Carel, M., Denuc, C., & Machado, J.-C. (2021). *Cours de sémantique argumentative*. Pedro e João editores.

Blakemore, D. (1988). *So* as a constraint on relevance, In R. Kempson (éd.) *Mental representation: The interface between language and reality* (pp. 183–195). Cambridge University Press.

Blakemore, D. (1992). *Understanding utterances*. Blackwell.

Blakemore, D. (2002). *Relevance and linguistic meaning: The semantics and pragmatics of discourse markers*. Cambridge University Press.

Carel, M. (1995). Pourtant: argumentation by exception. *Journal of Pragmatics* 24/1–2, 167–188.

Carel, M. (2011). *L'entrelacement argumentatif. Lexique, discours et blocs sémantiques*. Honoré Champion.

Carel, M. (2014). *Tu seras un homme mon fils*. Un prolongement de la doxa: le paradoxe. In A.-M. Cozma, A. Belhachhab & M. Pescheux (éds.) *Du sens à la signification. De la signification aux sens* (pp. 389–407). Peter Lang.

Carel, M. (2019). Interprétation et décodage argumentatifs. *Signo* 44/ 80, 2–15.

Carel, M. (2023). *Parler*, Pontes Editores.

Culioli, A. (2002). À propos de même. *Langue française*, n°133, Le lexique, entre identité et variation, 16–27.

Degand, L., Cornillie, B., & Pietrandrea, P. (2013). *Discourse markers and modal particles. Categorization and description.* John Benjamins

Ducrot, O. et al. (1980). *Les mots du discours.* Les éditions de Minuit.

Ducrot, O. (1996). Lexique et gradualité. In E. Alonso, M. Bruna & Muños, M. (eds.), *La lingüística francesa: gramática, historia, epistemología* (pp. 191–206). Universidad de Sevilla.

Ducrot, O. (2001). Critères argumentatifs et analyse lexicale. *Langages*, 35, n°142, 22–40.

Ducrot, O. (2005). De l'intérêt de choisir entre *peu* et *un peu*. *Bulletin Hispanique*, tome 107, n°1, 109–117.

Fauconnier, G. (1976). Pragmatic scales and logical structures. *Linguistic Inquiry* VI/3.

Fillmore, C. J. (1965). Entailment rules in a semantic theory. *Ohio State University Research Foundation Project on Linguistic Analysis*, Report n° 10, 57–82.

Fraser, B. (1999). What are discourse markers?. *Journal of Pragmatics* 31, 931–952.

Hansen, M.-B. M. (1997). *Alors* and *donc* in spoken French: A reanalysis. *Journal of Pragmatics* 28, 153–187.

Hansen, M.-B. M. (2006) A dynamic polysemy approach to the lexical semantics of discourse markers, (with an exemplary analysis of French *toujours*). In K. Fischer (ed.), *Approaches to discourse particles* (Studies in pragmatics 1) (pp. 21–41). Elsevier/Brill.

Kleiber, G. (2005). Les noms propres « modifiés » par même. *Langue Française* 146, 114–126.

Rossari, C. (2000). *Connecteurs et relation de discours : des liens entre cognition et signification*. Presses Universitaires de Nancy.

Schourup, L. (1999). Discourse markers. *Lingua* 107, 227–265.

Corpus

Camus, A. (1947). *La Peste.* Editions Gallimard.

ESLO2. http://eslo.huma-num.fr/

Yourcenar, M. (1974). *Mémoires d'Hadrien suivi de Carnets de notes de Mémoires d'Hadrien.* Editions Gallimard.

www.ingramcontent.com/pod-product-compliance
Ingram Content Group UK Ltd.
Pitfield, Milton Keynes, MK11 3LW, UK
UKHW041826100926
8556IPUK00002B/38